D1477768

CHRIST ————— ——.
OXFORD

XXX. 6.623

CHRIST CHURCH LIBRARY
OXFORD OX1 1DP

SHAKESPEARE AND QUOTATION

EDITED BY

JULIE MAXWELL

KATE RUMBOLD

University of Birmingham

CAMBRIDGE
UNIVERSITY PRESS

CAMBRIDGE
UNIVERSITY PRESS

University Printing House, Cambridge CB2 8BS, United Kingdom

One Liberty Plaza, 20th Floor, New York, NY 10006, USA

477 Williamstown Road, Port Melbourne, VIC 3207, Australia

314–321, 3rd Floor, Plot 3, Splendor Forum, Jasola District Centre, New Delhi – 110025, India

79 Anson Road, #06-04/06, Singapore 079906

Cambridge University Press is part of the University of Cambridge.

It furthers the University's mission by disseminating knowledge in the pursuit of
education, learning and research at the highest international levels of excellence.

www.cambridge.org
Information on this title: www.cambridge.org/9781107134249
DOI: 10.1017/9781316460795

© Cambridge University Press 2018

This publication is in copyright. Subject to statutory exception
and to the provisions of relevant collective licensing agreements,
no reproduction of any part may take place without the written
permission of Cambridge University Press.

First published 2018

Printed in the United Kingdom by TJ International Ltd. Padstow Cornwall

A catalogue record for this publication is available from the British Library.

Library of Congress Cataloging-in-Publication Data
Names: Maxwell, Julie, 1975– editor. | Rumbold, Kate Louise, 1978– editor.
Title: Shakespeare and quotation / edited by Julie Maxwell, Kate Rumbold.
Description: Cambridge; New York, NY: Cambridge University Press, 2018. |
Includes bibliographical references and index.
Identifiers: LCCN 2017057304 | ISBN 9781107134249 (hardback)
Subjects: LCSH: Shakespeare, William, 1564–1616 – Influence. |
Shakespeare, William, 1564–1616 – In literature. | Shakespeare, William,
1564–1616 – In mass media. | Shakespeare, William, 1564–1616 – Quotations.
Classification: LCC PR2976.S3357 2018 | DDC 822.3/3–dc23
LC record available at https://lccn.loc.gov/2017057304

ISBN 978-1-107-13424-9 Hardback

Cambridge University Press has no responsibility for the persistence or accuracy of URLs
for external or third-party internet websites referred to in this publication and does not
guarantee that any content on such websites is, or will remain, accurate or appropriate.

Contents

Illustrations

Contributors

JAMES P. BEDNARZ, Professor of English, Long Island University

DOUGLAS BRUSTER, Mody C. Boatright Regents Professor of American and English Literature, University of Texas at Austin

FRANS DE BRUYN, Professor of English, University of Ottawa

CHRISTY DESMET, Josiah Meigs Distinguished Teaching Professor, University of Georgia

BALZ ENGLER, Professor of English Emeritus, University of Basel

MARGRETA DE GRAZIA, Emerita Sheli Z. and Burton X. Rosenberg Professor of the Humanities, University of Pennsylvania

BEATRICE GROVES, Research Fellow and Tutor in English, Trinity College, University of Oxford

BREAN HAMMOND, Emeritus Professor of Modern English Literature, University of Nottingham

TON HOENSELAARS, Professor of Early Modern English Literature and Culture, Utrecht University

REGULA HOHL TRILLINI, Adjunct Lecturer in English Literature, University of Basel

GRAHAM HOLDERNESS, Research Professor of English and Creative Writing, University of Hertfordshire

PETER KIRWAN, Associate Professor in Early Modern Drama, University of Nottingham

TOBY MALONE, Assistant Professor of Theatre History, Criticism, and Dramaturgy, State University of New York at Oswego

GAIL MARSHALL, Professor of Victorian Literature and Culture, University of Reading

JULIE MAXWELL, independent scholar; formerly Fellow and Lecturer in English at Lucy Cavendish College, University of Cambridge and Exeter College, University of Oxford

STEPHEN O'NEILL, Senior Lecturer in English, Maynooth University

KEVIN PETERSEN, Lecturer in English, University of Massachusetts Lowell

DANIEL POLLACK-PELZNER, Ronni Lacroute Chair in Shakespeare Studies, Linfield College

CRAIG RAINE, poet and Emeritus Fellow, New College, University of Oxford

FIONA RITCHIE, Associate Professor of English (Drama and Theatre), McGill University

KATE RUMBOLD, Senior Lecturer in English Literature, University of Birmingham

R. S. WHITE, Winthrop Professor of English and Cultural Studies, University of Western Australia

Acknowledgements

Shakespeare and quotation is a long-standing shared interest of ours, and we are grateful, above all, to the contributors for enabling us to realise the vision of a wide-ranging study of the subject. With their expertise, insight and generosity, they have more than fulfilled the promise of one contributor to 'get [us] a volume to be proud of'. We would like to thank Sarah Stanton, former Commissioning Editor at Cambridge University Press, for her encouragement to develop the project, and Emily Hockley, her successor, for expertly overseeing its completion. We are also indebted to three anonymous Press readers for their helpful comments on the initial proposal for the project. We are grateful to the participants in seminars on 'Shakespeare and Quotation' at the annual meeting of the Shakespeare Association of America (2013) and the World Shakespeare Congress (2016) for thought-provoking discussion. Thanks are also due to the institutions and individuals who have kindly granted permission to reproduce images: the Bodleian Library, Folger Shakespeare Library, Tate Images, Brotherton Library, Nightboat Books, Boston Public Library, http://incorrectshakespeare.tumblr.com/ and *HyperHamlet*; to the College of Arts and Law, University of Birmingham for institutional leave; and to Sally Baggott for her invaluable assistance in preparing the typescript. Our greatest thanks are to our respective families, especially Marius, and young Shakespeare enthusiasts Jude and Florence, and Hugh and Michael.

General Introduction

Julie Maxwell and Kate Rumbold

William Shakespeare is the most quoted English author of all time. Quotations occur everywhere – from kitsch pencil-case tins ('2B Or Not 2B') to the controversial incident involving the British marine who said 'shuffle off this mortal coil you cunt' as he shot a wounded insurgent in Afghanistan.[1] The truth of Jane Austen's observation in *Mansfield Park* (1814), that '[h]is celebrated passages are quoted by every body [*sic*] ... we all talk Shakespeare, use his similes, and describe with his descriptions', can be acknowledged, if not exactly universally, then certainly in worlds other than hers.[2] *Shakespeare and Quotation* travels from Shakespeare's time to our own. It endeavours to chart the history of four centuries of quoting Shakespeare – from the 'A' of the early modern anthology to the 'Z' of Howard Jacobson's 2012 novel *Zoo Time*. Quoting Shakespeare is very much an evolving, living and global activity, present in long-established ways of writing like the novel but also in wider and still fledgling cultural forms.

The aim is to offer more than a diversity of examples of Shakespeare quotation down through the ages, however individually fascinating, shocking or entertaining. This volume provides a new way of understanding *how* Shakespeare has come to be so widely quoted – in the classroom as well as the courtroom; in poetry and in parliamentary discourse; in political propaganda, prisoner-of-war notebooks, advertisements, internet memes and Oulipian experiments, to mention only a few of the possibilities. In an episode of the ITV detective drama *Lewis*, 'The Quality of Mercy', it's murder at a student production of *The Merchant of Venice* staged in the gardens of an Oxford college. A quotation from *Hamlet* ('Neither a borrower nor a lender be' (1.iii.75)) is left on the body of the victim. 'Well, this

---

[1] We owe the latter example to Graham Holderness, private email correspondence, 17 November 2014. See further www.theguardian.com/uk-news/2013/oct/25/royal-marines-court-martial-video-transcript (last accessed 26 April 2017).

[2] Jane Austen, *Mansfield Park*, ed. John Wiltshire (Cambridge: Cambridge University Press, 2005), pp. 190–1.

is Oxford', the forensics expert teasingly observes. 'Don't I bloody know it!', the philistine Inspector Lewis grimly replies.[3] Of course, the joke is on him. Quotation of Shakespeare is (almost) everywhere, including the mass medium of television and the new media of our digital age.

The subject is so large, in fact, that its treatment here is necessarily representative rather than comprehensive, let alone exhaustive. As well as width, we have wanted to provide depth. *Shakespeare and Quotation* gives special coverage to literary quotation of Shakespeare, while *Hamlet* in particular is the focus of an individual chapter and many of the examples discussed elsewhere in the volume. As editors we have research interests in Shakespeare's 400-year reception history, in the wider fields of adaptation and source study and in Shakespeare's centrality to the history of literary quotation – a history in which Shakespeare can now be seen to play a double role.[4]

In brief: as well as being so extensively quoted, Shakespeare was himself a quoter of classical and contemporary literature, of the Bible, of snatches of popular songs and proverbs. This has one already recognised implication: some of the sayings that we may think are Shakespeare's coinages ('it's Greek to me') are documented as preceding his usage. In these cases we are (strictly speaking) borrowing Shakespeare's own borrowings. 'You are not quoting Shakespeare', as one Facebook member objects in a detailed retort to a litany of such examples, reproduced on a poster his wife has hung in their bathroom ('Every time I sit in our toilet, I see it staring at me'). 'Shakespeare was quoting somebody else.'[5] What is a matter of domestic irritation to some is a matter of scholarly interest here. Many of Shakespeare's leading characters are, like their creator, past masters of quotation – a favoured rhetorical practice and literary technique. And this has larger, and rather different, implications for Shakespeare studies than have been previously grasped.

One might reasonably assume, for example, that quoting Shakespeare has been, at least from the late eighteenth century onward, a by-product of the Bard's established cultural presence. 'Shakespeare was quotable

---

[3] First aired 29 March 2009. All references to Shakespeare in this volume are to the New Cambridge Shakespeare unless otherwise stated.

[4] Kate Rumbold, *Shakespeare and the Eighteenth-Century Novel: Cultures of Quotation from Samuel Richardson to Jane Austen* (Cambridge: Cambridge University Press, 2016); Kate Rumbold and Kate McLuskie, *Cultural Value in the Twenty-First Century: The Case of Shakespeare* (Manchester: Manchester University Press, 2014); Julie Maxwell, 'How the Renaissance (Mis)Used Sources: Shakespeare and the Art of Misquotation', in Laurie Maguire (ed.), *How to Do Things with Shakespeare* (Oxford: Blackwell, 2008), pp. 54–76; Julie Maxwell, 'Counter-Reformation Versions of Saxo: A New Source for *Hamlet?*', *Renaissance Quarterly*, 57:2 (2004), 518–60.

[5] www.facebook.com/ShakespearesGlobe/posts/10152484054115774 (last accessed 26 April 2017).

Figure 1   S. Harris, 'The Globe Playhouse – "Hamlet": A new play by Wm Shakespeare –
"You'll come out quoting."'

precisely because he was already familiar. William Blake could entitle an image "Jocund Day" or "Fiery Pegasus" and expect the two-word quotation to recall its context in *Romeo and Juliet* or *Henry IV*.[6] So Gary Taylor argued (in passing) in a landmark cultural history of Shakespeare that is now a quarter of a century old. The latest scholarship, published here in exciting chapters by James Bednarz, Douglas Bruster and Kevin Petersen, demonstrates how actively Shakespeare himself contributed to the memorability of his words. Educated and working in literary, oral and theatrical cultures where quotation was a central activity, Shakespeare was quotable not least because he made himself so. These chapters encourage

[6] Gary Taylor, *Reinventing Shakespeare: A Cultural History from the Restoration to the Present* (Oxford: Oxford University Press, 1990), p. 107.

us, then, to give serious consideration to what has sometimes been a comical notion. In one cartoon image of Shakespeare's Globe (Figure 1), the playbill promises ' "YOU'LL COME OUT QUOTING" ' from the 'NEW PLAY BY W^M SHAKESPEARE'. However, the discovery in 2017 of a seventeenth-century notebook featuring extracts from Shakespeare suggests that early audiences and readers did indeed 'come out quoting' – just as the playwright and his publishers had envisaged.[7]

Further chapters of the study trace how the quotation of Shakespeare, especially in the early novel, boosted his cultural authority as never before. This means that quotation has had a constructive, as well as reflective, relationship to Shakespeare's pre-eminence. What were previously understood to be one-directional relationships are more accurately seen as two-way, even multi-way exchanges. What connections can be drawn between Shakespeare's own borrowings and the pieces of his plays that have subsequently been admired as 'beauties' or wisdom? What is it about Shakespeare's language that invites extraction and repetition, especially in later literature? What role has selective quotation played in constructing and shaping Shakespeare's reputation during the past four centuries – and what creative new uses have been made of his language and status? These are the sorts of questions that this study seeks to answer, in three main parts that are arranged chronologically to unfold a new reception history: 'Shakespeare and Early Modern Quotation' (Part I), 'Quoting Shakespeare, 1700–2000' (Part II) and 'Quoting Shakespeare Now' (Part III). Further discussion of the significance of individual chapters, and the overarching history of Shakespeare and quotation to which they contribute, can be found in the editorial introductions provided for each part.

For despite the ubiquity of Shakespeare quotation – past, present and emerging into the future – it is relatively absent as an object of study. There is a particular irony in this. A quotation is, of all the forms that a use of literature may take, one of the most obvious and manifest. It tends to be explicit and visible in a way that fainter echoes and allusions are not. It calls for attention, sometimes very expressly. ' "Sweets to the sweet" ', writes Byron in *Don Juan* (1819–24), quoting *Hamlet* (v.i.210), 'I like so much to quote.'[8] And so he does, unambiguously, throughout the poem. We can't miss it: ' "There is a tide in the affairs of men / Which taken at the flood" – you know the rest' (*Don Juan*, vi.i.1–2; quoting *Julius Caesar*,

---

[7] www.bbc.co.uk/news/uk-england-berkshire-39477017 (last accessed 26 April 2017).
[8] George Gordon Byron, 6th Baron Byron, *Don Juan*, ii.xvii.3, in *The Major Works*, ed. Jerome McGann (Oxford: Oxford University Press, 2000). Subsequent references are to this edition and are given in parentheses in the text.

IV.iii.218–19). Byron explicitly directs our attention toward this particular kind of overt creative borrowing. All the same, it is neglected in the field of Shakespeare studies (see 'Quotation in Shakespeare Scholarship' later in this Introduction). Astonishingly, this is in fact the first full-length study of Shakespeare and quotation. The reasons for this lie partly in the nature of English literary studies as a profession (see 'Definitions' below). They can also be traced to the major functions of quotation in Western culture (see the 'Brief History of Quotation' given in the introduction to each part). Before we explore these intricate topics, however, we should answer some more straightforward questions. Does a quotation always need quotation marks and/or attribution? Shouldn't it be, at the very least, verbatim? Isn't anything else an *allusion*? What exactly is the object of study in this volume?

Definitions: *Quotation* and *Allusion*

The overlooking of quotation means that it will not generally be found in dictionaries of literary terms. The scope of this volume extends, in any case, into many forms of non-literary usage too. So we begin with a broad, working, straightforward definition: the *OED* defines *to quote* as 'To copy out or repeat (a passage, statement, etc.) from a book, document, speech, etc., with some indication that one is giving the words of another (unless this would otherwise be known)'.[9] This copying or repeating of the words of another encompasses direct quotation and indirect quotation, as well as accidental misquotation. In this study we are also interested in the creative functions of deliberate misquotation. All of these possibilities are discussed and illustrated later.

The 'indication that one is giving the words of another' may be achieved by various means. A quotation's presence may be signalled (in modern texts) by the use of quotation marks or (in earlier printed texts) by placing the quoted words in italics, so that the contrasting type visibly distinguishes them from the rest of the text. To give another example, a quotation may be signposted by a prefatory phrase: for example, 'as our Shakespeare says'. Such attributory phrasing is known as a *quotative* or as embedment under a verb of saying. Corresponding to the classic distinction between direct and indirect speech, a quotation may be *direct* ('In *Julius Caesar*, Casca says, "it was Greek to me"'), or *indirect* ('Casca says it was Greek to him').[10]

---

[9] *Oxford English Dictionary* (hereafter *OED*), s.v. *quote*, 4(a).

[10] An indirect quotation needs to bear a recognisable verbal relationship to the original words, if it is not to become paraphrase rather than a form of quotation. For example, 'Casca found it unintelligible' would not be quotation but paraphrase.

In either case it is overt, and this overtness results partly from the pointer(s) given to the audience. In oral communication, the words 'quote … unquote' or finger dancing serve the same pointing function. Particular pointers are not essential, however, and the presence of quotation may be inferred in various ways, including universal familiarity (for example '2B Or Not 2B') and register shift ('shuffle off this mortal coil' followed by 'you cunt'). As the *OED* definition reminds us, some kind of indication or pointing is necessary '*unless* this would otherwise be known' (our italics).

Beyond these easily appreciated markers and classifications of quotation, we may choose to employ the finer distinctions that belong to specialist linguistic or theoretical discussion. The contributors to this volume represent a diversity of critical schools, interests and expertise. They have adopted and adapted the available terminology of quotation – in most cases straightforwardly, but sometimes subtly or innovatively – in ways that best suit their individual explorations of the topic. In some cases, it is their theoretical preference *not* to define their terms. Scholars, especially those working on contemporary culture, sometimes argue that digital media are currently redefining what we mean by 'quotation' (see the chapters in Part III). Whatever the critical approach, though, contesting definitions, like offering them, will only take us so far.

One initially puzzling aspect of quotation will benefit, however, from further discussion here. A quotation copies or repeats the words of another, so as to reproduce them, either actually or apparently. Why 'apparently'? There are many reasons why even an overt quotation need not be word-perfect, verbatim, accurate or identical to the original from which it derives. This could be, for example, because of its reported nature in indirect quotation ('it was Greek to *him*' replacing me'). It may be the result of accidental misquotation. Deliberate misquotation ranges along a spectrum. At one end, there is straightforward colloquial shortening ('it's Greek to me' replacing 'it was …'), sometimes reflecting the passage of a Shakespeare quotation into proverbial usage: 'If you cannot understand my argument, and declare "It's Greek to me", you are quoting Shakespeare', as Bernard Levin claims in a well-known passage (reproduced, for example, on the poster mentioned by the Facebook member in the previous section).[11] At the other end, there are imaginative

---

[11] Bernard Levin, *Enthusiasms* (London: Jonathan Cape, 1983), pp. 167–8. The proverbial phrase is known, however, to predate Shakespeare's usage, as the Facebook member points out.

Figure 2   Harley Schwadron, 'Shakespeare in the 21st Century … "To blog or not to blog, that is the question."'

reworkings of quoted excerpts that have been termed 'creative misquota-tion'.[12] Pastiche and parody are obvious examples: 'To blog or not to blog' fills the thought bubble of various cartoon depictions of the Bard in front of a PC (Figure 2).[13] Or compare Philip Larkin's witty variant on Othello's 'I will chop her into messes!' (*Othello*, iv.i.188) when writing about his library colleagues to his lover Monica Jones: 'I'd like to chop them into messes.'[14]

Further, quotation cannot simply be conflated (as we might also rea-sonably assume) with verbatim reproduction of another's words because

[12] Matthew Hodgart, 'Misquotation as Re-Creation', *Essays in Criticism*, 3 (1953), 28–38, an idea developed by Christopher Ricks, *The Force of Poetry* (Oxford: Clarendon Press, 1984), p. 392, and by Maxwell in 'Art of Misquotation'.
[13] See, for example, www.cartoonstock.com/directory/t/to_be_or_not_to_be.asp (last accessed 26 April 2017).
[14] Philip Larkin, *Letters to Monica*, ed. Anthony Thwaite (London: Faber and Faber, 2010), p. 389.

'the degrees of looseness permitted or expected in quotation differ depending on the circumstances'.[15] The circumstances of a poem or a cartoon are very obviously different from those of an academic article or legal testimony. Samuel Johnson's ground-breaking *Dictionary* (1755) extensively quoted Shakespeare for the purposes of illustrating semantic usage. As Johnson wrote in his Plan for the work, 'in citing authorities, on which the credit of every part of this work must depend, it will be proper to observe some obvious rules, such as … noting the quotations with accuracy'.[16] By contrast, here is Batman overtly quoting Shakespeare: 'As the Bard once said, The fault lies not in our stars but in ourselves.'[17] (The line actually reads: 'The fault, dear Brutus, is not in our stars / But in ourselves' (*Julius Caesar*, I.ii.140–1)). The circumstances of children's television permit the near-verbatim quotation. It could also be described as misquotation, or as 'weak quotation',[18] or as indirect quotation of what Shakespeare 'said'. In contemporary popular culture, Shakespeare is often quoted very indirectly, for example via film adaptations.

Alternatively, consider how Byron makes a poet's decision to modify his quotation of a line from *King John*, 'to gild refinèd gold, to paint the lily' (IV.ii.11). Here is the line in its original Shakespearean context, a pair of infinitives belonging to a formal speech patterned by infinitives:

> Therefore, to be possessed with double pomp,
> To guard a title that was rich before,
> To gild refinèd gold, to paint the lily,
> To throw a perfume on the violet,
> To smooth the ice or add another hue
> Unto the rainbow, or with taper-light
> To seek the beauteous eye of heaven to garnish,
> Is wasteful and ridiculous excess. (IV.ii.9–16)

And here is Byron's mild, chattier misquotation in *Don Juan*:

> But Shakespeare also says 'tis very silly,
> 'To gild refined gold, or paint the lily'. (III.lxxvi.7–8)

[15] Eun-Ju Noh, *Metarepresentation: A Relevance-Theory Approach* (Amsterdam: John Benjamins, 2000), p. 17.
[16] Samuel Johnson, *Johnson's Dictionary: An Anthology*, ed. David Crystal (London: Penguin, 2005), p. 18.
[17] 'Prophecy of Doom', 1992, from *Batman: The Animated Series*, which aired on the former American children's TV channel Fox Kids.
[18] www.hyperhamlet.unibas.ch/index.php/hyperhamlet/about__corpus (last accessed 6 February 2017).

The modification in Byron's brief quotation ('or' replacing 'to') is a matter not only of tone but of economy. It takes a verse paragraph for Shakespeare's speaker to employ the conjunction 'or' that establishes these as alternative absurdities. It takes Byron a line. (He isn't gilding the lily.) Even when Shakespeare's words are used in explicitly punctuated quotations and/or in excerpts attributed to him by name, therefore, they are sometimes altered. So overtness is more defining than precision when we are identifying Shakespeare quotation.

The nature of quotation can be best described, perhaps, by explaining its relationship to the term *allusion*. In contrast to the overtness of quotation identified above, allusions are generally understood to be covert. Hence the *OED* definition of *allusion* as 'a covert, implied, *or* indirect reference'.[19] The visibility of quotation compared to allusion may be readily demonstrated by testing it at the extremes, in a single-word example. In his chapter here on *Hamlet*, Bruster discusses how Hamlet picks up on Gertrude's word 'seems' and quotes it back at her – 'Seems madam? nay it is, I know not seems' (1.ii.76). Although it is only a single word, we have no difficulty perceiving the presence of the quotation. It is not in doubt. (One might note, incidentally, how effectively Shakespeare has depicted an everyday use of quotation – quoting their own words back to family members as a staple of the domestic row.) Compare this, though, to the complexity of arguing for a single-word *allusion* to Shakespeare. Could 'dark *dexterity*' in the *Dunciad* be referencing the phrase '*dexterity* of wit' (our italics) in *The Merry Wives of Windsor*, as Brean Hammond suggests in his chapter below on Pope? The case for this kind of allusion is one of the most difficult to establish – except in the rare instance (not applicable here) that the word is unique or otherwise peculiar to the writer in question. It would be false, however, to create an absolute, artificial segregation of quotations from obliquer allusions. As Fiona Ritchie and R. S. White observe in their discussion of the Romantics in Chapter 7, quotations can occasionally be unobtrusive too. Very often both quotations and allusions occur within the same text or author. Sometimes the critic's task is therefore a material one: as when Hammond identifies quotations Pope drew attention to in his edition of Shakespeare, and then uses them to strengthen his argument for possible allusions to Shakespeare in Pope's own verse. Sometimes the relationship between quotation and allusion benefits from a subtle theoretical distinction, as in Beatrice Groves's deft

---

[19] *OED*, s.v. *allusion*, 4.

use of film terminology to identify 'unheard' quotations prompted by Shakespeare's biblical allusions.

The covert nature of allusions means that even establishing their exist-ence can require considerable critical expertise. This was particularly the case before the advent of digital research tools. And it is a major reason why allusions have traditionally consumed far more energy and attention than unmissable quotations do. Alternatively, one could say that establishing allusions has often functioned as a *demonstration* of critical expertise that serves to justify the role of the professional critic. What the common reader may not spot, the critic can. This can be enor-mously valuable. But it can also involve many wild goose chases, with the unhappy effect of devaluing literary criticism, and allusion studies in particular. Literary historians and theorists with other research interests therefore sometimes refer, a little contemptuously, to allusion 'spotting' or 'hunting'. Focusing heavily on detecting hidden references to prior texts can, ironically, distract attention from the meaning and significance of those intertextual connections and the function of an older author's words in a new text. In this volume, we have conducted a different kind of critical experiment – asking contributors to focus primarily on explicit quotations by or from Shakespeare. In Craig Raine's brilliant chapter below on twentieth-century literature, for example, quotation is revealed as a figure that is not only as complex and intricate as allusion, but is arguably more sophisticated. Specific effects are shown to depend on exact reproduction, or very close copies. Discussion of allusion is included in this volume where it casts light on the distinct practice and/ or history of Shakespeare quotation – the large but long-neglected topic that we have set out to explore.

Quotation in Shakespeare Scholarship

Shakespeare and quotation has not hitherto been defined as a field in its own right. It shades naturally into other kinds of scholarship: the study of the sources and contexts that shaped Shakespeare's work, and of the subse-quent influence, adaptation and performance of his plays and poems. For all the visibility of quotation, it can be obscured in such studies, thanks to prevailing critical tendencies to treat quotation as merely an outward sign of a larger relationship between texts, or to overlook it in favour of allusion. In particular, few critics have considered quotation as a *creative* practice. Recent years, however, have seen a growing critical interest in quotation in its own right. New studies have respectively examined, for example, Shakespeare's use of *sententiae*, the early modern commonplacing and circulation of fragments of his plays and poems, and the function of his words and phrases in twenty-first-century popular culture. This final part of the introduction examines key trends in Shakespeare scholarship, both to account for the long critical neglect of quotation and to bring together the fascinating but still disparate studies that attend to it. *Shakespeare and Quotation*, this introduction shows, both builds on this work and deepens its significance by connecting for the first time the study of quotation *in*, and *of*, Shakespeare's plays and revealing the creativity of this neglected mode of intertextuality.

By uniting in one book the study of Shakespeare's uses of quotation and of his subsequent quotation by all kinds of writers and speakers, *Shakespeare and Quotation* enables the reader to trace, over four centuries, the persistence of specific habits of creative quotation. At the same time, the volume's chronological structure revisits (and modifies) a history that may be familiar to some scholarly readers but will be new to others. In the past 400 years, quoters and quotations have operated in drastically changing value systems: from the fluid conceptions of borrowing and remaking that characterise the early modern period, to the proprietary notions of authorship that were established in the eighteenth century and that underpin present-day attitudes to quotation, copyright and plagiarism – attitudes that our digital age is, as we shall see, in the process of reinventing.[20]

Shakespeare as Quoter

First, then, *Shakespeare and Quotation* at once contributes to and challenges the study of Shakespeare's sources and influences as traditionally conceived. In this vast field of scholarship dating back to the eighteenth century, quotation has been regarded less as an index of Shakespeare's creativity and more as a body of evidence that can be used to prove or disprove his knowledge. For the past 250 years, scholars have used Shakespeare's most overt borrowings as tools to establish the extent, and the nature, of his reading. Richard Farmer challenged the tendency of Shakespeare's eighteenth-century editors to find verbal parallels in classical texts by instead quoting Shakespeare's quotations and misquotations as evidence (or a 'series of proofs') of his hopeless reliance on translations, commonplace sayings and

---

[20] Margreta de Grazia, 'Shakespeare in Quotation Marks', in Jean I. Marsden (ed.), *The Appropriation of Shakespeare: Post-Renaissance Reconstructions of the Works and the Myth* (New York: St Martin's Press, 1992), pp. 57–71. See the introduction to Part II in this volume for further discussion.

school books.[21] Victorian scholars used Shakespeare's quotations from the Bible in an effort to prove his piety.[22] And in the twentieth century, T. W. Baldwin compiled Shakespeare's quotations to demonstrate, more positively than Farmer, that his classical knowledge was that of a 'learned grammarian', and not out of the reach of one lacking a university education, as others had claimed.[23] Quotations in Shakespeare's plays and poems have thus constituted evidence for both the prosecution and the defence at the contested limits of Shakespeare's education (and beliefs). They have even been co-opted, in the form of repeated collocations, to prove or dispute his authorship of the plays.[24]

This restricted usage of quotation would have seemed strange, however, to Shakespeare and his contemporaries. In the early modern period, a writer's skilfulness in quoting, and own quotability, were accepted markers of literary distinction – and not only an indicator of learning (see the introduction to Part I). This was based on a creative principle that scholars have long discussed – the *imitatio* that characterised the period's pedagogy and writing.[25] Yet scholars tend to overlook, or downplay, Shakespeare's quotations in favour of more obviously extended connections that apparently suggest a 'deeper' creative engagement with his sources. Laurie Maguire and Emma Smith have recently observed that source study appears remarkably unmoved by theoretical developments in intertextuality. Despite the 'giddy proposal' of poststructuralism, 'that every text is and can only be a tissue of citations authored by the limited cultural resources of the literary language rather than by any particular individual authorial agent', the texts

---

[21] Richard Farmer, *An Essay on Shakespeare's Learning: Addressed to Joseph Craddock, Esq.* (Cambridge, 1767), p. 3.

[22] For example, T. R. Eaton, *Shakespeare and the Bible* (London, 1861); Charles Wordsworth, *Shakespeare's Knowledge and Use of the Bible*, 3rd edn (London, 1880 (1864)); and others discussed in Julie Maxwell, 'The Part of Allusion: Religious Controversy on the English Renaissance Stage', unpublished D.Phil. thesis, University of Oxford (2004), pp. 31–2.

[23] T. W. Baldwin, *William Shakespere's Small Latine and Less Greeke* (Urbana: University of Illinois Press, 1944); available online at www.durer.press.illinois.edu/baldwin/index.html (last accessed 12 May 2017). See Robert Miola, *Shakespeare's Reading* (Oxford: Oxford University Press, 2000), pp. 164–9, for discussion of 'The Dream of Shakespeare's Library' that has driven such scholarly pursuits.

[24] See, for example, Brian Vickers, *Counterfeiting Shakespeare* (Cambridge: Cambridge University Press, 2002), p. 220; Gary Taylor and John V. Nance, 'Imitation or Collaboration: Marlowe and the Early Shakespeare Canon', *Shakespeare Survey*, 68 (2015), 32–47; Santiago Segarra, Mark Eisen, Gabriel Egan and Alejandro Ribeiro, 'Attributing the Authorship of the *Henry VI* Plays by Word Adjacency', *Shakespeare Quarterly*, 34:2 (2016), 232–56.

[25] G. W. Pigman III, 'Versions of Imitation in the Renaissance', *Renaissance Quarterly*, 33:1 (Spring 1980), 1–32; Thomas M. Greene, *The Light in Troy: Imitation and Discovery in Renaissance Poetry* (New Haven: Yale University Press, 1982); see also, more recently, Vernon Guy Dickson, *Emulation on the Shakespearean Stage* (Farnham: Ashgate, 2013).

that tend to be printed as sources in modern editions of Shakespeare's plays and poems are still those that offer substantial parallels of plot and character.[26] More glancing, but overt, verbal connections can be dwarfed by these precursor texts: Pramit Chaudhuri notes, for example, that scholars have documented thoroughly the Latinate sources of *Titus Andronicus*, but still treat the direct Latin quotations by characters in that play as merely decorative or atmospheric.[27] Quotations might be mentioned as the outward sign of a deeper systemic relationship with an influential author, such as Ovid.[28] Or they might be regarded as prizes in the retrograde activity of spotting 'sources, references, allusion' rather than examining the dynamics of the relationship.[29] Focusing only on the 'narrow range of texts indicated by evidence of verbal echo' might prevent one seeing beyond to the 'structural, thematic, ideational, imagistic, and generic linkages' that connect Shakespeare to a wider range of materials.[30]

What, though, if we examine quotation on its own terms, in the context of the culture in which Shakespeare worked? If we try to consider it, that is, not merely as a superficial sign of a deeper connection, but as a practice in its own right? The (near) exact wording that we identify as quotation is weighted with a completely different significance, for example, in the context of a society where the particular words of one book – the Bible – could be taken to govern all aspects of life. As Maxwell has argued, 'creative misquotation' of passages from the Bible was in tension with the need to establish reliable authoritative texts and translations, as well as the use of precisely worded quotations as authorities, or 'proofs'.[31] This paradox is further opened out in Part I of this volume, where both kinds of borrowing are seen at work in Shakespeare. It also echoes through the subsequent centuries of Shakespeare's reception, in which his words have sometimes gained the status of a secular scripture.[32]

As well as invoking texts such as the Bible and classics, Shakespeare's quotations often evoke the environment in which those texts were first

---

[26] Laurie Maguire and Emma Smith, 'What Is a Source? Or, How Shakespeare Read His Marlowe', *Shakespeare Survey*, 68 (2015), 15–31. Maguire and Smith note how the term 'source' has been heavily qualified in recent years to try to account for subtler intertextual relationships.

[27] Pramit Chaudhuri, 'Classical Quotation in *Titus Andronicus*', *ELH*, 81:3 (2014), 787–810.

[28] See, for example, Jonathan Bate, *Shakespeare and Ovid* (Oxford: Clarendon Press, 1993).

[29] Charles Martindale and A. B. Taylor (eds.), *Shakespeare and the Classics* (Cambridge: Cambridge University Press, 2004), p. 4.

[30] Miola, *Shakespeare's Reading*, p. 369.

[31] Maxwell, 'Art of Misquotation'. For Hannibal Hamlin, the term 'quotation' is subsumed by 'allusion': *The Bible in Shakespeare* (Oxford: Oxford University Press, 2013).

[32] Jem Bloomfield, *Words of Power: Reading Shakespeare and the Bible* (Cambridge: Lutterworth Press, 2016).

encountered, such as church or the early modern schoolroom. Recently, Lynn Enterline has nuanced the notion of *imitatio* as a pedagogical practice by arguing that it provided not only a store of familiar biblical and classical tropes, but also, ironically for humanist training, the performative skills with which to distance oneself from and undercut the emotions expressed.[33] When Shakespeare has his characters quote school-learned phrases, then, he not only evokes their educational experience, but also relies on his contemporary audience's recognition of the possibility for irony. This brings us to the crucial point that in Shakespeare's plays, quotations are usually, by necessity, delivered by characters. They do not have to be verbal departures from their source to have a character-creating function. The practice, as much as the source text itself, is being creatively deployed. Critics have tended to focus on ways in which Shakespeare's words transform those of his source text: the description of Cleopatra's barge stays close to the equivalent passage in North's translation of Plutarch, but adds rich metaphor and the perspective of a dramatic character.[34] There are, however, signs in recent criticism of attention to what it means when Shakespeare's characters quote exactly or repeat *sententiae*.[35] The present volume examines the act of quotation as practised by characters from Shakespeare's Falstaff to Ian McEwan's Henry Perowne.

In recent years, scholars have examined a more diverse range of resources for Shakespeare's plays than those encountered in the Renaissance classroom, including proverbs, sayings, songs and epitaphs.[36] These often fragmentary texts, by their nature, resist critical assumptions that a 'source' must entirely underpin the plot of a play, and encourage attention to what it means for a character, such as the proverb-laden Polonius, to deliver them. Importantly, Shakespeare's sources are not necessarily prior texts: Janet Clare has illuminated the 'dynamic exchange between plays' in the early modern period and argued that Shakespeare's plays were 'once

---

[33] Lynn Enterline, *Shakespeare's Schoolroom: Rhetoric, Discipline, Emotion* (Philadelphia: University of Pennsylvania Press, 2012).

[34] Catherine Belsey, 'The Elephants' Graveyard Revisited: Shakespeare at Work in *Antony and Cleopatra*, *Romeo and Juliet* and *All's Well that Ends Well*', *Shakespeare Survey*, 68 (2015), 62–72 (pp. 63–6); Leah Scragg, 'Source Study', in Stanley Wells and Lena Cowen Orlin (eds.), *Shakespeare: An Oxford Guide* (Oxford: Oxford University Press, 2003), pp. 373–90.

[35] See, for example, Heather James, 'Shakespeare's Learned Heroines in Ovid's Schoolroom', in Martindale and Taylor, *Shakespeare and the Classics*, pp. 66–85; and Heather James, 'Shakespeare, the Classics, and the Forms of Authorship', *Shakespeare Studies*, 36 (2008), 80–9.

[36] Stuart Gillespie and Neil Rhodes (eds.), *Shakespeare and Elizabethan Popular Culture* (London: Arden Shakespeare, 2006); Scott L. Newstok, *Quoting Death in Early Modern England: The Poetics of Epitaphs beyond the Tomb* (Basingstoke: Palgrave Macmillan, 2009).

part of the give-and-take of theatre traffic'.[37] Her focus, however, is the circulation of gesture and dramaturgy between playwrights; ours is the 'give-and-take' of dramatic words and phrases (see Chapter 1).

What of the longer-term fortunes of these circulating words and phrases? The words 'To thine own self be true' are already proverbial when Polonius heaps advice on his son, Laertes; today, they can be found on jewellery, keyrings and tattoos, ascribed to 'William Shakespeare'. *Shakespeare and Quotation* reveals how intervening centuries of selective quotation detach phrases and even quotations from their dramatic speakers and render them the timeless wisdom of Shakespeare. Bruster has previously examined the creative practices of *bricolage* (or 'patchwork', 'mingle-mangle' and 'hodge-podge') by which early modern dramatists constructed new texts from fragments, and the insight this offers into the 'cultural, historical, and political positions' of the writers. But he has space only briefly at the end of his book to connect this practice with the comparable techniques of American modernists; to sample, rather than survey, the relationships between Shakespeare's working habits and those of subsequent authors.[38] More recently, Laura Estill has traced the ways in which already proverbial lines quoted by Shakespeare gained a new, independent afterlife by following a single phrase from *Love's Labour's Lost* as it is transcribed from the play into early anthologies, and then copied by authors from these intermediary texts.[39] This fascinating account of a phrase that criss-crosses the boundaries of oral, print and manuscript cultures is revealing of larger patterns of circulation in the seventeenth century. With its 400-year span, *Shakespeare and Quotation* has the scope to reveal the longer-term movements of Shakespeare's phrases, whose meaning is inflected by pre- and post-Romantic notions of authorship and authority, and by changing practices of quotation.

Shakespeare as Quoted

If Shakespeare's own acts of quotation have been used by scholars as evidence; been disregarded in preference for thorough-going connections with prior texts; and, latterly, come closer to the fore in studies more concerned

[37] Janet Clare, *Shakespeare's Stage Traffic: Imitation, Borrowing and Competition in Renaissance Theatre* (Cambridge: Cambridge University Press, 2014), pp. 1, 20.
[38] Douglas Bruster, *Quoting Shakespeare: Form and Culture in Early Modern Drama* (Lincoln: University of Nebraska Press, 2000), pp. 22, 11.
[39] Laura Estill, *Dramatic Extracts in Seventeenth-Century English Manuscripts: Watching, Reading, Changing Plays* (Newark: University of Delaware Press, 2015), pp. 201–24.

with fleeting verbal connections, with intermediary influences and with what it means for characters to quote, a remarkably similar story can be told about the critical fortunes of quotations *of* Shakespeare. Here, as in the study of Shakespeare's own creative practice, 'quotation' can be threatened with being subsumed by other kinds of relationship. Zoltán Márkus has recently noted that quotation has much in common with 'other cultural practices of textual reiteration such as adaptation, editing, performing, and translation'.[40] But, as in the study of Shakespeare's borrowings, the rewards of resisting conflation and paying attention to quotation specifically are substantial.

In particular, we gain a much fuller appreciation of literary quotation. *Shakespeare and Quotation* differs from previous studies of Shakespeare in literature in two regards. First, by uniting the expertise of the contributing scholars, this collection can span several centuries of literary borrowings. Many important studies already examine the role of Shakespeare within the work of a particular author or period in fiction, poetry and drama.[41] *Shakespeare and Quotation* can begin to draw lines of connection through centuries of literary borrowings, and even show how novels, poems and plays became intermediary texts that shaped later authors' relationships with Shakespeare. Second, in a field that privileges authors who demonstrate 'sustained engagement' with Shakespeare rather than using him in a 'purely allusive or embedded manner', this collection demonstrates the value of paying attention specifically to literary quotation.[42]

To date, literary quotations have sometimes been regarded as a measure of the extent to which the mind of an author is steeped in Shakespeare. Valerie L. Gager notes, for example, that 'quotations, allusions and echoes'

[40] Zoltán Márkus, 'Shakespeare in Quotation Marks', in Bruce R. Smith (ed.), *The Cambridge Guide to the Worlds of Shakespeare*, 2 vols. (Cambridge: Cambridge University Press, 2016), vol. II, pp. 1694–8 (p. 1695).
[41] Marianne Novy, *Engaging with Shakespeare: Responses of George Eliot and Other Women Novelists* (Iowa City: University of Iowa Press, 1998); Adrian Poole (ed.), *Great Shakespeareans*, Vol. V: *Scott, Dickens, Eliot, Hardy* (London: Continuum, 2011); Gail Marshall, 'Shakespeare and Nineteenth-Century Fiction', in Gail Marshall (ed.), *Shakespeare in the Nineteenth Century* (Cambridge: Cambridge University Press, 2012); Julie Sanders, *Novel Shakespeares: Twentieth-Century Women Novelists and Appropriation* (Manchester: Manchester University Press, 2001); David Fairer, 'Shakespeare in Poetry', in Fiona Ritchie and Peter Sabor (eds.), *Shakespeare in the Eighteenth Century* (Cambridge: Cambridge University Press, 2012), pp. 99–117; Neil Corcoran, *Shakespeare and the Modern Poet* (Cambridge: Cambridge University Press, 2010); Tiffany Stern, 'Shakespeare in Drama', in Ritchie and Sabor, *Shakespeare in the Eighteenth Century*, pp. 141–57.
[42] Sanders, *Novel Shakespeares*, p. 12. Quotation can be distinguished in these terms from adaptation and appropriation (Sanders, *Novel Shakespeares*, p. 4); alternatively, it can be placed on a spectrum of appropriation (Christy Desmet, 'Introduction', in Christy Desmet and Robert Sawyer (eds.), *Shakespeare and Appropriation* (London: Routledge, 1999), pp. 1–12 (pp. 8–9)).

are 'successively the most obvious manifestations of influence in Dickens' work'.[43] A quotation might be treated as a clue to an extended plot or character parallel, as when the line 'the isle is full of noises' in James Joyce's play *Exiles* (1918) is thought to invite comparison between the exiled figures of Shakespeare's Prospero and Joyce's Richard.[44] A quotation might be considered the outward sign of a larger structure or 'skeleton of allusion' to a particular play; or, conversely, treated as 'merely ornamental', compared to references that are more thoroughly and subtly worked into the text.[45] In other words, literary quotations are often treated as symbolic of, or incidental to, a larger relationship with Shakespeare. Rarely are they an object of focused study in themselves. This collection includes the work of scholars who, building on Leah Price's *The Anthology and the Rise of the Novel* (2000), have begun to examine those texts that mediate the way in which novelists quote Shakespeare; to consider what it means when Shakespeare's words are voiced by fictional characters; and to explore the long-term implications for both Shakespeare and the novel.[46] This volume extends that analysis of the specific functions of quotation through a wide range of literary forms to the present day.

Shakespeare and Quotation also pays attention to the material forms in which Shakespeare's words circulated. In doing so, it builds on new insights from book history. Important studies of early modern commonplacing culture necessarily devote little space to Shakespeare.[47] But scholars of Shakespeare and the history of the book have increasingly examined the transmission of Shakespeare's plays and poems not only in folio and quarto editions, but also in more fragmentary forms, from quotation books to the printed plays and poems bound together in volumes according to the tastes of the purchaser and the extracts transcribed by readers in their manuscript commonplace books.[48] Such studies usefully challenge

---

[43] Valerie L. Gager, *Shakespeare and Dickens: The Dynamics of Influence* (Cambridge: Cambridge University Press, 1996), p. 20.

[44] Giuseppina Restivo, 'Joyce's *Exiles* and Shakespeare's *Tempest*', in Laura Pelaschiar (ed.), *Joyce/Shakespeare* (Syracuse: Syracuse University Press, 2015), pp. 56–72.

[45] Valerie Grosvenor Myer, '"Well Read in Shakespeare"', in Valerie Grosvenor Myer (ed.), *Samuel Richardson: Passion and Prudence* (London: Vision, 1986); Berit R. Lindboe, '"O *Shakespear*, had I thy Pen!": Fielding's Use of Shakespeare in *Tom Jones*', *Studies in the Novel*, 14:4 (Winter 1982), 303–14.

[46] Rumbold, *Shakespeare and the Eighteenth-Century Novel*; Daniel Pollack-Pelzner, 'Dickens and Shakespeare's Household Words', *ELH*, 78:3 (2011), 533–56.

[47] Ann Moss, *Printed Commonplace-Books and the Structuring of Renaissance Thought* (Oxford: Clarendon Press, 1996); Barbara Benedict, *Making the Modern Reader: Cultural Mediation in Early-Modern Anthologies* (Princeton: Princeton University Press, 1996); Leah Price, *The Anthology and the Rise of the Novel* (Cambridge: Cambridge University Press, 2000).

[48] Peter Stallybrass and Roger Chartier, 'Reading and Authorship: The Circulation of Shakespeare 1590–1619', in Andrew Murphy (ed.), *A Concise Companion to Shakespeare and the Text* (Malden,

assumptions about where the meanings of quotation reside. For example, are the sententious markings next to certain lines in *Lucrece*, *Hamlet* and *Troilus* authorial additions designed to promote the literariness and quotability of the work, or the calculated additions of the circle of printers and publishers marketing printed commonplace books of extracts from English plays (see Chapters 2 and 4)?[49] Is the meaning of a line shaped by a printed commonplace heading or by the new applications readers put them to in their letters and manuscript commonplace books?[50] What are the mediating effects of these fragmentary texts – and others, such as the illustrative quotations in Johnson's *Dictionary* and the *OED* – on later authors' relationships with Shakespeare?[51]

In recent years, new technology has furnished the scholarly community with more tools for tracing the circulation of fragments of Shakespeare. Sayre Greenfield uses the full-text search capacity of resources such as *Literature Online* (*LION*), *Early English Books Online* (*EEBO*) and *Eighteenth Century Collections Online* (*ECCO*) to find specific lines from *Hamlet* in seventeenth- and eighteenth-century printed texts, and to observe patterns in their usage, from playful repetition by other theatre practitioners to literary reverence.[52] Scholars have also created new resources specifically to examine the material forms in which quotation circulated. *DEx: A Database of Dramatic Extracts* makes searchable (by manuscript, playwright, play or character) excerpts copied into seventeenth-century manuscripts, while *Verse Miscellanies Online, An Online Index of Poetry in Printed Miscellanies, 1640–1682* and the *Digital Miscellanies Index* record the contents of the printed miscellany in the sixteenth and early

---

MA: Blackwell, 2007); Jeffrey Todd Knight, *Bound to Read: Compilations, Collections, and the Making of Renaissance Literature* (Philadelphia: University of Pennsylvania Press, 2013); Sasha Roberts, *Reading Shakespeare's Poems in Early Modern England* (Basingstoke: Palgrave Macmillan, 2002); Estill, *Dramatic Extracts*; David Allan, *Commonplace Books and Reading in Georgian England* (Cambridge: Cambridge University Press, 2010).

[49] Zachary Lesser and Peter Stallybrass, 'The First Literary *Hamlet* and the Commonplacing of Professional Plays', *Shakespeare Quarterly*, 59:4 (2008), 371–420; H. R. Woudhuysen, 'The Foundations of Shakespeare's Text', *Proceedings of the British Academy*, 125 (2004), 69–100; Adam Hooks, *Selling Shakespeare: Biography, Bibliography and the Book Trade* (Cambridge: Cambridge University Press, 2016).

[50] See Roberts, *Reading Shakespeare's Poems*; Allan, *Commonplace Books*.

[51] John Considine, 'Literary Classics in *OED* Quotation Evidence', *Review of English Studies*, 60 (2009), 620–38.

[52] Sayre Greenfield, 'Quoting *Hamlet* in the Early Seventeenth Century', *Modern Philology*, 105:3 (2008), 510–34. See also Sayre Greenfield, '*ECCO*-locating the Eighteenth Century', *Eighteenth-Century Intelligencer*, 21:1 (2007), 1–9; and Sayre Greenfield, 'Quoting *Hamlet* outside Britain in the Eighteenth Century', in Richard Fotheringham, Christa Jansohn and R. S. White (eds.), *Shakespeare's World/World Shakespeares: The Selected Proceedings of the International Shakespeare Association World Congress, Brisbane, 2006* (Newark: University of Delaware Press, 2008), pp. 237–46.

seventeenth, late seventeenth, and eighteenth centuries respectively.[53] These digital projects build on research that emphasises the malleability of early modern texts and the agency of active readers; they have already generated insights into Shakespeare's status.[54] Unlike the *Shakspere Allusion Book* (1874), which focused exclusively on Shakespeare, these resources usefully situate extracts from his plays and poems in a wider culture of print and manuscript quotation. By contrast to these period-focused projects, the *HyperHamlet* database, whose creators appear in this volume, crowd-sources references to *Hamlet* from Shakespeare's lifetime to the present day (see Chapter 16).[55] Within its similarly long view, *Shakespeare and Quotation* can begin to speculate about the cumulative influence of these quotations on Shakespeare's reputation.[56]

New technology also changes, of course, the ways in which Shakespeare circulates. In the twentieth century, expanding broadcast media saw Shakespeare's words appear on film; on television; on radio; and in adverts, comics and popular fiction. Important work on Shakespeare and popular culture has taken seriously Shakespeare's appearances in these popular forms; some have paid close attention to the precise role of quotation therein.[57] For Douglas Lanier, allusion to and citation of Shakespeare's words embody and exacerbate the 'tension between reverence and resistance' characteristic of popular-culture uses of Shakespeare. Since films

---

[53] Laura Estill and Beatrice Montedoro (eds.), *DEx: A Database of Dramatic Extracts*, Iter: *Gateway to the Middle Ages and Renaissance* (2015), www.dex.citd.tamu.edu/; Michelle O'Callaghan (ed.), *Verse Miscellanies Online*, www.versemiscellaniesonline.bodleian.ox.ac.uk; Adam Smyth, 'An Online Index of Poetry in Printed Miscellanies, 1640–1682', *Early Modern Literary Studies*, 8:1 (2002), www. purl.oclc.org/emls/08-1/smyth.htm; Abigail Williams (ed.), *Digital Miscellanies Index*, www.dmi. bodleian.ox.ac.uk/ (all last accessed 12 May 2017).

[54] The underpinning research includes Estill, *Dramatic Extracts*; Michelle O'Callaghan, 'Textual Gatherings: Print, Community and Verse Miscellanies in Early Modern England', *Early Modern Culture* 8 (2010), www.emc.eserver.org/1–8/ocallaghan.html (last accessed 12 May 2017); Adam Smyth, *Profit and Delight: Printed Miscellanies in England, 1640–1682* (Detroit: Wayne State University Press, 2004); and a bibliography of eighteenth-century miscellanies compiled by Michael Suarez (www.digitalmiscellaniesindex.org/about/ (last accessed 12 May 2017)). New publications arising from research in the databases include Christopher Salamone, '"The Fragments, Scraps, the Bits and Greasy Relics": Shakespeare and the Eighteenth-Century Poetic Miscellany', *Eighteenth-Century Life*, 41:1 (2017), 7–31.

[55] www.hyperhamlet.unibas.ch/ (last accessed 12 May 2017).

[56] See Douglas Lanier, 'Shakespearean Rhizomatics: Adaptation, Ethics, Value', in Alexa Huang and Elizabeth Rivlin (eds.), *Shakespeare and the Ethics of Appropriation* (New York: Palgrave Macmillan, 2014), pp. 21–40.

[57] See, for example, Robert Shaughnessy (ed.), *The Cambridge Companion to Shakespeare and Popular Culture* (Cambridge: Cambridge University Press, 2007); Michael P. Jensen, 'Shakespeare and the Comic Book', in Mark Thornton Burnett, Adrian Streete and Ramona Wray (eds.), *The Edinburgh Companion to Shakespeare and the Arts* (Edinburgh: Edinburgh University Press, 2011), pp. 388–405; Adam Hansen, *Shakespeare and Popular Music* (London: Continuum, 2010).

and pop songs repeatedly used Shakespearean language as a 'foil' against which to demonstrate their popularity, 'the act of citing Shakespeare became a conventional mark of the other', his words voiced in popular forms by 'eccentrics, lunatics, over-achievers, intellectuals, aliens, losers, homosexuals, and, most importantly, villains'.[58] Lanier also provides an annotated bibliography of 'Film Spin-Offs and Citations', as distinct from 'Film Adaptations', in Richard Burt's encyclopedic *Shakespeares after Shakespeare* (2007).[59] Several contributors to Burt's collection *Shakespeare after Mass Media* focus on quotation, in settings from *Bartlett's Familiar Quotations* (1855) (where the Shakespeare selections expanded significantly under new commercial imperatives after Bartlett's death) to Harlequin romances (where his words represent authority and emotional authenticity in a genre of changing status) and *Star Trek* (where the Shakespeare quotations are mediated by the commonplace tradition and evoke the manuals that enable characters to speak in Shakespearean phrases).[60]

In the twenty-first century, new media technologies have the potential to transform quotation yet again. For some, the fragmentariness, heterogeneity and multiplicity of the 'Shakespeares' in digital culture are defining; yet as scholarship races to catch up, attention to verbal fragments online has so far been relatively limited.[61] For Stephen O'Neill, who appears in this volume, digital Shakespeare can represent not so much a departure from, as an expansion in the scale of, earlier quotation practices: the YouTube Shakespeare excerpt 'perpetuates the concept of the exemplary Shakespearean speech' as it has appeared in collections of quotations since Shakespeare's own lifetime (see introductions to Parts II and III). A charge long levelled at anthologies is that they divorce Shakespeare's words from their context: O'Neill observes that, while dramatic context can be lost on this platform, the 'relational organization' of YouTube puts these isolated speeches into contact with their sources and with other texts.[62] But do

---

[58] Douglas Lanier, *Shakespeare and Modern Popular Culture* (Oxford: Oxford University Press, 2002), pp. 55, 66. See Graham Holderness's chapter in this present volume for discussion of the distinctions between culture and commerce, and high and low culture, that persist in modern scholarship (Chapter 15).

[59] Richard Burt, *Shakespeares after Shakespeare: An Encyclopedia of the Bard in Mass Media and Popular Culture* (Westport, CT: Greenwood Press, 2007).

[60] Helen M. Whall, 'Bartlett's Evolving Shakespeare'; Laurie E. Osborne, 'Harlequin Presents: That '70s Shakespeare and Beyond'; and Craig Dionne, 'The Shatnerification of Shakespeare: *Star Trek* and the Commonplace Tradition'; all in Richard Burt (ed.), *Shakespeare after Mass Media* (Basingstoke: Palgrave Macmillan, 2002), pp. 287–94, 127–49 and 173–91 respectively.

[61] Maurizio Calbi, *Spectral Shakespeare: Media Adaptations in the Twenty-First Century* (New York: Palgrave Macmillan, 2013).

[62] Stephen O'Neill, *Shakespeare and YouTube* (London: Arden, 2014).

other social media 'Shakespeares' represent more of a departure from previous practice? In this volume, O'Neill reveals the 'creative intertextuality and critical misquotation' at work at the point where Shakespeare, the individual human user and the technological apparatus of Twitter meet (see Chapter 16).

If fragments of Shakespeare are now a free resource for memes, mash-ups and tweeted misquotations, has quotation come full circle to reinhabit early modern notions of creative quotation? It is quickly apparent in Part III that proprietary notions of authorship persist in even the most playful uses of Shakespeare on social media. They are attended, sometimes explicitly, by the author function of 'Shakespeare'. Very often, the creative play is precisely with the residual authority that name confers – just as Shakespeare and his contemporaries themselves played creatively with biblical and classical authorities.[63] The persistent tension between reverence and reuse in quotation, traced in this volume over four centuries, becomes a productive creative resource in itself in the present day.

Digital media can give the impression of being open to all, but for whom is this 'communal ground', as in de Grazia's description of the early modern commonplace, and who is now excluded?[64] Taking an anthropological, cultural-studies and ethnographic approach to the 'strange human propensity' to repeat others' words, Ruth Finnegan answers the question of *Why Do We Quote?* with reference to the communities of family, educational group and nation, for whom quotation represents an in-joke, or a shared family or collegial history.[65] This is borne out in the handful of studies of Shakespeare in modern-day legal and political settings.[66] But if there are fascinating continuities with the 'communities of quotation' of the eighteenth-century House of Commons, in which Members of

---

[63] See Marjorie Garber, *Quotation Marks* (New York: Routledge, 2003) on the 'doxa' effect of quotation, pp. 19–20.

[64] De Grazia, 'Shakespeare in Quotation Marks', p. 58.

[65] Ruth Finnegan, *Why Do We Quote? The Culture and History of Quotation* (Cambridge: OpenBook, 2011).

[66] John Curtis, 'Twitter, *King Lear*, and the Freedom of Speech', *Exchanges: The Warwick Research Journal*, 1:2 (2014), 246–59; William Domnarski, 'Shakespeare in the Law', *Connecticut Bar Journal*, 67 (1993), 317–51; W. N. Osborough, *Literature, Judges and the Law* (Dublin: Four Courts Press, 2008). Jem Bloomfield sees Shakespeare quotation as part of the 'general language game' played in Parliament; *Words of Power*, p. 147. Conversely, Judi Atkins and Alan Finlayson, tracing the changing use of quotation in party conference keynote speeches, notice that, in the latter decades of the twentieth century, literary references, once common to all parties, were gradually replaced by references to the 'ordinary' voices of 'the British people'; Judi Atkins and Alan Finlayson, '"As Shakespeare so memorably said …": Quotation, Rhetoric and the Performance of Politics', *Political Studies*, 64:1 (2016), 164–81.

Parliament bandied lines from Shakespeare knowing they would be under-stood, there are also important points of departure.[67] Does Shakespeare still sustain communities of quotation? For all his global and digital reach, do Shakespeare quotations speak to entire nations, or to minority interest groups with shared educational experience and cultural values?[68] Does Shakespeare quotation represent an exclusive community, or a creative resource that everyone can deploy?

How scholars treat quotation tells us much about what they value. Visible across a wide range of studies of Shakespeare's formation and reception is a persistent sense that quotation represents a loss of context (we even speak of 'quoting out of context'); and that allusion, which implies a deeper knowledge of and engagement with a prior text in order to weave it more subtly into the new, is of more intrinsic interest. Meaning is often assumed to lie primarily in the sustained reworking or rethinking of Shakespeare's plots and characters. But quotations are not 'post-hermeneutic' (in Burt's phrase), nor emptied of meaning when detached from their source.[69] They are imbued with the significance not just of their original source in Shakespeare, but of several centuries, and many layers, of subsequent borrowing, which Shakespeare studies are beginning to document.

Shakespeare and Quotation is the first full-length study of the quotation of Shakespeare from his own lifetime to the present day. It historicises the significance of quotation in a wide range of literary genres, and in non-literary texts, in all periods from the sixteenth and seventeenth centuries to the twenty-first, and argues for the cumulative impact of those cen-turies of quotation on the status of Shakespeare in literature and culture. The chapters that follow demonstrate the meaningfulness of quotation-sized connections between texts; treat quotation as a cultural practice, rather than a transparent window on a prior text; and reveal the consti-tutive power of quotation in shaping not only Shakespeare's reputation but also language, culture and society more broadly. Together, they reveal the immense significance of quotation, both in the fabric of Shakespeare's plays and poems, and in what the world has made of them.

---

[67] Christopher Reid, ' "Community of Mind": Quotation and Persuasion in the Eighteenth-Century House of Commons', *The Age of Johnson*, 17 (2006), 317–40.

[68] See, for example, studies of 'Shakespeare in Quotations' in English, Spanish, French, German and Japanese, in *The Cambridge Guide to the Worlds of Shakespeare*, vol. II, pp. 1696–1706; and Huang and Rivlin, *Shakespeare and the Ethics of Appropriation*.

[69] Richard Burt, *Unspeakable ShaXXXpeares: Queer Theory and American Kiddie Culture* (New York: St Martin's Press, 1998), p. 243.

PART I

Shakespeare and Early Modern Quotation

Introduction

Julie Maxwell

How has Shakespeare become the most quoted English author of all time?

This part of the volume traces the earliest phase of a 400-year history. From the very beginning of his career, as James Bednarz shows us in Chapter 1, Shakespeare's lines were admiringly quoted – as well as enviously misquoted. 'My kingdom for a horse!' (*Richard III*, v.iv.13) was already inspiring endless variants. His phrases were parodied as well as praised; maxims and metaphors from his writings appeared in printed quotation books. His words were also starting to supply a language of political catchphrase. And, in a withering description of the new 'alchemists of eloquence' (including Shakespeare) in the late 1580s, we may perceive a further analogy to the present day. In contemporary reviewing culture and literary journalism, fine writing is frequently disparaged as 'showing off' – and quoted just as disapprovingly as Shakespeare's was in his time.[1]

But while there is much that is recognisable, there is also much that is not. Most significantly, it is hard for us to grasp the central importance of quotation in Shakespeare's culture. Quotation had key functions in education, religion and the law not immediately obvious to the contemporary reader.[2] It was an essential part of literacy training, and of reading habits, for example, in a way that is no longer the case. The title of Ann Moss's 1996 study of collections of quotations is indicative of how fundamental they were, historically, to large areas of mental life: *Printed Commonplace-Books and the Structuring of Renaissance Thought*. Early modern scholars are likely to be well aware of this. Yet quotation was also more crucial to Shakespeare's particular professional worlds – and his own writing – than has been recognised previously, even in specialist studies.

---

[1] Editorial, 'Who Put the Plain in Complain?', *Areté*, 27 (2008), 107–8.

[2] On education and religion, see Ann Moss, *Printed Commonplace-Books and the Structuring of Renaissance Thought* (Oxford: Clarendon Press, 1996); on the law, Quentin Skinner, *Forensic Shakespeare* (Oxford: Oxford University Press, 2014), pp. 291–314.

For quotation was not a one-directional practice, with Shakespeare's best (or worst!) lines passively quoted and misquoted by others. As we commented in the 'General Introduction', Shakespeare contributed actively to the memorability of his words – and not simply in the obvious sense that he often wrote pre-eminently well. The fact that quotation was a practice centrally embedded in early modern England provided part of the impetus to make his own words quotable too. It also meant that he responded more deeply to quotation as a form than has been thought until now. Part I of this study presents the evidence to make good those claims.

A Brief History of Quotation (1)

The next four chapters will explore the most relevant early modern contexts for understanding Shakespeare as both a quoting and quotable author. Quotation's history as a rhetorical practice, however, long precedes Shakespeare's time. And since this earlier history bears directly on his writing, as well as the following chapters of this study, it is worth identifying some main points straightaway.

In the 'General Introduction', we described the overtness of quotation compared to allusion. This overtness is related to the functions that, historically, it has been developed to perform. To quote is to invoke an authority and/or to cite the proof (with an implicit invocation of the general authority of truth). For the literary critic as for the lawyer and the theologian, quotation is evidence. Quoting the evidence in the form of proof-texts may be traced back ultimately to the Bible. Christian quotation of the Hebrew scriptures was used extensively and ingeniously by St Paul, a legally minded writer, in an attempt to prove the coming of the Messiah. Quoting the Bible was also a vitally important argumentative strategy throughout the early modern period. From the Reformation onward, scriptural proof-texts were used to argue in support of all manner of religious and political causes. 'Prove yt by scriptur', says the proto-Protestant ruler in John Bale's drama *King Johan* (c. 1538–9), 'and then wyll I yt alowe'.[3]

As Beatrice Groves shows in Chapter 3, Shakespeare quoted the Bible with witty awareness of how quotations were regarded as proof by contemporary clergymen and other religious writers. With Groves to guide us through the detail and significance of rarely read early modern religious

---

[3] John Bale, *The Complete Plays of John Bale*, ed. Peter Happé, 2 vols. (Cambridge: D. S. Brewer, 1985–6), vol. 1, line 1435.

texts, we are helped to grasp a little-understood dimension of Shakespeare's art. Quoting the Bible on stage could be used to moving as well as comical effect. Groves pays illuminating attention to how quotation functioned in Shakespeare's drama at the level of character, scene and (projected) audience experience, creating a sophisticated 'soundscape' that works in *1* and *2 Henry IV* as part of a wider dramatic technique.

When we turn from the Bible to other texts familiar to Shakespeare, it is apparent that quotation served powerful evidence functions here too. Quotations from exemplary writers in the vernacular (for example, Philip Sidney) were used to prove, in this case, that English literature could rival the greatness of classical literature. Quoted excerpts appeared in rhetoric manuals as illustrative examples of a wide variety of possible techniques.[4] Schoolboys also created their own commonplace books, individually compiled anthologies from their reading that served as a resource for later writing, speeches, letters etc., as well as a repository of received wisdom and suitably moral thoughts. Quoting the best authors – and the best *of* the best authors – was a practice carried into adult life. Schoolboy quotation is remembered by Shakespeare, for example, in *Titus Andronicus*'s misunderstood quotation of Horace (IV.ii.21–2).

As well as proving the strength of vernacular literature in general, a writer's individual greatness could also be measured by quotability. In Ben Jonson's *Poetaster* (1601), Virgil has supreme authority as a writer on this basis. 'To approve [i.e. both *prove* and *approve of*] his works of sovereign worth', says Tibullus, one need only observe that Virgil's lines already contain everything important a man could possibly need in his life.[5] Caesar clarifies that this means quotation: 'You mean he might repeat part of his works / As fit for any conference he can use?' (v.i.124–5). Exactly so.

Part I explains how this perception applied to Shakespeare among his contemporaries and within his own lifetime. As James P. Bednarz demonstrates in Chapter 1, quotation was used as evidence of the achievement and distinctiveness of playwrights who nonetheless worked in a culture of literary borrowing. It expressed professional rivalry and authorial self-positioning, as well as private fan admiration and commercial hopes. It also provides evidence, useful to us now, of early appreciation of both Shakespeare's plays and his poems, and of how that appreciation

---

[4] For a selection, and discussion of their significance, see Brian Vickers, *English Renaissance Literary Criticism* (Oxford: Oxford University Press, 1999); and Gavin Alexander, *Sidney's 'The Defence of Poesy' and Selected Renaissance Literary Criticism* (London: Penguin, 2004).

[5] Ben Jonson, *Poetaster*, ed. Thomas Cain (Manchester: Manchester University Press, 1995), v.i.116. Subsequent references are to this edition and are given in parentheses in the text.

was partly fostered by book trade practices. Bednarz's argument reveals a growing literary celebrity challenged by a younger generation of writers who sometimes quoted Shakespeare less than reverentially. And it hints – as remarked above, of the four centuries to come – of a nascent Shakespeare often quoted for his exemplary wisdom.

In Chapter 2 Kevin Petersen opens up a topic of apparently leaden dullness – maxims – and shows how Shakespeare's poetry interrogates widespread cultural assumptions about the value and efficacy of quoted wisdom. Forewarned is not forearmed, as it turns out. Shakespeare's use of quotation here can be understood as a challenge, not only to the claims that humanist pedagogues made for sententious quotation, but to a historiography reliant on paradigms. We get a glimpse of a proleptically modern-thinking Shakespeare among a much older mental machinery. Like other contributors to this part, Petersen draws on, and refines, recent research on the early modern book trade and the material text. His research illustrates how attention to quotation as a particular form can bring new insights to those areas of scholarly enquiry. Satisfyingly, he is able to combine literary with material criticism: to write about a narrative poem *as* a narrative as well as printed lines in a book.

Petersen's main example – *The Rape of Lucrece*'s paratextual apparatus of quotation marks enclosing sententious wisdom – demonstrates something else too. As we've already indicated, quotation was one way that a writer and/or printer might lay claim to classic literary status for a new work. This idea is fascinatingly pursued, in relation to *Hamlet*, by Douglas Bruster in Chapter 4. The world's most frequently quoted play is here revealed as a play that thinks deeply *about* quotation. Its quotability is, then, no accident but woven into its literary and theatrical textures. Bruster invites us to scrutinise what we generally take for granted: why should a dramatic work feature borrowed words at all, much less obsess over them? Quotation, Bruster argues, is how Shakespeare both achieves as a literary dramatist, and displays that achievement. Usefully, Bruster provides a typology of kinds of quotation in *Hamlet*, which leads him to uncover their unexpected overall function: as a metaphor for the full range of professional activities in and around the early modern theatre.

These chapters can be read individually, but are best read together. Points or examples touched on by one contributor are often developed by another. We have supplied cross-references to aid the interested reader. Common themes emerge. The competitiveness of quotation, for example, is apparent in examples as diverse as the War of the Theatres and the godly's denunciation of plays with biblical content.

Part I also lays the foundation for the reception history that follows in the rest of the volume. Take just one example: Milton's use of Shakespeare, a generation later, in *Eikonoklastes* (1649). The preceding emphasis on quotation as a form of proof helps us better to understand what might otherwise seem like a historical curiosity. Milton's father had been a trustee of the Blackfriars Theatre, and he grew up in a house just a few feet away from the legendary Mermaid Tavern. But Milton would later quote Shakespeare in a very different world. Literary quotation was now co-opted as quasi-legal proof. Following the trial and execution of King Charles I, Milton's regicide tracts were written to argue the case for the prosecution in the court of European opinion. In *Eikonoklastes*, Milton repeatedly uses quotation as a strategy to try to prove the charge of the king's tyranny. A quotation from a book supposedly written by King Charles and posthumously published, *Eikon Basilike* (1649), is followed by an excerpt from Shakespeare:[6]

> *I intended*, he [Charles I] saith, *not onely to oblige my Friends but mine enemies.* The like saith *Richard* [III], *Act 2. Scene 1*,
>
> *I do not know that Englishman alive*
> *With whom my soule is any jott at odds,*
> *More then the Infant that is borne to night;*
> *I thank my God for my humilitie.*

If Charles *sounds* like Richard III, then he must *be* like him. And when quotation is being used, as it is here, to argue the evidence, the necessary corollary is that what's being quoted must be absolutely clear. A passing allusion will not clinch the case. A hint, which might easily be missed, will not do. All this is in direct contrast to the nature of an allusion, which is not similarly essential to our comprehension. (We could read the epitaph on Shakespeare that Milton contributed to the Second Folio (1632), for example, without ever knowing what was not discovered in modern scholarship until 1999 – that the lines allude to a poem then circulating in manuscript and ascribed to Shakespeare himself.[7] To quote Christopher Ricks quoting William Empson on this point: 'It is tactful [for a poet], when making an obscure reference, to arrange that the verse shall be intelligible even when the reference is not understood.'[8]) In political discourse,

---

[6] The example is quoted and fully discussed in Nicholas McDowell, 'Milton's Regicide Tracts and the Uses of Shakespeare', in Nicholas McDowell and Nigel Smith (eds.), *The Oxford Handbook of Milton* (Oxford: Oxford University Press, 2009), pp. 252–71 (p. 270).
[7] By Gordon Campbell, as reported by Barbara K. Lewalski, *The Life of John Milton* (Oxford: Blackwell, 2000), p. 559, n86.
[8] Christopher Ricks, *Allusion to the Poets* (Oxford: Oxford University Press, 2002), p. 2.

an allusion can of course do different work: it might, for example, set off a train of associations that are polemically useful precisely because they go unexamined as evidence.

Paradoxically, however, in modern scholarship it is *quotation*'s nature and effects that have gone underexamined.

CHAPTER I

Shakespeare and the Early Modern Culture of Quotation

James P. Bednarz

At the end of the sixteenth century in England, an extraordinarily talented community of professional writers was at the centre of a culture of quotation. Words – in short bursts of memorable phrasing – became instantly recognisable tropes of individual authorship. Some well-known catchphrases circulated anonymously in the period, but others clung tenaciously to acknowledged authorial sources of attribution. Humanist educators encouraged imitation, but conceived of it as emulation – a struggle to overgo, not just repeat, antecedents. They encouraged the study of rhetorical commonplaces as an aid to expression and never condoned mimetic servility. How much linguistic and conceptual variation was necessary to avoid charges of plagiarism, however, remained a vexing issue of debate for Shakespeare and his contemporaries. At best, through quotation, professional writers were identified as the producers of an energised vernacular language worth remembering, transcribing and repeating. At worst, however, they could be subjected to the kind of abuse Shakespeare encountered when he found his own phrasing turned against him. Artful misquotation was part of a virulent coded attack on him in *Greene's Groatsworth of Wit, Bought with a Million of Repentance*, published in 1592.

Our understanding of the inception of Shakespeare's professional career as a poet-player begins with this satiric misquotation. In 1592, even before Shakespeare's work had reached print, he was quoted in a now famous apostrophe attributed to the dying Robert Greene (in a text heavily edited by Henry Chettle). It warned Christopher Marlowe, Thomas Nashe and George Peele about the threat that an ambitious poet-player posed to the livelihood of fellow poet-scholars. In denouncing actors as a class, he advised his colleagues to

> trust them not; for there is an upstart Crow, beautified with our feathers, that with his *Tygers hart wrapt in a Players hyde*, supposes he is as well able to

bombast out a blanke verse as the best of you: and being an absolute *Johannes fac totum*, is in his owne conceit the onely Shake-scene in a countrey.[1]

This passage is the first known instance of anyone quoting Shakespeare, and it depends upon the reader remembering the implied phrase – 'tiger's heart wrapped in a woman's hide' – from prior performance and associating it with its author, upon whose name the text plays. In vilifying Shakespeare, 'Greene' takes for granted a core community of artisan professionals, centred on Marlowe, Nashe and Peele, as well as a broader constituency of habitual hybrid theatregoer-book-buyers excited by the politics of performance. His remarks are addressed to an audience of readers so familiar with the contemporary theatre scene that some could not only decipher Shakespeare's name in 'Shake-scene' but also link the dramatist to a brief phrase from the unprinted *3 Henry VI*, spoken to Queen Margaret in the middle of a long blank-verse tirade by Richard Plantagenet, duke of York, as she oversees his assassination. The line of verse Greene played on would be published for the first time three years later without authorial attribution in *The true Tragedie of Richard Duke of Yorke*, a variant of the play later printed in the First Folio as *The Third part of King Henry the Sixt*. Rebuking her for taunting him to dry his eyes with a handkerchief stained with the blood of his young son Rutland, York laments:

> Oh Tygers hart wrapt in a womans hide?
> How couldst thou draine the life bloud of the childe,
> To bid the father wipe his eies withall,
> And yet be seene to beare a womans face?[2]

Greene's Groatsworth of Wit, however, takes such common cultural awareness of dramatic authorship for granted in its readership. Here, Shakespeare's ability to shake a 'scene' (the wooden platform on which he performed) with overpowering rhetoric is treated with the same contempt that Greene had previously voiced for Marlowe's notable success with blank verse. In *Perimedes the Blacksmith* (1588) Greene stated that he had been lampooned for being unable to write as forcefully as Marlowe, since he could not make

---

[1] Attributed to Henry Chettle and Robert Greene, *Greene's Groatsworth of Wit, Bought with a Million of Repentance*, ed. D. Allen Carroll (Binghamton: Center for Medieval and Renaissance Studies, 1994), p. 84.
[2] *The true Tragedie of Richard Duke of Yorke, and the death of good King Henrie the Sixt, with the whole contention between the two Houses Lancaster and Yorke* (London, 1595), B2v. The second edition of 1600 was also anonymous. Shakespeare was first explicitly identified in print as the author of these lines when *The true Tragedy* was turned into the second part of *The Whole Contention* by Thomas Pavier in 1619. He was again cited as their author in the alternative 'good' longer version of *3 Henry VI* in the First Folio of 1623.

his verses 'jet upon the stage in tragicall buskins, everie word filling the mouth … with that Atheist *Tamburlan*'. In retaliation, he enlisted Nashe to write a preface to *Menaphon* (1589) that indirectly satirises Marlowe for being one of those 'vain glorious Tragedians' and 'ideot Art-masters, that intrude themselves to our eares as the Alcumists of eloquence' as they seek to 'out-brave better pennes with the swelling bombast of bragging blanke verse'.[3]

Shakespeare's response to Greene's derogatory misquotation of his Marlovian rhetoric has long been assumed to be implicit in the Latin epigraph from Ovid's *Amores* displayed on the title page of *Venus and Adonis* in 1593 (Figure 3):

Vilia miretur vulgus: mihi flavus Apollo
Pocula Castalia plena ministret aqua.

In these lines Shakespeare as Ovid expresses the high standards he has set for himself in rejecting the common for the elite: 'Let the vulgar admire worthless things; may golden Apollo serve me cups full of Castalian water.' In Ovid's time drinking water from the Castalian spring on Mount Parnassus was thought to bring inspiration. Quoting *Amores*, I.xv.35–6 unites the author of *Venus and Adonis* with a standard of ancient literary excellence: Ovid's solicitation of divine inspiration from Apollo, the god of poetry. Adam Hooks speculates that the 'originary moment' of this epigraph 'is better understood within a broader Ovidian milieu' that was visibly accessible in Richard Field's printing house and William Harrison's bookshop 'rather than as the result of an isolated authorial ambition'.[4] 'To find his motto', Hooks continues, 'Shakespeare would not have to look any farther' than Harrison's stock of Ovidian poetry, printed by Field. Yet Hooks nevertheless admits that the epigraph's 'initial impulse and authorial aspiration belonged to Shakespeare'.[5] And, if this is the case,

[3] Robert Greene, *The Life and Works of Robert Greene*, ed. Alexander Grosart, 15 vols. (London: Huth Library, 1881–6), vols. VII, pp. 7–8; III, p. 311.

[4] Adam G. Hooks, 'Shakespeare at the White Greyhound', *Shakespeare Survey*, 64 (2011), 260–75 (p. 262). Hooks, despite his denial, tends to 'relocate a singular agency from the poet to his publisher or bookseller'. Yet George Chapman, as I indicate above, evokes *Amores*, I.xv.35–6 specifically to critique Shakespeare as the author of *Venus and Adonis*. Hooks plausibly assumes that, at the least, 'Field would have been comforted to know that there was a proximate precedent for his venture in contemporary Ovidian poetry, and that it was dedicated to a member of a circle with which he was associated' (p. 266). For Field's later involvement with Shakespeare and Chapman (along with Marston and Jonson) in the evocation of the same Ovidian lines in 1601, see James P. Bednarz, 'Contextualizing "The Phoenix and Turtle": Shakespeare, Edward Blount and the *Poetical Essays* Group of *Love's Martyr*', *Shakespeare Survey*, 67 (2015), 131–49.

[5] Hooks, 'Shakespeare at the White Greyhound', pp. 269, 272.

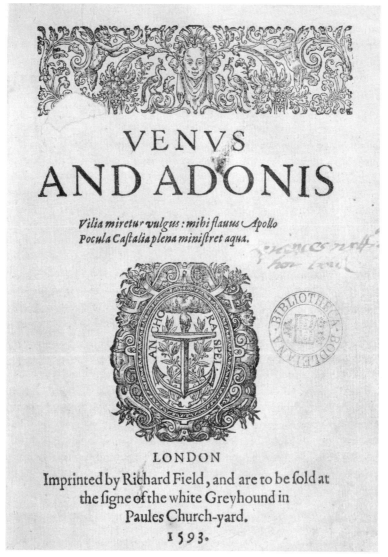

Figure 3   William Shakespeare, *Venus and Adonis* (London, 1593), title page.

Shakespeare's creative decision to quote *Amores*, i.xv.35–6 was simultaneously self-referential and contextual. It resonated with Shakespeare's bid
to distinguish himself as *the new Ovid* in a contemporary English poem
through a process of emulation within an 'Ovidian milieu'. Shakespeare
had apparently carefully chosen both his motto and his affiliation with
Field and Harrison. Maligned for being a poet-player instead of a poet-
scholar, Shakespeare, in his first-known involvement with the book trade,
demonstrates his prestigious classical learning through Latin quotation,
even as he balances his ostentatious Ovidian rhetoric with an accom-
panying act of humility by leaving his name off the poem's title page.
Authors regularly selected their own mottoes when they worked closely
with stationers. Greene himself had used Latin tags to signal a major
shift in his outlook in 1590, exchanging versions of Horace's 'Omne tulit
punctum qui miscuit utile dulci' ('He carries away every point who mixes
profit with delight') for the sterner 'Sero sed serio' ('Late but serious'). But
where Greene's name had been aggressively used as an advertising ploy
to attract readers, Shakespeare rejects this strategy. He reveals his name
only in his dedication to Henry Wriothesley, the earl of Southampton,
when establishing his identity as a patronage poet. Yet this new authorial
strategy of self-presentation was mocked by George Chapman a year later.
His poem *The Shadow of Night* obliquely censured the author of *Venus and
Adonis* for failing to match the high standard set by its epigraph:

> Presume not then ye flesh confounded soules,
> That cannot beare the full Castalian bowles,
> Which sever mounting spirits from the sences,
> To looke in this deepe fount for thy pretenses.[6]

---

[6] George Chapman, *The Shadow of Night*, 'Hymnus in Cynthiam', lines 162–5, in *The Poems of George Chapman*, ed. Phyllis Bartlett (New York: Russell & Russell, 1962), p. 34. The identification of these lines as an allusion to Shakespeare as the author of *Venus and Adonis* is widely accepted in contemporary scholarship. Recently, Katherine Duncan-Jones and H. R. Woudhuysen, *Shakespeare's Poems* (London: Thomson Learning, 2007), p. 127n, endorse it and cite MacDonald P. Jackson, 'Francis Meres and the Cultural Contexts of Shakespeare's Rival Poet Sonnets', *Review of English Studies*, 56 (2005), 224–46, who states that 'Shakespeare and his use of the Ovidian lines on the title-page' of *Venus and Adonis* are 'the objects of derision'. Katherine Duncan-Jones, *Shakespeare: Upstart Crow to Sweet Swan 1592–1623* (London: Bloomsbury, 2011), p. 131, also uses this quotation to anchor her extended exposition of how Chapman's poem 'echoes and answers Shakespeare's *Venus and Adonis*'. Jackson, in turn, evokes Douglas Bush's well-received description of Chapman's lines in *Mythology and the Renaissance Tradition in English Poetry* (New York: Norton, 1960), p. 208n, as 'a clear allusion to the *pocula Castalia* of the Ovidian motto prefixed to *Venus and Adonis*'. Bush notes that Chapman's change from 'ye' to 'thy' particularises his criticism as 'the protest of a mystic and moralist against a leader of the fleshly school' (p. 130). John Huntington, *Ambition, Rank and Poetry in 1590s England* (Urbana: University of Illinois Press, 2001), p. 130, similarly notes that Chapman 'invokes the Ovidian moment of Shakespeare's epigraph'. Huntington construes Chapman's censure as a literary judgement based on a conception of what great poetry should be.

Chapman deployed Shakespeare's motto as a marker of literary difference. In affiliating himself with Ovid through quotation, Shakespeare consequently created an enduring self-identification. The volume became, during his lifetime, his most frequently reprinted and copied work. It was an association that Francis Meres evoked most grandly in 1598 by concluding that 'the sweete wittie soule of *Ovid* lives in mellifluous & hony-tongued *Shakespeare*'.[7]

Yet the initially negative reviews of his drama and poetry by 'Greene' and Chapman were overshadowed by a growing fascination with Shakespeare's eloquence. At about the same time that Greene ridiculed *3 Henry VI*, Nashe, in *Pierce Penniless*, also published in 1592, marvelled at the emotional power of the similarly unpublished *1 Henry VI*, which had moved thousands of spectators, claiming that 'there is no immortalitie can be given a man on earth like unto Playes'.[8] An indication of the existence of a more widespread Shakespearean culture of quotation is revealed in the non-professional 'commonplacing' activity of Edward Pudsey. Pudsey kept a notebook into which he copied, mostly between 1600 and 1603, memorable phrases from *Titus Andronicus, Romeo and Juliet, The Merchant of Venice, Richard II, Richard III, Much Ado about Nothing, Hamlet* and *Othello*.[9] Pudsey's interests in Shakespeare and a range of other writers are primarily ethical and rhetorical, focused on exemplary models of instruction or eloquence. Sometimes he transcribes adages consisting of moral observations or practical knowledge. 'When the blood burnes ye soule ys prodigall to lend the loving vowes', he notes from *Hamlet* (1.iii.116–17). Yet he also appreciates Shakespeare's linguistic flair in his list of love's oxymorons from *Romeo and Juliet* (1.i.171–2): 'ffeath^r of lead, bright smoake, cold fyer, sick health, still waking sleep'. Since all these dramas except *Othello* were available to Pudsey in print, his jottings demonstrate how the publication of Shakespeare's plays, which began with *Titus Andronicus* in 1594, accelerated the practice of copying his work. But since *Othello* was first published in 1622, nine years after Pudsey's death in 1613, he might have

---

Field printed a Latin version of the *Amores* in 1594, a year after *Venus and Adonis*. But the fact that he also printed *The Shadow of Night* that year (this time for William Ponsonby) complicates his relation to Shakespeare's Ovidianism as well as our impression of the vendible inventory of Harrison's White Greyhound.

[7] Francis Meres, *Palladis Tamia*, ed. A. J. Smith, in *Elizabethan Critical Essays*, 2 vols. (Oxford: Oxford University Press, 1904), vol. II, p. 317.

[8] Thomas Nashe, *The Works of Thomas Nashe*, ed. Ronald B. McKerrow, 5 vols. (Oxford: Blackwell, 1958), vol. I, p. 312.

[9] Pages of Edward Pudsey's commonplace book are currently divided between eighty-eight numbered leaves at the Bodleian Library and four separate leaves at the Shakespeare Birthplace Trust Record Office and Library.

transcribed quotations from *Othello* during a performance or soon after, if he had not read it in a lost manuscript.[10]

The political utility of Shakespeare's wit was recognised early. In 1598, Tobie Matthew, paraphrasing Falstaff, wrote to Dudley Carleton that those seeking military intervention in the Low Countries seemed doomed: 'honour pricks them on; and ye world thinks yt honour will quickly prick them of[f] again'.[11] This impulse to quote Shakespeare because he phrased expressions so memorably is also evident on a less directed level in the doodling of the anonymous 'scribbler' of the Northumberland manuscript. Sometime at the end of the Elizabethan period, this writer scrawled variations on Shakespeare's name, noted the titles *Richard II* and *Richard III*, approximated what was taken to be the longest word in Latin (*honorificabilitudinus*) featured in *Love's Labours Lost* (v.i.36) and jotted down a line from *Lucrece* on the cover of a manuscript that consisted mainly of tracts by Francis Bacon. Shakespeare writes that on the morning after Lucrece's rape by Tarquin, 'Revealing day through every cranny spies, / And seems to point her out where she sits weeping' (lines 1086–7). Lucrece then asks the sun to stop its 'peeping' (1089). Recalling this, the scribbler, possibly one of Bacon's secretaries and perhaps trying out his quill pen, writes, among a welter of miscellaneous musings:

> *revealing*
> *day through*
> *every crany*
> *peepes and see*

The works he recalls were all published by 1597. A similar caprice in the mid 1590s induced Henry Colling of Bury St Edmunds, Suffolk, to copy from memory the famous erotic blazon from *Venus and Adonis* into a volume of late-fifteenth-century historical manuscripts.[12] What is particularly important about the Northumberland manuscript, as Patrick Cheney points out, is its evidence of how Shakespeare's contemporaries recognised him equally for writing narrative poetry and drama.[13]

---

[10] Pudsey's quotation of *Hamlet* is from Shakespeare Birthplace Trust, MS ER 82/1/21, fo. 2. His echo of *Romeo and Juliet* appears in Bodleian Library, MS Eng. Poet. d. 3, fo. 86v. His four paraphrases of *Othello* are found at the bottom of fo. 1 in the Shakespeare Birthplace Trust pages.

[11] This application of *1 Henry IV* (v.i.129–30) is cogently analysed by Charles Whitney, *Early Responses to Renaissance Drama* (Cambridge: Cambridge University Press, 2006), p. 84.

[12] See Sasha Roberts, *Reading Shakespeare's Poems in Early Modern England* (Basingstoke: Palgrave, 2003), p. 84.

[13] For a facsimile edition with transcription, see *Northumberland Manuscripts*, ed. Frank J. Burgoyne (London: Longmans, Green, 1904); Patrick Cheney, *Shakespeare, National Poet-Playwright* (Cambridge: Cambridge University Press, 2008), pp. 65–6.

But while Pudsey, the Northumberland scribbler and Colling quoted
Shakespeare for personal pleasure, a group of stationers associated with
John Bodenham began to realise the commercial potential of mining
Shakespeare's work for commonplaces, thereby producing what Neil
Rhodes calls some of 'the first anthologies of English literature'.[14] In 1600,
two printed commonplace books – *Bel-vedére*, assembled by A. M. (probably Anthony Munday), and *England's Parnassus*, compiled by Robert
Allott – testify to Shakespeare's growing influence.[15] Both are assembled by
topic, but differ mainly insofar as *Bel-vedére* limits its excerpts to between
one and two lines while *England's Parnassus* provides longer entries. *Bel-
vedére* does not add ascriptions to specific quotations, but it is particularly
noteworthy for its enthusiastic treatment of Shakespeare, who still by no
means dominates the collection. *Bel-vedére* offers some 4,482 quotations,
with 214 selections from Shakespeare, more than from either Samuel
Daniel or Edmund Spenser. These are divided among: *Lucrece* (91); *Richard
II* (47); *Venus and Adonis* (34); *Richard III* (13); *Romeo and Juliet* (13); *The
True Tragedy* (10); *Love's Labour's Lost* (5); and *1 Henry IV* (1). If *Edward III*
(23) is added, there are 237. Although about half of the quotations are from
the two narrative poems, the prominence of *Richard II* is proof that some
early modern readers fused their assessment of Shakespeare as the author of
narrative poetry and commercial drama, without perceiving a generic split
between them. Robert Allott's *England's Parnassus* consists of 2,350 excerpts
from narrative and dramatic poetry similarly organised under headings,
but arranged alphabetically, from 'Albion' to 'Youth'. Within this structure
it prints 95 quotations correctly attributed to Shakespeare from: *Lucrece*
(39); *Venus and Adonis* (26); *Romeo and Juliet* (13); *Richard II* (7); *Richard
III* (5); *Love's Labour's Lost* (3); and *1 Henry IV* (2). Allott was, however,
more interested in the writing of Spenser, Drayton, William Warner, Sir
John Harington and Thomas Lodge, whom he quotes more frequently.
These 'florilegia' (collections of the flowers of rhetoric), as they were sometimes called, helped create a market for Shakespearean wisdom literature
that still flourishes four centuries later. Yet even though their intent was to
provide models of eloquence and insight, they repeatedly alter, misquote
and maul their sources. However similar they may be, each of these two
collections operates in an opposite manner and, in doing so, they epitomise
the nature of quotation in the period. While *England's Parnassus* helped

[14] Neil Rhodes, *Shakespeare and the Origins of English* (Oxford: Oxford University Press, 2004), p. 154.
[15] *Bel-vedére; or, The Garden of the Muses* (London, 1600); and *Englands Parnassus; or, The Choysest
Flowers of Our Moderne Poets, With their Poetical Comparisons* … (London, 1600).

initiate the cultural process that would cause 'Shakespeare' to be construed as a source of omniscient understanding, *Bel-vedére* lists him at its opening but transforms his pithy insights into unattributed commonplaces. Shakespeare included popular expressions, proverbs, aphorisms, maxims, witticisms, catchphrases and popular songs in his writing throughout his career, and with *Bel-vedére* some of his words returned to anonymity. In its section on 'Love', for example, adapted echoes of *Romeo and Juliet* can only be discerned by carefully scanning its list of unidentified apothegms:

> Love is too full of faith, too credulous.
> Great force and vertue hath a loving looke.
> No stonie limits can hold out true love.
> What love can doe, that dare it still attempt.[16]

Continuing quotation of his writing accompanied Shakespeare's growing stature as a literary celebrity by the beginning of the seventeenth century. In 1594, Richard Barnfield echoed *Venus and Adonis* in *The Affectionate Shepherd*, and in 1600 Samuel Nicholson wove phrases from *Venus and Adonis*, *Lucrece* and *The Affectionate Shepherd* into *Acolastus His After-Witte*. Nicholson even revives 'O woolvish heart wrapt in a womans hyde', to remonstrate against an unfaithful lover.[17] An active manuscript culture lifted passages from *Venus and Adonis*, *Lucrece*, *The Passionate Pilgrim*, the *Sonnets* and *A Lover's Complaint*, sometimes with telling changes devised by anonymous collaborators. Around the turn of the century the romantic fictions Shakespeare favoured were challenged by a younger generation of poets who found their voice in formal verse satire. Within this changing cultural scene, writers such as John Marston mocked gallants infatuated by *Venus and Adonis* and *Romeo and Juliet*. Marston's Luscus in *The Scourge of Villanie* is a theatregoer so besotted with Shakespeare's amorous rhetoric that from his 'lips … doth flow / Naught but pure *Juliat* and *Romio*'. Luscus's conversation is drawn from the 'stock / Of well-penned plays' he has copied into his table book.[18] The infatuated Gullio of the anonymous Cambridge student play *Return from Parnassus, Part 1*, is similarly mocked for using lines 5–6 of *Venus and Adonis* to court his intended mistress: 'Pardon faire lady, thoughe sicke thoughted Gullio makes a maine unto thee, & like a bould faced sutore gins to woo thee'. 'We shall have nothinge but pure Shakspeare', Ingenioso observes, as Gullio further

---

[16] Quoted from *Bel-vedére*, p. 30. The last two lines paraphrase *Romeo and Juliet*, II.ii.67–8.
[17] Samuel Nicholson, *Acolastus His After-Witte* (London, 1600), sig. C1v (line 265).
[18] John Marston, *The Scourge of Villanie*, Satire XI, lines 38–9, 50–1, quoted from *The Poems of John Marston*, ed. Arnold Davenport (Liverpool: Liverpool University Press, 1961).

paraphrases *Venus and Adonis* and adds from *Romeo and Juliet* (ii.iv.35–7): 'the moone in comparison of thy bright hue' is 'a meere slutt, *Anthonies* Cleopatra a blacke browde milkmaide, Hellen a dowdie'. Alert to Gullio's ploy of crudely paraphrasing Shakespeare's well-known verses as his own, Ingenioso again responds: 'Marke Romeo, and Juliet. o monstrous theft'.[19]

The quotations that Shakespeare's contemporaries cited most frequently are not usually the ones that come to mind today. It is perhaps impossible to account fully for changes in the frequency of popular reiteration in this regard. Yet, Richard III's plea, 'A horse, a horse, my kingdom for a horse!' (v.iv.13), still serves as a magnet for witty variations. John Marston first isolated the line in *The Scourge of Villanie* of 1598, when he opened 'A Cynicke Satire' by assuming the desperate voice of Shakespeare's Richard III: '*A Man, a man, my kingdome for a man*'.[20] Shakespeare's Richard III could not find a steed, but Marston's satiric commentator complains that he cannot find a man, since they have all turned into beasts. In *Cynthia's Revels*, Jonson accuses Marston of depending too much on Shakespeare, and in *What You Will* Marston's spokesman Quadratus replies by claiming his freedom to recite the same quotation – 'A horse, a horse, my kingdom for a horse!' – before adding defiantly: 'Looke the[e] I speake play scrappes.'[21] While denouncing others in *The Scourge of Villanie* for attempting to steal Shakespeare's phrasing by passing it off as their own, in *What You Will* Marston nevertheless insists on his own right to quote Shakespeare whenever he pleases. Indeed, he found Shakespeare's phrasing so memorable that he alludes to it again as an in-joke in *Parasitaster* (1604): 'A fool, a fool, a fool, my coxcomb for a fool'. Others would follow his lead. In Thomas Heywood's *Second Part of the Iron Age* (1611), Synon's call, 'A horse, a horse', is answered by Pyrhus, 'Ten Kingdomes for a horse to enter *Troy*'. The phrase would subsequently be picked up by Richard Brathwaite in *A Strappado for the Divell* (1615) and Richard Corbett in 'Iter Boreale' (before 1621).[22]

---

[19] Quoted from the transcription of *The Return from Parnassus, Part 1*, in Bodleian Library, MS Rawlinson D, 398, fos. 214v–215r, in Appendix C of *The Riverside Shakespeare*, ed. G. Blakemore Evans (Boston: Houghton Mifflin, 1997), p. 1961. This play was performed at St John's College, Cambridge, sometime between 1598 and 1602.

[20] Marston, *The Scourge of Villainie*, Satire vii, line 1. Indeed, when writing *Richard III* it is possible that Shakespeare himself adapted phrasing from George Peele's *The Battell of Alcazar* (London, 1594), sig. F3r: 'A horse, a horse, villaine, a horse!'.

[21] John Marston, *What You Will* (London, 1607), sig. C1r–v. For the theatrical context of these quotations in 1601, see James P. Bednarz, *Shakespeare and the Poets' War* (New York: Columbia University Press, 2001), pp. 166–7.

[22] John Marston, *Parasitaster; or, The Fawn*, ed. David A. Blowstein (Manchester: Manchester University Press, 1978), v.43–4; Thomas Heywood, *The Second Part of the Iron Age*, in *The Dramatic*

It comes as no surprise then to hear the stranded usurer Security in *Eastward Ho!* (1605) call out: 'A boat, a boat, a boat, a full hundred marks for a boat!'.[23] A comic collaboration by Marston, Jonson and Chapman, *Eastward Ho!* prompts laughter at the expense of *Hamlet* in a network of ridiculous verbal echoes. ''Sfoot, Hamlet, are you mad?' (III.ii.6), Gertrude asks her footman. 'My coach, for the love of heaven, my coach!' (III.ii.24), she continues, repeating Ophelia's 'Come, my coach!' (*Hamlet*, IV.v.71), before singing:

> 'His head as white as milk,
> All flaxen was his hair;
> But now he is dead,
> And laid in his bed,
> And never will come again.' (*Eastward Ho!*, III.ii.64–8)

Hamlet's 'Thrift, thrift, Horatio, the funeral baked meats / Did coldly furnish forth the marriage tables' (*Hamlet*, I.ii.180–1) is similarly evoked in Quicksilver's jest to Gertrude that her father had married Golding to her younger sister in haste so 'that the cold meat left at your wedding might serve to furnish their nuptial table' (*Eastward Ho!*, III.ii.51). Such 'play ends' (*Eastward Ho!*, II.i.107), as Touchstone calls them, were calculated to register a smile of recognition at their obvious incongruity. Four years earlier, in 1601, Shakespeare, Marston, Chapman and Jonson had been commissioned by Sir John Salusbury to write a series of lyrics on the archetype of the 'phoenix and turtle' for a miscellany of *Poetical Essays* appended to Robert Chester's *Love's Martyr*. In a metatheatrical jest, Shakespeare's erstwhile poetic collaborators appear to have deliberately included him in their dramatic collaboration on *Eastward Ho!* by conspicuously repeating his phrasing. The one absent member of their earlier group was consequently included by proxy in their amusing city comedy through the addition of this series of burlesque quotations drawn from the recently published *Hamlet*.

Jonson was one of Shakespeare's most ardent admirers as well as being one of his severest critics, and a criticism he repeatedly made was that

---

Works of Thomas Heywood, ed. John Pearson, 3 vols. (London: J. Pearson, 1874), vol. III, p. 369; Richard Brathwait, 'Upon a Poets Palfrey', line 4, in *A Strappado for the Divell*, ed. J. W. Ebsworth (Boston, Lincolnshire: R. Roberts, 1878); and Richard Corbett, 'Iter Boreale', in *Certain Elegant Poems* (London, 1647), sig. B6v.

[23] Ben Jonson, *Eastward Ho!*, III.iv.3–4, ed. Suzanne Gossett and W. David Kay, in *The Cambridge Edition of the Works of Ben Jonson*, ed. David Bevington *et al.*, 7 vols. (Cambridge: Cambridge University Press, 2013), vol. II. Subsequent references to Jonson are to this edition and are given in parentheses in the text.

Shakespeare's writing lacked control. In *Discoveries*, his commonplace book, for example, Jonson noted that:

> His wit was in his own power; would the rule of it had been so too. Many times he fell into those things, could not escape laughter: as when he said in the person of Caesar, one speaking to him, 'Caesar thou dost me wrong'; he replied, 'Caesar did never wrong, but with just cause'; and such like, which were ridiculous. But he redeemed his vices with his virtues. There was ever more in him to be praised, than to be pardoned. (vol. VII, p. 522)

Jonson enjoyed this jest so much that he repeated it in the Induction to *The Staple of News* (1626) (lines 36–7). In the text of the Shakespeare First Folio, however, these lines in *Julius Caesar*, spoken to Metellus Cimber, read: 'Know, Caesar doth not wrong, nor without cause / Will he be satisfied' (III.i.47–8). Jonson was too careful a critic to have mistaken Shakespeare's language in this instance, and the dialogue of *Julius Caesar*, as we have it, seems to have been altered in deference to his critique, leaving a half line as a result of its revision.[24]

With this escalating attention to his language from contemporary writers, whom among them did he quote? The two he engaged most seriously through quotation are the two whose work he found most challenging: Marlowe and Jonson. Shakespeare's only attributed direct quotation of any contemporary writer is found in the brief pastoral elegy spoken by the shepherdess Phebe in *As You Like It*. She accepts the aphoristic wisdom of line 176 of *Hero and Leander* after having experienced instantaneous desire for Rosalind, disguised as Ganymede:

> Dead shepherd, now I know thy saw of might:
> 'Who ever lov'd that loved not at first sight?' (III.vi.80–1)

The couplet was a rhyme scheme at which Marlowe excelled, and Shakespeare consequently duplicates both the signature form and content of *Hero and Leander* in framing Marlowe's question. Within Shakespeare's pastoral play the natural and artificial are paradoxically inseparable; Marlowe, who died on 30 May 1593, is thus eulogised through quotation in the allusive Forest of Arden. The publication of three different editions of *Hero and Leander* in 1598 initiated a revival of interest in his work that was sustained well into the next century. Marlowe is the 'Dead shepherd' because he was the author of one of the period's most famous pastoral lyrics. It came to be known as *The passionate Sheepheard to his love* when it was printed in *England's Helicon* in 1600, after having been attributed to

[24] See J. Dover Wilson, 'Ben Jonson and *Julius Caesar*', *Shakespeare Survey*, 2 (1966), 36–43.

Shakespeare, a year earlier, in *The Passionate Pilgrim*.[25] It is a lyric, Douglas Bruster notes, 'that clearly fascinated its contemporaries: Greene, Drayton, Lodge, Deloney and Walton are only a few of the many authors who quote it'.[26] That Sir Hugh Evans sings it (to calm his nerves) in *The Merry Wives of Windsor* (III.i.12–24) may have encouraged the false attribution. Shakespeare's quotation recalls Marlowe as the deceased *magister amoris* whose wise 'saw' universalises one of love's most extravagant expressions. But Shakespeare's memorial is, nevertheless, subtly playful, since Marlowe's 'saw' proves to be wrong in the case of its quoter (see Chapter 2). Upon discovering that Ganymede is Rosalind, Phebe finally accepts Silvius, the devoted shepherd she had long despised. Dramatic context ironises Marlowe's generalisation. Aside from Evans and Phebe, Pistol in *2 Henry IV* – the character best known for quoting Marlowe in Shakespeare's drama – garbles *2 Tamburlaine*: 'Shall pack-horses / And hollow pampered jades of Asia, / Which cannot go but thirty mile a day, / Compare with Caesars and with Cannibals, / And Troyant Greeks?' (II.iv.130–4).[27] This misquotation says more about Pistol as an incompetent retailer of Marlovian hyperbole than it does about Marlowe's writing itself. But it also indicates Shakespeare's awareness of the dangers inherent in echoing what Jonson in the Shakespeare First Folio famously calls 'Marlowe's mighty line' (sig. A4r).

When Shakespeare quoted Marlowe, he evoked the past, but when he answered Jonson's 'armed Prologue' to *Poetaster* with his own 'Prologue armed' of *Troilus and Cressida*, around the end of 1601, at the climax of the Poets' War, he addressed a living rival.[28] Jonson's 'armed Prologue', vigilant against detractors, beats down Envy and interprets his own heroic action as illustrating how:

> the allegory and the hid sense
> Is, that a well erected confidence
> Can fright their pride and laugh their folly hence. (lines 73–5)

In his Prologue to *Troilus and Cressida*, Shakespeare counters this inflated self-confidence with radical scepticism about the quality of the play, its author and actors:

[25] See James P. Bednarz, 'Canonizing Shakespeare: *The Passionate Pilgrim*, *England's Helicon* and the Question of Authenticity', *Shakespeare Survey*, 60 (2007), 252–67.

[26] Douglas Bruster, *Quoting Shakespeare* (Lincoln: University of Nebraska Press, 2000), p. 55.

[27] Tamburlaine mocks the three captive kings who pull his chariot: 'Holla, ye pampered jades of Asia! / What, can ye draw but twenty miles a day?' (IV.iii.1–2). Cited from Christopher Marlowe, *Tamburlaine*, ed. J. S. Cunningham (Manchester: Manchester University Press, 1999).

[28] For background on this theatrical debate, see Bednarz, *Shakespeare and the Poets' War*.

and hither am I come,
A prologue armed, but not in confidence
Of author's pen or actor's voice, but suited
In like conditions as our argument. (lines 22–5)

Here 'confidence' is the key word Shakespeare quotes from *Poetaster*,
where it expresses Jonson's faith in the power of his literary authority.
Shakespeare obviously expected enough members of his audience to have
recently seen *Poetaster* at Blackfriars to make his critique of Jonson's literary
programme recognisable. Shakespeare's overt linking of these Prologues
splits his original spectators' interests between his play's internal fiction of
the Trojan War and a metatheatrical referentiality that contests Jonson's
self-assured didactic dramaturgy. Strategic quotation consequently enables
a distinct layer of literary criticism to emerge within the drama as an
element integral to its meaning. At the beginning of the seventeenth century, Shakespeare, like his predecessor Robert Greene, used quotation as a
powerful vehicle for defining his position in literary culture. But he did so
with far greater sophistication. His spokesman, inhabiting a more uncertain world, characterises himself as lacking those heroic attributes – virtue
and power – that Jonson's interlocutor claims to possess.

'Language most shows the man: speak, that I may see thee', Jonson
wrote in *Discoveries*. 'It springs out of the most retired and inmost parts
of us, and is the image of the parent of it, the mind' (vol. vii, p. 567).
Does it matter that he translated much of this famous passage on how
speech particularises a speaker from Juan Luis Vives's *De ratione dicendi*?[29]
Humanists typically viewed themselves as drawing on common sources
of knowledge. And although Dryden called Jonson a 'learned' plagiarist,
there was never a consensus in the early modern period about how much
of another's recognisable language and ideas one might use before being
accused of being merely parasitic. This was particularly true in the case of
translation. Shakespeare and his contemporaries' mutual pursuit of eloquence caused them to be especially attentive to each other's modes of
expression, as they called on the resources of rhetoric both to reiterate
each other's language and to distinguish themselves from each other. While

---

[29] See Juan Luis Vives, *De ratione dicendi*, in *Opera omnia*, 2 vols. (Basle, 1555), vol. ii, p. 103: 'Quippe
oratio ex intimis nostri pectoris recessibus oritu … Et imago est animi parentis sui' ('Indeed, speech
springs from the innermost recesses of our breast … It is the image of the soul, of its parent'). Jonson
borrowed extensively from Vives; his copy of *Opera omnia* is preserved in the library of St John's
College, Cambridge.

Shakespeare was still living, quotations from his work had multiple uses and served as evidence for conflicting conceptualisations of his merit. Over the next four centuries, however, the criticism Shakespeare was initially subjected to by 'Greene' and Jonson would occasionally be revived through burlesque, but its expression would be subsumed increasingly by adulation.

CHAPTER 2

Shakespeare and Sententiae: The Use of Quotation in Lucrece

Kevin Petersen

What happens when Shakespeare wants you to quote him? A compelling answer to that question appears in the first edition of Shakespeare's poem *Lucrece*, published in 1594 by his fellow Stratfordian, Richard Field. Not often noted, the first edition of the poem supplements the narrative with printed marks of sententiousness (Figure 4). Inverted commas printed in the margins serve as paratexts, which highlight portable precepts and encourage readers to memorise or to copy the passages into a commonplace book.[1] The poem's use of this paratext complements Gabriel Harvey's well-known comment that the 'wiser sort' valued *Lucrece* and *Hamlet* while the immature and simple took pleasure in *Venus and Adonis* (1593).[2] The 'graver labour' Shakespeare promised to the earl of Southampton in his first narrative poem was demonstrated in the latter publication by the visual apparatus indicating its wisdom and value.[3] Where Shakespeare's first narrative poem delights readers with an over-lusty goddess, the second aspires to the literary and epic, worthy of study and remembrance through quotation. The presence of these paratextual markers suggests that Shakespeare, with the help of industrious readers who replicate passages in their commonplace books, wishes his text to thrive well into the future, beyond the life of its material publication, outside the reach of 'sluttish time' (Sonnet 55, line 4).

---

[1] On the practice of marking commonplaces in Elizabethan literature see G. K. Hunter, 'The Marking of *Sententiae* in Elizabethan Printed Plays, Poems, and Romances,' *The Library*, 5th series, 6 (1951–2), 171–88.

[2] Writing in the margins of his edition of Chaucer, Harvey notes, 'The younger sort takes much delight in Shakespeares Venus, & Adonis: but his Lucrece, & his tragedie of Hamlet, prince of Denmarke, have it in them, to please the wiser sort.' See Virginia F. Stern, *Gabriel Harvey: His Life, Marginalia and Library* (Oxford: Clarendon Press, 1979), pp. 126–8.

[3] See *Venus and Adonis*'s dedication to Wriothesley, where Shakespeare vows 'to take advantage of all idle hours, till I have honoured you with some graver labour'. William Shakespeare, *The Poems*, ed. John Roe, The New Cambridge Shakespeare (Cambridge: Cambridge University Press, 2006), p. 86.

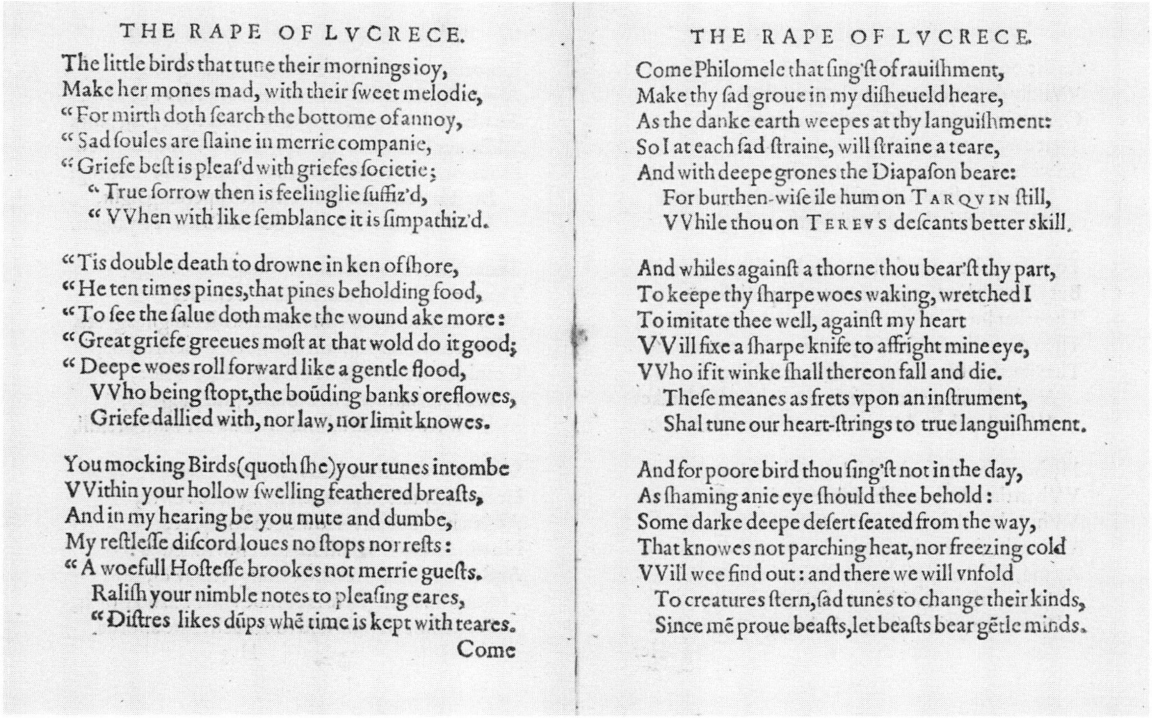

The little birds that tune their mornings ioy,
Make her mones mad, with their sweet melodie,
"For mirth doth search the bottome of annoy,
"Sad soules are slaine in merrie companie,
"Griefe best is pleas'd with griefes societie;
  "True sorrow then is feelingly suffiz'd,
  "VVhen with like semblance it is sympathiz'd.

"Tis double death to drowne in ken of shore,
"He ten times pines, that pines beholding food,
"To see the salue doth make the wound ake more:
"Great griefe greeues most at that wold do it good;
"Deepe woes roll forward like a gentle flood,
  "VVho being stopt, the bouding banks oreflowes,
  Griefe dallied with, nor law, nor limit knowes.

You mocking Birds(quoth she)your tunes intombe
VVithin your hollow swelling feathered breasts,
And in my hearing be you mute and dumbe,
My restlesse discord loues no stops nor rests:
"A woefull Hostesse brookes not merrie guests.
  Ralish your nimble notes to pleasing eares,
  "Distres likes dups whē time is kept with teares.
                                        Come

Come Philomele that sing'st of rauishment,
Make thy sad groue in my disheueld heare,
As the danke earth weepes at thy languishment:
So I at each sad straine, will straine a teare,
And with deepe grones the Diapason beare:
  For burthen-wise ile hum on TARQVIN still,
  VVhile thou on TEREVS descants better skill.

And whiles against a thorne thou bear'st thy part,
To keepe thy sharpe woes waking, wretched I
To imitate thee well, against my heart
VVill fixe a sharpe knife to affright mine eye,
VVho if it winke shall thereon fall and die.
  These meanes as frets vpon an instrument,
  Shal tune our heart-strings to true languishment.

And for poore bird thou sing'st not in the day,
As shaming anie eye should thee behold:
Some darke deepe desert seated from the way,
That knowes not parching heat, nor freezing cold
VVill wee find out: and there we will vnfold
  To creatures sterne, sad tunes to change their kinds,
  Since men proue beasts, let beasts beare gentle minds.

Figure 4   William Shakespeare, *Lucrece* (London, 1594). sigs. H3v–H4r.

Lucrece prints at least thirteen marked passages of *sententiae* with double inverted commas at the beginnings of lines.[4] The inverted commas, as Philip Sidney observed, 'stand there like a hand in the margine of a Booke, to note some saying worthy to be marked'.[5] Early modern readers knew a marked passage urged careful reading, copying and potential redeployment in the future. In both books and manuscripts, sententious markers transformed narratives from momentary entertainments to epistemological resources that a careful reader would categorise into a commonplace book. Thus the presentation of the poem defines it as a humanist tool and intellectual commodity. In its material form, *Lucrece* was a poem worthy of payment and worthy of reuse. Why Shakespeare's poem utilised this paratext, and whether or not he was involved in publishing decisions, however, remain questions that involve how we understand Shakespeare's relationship to print and what role publication played in defining the literary.

Research on early modern readers and printers, and the confluence between the material text and literary interpretation, have evolved significantly in recent years. Critics have demonstrated that paratexts play a significant role in interpretation. As Leah Price has argued, 'Far from replacing hermeneutics by pedantry, book history insists that every aspect of a literary work bears interpretation – even, or especially, those that look most contingent.'[6] And G. Thomas Tanselle insists that 'What a text says is forever linked to the mundane realities underlying the physical product that gives the text a material embodiment.'[7] Critics have compellingly explored material conditions of how the literary operates, and how it engages readers with a network of language, paratextual signals and generic formats to show how paratexts like *sententiae* markers impel specific reading processes and create productive readers.

---

[4] With the notable exception of Arden 3, most modern editors do not reproduce or consider the original edition's textual apparatus; see William Shakespeare, *Shakespeare's Poems*, ed. Katherine Duncan-Jones and H. R. Woudhuysen (London: Thomson Learning, 2007). Colin Burrow discusses the *sententiae* markers in his edition's notes but does not reproduce them in the text; see William Shakespeare, *The Complete Sonnets and Poems*, ed. Colin Burrow (Oxford: Oxford University Press, 2002). On the material text, see *Shakespeare's Poems*, ed. Duncan-Jones and Woudhuysen, Appendix 1, pp. 508–10. The editors note that the number of *sententiae* in the poem is not always clear from the way the text is marked (p. 509).

[5] Philip Sidney, *The Countesse of Pembrokes Arcadia*, Book 1, in *The Prose Works of Sir Philip Sidney*, vol. 1, ed. Albert Feuillerat (Cambridge: Cambridge University Press, 1965), p. 119.

[6] Leah Price, 'Introduction: Reading Matter,' *PMLA: Publications of the Modern Language Association of America*, 121:1 (2006), 9–16 (p. 11).

[7] G. Thomas Tanselle, 'The Bibliography and Textual Study of American Books,' *Proceedings of the American Antiquarian Society*, 95:2 (October 1985), 113–51 (p. 113).

Contributing to book history with a renewed interest in materialism a few scholars have returned to the question of highlighted *sententiae* in Shakespeare's poem following G. K. Hunter's exploration in the 1950s. Peter Stallybrass, for example, in articles co-authored with Roger Chartier and Zachary Lesser, has invigorated our understanding of how publishers helped produce literary commodities.[8] Their argument suggests the design of the text stemmed largely from the publisher's impulse to imitate classical and humanist texts. As Chartier and Stallybrass argue, 'By printing *Lucrece* with commonplace markers in 1594, Richard Field produced a book that drew attention to the fact that it had already been read as a canonical text.'[9] The methodology focuses on the publisher's product and its strategy for sales, and since the printed book's design was constructed by the publisher and not the author, Lesser and Stallybrass conclude that commonplace markers were 'made by a reader, not a dramatist'.[10] Thus the subsequent miscellanies produced at the turn of the century, which abstracted and organised quotations from a range of English poets, utilised paratextual makers to align highly regarded classical texts with modern vernacular poetry. The products constructed another source of wisdom and invention that paid little attention to authorial intent or the original narrative. Shakespeare wrote the poem; but the publisher devised a material form to market the product that bore a sales strategy and reader's infrastructure rather than an artistic impulse.

More recently, Adam Hooks has built on this argument to assert that Shakespeare 'was almost certainly not responsible for inserting [*sententiae* markers] himself'.[11] Hooks is right to critique the idea of Field as a 'conduit' for Shakespeare's intent, and his scepticism of the critical desire for biography rather than material history helps us understand the considerable role publication played in constructing Shakespeare's literary fame.[12] One effect of this methodology that severs the author from material form, however, is to ignore how the narrative might use its physical attributes to

---

[8] See Roger Chartier and Peter Stallybrass, 'Reading and Authorship: The Circulation of Shakespeare 1590–1619', in Andrew Murphy (ed.), *A Concise Companion to Shakespeare and the Text* (Malden: Blackwell Publishing, 2007), pp. 35–56. See also Zachary Lesser and Peter Stallybrass, 'The First Literary *Hamlet* and the Commonplacing of Professional Plays', *Shakespeare Quarterly*, 59:4 (2008), 371–420. Much of this research relies on Ann Moss, *Printed Commonplace-Books and the Structuring of Renaissance Thought* (Oxford: Oxford University Press, 1996).

[9] Chartier and Stallybrass, 'Reading and Authorship', p. 47.

[10] Lesser and Stallybrass, 'First Literary *Hamlet*', p. 381.

[11] Adam G. Hooks, 'Shakespeare at the White Greyhound', *Shakespeare Survey*, 64 (2011), 260–275 (p. 264).

[12] Ibid., p. 265.

poetic ends. In an effort to align publication and narrative more closely, I will examine how *Lucrece* uses its particular material format, and the relationship with readers facilitated by the paratextual resource, to offer evidence that Shakespeare did indeed concern himself with publication, and did so in a complex fashion to underscore larger pedagogical questions and humanist assumptions.

This chapter began with the question of what it means to solicit quotation in Tudor England, and what happens to a text when it is quoted by readers. Does quotation preserve the meaning of the original work or its essential merits? Or does the quotation change according to its use? Moreover, do abstractions from texts change readers? To pursue these questions, I will consider the act of quotation in *Lucrece*, both with the paratextual markers printed in the first edition and evoked in the poem's narrative. In particular, I will explore Shakespeare's paratextual strategy, which challenges humanist claims for the utility of quotation, and the means by which he asks readers to reconsider the efficacy of mining texts for a 'pattern, precedent, and lively warrant' (*Titus Andronicus*, v.iii.43). To attend to the poem's material condition illustrates how Shakespeare makes conspicuous the idealised relationship between text and readers. He uses quotation to construct a narrative poem that undermines the conservation of the past and instead imagines an engaged reader's dynamic impact on recovery, and thus revision, of the past.

At the poem's outset, Prince Tarquin storms in with the intent but not the ultimate resolve to ravish Lucrece. The speed of Tarquin's entrance resembles the economy of Shakespeare's sources. Both Livy's *Historia* and Ovid's *Fasti* describe briefly how Tarquin's wicked desire, ignited from a competition among young men about their wives, impels him to rape Lucrece. In the aftermath, she summons her husband, who is joined by her father and others, to hear her story. Before the small audience, Lucrece describes the crime so that they may vow revenge, and she commits suicide to protect her virtue. Her stoic act triggers the witnesses to march Lucrece's dead body through the Roman streets. Collectively the Romans respond by banishing the monarchy, and in its place establish the Roman Republic. From violation, abstracted to an analogy of the people and its rulers, a new political system takes root; Lucrece's abused body encourages the Romans to redefine their own political body. The well-known, etiological story describes how Lucrece's constancy, made public before the Roman people, incites spontaneous change.

In contrast to the lust-fuelled haste that opens Shakespeare's narrative, the remainder of his poem slows considerably to offer dilations of the

original ancient tale. Shakespeare's digressions invest his main characters
with perambulations of the mind. The method of their enquiry, quoting
and reacting to exemplary pieces of wisdom, establishes itself as a main
concern of the poem, both in the narrative and in the physical presentation of the text.

The first instance of a character's use of quotation comes in the form
of rejection, not of a particular commonplace, but of the industry itself.
Isolated in the still of the night, Tarquin oscillates wildly, 'revolving /
The sundry dangers of his will's obtaining' (lines 127–8). He must decide
whether or not to act on his lust and 'Is madly tossed between desire and
dread' (171). To determine his course, Tarquin holds 'disputation' with
himself to anticipate gain and loss. Eventually the diminishing capacity
of Tarquin's reason cannot withstand his inflated desire, and his argument
quickly shifts from debate to rationalisation. He quotes his conclusion that
his 'shame and fault finds no excuse' (238) in the contrary to create his own
aphorism:

> Shameful it is: ay, if the fact be known.
> Hateful it is: there is no hate in loving.
> I'll beg her love: but she is not her own.
> The worst is but denial and reproving.
> My will is strong past reason's weak removing:
>> Who fears a sentence or an old man's saw
>> Shall by a painted cloth be kept in awe. (239–45)

Aside from the perverse allusion to Lucrece's later disputations with Night,
Time and Opportunity, and the fact that she ultimately reads a 'painted
cloth' of an overthrown Troy, Tarquin's retreat from checks to his will
merits attention: he rejects the *sententiae* that, overused, become 'an old
man's saw', and he links them to pictures depicting moralistic simplicities.
He refuses to allow stale quotations from the past, even those of his own,
to guide his debate about what to do in the present moment. Thus, free
from precedent or authority, he decides to rape his hostess.[13]

---

[13] Tarquin might reject sententious ways of thinking, but he is willing to exploit them for nefarious
ends. After threatening that he will kill Lucrece and her male servant to create the illusion of an
affair, thus shaming her husband and kinsmen through 'succeeding times' (513–25), he reasons with
her that the ends justify the means: 'A little harm done to a great good end / For lawful policy
remains enacted' (528–9; Q, sig. EIV). Marked with sentential marks, as is the subsequent rationale
('The poisonous simple sometime is compacted / In a pure compound; being so applied, / His
venom in effect is purified' (530–2; Q, sig. EIV)), these words draw attention to Tarquin's manipulation of transportable wisdom for the purposes of seduction.

Distinct from Tarquin, Lucrece amply quotes *sententiae*, and the physical poem marks passages as moments worthy of collection. Throughout the poem, marked passages correspond either to Lucrece's or to the narrator's speech, and they provide analogies to describe Lucrece's plight. The first example of printed quotation marks to signal *sententiae* comes early in the poem after Tarquin arrives and silently rages over Lucrece's beauty – an interior storm Lucrece cannot see. The marked passage offers a general explanation as to why: 'For unstained thoughts do seldom dream on evil; / Birds never limed, no secret bushes fear' (87–8; Q, sig. B3r).[14] One never harmed or one who has no experience with sin or transgression has no reason to be aware of its presence. According to the maxim, evil is not part of one's perceptive landscape until one strays or is harmed by one who strays. Lucrece, whose victory among the young men's wives established her as the most chaste and 'guiltless' (89), has no reason to suspect a traitor in her home. Because this threat is largely unseen by the innocent, the printed text makes this wisdom visible so that readers may avoid the trap into which Lucrece unwittingly fell. The presence of wisdom marked in the text seems to be to help readers attend to an otherwise unseen danger. As William Kerrigan reminds us in another context, 'Forewarned is forearmed.'[15]

The majority of the *sententiae* markers cluster in the middle of the poem as Lucrece 'Holds disputation with each thing she views / And to herself all sorrow doth compare' (1101–2). Reeling from the attack and isolated in her home, Lucrece begins to reflect on how such steadfast chastity could have been so mercilessly overthrown. In the course of these complaints, Lucrece evokes several *sententiae* that are also marked in the text. She calls to mind aphorisms, ones the text encourages readers to copy, which help her to contextualise this evil and to compare her tragedy to precedent. For example, Lucrece considers the injustice to her husband Collatine's name and his posterity, which impels her to note, in lines that are supplemented with quotation marks, 'How he in peace is wounded, not in war. / Alas how many bear such shameful blows, / Which not themselves but he that gives them knows!' (831–3; Q, sig. F4v). She decries the paradox that individuals are more often in danger in times of peace than on the battlefield: the unprovoked malice of colleagues or friends presents the more serious threat. On the next page of the quarto, also marked on the page

---

[14] I refer to the 1594 Quarto when discussing the physical presentation of Shakespeare's book.
[15] William Kerrigan, 'Complicated Monsters: Essence and Metamorphosis in Milton', *Texas Studies in Literature and Language*, 46:3 (2004), 324–39 (p. 327).

as *sententiae* in the stanza's final couplet, Lucrece offers a general reflection on the corruption of kings, who themselves purport to stand as spotless models of virtue: 'But no perfection is so absolute / That some impurity doth not pollute' (853–4; Q, sig. G*r*). Both of these maxims are general enough to warrant countless applications, and we understand Lucrece's need to contextualise the otherwise inexplicable crime and her undeserved suffering. Shakespeare describes a character using aphorisms to ground her story in broader contexts, and the poem itself offers this wisdom to readers who, in turn, may find a use for it in their own lives.

What readers often neglect, however, is how unsatisfying Lucrece's use of quotation is. Attention to the rehearsal of *sententiae* reminds us that Lucrece did not suddenly open a commonplace book full of adages and accordingly apply them.[16] She had these words of wisdom committed to memory long before – there is no other explanation for her sudden eloquent retrievals. Shakespeare employs *sententiae* that are not exact copies of well-known commonplaces, but resemble those in circulation. The poem's focus on the presence of wisdom, signalled in the margins of the text and in the speech of its heroine, invites us to ask what purpose this wisdom served. *Sententiae* do not warn Lucrece or put her on the defensive the moment Prince Tarquin arrives from the battlefield to visit her peaceful home; they do not remind her that the presentation of royalty does not guarantee virtue. In the narrative of *Lucrece*, therefore, *sententiae* fail in their culturally prescribed roles. Attending to the poem's paratexts, which heighten our awareness of Lucrece's own belated use of aphorisms, demonstrates Shakespeare's challenge to this pedagogical tool. Experience, not categorised wisdom, determines what Lucrece can see and understand.

Another example of a highlighted adage that possesses meaning only after the fact comes at daybreak while Lucrece is still alone. With the morning light the birds begin to sing, a reminder of daily life that now pains Lucrece. In a mass of marked lines on the page, the aphorisms used by the narrator reflect that 'Sad souls are slain in merry company' (1110; Q, sig. H3*v*), and that grief wants only other miserable company. To those who are harmed, potential remedies only augment pain: a drowning man suffers more 'in ken of shore' and 'Great grief grieves most at that would do

---

[16] I have consulted both R. W. Dent and Morris P. Tilley where I found similar-sounding adages to Shakespeare's, but no direct quotations. See R. W. Dent, *Proverbial Language in English Drama Exclusive of Shakespeare, 1495–1616: An Index* (Berkeley: University of California Press, 1984); and Morris P. Tilley, *A Dictionary of the Proverbs in England in the Sixteenth and Seventeenth Centuries: A Collection of the Proverbs Found in English Literature and the Dictionaries of the Period* (Ann Arbor: University of Michigan Press, 1950).

it good' (1114, 1117). It becomes clear that the maxims the poem offers make
sense only in the wake of tragedy, after the subject suffers harm. To return
to the poem's initial *sententia*, we see that the aphorism has no admonitory power; it can only make sense in retrospect. If 'unstained thoughts do
seldom dream on evil' (87), what chance do the innocent have? If 'Birds
never limed' (88) have no recourse to fear bushes, how will they avoid
the traps?

The poem's paratexts, conventional signals that press the reader to conserve wisdom in anticipation of future challenges, actually undermine the
idealised usefulness of the *sententiae* by emphasising the role of experience
and hindsight. Knowledge in the abstract has little effect. Without experience one does not anticipate danger or expect ambivalent intentions behind
surface appearance. Relying on extracted knowledge, therefore, Lucrece
'Could pick no meaning' from Tarquin's eyes, 'Nor read the subtle shining
secrecies / Writ in the glassy margents of such books' (100–2). The passage
describes the place of obscurity as marginalia, exactly where the paratextual
markers reside. Furthermore, the heroine's use of *sententiae* foregrounds
the reader's charge to collect and store. Because Lucrece ends up using
hindsight and not foresight, the failure of gathered *sententiae* suggests the
reader too may be engaged in a barren industry. In Shakespeare's poem,
precedents fail to anticipate the future.

The conventions Shakespeare qualifies were articulated by Roger Ascham,
who judges in *The Scholemaster* that while experience 'doth proffet moch',
mining truths and sentences from texts has the most value: 'Learning
teacheth more in one yeare, then experience in twentie.' Ascham's concept
of wisdom complements the exemplarity tradition students were taught to
commonplace: 'For good precepts of learning, be the eyes of the minde,
to looke wiselie before a man, which way to goe right, and which not.'
Knowledge predicts outcomes based on historical example, which is why
they are the 'eyes' because they provide foresight. Historical exemplars
'teacheth safelie, when experience maketh more miserable then wise'.[17]
Ascham articulates the pedagogical theory behind *sententiae*: they allow
the innocent to avoid danger and pursue virtue without experience. The
rhetorical use of the *exemplum*, as Karlheinz Stierle notes, 'presupposes that

---

[17] Roger Ascham, *The Scholemaster* (1589), fo. 17r. Judith Anderson, *Words that Matter: Linguistic
Perception in Renaissance English* (Stanford: Stanford University Press, 1996), pp. 35–6, also discusses
the passage to argue that *sententie* 'operate as templates of meaning, freeze language, and appear
to solidify it'. Anderson perceptively notes that 'The essential significance of an experience appears
to be settled beforehand', a theory that informs the commonplace book's use and application.
Shakespeare, I argue, is challenging this theory.

over time, there is more analogy in human experience than diversity, or that in all situations of civil and political life the pole of equality is stronger than that of difference'.[18] Thus a reader catalogues precepts and aphorisms into prescribed headings to manage future challenges.[19]

One of Shakespeare's sources echoes this pedagogical convention in its presentation of Lucrece and other moral figures designed to teach and admonish. William Painter's *The First Tome of the Palace of Pleasure* (1566) claims that the moral tales will 'reveale the miseries of rapes and fleshy actions, the overthrow of noble men and Princes by discordred government', so that the reader will 'learne how to behave thy self with modestie'. Nothing surpasses histories because they offer 'matter pleasaunt and plausible, even so for example and imitation good and commendable. The one doth rejoyce the werie and tedious minde, many times involved with ordinarie cares, the other *prescribeth a directe pathe to treade the tracte of this present life*.'[20] History presents that which predicts and delimits 'this present life'. All of these stories supply lessons readers may apply to their own lives – the stories may indeed predict readers' lives. Painter packages Lucrece in a collection that serves as a warning system, a set of moral precepts, and cautions to avoid wrongdoing or danger. Similar to Ascham, Painter suggests that one may know future outcomes by reading paradigmatic tales. Likewise, George Puttenham notes in his discussion of paradigm that 'we compare the past with the present, gathering probability of like success to come in the things we have presently in hand'.[21] The historiographic method relied on paradigms to collapse the past and present. Quoting the past ultimately meant quoting the future.

But Shakespeare's *Lucrece*, both in narrative and in presentation, deflates the promise of *sententiae* by making conspicuous the process and promise of commonplacing for future use. According to humanist pedagogical theory, *sententiae* provided transcendent resources to shape and warn the reader. In Lucrece's case, however, *sententiae* cannot anticipate or codify experience, and they only become relevant retrospectively: the experience is what makes the precept. While we never doubt Lucrece's moral purity, it

---

[18] Karlheinz Stierle, 'Three Moments in the Crisis of Exemplarity: Boccaccio-Petrarch, Montaigne, and Cervantes', *Journal of the History of Ideas*, 59:4 (1998), 581–95 (p. 581).

[19] For a learned summary on the pedagogical theory and its context, see Mary Thomas Crane, 'Early Tudor Humanism', in *A New Companion to English Renaissance Literature and Culture*, Vol. 1, ed. Michael Hattaway (Oxford: Wiley-Blackwell, 2010), pp. 91–105.

[20] William Painter, *The First Tome of the Palace of Pleasure* (1566), 'The Epistle to the Reader', sigs. A4r, A3v, emphasis added; *STC* 19123.

[21] George Puttenham, *The Art of English Poesy*, ed. Frank Whigham and Wayne A. Rebhorn (Ithaca: Cornell University Press, 2007), p. 330.

is clear that she fails to recall these words of wisdom until after the fact.[22] Shakespeare intertwines the rational and the physical in both the presentation of his text and the narrative itself. The failure in this poem stems not from its heroine, but from a pedagogical system of assimilation of and comfort with the past.

In *Lucrece*, a poem that is fraught with efforts to control posterity and legacy, reading the past is a central preoccupation.[23] Working out of the complex relationship between the past and the present, Shakespeare's model revises the conventional transfer of knowledge: from the marked *sententiae* fixed on the page to the active reader who literally incorporates that knowledge and applies it to living experience. The shift from page to reader stresses the role of perspective and physical context in the work of knowing. A reader in Shakespeare's construction is not a passive vessel, but rather one who mixes precedent with the personal to revise both.

William Sherman notes that marking *sententiae* and 'the recording and reusing of exemplary passages from authoritative books, became a basic skill in the Elizabethan schoolroom ... [But] the practice is self-explanatory and it is rare to find anyone reflecting explicitly upon its technical or symbolic potential.'[24] This act of explicit reflection, however, is exactly what Shakespeare constructs in *Lucrece*. Shakespeare examines the concepts of reflection and self-explanation in the fullest sense – that is, he suggests these resources were used to help readers know themselves as the wisdom was bent to individual purposes. He fuses the transcendent with the perspective of the person reading *sententiae* to qualify their authority. The collusion between the material text and the narrative raises fascinating questions about the reading process as Shakespeare imagines Lucrece's acts of quotation in tragic hindsight.

[22] Augustine's discussion of Lucrece in *The City of God* suggested that Lucrece was complicit in the crime since the body cannot infect the mind. See St Augustine of Hippo, *The City of God*, trans. George E. McCracken, Loeb Classical Library (Cambridge: Harvard University Press, 1957), i.xix, pp. 88–9. Katharine Eisaman Maus, 'Taking Tropes Seriously: Language and Violence in Shakespeare's *Rape of Lucrece*', *Shakespeare Quarterly*, 37:1 (1986), 66–82, provides the strongest rebuke to this position (especially pp. 68–72).
[23] Heather Dubrow, 'The Rape of Clio: Attitudes to History in Shakespeare's *Lucrece*', *English Literary Renaissance*, 16:3 (1986), 425–41.
[24] William H. Sherman, *Used Books: Marking Readers in Renaissance England* (Philadelphia: University of Pennsylvania Press, 2008), p. 44. My position also differs from Lesser and Stallybrass's conclusion that the *sententiae* markers are the work of the printer solely and that literariness is something imposed during the printing process: 'For Shakespeare, as for most other playwrights, the literary elevation provided by commonplacing is more likely to have been thrust upon him than to have been a self-conscious authorial strategy' (p. 404). Their analysis of Q1 *Hamlet* appears to be correct (although see Chapters 1 and 3 in the present volume for further discussion); but the difference from the use in *Lucrece* is important to note.

Focusing on how Shakespeare interrogates quotation compels us to re-evaluate that startling quotation he adds to the etiological tale: Lucrece's reading of Troy's destruction. Because cognition in Shakespeare's poem demonstrates how exemplarity exists in hindsight, not as a pedagogical premonition, the Trojan paradigm gains currency after Lucrece's body is transformed. Thus Shakespeare shows us how Lucrece reads herself backward into Troy, and how it becomes a map onto which she can plot her death. In an effort to rationalise her tragedy, she searches the classic story for a precedent, which also provides her a sense of an ending. Her method is to supplement the narrative by using 'the eye of mind' (1426) to complete the picture, as its design demands. Shakespeare repeatedly draws attention to the painter's metonymic skill in using a piece to suggest a whole: Trojan eyes peering through tower 'loop-holes' (1383); faces of 'great commanders'; the 'physiognomy' (1395) of Ajax's 'eyes' (1398) and Ulysses' 'mild glance' (1399) that 'ciphered either's heart' (1396). The 'eye of the mind' took only a part, which '[s]tood for the whole to be imagined' (1426, 1428). But here Lucrece discovers the paradigm by participating in the story, which dynamically alters both the Trojan narrative and her own.

Shakespeare's ekphrasis not only shows what Lucrece has learned, but also describes her in the process of learning. Lucrece reads the painting to distract her mind, and in the process she finds an analogous context to help her understand her situation. When Lucrece centres her attention on Sinon, the devious Greek and 'devil' who convinced 'the credulous old Priam' (1513, 1522) that the invading army had retreated home, she finds in Sinon a paradigm to explain the devil who overthrew her edifice of chastity. As with the *sententiae*, Lucrece evokes these paradigms in hindsight, long after they are useful. In making the comparison, however, she notes how the 'Painter laboured with his skill / To hide deceit, and give the harmless show / An humble gate' (1506–8). She is surprised to find the villain painted in such a pleasing aspect. She 'advisedly perused' the painting and 'chid the painter' because he constructed Sinon pleasingly: 'So fair a form lodged not a mind so ill / And still on him she gazed, and gazing still, / Such signs of truth in his plain face she spied, / That she concludes the picture was belied' (1527–8, 1530–3). Shakespeare seems to construct Lucrece's logic similarly to Holinshed's description of Richard III to suggest the picture was wrong: a corrupt mind must manifest a corrupt body.[25] And yet,

[25] While Richard was 'in wit and courage equall with either' of his brothers, King Edward IV and George, Duke of Clarence, he was 'in bodie and prowesse farre under them both, litle of stature, ill featured of limmes, crooke backed.' Raphael Holinshed, *The Third Volume of Chronicles* (1587), p. 712.

she continues to investigate the painting and the physiognomic relationship as 'Tarquin's shape came in her mind': the force of her experience and
reading the painting reverses her thinking.

> And from her tongue 'can lurk' from 'cannot' took.
> 'It cannot be' she in that sense forsook,
>   And turned it thus: 'It cannot be, I find,
>   But such a face should bear a wicked mind.
>
> 'For even as subtle Sinon here is painted,
> So sober-sad, so weary, and so mild
> (As if with grief or travail he had fainted),
> To me came Tarquin armed to beguild
> With outward honesty, but yet defiled (1537–45)

As Lucrece is about to speak, she quotes herself and upends her thinking
to its opposite. Her experience forces her to the other extreme: a fair
face can only mean deceit. Lucrece's reading challenges the Neoplatonic
connection between inner and outer forms and instead registers a gap
between appearance and intention. Lucrece's prosopographia now has an
interpretative edge that was missing in the poem's opening.[26] She reads the
past in context of the present. Rather than letting transcendent *sententiae*
prescribe what is worthy of memory, current circumstance selects and
revises the past to fit present needs.

Why would Shakespeare incorporate a pedagogical device that the
narrative of the poem calls into question? For Shakespeare, the strategy
offers an opportunity to raise epistemological questions about the work of
knowing and how context affects the collection or recovery of historical
wisdom. He insists on present time and its involvement in recovering the
past, thus altering that past to present circumstances and needs. The paradigmatic method of reading the past suggests it is always available, always
read to be deployed with equal reliability. As Shakespeare takes aim at the
industry of the commonplace book, and pedagogical claims for *sententiae*
generally, he highlights problems with exemplarity. Reading paradigmatic-
ally has a tendency to reduce knowledge and possibility. In contrast to the
closed structures that seek to conserve elements from the past, the Ovidian
poem imagines a dynamic engagement between agents. While Shakespeare
does not radically undermine the industry of the historian or relish the
potential of scepticism to reduce all knowledge to isolated, particular

---

[26] 'The visage, speech and countenance of any person absent or dead. And this kind of representation
is called the Counterfeit Countenance'; Puttenham, *The Art of English Poesy*, p. 324.

experiences, he does question the assumption that from *sententiae* or paradigms one may gather accessible, coherent and stable meanings, out of which the future may be known. To make this complex challenge, however, Shakespeare would need to engage both his poetic resources and the resources of the printed book. Exploring how the mechanics of the printing reinforce the narrative's broader interrogation of *sententiae* suggests that in fact Shakespeare did use the material book to underscore his artistry.

CHAPTER 3

'The ears of profiting'
Listening to Falstaff's Biblical Quotations

Beatrice Groves

In the early modern period preachers and playwrights competed for audiences: both couched their morals in memorable rhetoric while each claimed that their art uniquely married its edifying moral core with emotionally compelling delivery.[1] Preachers and players alike reconciled admonition with entertainment, communicated moral truths through a performative medium, and quoted the Bible. This last parallel particularly rankled among the godly, who by the late Elizabethan period declared biblical quotation on the stage anathema: 'whatsoeuer choice of matter yea out of the Scripture-stories, is made for their Plaies and enterludes, it hath no blessing from the Lord to the hearers and beholders because he hath ordained, the Preaching not the Playing of his word'.[2] Playwrights, nonetheless, continued to use biblical material, and the genre of Bible-play was much more popular in the late Elizabethan period than is generally realised: including, for example, *Abraham and Lot* (1594), *Esther and Ahasuerus* (c. 1594), *The History or Tragedy of Job* (c. 1594), *Nebuchadnezzer* (c. 1596), *The Love of King David and Fair Bethsabe* (1599), *Judas* (c. 1600–2), *Pontius Pilate* (c. 1601), *Jephthah* (c. 1602), *Tobias* (c. 1602), *Samson* (c. 1602) and *Joshua* (c. 1602). In addition, many ostensibly 'secular' Elizabethan plays contained biblical quotation. The joke about the identity of 'Judas' at the end of *Love's Labour's Lost*, for example, indicates the currency of biblical quotation on the stage by generating comedy from John's gospel (v.ii.590–5; John 14:22). The humour depends on the disjunction in biblical literacy between the on-stage spectators and performers of the Pageant of the Nine Worthies, and illustrates the way that Shakespeare uses biblical quotation confident that his audience will catch the reference and laugh at the joke.[3]

[1] For further, see Beatrice Groves, *The Destruction of Jerusalem in Early Modern English Literature* (Cambridge: Cambridge University Press, 2015), pp. 86–118.
[2] Osmund Lake, *A Probe Theologicall* (London: William Leake, 1612), p. 268.
[3] For further, see Beatrice Groves, *Texts and Traditions: Religion in Shakespeare 1592–1604* (Oxford: Oxford University Press, 2007), pp. 10–11.

This chapter uses new contextual evidence to argue that Falstaff (Shakespeare's most scripturally aware character) uses biblical quotation in a way that ironically reflects the contemporary, godly use of biblical quotation. In post-Reformation England, quoting brief, out-of-context biblical verses became accepted as an argumentative strategy – and this use of biblical quotation as 'proof-text' is wittily turned on its head by Falstaff.

The godly were called to preach the Bible: to utter biblical quotations that needed to be recognised as such in order to retain, and communicate, their authoritative status. As Marjorie Garber notes: 'the quotation creates authority by its very nature and form. It instates an authority elsewhere, and, at the same time, it imparts that authority, temporarily, to the speaker or the writer.'[4] Ann Moss has traced in depth the reciprocal relation between the importance of scriptural proof-texts and commonplaces in the period and argues that the acceptance of proof by quotation (or *auctoritas*) in Reformation debates (drawn from the Reformers' belief in Scripture's absolute authority) redounded to the credit of quotation as an argumentative strategy in the culture as a whole.[5] The authority that quotation confers, however, is at its most powerful in biblical quotation, and Falstaff makes dramatic capital from subverting and ironising this authority.

As Falstaff leaves his first scene on the stage, he prays:

> God give thee the spirit of persuasion, and him the ears of profiting, that what thou speakest may move, and what he hears may be believed, that the true prince may – for recreation sake – prove a false thief, for the poor abuses of the time want countenance. (*1 Henry IV*, 1.ii.123–6)

Falstaff's valedictory speech echoes the early modern godly commonplace that true persuasion comes through hearing rather than seeing: through the ears not the eyes. This belief derived from the biblical proof-text: 'so then faith cometh by hearing' (Romans 10:17). Proof-texts were one of the period's most important forms of quotation: they appealed to the higher authority of scripture as evidence or 'proof' of the argument in hand. Romans 10:17 was used by early modern preachers to attack the visual appeal of both Catholic liturgy and secular drama; as William Lambarde concluded: 'sence true Faithe cometh by hearinge and not by seinge, [Faith] is more then al the Spectacles in the Worlde can bringe to pass'.[6]

---

[4] Marjorie Garber, *Quotation Marks* (London: Routledge, 2003), p. 2.

[5] Ann Moss, *Printed Commonplace-Books and the Structuring of Renaissance Thought* (Oxford: Clarendon Press, 1996), p. 22. See also p. 204 and *passim*.

[6] William Lambarde, *Dictionarium Angliae topographicum & historicum* (London, 1730), pp. 459–60.

Shakespeare's Falstaff-plays, however, playfully and subversively suggest
that the aural route to salvation is not best left in the hands of the clergy.
The name of 'Master Dumbe, our minister' (*2 Henry IV*, II.iv.88) comically highlights this minister's inability to help his congregation to hear
the word of God. When, in *The Merry Wives of Windsor*, Pistol quotes a
passage familiar from both the Psalter and the Prayer Book litany, 'he hears
with ears' ('wee haue heard with our eares', Psalm 44:1 (1.i.148–50)), Parson
Evans fails to spot the quotation and dismisses it as an affectation.[7] But
the joke is not merely that Evans is affronted by tautology when he should
be delighted by holy quotation. It is also that the scriptural quotation he
is unable to hear is precisely one about listening to the word of God. In
Pistol's – and the audience's – ability to hear biblical quotation of which
the Parson is unaware, the stage wittily claims for itself the ability to confer
on its audience 'the ears of profiting'.

This comic assumption of the godly emphasis on hearing is part of
Shakespeare's insistence on theatre audiences as 'auditors' as well as
'spectators'. Shakespeare trains his audience to listen as well as watch, and
his biblical references are a particularly rich source of meanings that resonate beyond the literal sense of the text. While Shakespeare's use of biblical
language is usually spoken of in terms of 'allusion' rather than 'quotation',
Julie Maxwell has argued persuasively that Renaissance educators' emphasis
on the creative appropriation of commonplaces means that 'the quotation
that appears loosest may actually have been most closely worked over. The
writer has digested his authority and imitated it, not with easy diligence,
but with true invention.'[8] What might appear a relatively loose allusion,
therefore, can nonetheless be legitimately considered a creative act of misquotation in the sense that the author is concentrating on his original as
he changes it, and expects the original text to be heard by his audience.
Maxwell's point is supported by the fact that in the rare moments that
Shakespeare explicitly cites the Bible – the book of Numbers in *Henry V*
and the Psalms in *2 Henry IV* – he does not quote accurately.[9]

Shakespeare, therefore, gives us an ample and generous interpretation
of what can be heard by the audience as biblical quotation. When Falstaff

---

[7] See Naseeb Shaheen, *Biblical References in Shakespeare's Plays* (Newark: University of Delaware Press,
    1999), p. 189. All subsequent biblical quotations are taken from Shaheen's indispensable work.
[8] Julie Maxwell, 'How the Renaissance (Mis)Used Sources: The Art of Misquotation', in Laurie
    Maguire (ed.), *How to Do Things with Shakespeare: New Approaches, New Essays* (Oxford: Blackwell,
    2008), pp. 54–76 (p. 62).
[9] Shaheen, *Biblical References*, pp. 441, 453.

describes the aftermath of the Gad's Hill robbery he tells of how 'I have scaped by miracle. I am eight times thrust through the doublet, four through the hose, my buckler cut through and through, my sword hacked like a handsaw – *ecce signum*!' (*1 Henry IV*, II.iv.140–3). Shaheen is cautious of perceiving a reference to Paul's recitation of his sufferings in Falstaff's bombast because of a lack of verbal echoes: 'Fiue times receiued I fourtie stripes saue one. I was thrise beaten with roddes: I was once stoned: I suffred thrise shipwracke' (2 Corinthians 11:24–5). But both Falstaff's claim of providential survival ('I have scaped by miracle') and the precision with which he enumerates his injuries do bear a resemblance to Paul's careful numbering of what he has suffered in proclaiming the gospel. To the impious mind, there is something almost comic about the particularity with which Paul insists on how much more he has suffered than everyone else and, as with Falstaff, Paul's injuries not only outdo those of his fellows but pass the bounds of probability: 'night and day I have laboured in the depths of the sea' (2 Corinthians 11:25) (although in his case we read it as metaphor rather than, as in Falstaff's, duplicity). The link adds to the bravura comedy of the scene as Falstaff's outrageous falsehoods gain an added piquancy through their distorted link with scriptural truth. But the Pauline echo also fits perfectly with Falstaff's habitual Puritan idiom, part of his 'Oldcastle' ancestry.[10] Kristen Poole argues that this idiom is not simple satire but that 'as a multivalent, polyvocal entity, "Falstaff", the epitome of carnival grotesque, encompasses and embodies contradictions, rather than flattens them'.[11] Elizabethan preachers had a particular fondness for Paul ('Goddes electe vessel') and this passage from 2 Corinthians was gathered into lists of godly 'common places.'[12] The godly perception of their own persecution led to Paul's enumeration of his injuries being much quoted in the period, and Falstaff's claims after Gad's Hill neatly echo both the godly and Pauline apprehension of their suffering as evidence of their unique fidelity.[13]

[10] See Gary Taylor, 'The Fortunes of Oldcastle', *Shakespeare Survey*, 38 (1985), 85–100.
[11] Kristen Poole, 'Facing Puritanism: Falstaff, Martin Marprelate and the Grotesque Puritan', in Ronald Knowles (ed.), *Shakespeare and Carnival: After Bakhtin* (London: Macmillan, 1998), pp. 97–122 (p. 108).
[12] Thomas Paniell, *A Frutefull booke of the common places of all S. Pauls Epistles* (London: John Tisdale, 1562), sigs. A4r, T8r.
[13] See, for example, Rudolf Gwalther, *An hundred, threescore and fiftene Homelyes or Sermons, vppon the Actes of the Apostles*, trans. John Bridges (London: Henrie Denham, 1572), p. 403; Heinrich Bullinger, *The Tragedies of Tyrantes*, trans. Thomas Twyne (London: Abraham Veale, 1575), sigs. Gv–G3v; and Heinrich Bullinger, *Fiftie Godlie and Learned Sermons*, trans H. I. (London: Ralphe Newberrie, 1577), p. 314.

Hannibal Hamlin uses film terminology to distinguish between
different types of allusion: there are biblical allusions that a character
intends to make (like the 'diegetic' music in a film when the protagonist plays the drums) and those of which the speaker themselves is
unaware (like the 'extradiegetic' film score which only the audience
hears). It is a helpful distinction and, while Hamlin uses 'diegetic' and
'extradiegetic' to distinguish between different types of 'allusion' rather
than between 'allusion' and 'quotation', in this chapter I will refer to
a character's self-conscious, diegetic biblical references as 'quotation',
and extradiegetic biblical references – references deliberately deployed
by the author but of which the character themselves is unconscious –
as allusion.[14] Such a distinction clearly operates, for example, in the
way that scriptural stories about Jacob and his inheritance surface in
Merchant of Venice both as explicit biblical quotation (in the argument
between Shylock and Antonio about Jacob's grazing of Laban's sheep)
and as extradiegetic allusion (when blind Old Gobbo's inability to recognise his son recalls Jacob's gulling of his blind father Isaac).[15] While
Falstaff makes intentional, diegetic, use of the Bible, his quotations
often provide a further layer of extradiegetic meaning as the audience
hear things that the other characters do not. The most explicit example
of the obliviousness of Falstaff's companions to his biblical language
occurs at his death, when – it can be argued – he may finally quote the
Bible 'straight' only to have the sole witness miss the fact entirely. If
modern editorial practice is right to emend Mistress Quickly's 'a Table
of greene fields' to 'a babbled of green fields' (*Henry V*, ii.iii.14), Falstaff
may be quoting Psalm 23 as he dies.[16] This traditional *in extremis* recitation of the green pastures of Psalm 23, however, appears to have
bypassed the comprehension of both Mistress Quickly and the Folio
compositor. It can, nonetheless, be heard by modern audiences in a
perfect example of a biblical reference that is at once diegetic (intended
by the speaker) and extradiegetic (heard by the audience, but not those
on stage).

---

[14] Hamlin argues that allusion is also always quotation so the distinction is merely
semantic: Hannibal Hamlin, *The Bible in Shakespeare* (Oxford: Oxford University Press, 2013),
pp. 233–4.

[15] See Steven Marx, *Shakespeare and the Bible* (Oxford: Oxford University Press, 2000), pp. 120–4.

[16] This is Theobald's emendation and has generally been followed by editors since; see Hamlin, *Bible
in Shakespeare*, pp. 250–1. The possible reference to Psalm 23 was first explicitly noted by John Dover
Wilson: William Shakespeare, *King Henry V*, ed. John Dover Wilson (Cambridge: Cambridge
University Press, 1947), p. 143.

Wisdom Cries Out in the Streets

The simplest, and least edifying, evidence that biblical quotation has been heard is that it has been censored. Richard II's biblical quotations as he soliloquises in his cell (*Richard II*, v.v.15–17 (Mark 10:14, 24–5)) appear to have been recognised, for his pained sense of their contradictory nature ('which set the word itself / Against the word') was amended in the quarto to the less contentious 'set the Faith itselfe / Against the Faith'. Two passages of biblical allusion in the quarto of *2 Henry IV* were deleted from the Folio and, likewise, a section in the opening exchange between Hal and Falstaff in *1 Henry IV* was censored to remove the biblical reference:[17]

FALSTAFF. An old lord of the Council rated me the other day in the street about you, sir, but I marked him not, and yet he talked very wisely, but I regarded him not, and yet he talked wisely – and in the street too.
PRINCE. Thou didst well, for wisdom cries out in the streets and no man regards it.
FALSTAFF. O, thou hast damnable iteration, and are indeed able to corrupt a saint.
(1 Henry IV, 1.ii.66–73)

Hamlin writes that 'Hal is surely a bit thick' because he completes the quotation from Proverbs – 'Wisdome cryeth without, and putteth forth her voyce in the stretes … and no man regarded it' (1:20, 24) – while 'failing to notice that the allusion has already been made by Falstaff.'[18] But, in fact, Hal is fully aware that he is merely completing, not creating, the biblical reference. The odd syntax of Falstaff's speech – the double repetition of the key words 'wisely' and 'street' and the short phrases with their regular pauses – are an invitation to Hal to produce the biblical 'punch line', as Maxwell dubs it: an invitation that is persistently ignored.[19] Falstaff repeats himself and brings his phrasing closer to the biblical passage as he does so – changing 'but I marked him not' to 'but I regarded him not' – as he 'feeds' Hal the set-up line. He provides Hal with an easy witticism through the completion of the familiar biblical quotation in an attempt to draw Hal into a comic double-act. Hal's refusal to conclude the joke – until after Falstaff has given him numerous verbal nudges – is an early signal that he is drawing away from Falstaff, that he is no longer the sparring partner he once was. It is a moment of pathos: an awkward break-down of comic timing that reveals an emotional separation; and the effect is enhanced for

---

[17] Shaheen, *Biblical References*, pp. 432, 435, 409.
[18] Hamlin, *Bible in Shakespeare*, p. 238.
[19] Maxwell, 'Art of Misquotation', p. 60.

the audience, who hear the jarring hiatus between Falstaff's set-up of the
quotation and Hal's completion of it.

This awkward joke of failed comic timing takes place in the virtuosic
second scene of *1 Henry IV* in which the complex interactions between
Hal and Falstaff – at once knowing and mock-innocent, selfish and self-
aware, warm and strangely insulated – are explored through protracted
and playful biblical idiom. Falstaff's compulsively biblical turn of phrase
is fully displayed, from his passing reference to Romans 3 – 'if men were
to be saved by merit' (1.ii.85–6) – which insouciantly calls up the scriptural proof-text at the fault line of the Reformation ('man is iustified by
faith without the workes of the Lawe' (Romans 3:28)), to his defence that
thievery is but 'to labour in his vocation' (1.ii.84–5: 'Let euery man abide
in the same vocation wherein he was called' (1 Corinthians 7:20)). Falstaff's
well-known 'puritan cant' is a tissue of biblical quotation. Falstaff's assertion
that since knowing Hal he has become 'little better than one of the wicked'
(1.ii.75) draws on a ubiquitous name for the ungodly, but it is also an
expression that comes straight from the book of Proverbs.[20] Falstaff's generic godly reference to 'fear and trembling' (*2 Henry IV*, iv.i.365) is likewise a direct biblical quotation ('feare and trembling' (Ephesians 6:5)), and
when he signs his letter 'Thine by yea and no' (*2 Henry IV*, ii.ii.101) he is at
once quoting a biblical passage particularly popular among the godly but
also, perhaps, drawing on his biblical literacy to make one of his customarily impious puns. Jesus commands 'Let your communication be, Yea,
yea: Nay, nay' (Matthew 5:37) and Falstaff may be taking him literally by
ending his letter (his 'communication') 'by yea and no'.

Falstaff's final piece of Puritan idiom in his opening scene is the valedictory speech quoted earlier in this chapter: 'God give thee the spirit
of persuasion, and him the ears of profiting, that what thou speakest may
move, and what he hears may be believed, that the true prince may – for
recreation sake – prove a false thief, for the poor abuses of the time want
countenance.' As Paul A. Jorgensen has noted, 'time' is a crucial concept
in the Henriad: it makes forty-one appearances in the first part of *Henry
IV* and thirty-four in the second.[21] Falstaff's assertion that 'the poor abuses
of the time want countenance' (that the bad ways of the present need
a role model) is a tacit inversion of a biblical injunction. The believer
should spend his hours 'redeemyng the time, because ye dayes are euyll'

---

[20] See Shaheen, *Biblical References*, pp. 410, 439.
[21] Paul A. Jorgensen, *Redeeming Shakespeare's Words* (Berkeley: University of California Press,
1962), p. 52.

(Ephesians 5:16). It is a biblical text that, resonantly, Hal will promise to fulfil (not subvert, as Falstaff suggests) at the end of the scene: 'Redeeming time when men least think I will' (1.ii.177).

The literal references to time at the beginning of this scene – and the festive eschewal of such measurements (imagining 'hours were cups of sack, and minutes capons, and clocks the tongues of bawds' (1.ii.6–7)) – engages with the newly accurate measurement of time in this period. It has been argued that this encouraged a 'radically anthropocentric' reading of time, in which it became 'a subjective reality and its value depended on what one made of the opportunity'.[22] This was certainly the belief of the godly, expounded in works such as the epistle 'Unto the Christian Reader' of *A Confession of Fayth, made by common consent of diuers reformed Churches beyond the Seas* (1568). This epistle opens with the assertion that sinful man mistakes night for noon (esteeming 'the darknes of a cloudie night, as the brightnes of noone daies') and argues that in order to redeem the time every man ought 'to labour in his vocation'.[23] This preface (written, satisfyingly enough, by the prolific godly author, John Old) culminates with a prayer that readers may gain 'the spirite of wisdome' (B4r). The valediction is stylistically close to that of its author's near namesake, the erstwhile John Oldcastle, i.e. Falstaff. John Old's prayer – 'God indue vs all with his heauenly grace not onely to heare and read this vnfalliable truth, but to beleue it also; that beleuing it, we may openly professe it, and openly professing it, may constantly continue therein' – shares its rhetorical construction of connecting clauses (intended to embody the way in which attentiveness will lead to action) with Falstaff's prayer to Poins: 'God give thee the spirit of persuasion, and him the ears of profiting, that what thou speakest may move, and what he hears may be believed.' The second scene of *1 Henry IV*, like John Old's epistle, opens with the suggestion that sinners are hazy about the difference between noon and night. Hal responds to Falstaff's request for the time with the assertion that the fat knight treats all times the same: 'unbuttoning thee after supper, and sleeping upon benches after noon' (1.ii.2–3). John Old commends all to 'labour in his vocation' and Falstaff uses the same biblical proof-text (1 Corinthians 7:20) to claim the value of time spent pursuing one's vocation (even if it happens to be thievery): ''tis no sin for a man to labour in his vocation' (1.ii.84–5).

---

[22] John Spencer Hill, *Infinity, Faith, and Time: Christian Humanism and Renaissance Literature* (Montreal: McGill-Queen's University Press, 1997), p. 96.

[23] [Heinrich Bullinger and Theodore Beza], *A Confession of Fayth, made by common consent of diuers reformed Churches beyond the Seas*, trans. John Old (London: Lucas Harrison, 1568), sigs. A2r, B4r.

This idea of time as *tempus commodum* – time construed as opportunity – is basic to the way in which Ephesians 5:16 ('redeemyng the time')
was understood in this period.[24] What is rarely noted, however, is the
extent to which Hal's closing biblical quotation in this scene ('Redeeming
time when men least think I will') responds to and remembers Falstaff's
own biblical language. It recalls both Falstaff's tacit inversion of this idea
('the poor abuses of the time want countenance') and the reference to
Proverbs that Hal and Falstaff had created together ('wisdom cries out in
the streets'). Sixteenth-century homiletics preached that 'now' was the time
of the gospel, the time of redemption, and Proverbs 1:20 was considered a
proof-text of this idea: 'this acceptable time of grace: for euen now wisdom
cryeth without, the sounde of the Gospell is heard in our temples: nowe is
the time of peace, nowe is the day of repentance'.[25] To listen to the voice of
wisdom is to redeem the time. The calling out of wisdom in the streets was
typologically fulfilled in the contemporary preaching of the gospel.[26] The
crying of wisdom in the streets was seen by preachers as biblical sanction
of their own biblically saturated sermons but also as proof that the people
were not listening: 'Wisedome crieth in the streetes *I haue called and ye
refused, I have stretched out mine hande, and none woulde regarde*. Such
is the power of Satan, so shall hee stoppe their eares, that they shall not
vnderstande what is spoken in the name of the Lord.'[27] Falstaff's prayer
to Poins about the spirit of persuasion and the ears of profiting is a virtuoso inversion of the homiletic use of biblical proof-texts. Hal's final,
resounding quotation of Ephesians – 'redeemyng the time' – shows that
that he does gain the 'ears of profiting': but just not quite in the way in
which Falstaff had intended. Hal listens to Falstaff's biblical quotations
and reworks them for his own ends.

Preachers, of course, were highly antithetical to both the 'waste' of time
spent at the theatre and the theatre's claim that it might be able to edify its
audience with scriptural quotation. Alexander Leighton's *A Shorte Treatise*

---

[24] See, for example, Richard Turnbull, *An Exposition vpon the canonicall epistle of Saint Iames*
(London: John Windet, 1591), pp. 295, 300–3.
[25] Laurence Chaderton, *An Excellent and Godly Sermon* (London: Christopher Barker, 1578), sig. G8v.
[26] Everard Digby, *Everard Digbie his Dissuasiue* (London: Robert Robinson and Thomas Newman,
1590), p. 173. See also Michael Cope, *A Godly and Learned Exposition vppon the Prouerbes of Solomon*
(London: George Byshop, 1580), fo. 10v; Arthur Dent, *A Sermon of repentaunce* (London: John
Harrison, 1582), sig. C5r; Zacharias Ursinus, *The Svmme of Christian Religion* (Oxford: Joseph
Barnes, 1587), p. 42; and Henry Smith, *The Sermons of Maister Henrie Smith* (London: Thomas
Man, 1593), p. 471.
[27] John Jewel, *An Exposition vpon the two Epistles of the Apostle S. Paul to the Thessalonians* (London: Ralfe
Newberie, 1584), p. 356.

against Stage-Plays (1625) turns to precisely the biblical texts discussed above when arguing that play-going must be shunned because it involves the 'losse of pretious time, which should be spent in Gods service': 'everie one, both young and olde, must giue account to God of his labours, and of his time spent in this life. The Holy Ghost sayth Ephes. 5.16. *Redeeme the time, for the dayes are evill*; but some men say, Let us haue pastime.'[28] Leighton argues that it is only the

> perversly irreligious, will say, that sometimes the sacred Scripture is or may be acted by players on the stage, and thereby a man may learne more then at a sermon … concerning those persons that so greatly desire to learne religion at Stage-playes … They seldome come to the Church to learne religion according to Gods ordinance … though God intreate them so to doe, Prov. 1.20. *Wisedome cryeth without: she uttereth her voice in the streets.* (11)

Shakespeare, entertainingly, is wielding the weapons of the prosecution when claiming that Hal can redeem the time.

Falstaff and Henry IV

Falstaff frequently borrows the homiletic practice of using biblical quotations as proof-texts, but never more explicitly than when he is impersonating Henry IV. When he performs the role of the king in Act 11, Scene iv, biblical quotation forms the bedrock of his arguments: 'if then the tree may be known by the fruit' (11.iv.352–3: 'Euery tree is knowen by his owne fruite' (Luke 6:44)); 'this pitch – as ancient writers do report – doth defile' (11.iv.341–2: 'He that toucheth pitche, shalbe defiled with it' (Ecclesiasticus 13:1)). Falstaff joins euphuistic phrasing to specious moralising to make Henry's biblical quotations sound sententious: 'if then the tree may be known by the fruit, as the fruit by the tree, then peremptorily I speak it, there is virtue in that Falstaff' (11.iv.352–3). Falstaff, entertainingly, parodies Henry IV for the biblical turn of phrase that is actually his own mode of speech, but he also implies that the king's biblical commonplaces are uncreative compared to his own. He presents Henry IV's sententiousness as the opposite of his own transgressive deployment of biblical authority.

Falstaff's diegetic biblical quotation in Act 11, Scene iv, however, also performs an extradiegetic function in that it primes the ears of the audience to hear biblical allusion when the confrontation between the prince and his father (the scene being burlesqued in anticipation) actually does take

[28] Alexander Leighton, *A Shorte Treatise against Stage-Plays* ([Amsterdam], 1625), p. 20.

place. Stephen Greenblatt has written of the way in which Falstaff's language habitually acts as 'anticipatory, or proleptic parody' of the dominant ideology of the play, and particularly that of Henry IV.[29] This is true, likewise, of his biblical quotation. Henry IV uses biblical language sparingly compared to Falstaff, but he does indeed turn to scriptural precedent when he scolds his son. The easily recognised, sententious quotations of Falstaff's royal impersonation have opened the audience's ears for the complex biblical allusions of Act III, Scene ii, which are thick with extradiegetic force.

When Henry IV tells his son of how he won the throne, he draws on a well-known biblical type of usurpation:

> And then I stole all courtesy from heaven,
> And dressed myself in such humility
> That I did pluck allegiance from men's hearts,
> Loud shouts and salutations from their mouths,
> Even in the presence of the crownèd King. (*1 Henry IV*, III.ii.50–4)

The reference is to the famous story of David and Absalom.[30] The second book of Samuel describes how 'Absalom stale the heartes of the men of Israel' (15:5–6, a passage echoed by both Henry's 'stole' and 'men's hearts'). It is Absalom's pretended desire to give other men 'justice' that wins this allegiance – an aspect of the story brought to mind in Hotspur's bitter remembrance of how, 'by this face, / This seeming brow of justice, did he win / The hearts of all that he did angle for' (IV.iii.82–4). Allusions to the story of David and Absalom are used in reference to Henry's usurpation a further three times in the Henriad (and Falstaff also keeps the story in mind with his abuse of his tailor as a 'whoreson Achitophel!' (*2 Henry IV*, I. ii.27).[31] It is unsurprising that a connection between Henry IV's usurpation and Absalom comes naturally to his enemies; but it is unexpected that it should be used by the king himself.

In this passage, Henry IV (unaware of how little his son needs the lesson) is teaching Hal to use policy to rule: arguing that he should, like himself and Absalom, appear to give people what they want. But the extradiegetic biblical meaning available to the audience is that of a story about a son unseating his father. Henry IV's turn to the story of Absalom is an unconscious acknowledgement of the question mark that lingers in his mind over

---

[29] Stephen J. Greenblatt, *Shakespearean Negotiations: The Circulation of Social Energy in Renaissance England* (Berkeley: University of California Press, 1988), pp. 54–5.

[30] For evidence that George Peele's popular 1594 dramatisation of this well-known story uses the audience's biblical knowledge to create dramatic irony, see Groves, *Texts and Traditions*, pp. 17–18.

[31] Shaheen, *Biblical References*, pp. 386, 433.

his own son. In the source play – *The Famous Victories of Henry the Fifth* (1586) – the prince contemplates murdering his father in this scene. He enters '*with a dagger in his hand*' and the anxiety of this moment is recalled in Henry's reference to the famous biblical story of a child's attempted usurpation of his father's throne.[32]

Falstaff, as Hamlin writes, is Shakespeare's 'master of diegetic allusion … No character alludes to the Bible more self-consciously, more frequently, or with more boldly revisionary misapplication.'[33] But Falstaff's biblical quotations also resonate far beyond their original contexts. Falstaff's outrageous misuse of proof-texts allows him disingenuously to defend his thievery and gluttony with biblical authority, for 'if to be fat be to be hated, then Pharaoh's lean kine are to be loved' (*1 Henry IV*, II.iv.392–3 (Genesis 41:1–21)). Proof-texts are a touchstone of Falstaffian discourse, and the irony of Falstaff 'labouring in his vocation' resonates beyond the play to subtly undermine the godly use of biblical quotation as an argumentative strategy. Falstaff's biblical phraseology likewise resonates within the Henriad to create a soundscape in which diegetic quotations reverberate with extradiegetic meaning. Attending to Falstaff's biblical quotations does indeed bring to his audience 'the ears of profiting'.

[32] Geoffrey Bullough (ed.), *Narrative and Dramatic Sources of Shakespeare*, 8 vols. (London: Routledge and Kegan Paul, 1964–75), vol. IV, p. 315.
[33] Hamlin, *Bible in Shakespeare*, p. 234.

CHAPTER 4

Quoting Hamlet

Douglas Bruster

We think of *Hamlet* as the centre of Shakespearean quotation; as the old joke goes, the play is 'nothing but quotations'. Yet we rarely consider how quotation functions within it. This essay takes *Hamlet* as a representative example of Shakespeare's practice of quotation in order to trace quotation's role in the complexity and success of his writing. As we will see, Shakespeare uses quotation to stage crucial activities connected with his work: writing, playing, listening and reading. Quotation thus comes to function as a metaphor for *Hamlet*'s representational ambitions as well as an imperfectly understood component of its texture. If *Hamlet* crowns Shakespeare's efforts as 'literary' dramatist, quotation remains both a means by which he achieves the literary and a way of displaying that achievement as it unfolds.

Defining Quotation

How should we identify quotation in *Hamlet*? A thin definition – all words found between quotation marks – might seem misguided, for it depends upon the typographical system we take for granted but which had not developed in his time. Early Shakespeare texts, that is, actually feature very few of the inverted commas that call out quotations in printed texts today. And where such quotation marks do grace dramatic texts of Shakespeare's era, they serve largely to mark sententious material that readers might copy out (see Chapter 2).[1] As Peter Stallybrass and Zachary Lesser have shown,

---

[1] For typographical histories of quotation marks in an English context, see Margreta de Grazia, 'Shakespeare in Quotation Marks', in Jean I. Marsden (ed.), *The Appropriation of Shakespeare: Post-Renaissance Reconstructions of the Works and the Myth* (New York: St Martin's Press, 1991), pp. 57–71; and Laura Estill, 'Commonplace Markers and Quotation Marks', *ArchBook*, www.drc. usask.ca/projects/archbook/commonplace.php (7 March 2014; last accessed 9 November 2015). The implications of quotation marks for our understanding of Q1 *Hamlet* have been explored in a foundational essay by Zachary Lesser and Peter Stallybrass, 'The First Literary *Hamlet* and the Commonplacing of Professional Plays', *Shakespeare Quarterly*, 59 (2008), 371–420.

Hamlet was the first of Shakespeare's plays to be marked up in this way; so flagged, its *sententiae* stood as one signal of its literariness. These early texts tend to mark extra-dialogical material (including songs, letters and proclamations) with italic type. Many other kinds of speech that modern editions also place in quotation marks went typographically uninflected in the printed playbooks of Shakespeare's time.

Yet knowing the history of typographical convention need not entail blindness to the textual complexity it has been developed to address. The absence of quotation marks is not different from the abbreviated or incomplete stage directions and speech prefixes in early dramatic texts, most of which we supply without falsifying the text. To see only the modernity of quotation marks – dwelling, for instance, on their role in the assertion of intellectual property in the West – is to underestimate the complicated system of verbal repetition and inflection they record. As this chapter seeks to demonstrate, the quotation that modern editions carefully highlight with various marks (such as double and/or single inverted commas) remains one of early drama's most powerful aspects.

Whatever method modern texts employ, they insist that readers visualise – literally *see* – quoted speech as different in kind from ordinary dialogue. As such, quotation marks attend to something already there, in the texts, and make manifest the distinction that philosophers have drawn between the 'use' and 'mention' of words.[2] By virtue of their quotation marks, quoted passages announce language and speech from elsewhere, from other speakers, venues and times (past, present and future). Quoted speech is both made and mentioned as a unit rather than being used like ordinary words and phrases.

We could take as an example the following five words from *The Winter's Tale*:

> the former queen is well (v.i.30)[3]

---

[2] The 'use'/'mention' theory of quotation was popularised by Donald Davidson in 'Quotation', *Theory and Decision*, 11 (1979), 27–40. Since the publication of Davidson's essay, quotation has formed a signal problem for the philosophy of language. Three works that I have found especially useful among the many in this busy subfield include Herman Cappelen and Ernie Lepore, *Language Turned in on Itself* (Oxford: Oxford University Press, 2007); the essays of Elke Brendel, Joerg Meibauer and Markus Steinbach (eds.), *Understanding Quotation* (Berlin: Mouton de Gruyter, 2011); and Paul Saka, 'Quotation', *Philosophy Compass*, 8:10 (2013), 935–49. On p. 945, Saka provides a helpful schematic of ten current theories of quotation.

[3] All references to Shakespeare are to *The Riverside Shakespeare*, ed. G. Blakemore Evans *et al.* (Boston: Houghton Mifflin, 1997). The *Riverside* was selected as base text for this chapter because, with the exception of *Edward III*, all of its works were punctuated by a single editor.

This phrase (actually ending a question) uses each of its words on an equal level. A verbally comparable utterance comes in *Hamlet*'s

> mobled queen is good (ii.ii.504)

Typographically, however, modern readers encounter Polonius's line as something like this:

> 'mobled queen' is good

Because *mobled queen* has been heard twice already – once in the Player's speech (501), and once from Hamlet (502), who considers it worthy of notice – Polonius's line clearly refers to *mobled queen* as a unit of language, to words *qua* words, rather than primarily to a queen who is mobled. Thus *the former queen is well* denotes USE, *'mobled queen' is good* includes MENTION. In terms of dramatic texts, we could understand quotation to be language whose origin is marked, by conventions of dialogue and punctuation, as temporally and/or spatially ancillary. Quotation flags material for mention and subsequent interpretive emphasis; it both alienates words in the linguistic environment of a text and authorises their presence.

The Circle of Quotation in *Hamlet*

The *Riverside* edition of *Hamlet* encloses seventy-five units of speech within quotation marks, one of which ('Let her come in' at iv.v.53) we might be tempted to bracket as being an instance of dialogue spoken off stage. Yet the editorial conundrum posed by this off-stage speech (some editions do not employ quotation marks for it) sheds light on an important, inescapable aspect of quotation: its distancing element.

If we imagine for a moment an axis that stretches from near to far, proximate to distant, the ordinary dialogue of a drama falls on the near and proximate end. In accordance with customary representations of chronology, let us define the far right end of this axis as the present, the left end as the past. In drama, characters largely speak in the here and now, from 'Who's there?' to 'Go bid the soldiers shoot' (i.i.1, v.ii.403). Temporally, these words would fall at the far right side of our axis. But when characters quote something spoken just prior (say, ' "the mobled queen" '), we will place those words in proximity to the speaker, yet slightly down our axis to the left, for we have just heard them being spoken. Further still across this axis are words written or spoken not only prior but elsewhere: letters, proclamations or off-stage speech reported directly. Most distant, and at the far left end, are words that have been composed for anonymous performance; these are largely but not exclusively the lyrics to songs, and lines for performance within a play's fiction.

Because performers – including dramatic singers (such as Ophelia) and actors (such as the First Player) – both 'quote' ancillary texts and deliver those texts in a display that can virtually as well as typographically erase their quotation marks via sustained and committed performance, when we reach this end of the axis we may find ourselves reimagining our illustration. We may conceive, that is, not a line that demarcates unbridgeable distance but rather a circle that takes us back to characters speaking in what we have just called the 'here and now'. Ophelia quoting in song becomes Ophelia owning that song. Words can be so thoroughly inhabited and extended that they stretch the very definition of quotation, performance transforming the prior to the present, that of another to one's own.

A typology of quotations in *Hamlet* could begin with such performed passages, as they are its most prevalent kind of quotation. Here brief description of each variety of quotation is followed by the passages' first words, along with act-scene-line citation and speaker, and, in some instances, the party quoted or quoting. As with most typologies, some of its items plausibly belong to multiple categories.

Performances

There are twenty-eight instances of performed quotations in the *Riverside Hamlet*. These range from song lyrics and stanzas to the longer dramatic passages of the imagined Troy play. Their distribution reflects the drama's structure: the earliest performed quotes are from Hamlet and the First Player (after III.ii.284, Hamlet does not have quoted performance); thereafter Ophelia's songs dominate; finally, the First Clown (or Gravedigger) sings as he digs Ophelia's grave and turns up the skull of still another performer (Yorick). Seen as a chain, these performed quotations trace back, like a virus, to Hamlet's first performances and his solicitation of performance by the First Player. Two quotations ascribed to Ophelia reflect the voices of figures within her longest song – secondary quotations, that is, within her larger, primary quotation (the song).

Then came each actor (II.ii.395; Hamlet); *One fair daughter* (II.ii.407–8; Hamlet); *As by lot, God wot* (II.ii.416; Hamlet); *It came to pass* (II.ii.418; Hamlet); *The rugged Pyrrhus* (II.ii.450; Hamlet); *The rugged Pyrrhus* (II.ii.452–64; Hamlet); *Anon he finds him* (II.ii.468–97; First Player); *But who, ah woe* (II.ii.502; First Player); *Run barefoot* (II.ii.504–18; First Player); *For O, for O, the hobby-horse* (III.ii.135; Hamlet); *Why, let the strooken deer* (III.ii.271–4;

Hamlet); *For thou dost know* (iii.ii.281–4; Hamlet); *How should I* (iv.v.23; Ophelia); *He is dead* (iv.v.29; Ophelia); *White his shroud* (iv.v.36; Ophelia); *Larded all with sweet flowers* (iv.v.38–40; Ophelia); *To-morrow is Saint Valentine's day* (iv.v.48–55; Ophelia); *By Gis, and by Saint Charity* (iv.v.58–62; Ophelia); *Before you tumbled me* (iv.v.62–3; Ophelia); *So would I 'a done* (iv.v.65–6; Ophelia); *They bore him barefac'd* (iv.v.165–7; Ophelia); *A-down, a-down* (iv.v.171; Ophelia); *For bonny sweet Robin* (iv.v.187; Ophelia); *And will 'a not come again?* (iv.v.190–9; Ophelia); *In youth when I did love* (v.i.61–4; First Clown); *But age with his* (v.i.71–4; First Clown); *A pickaxe and a spade* (v.i.94–7; First Clown); *O, a pit of clay for* (v.i.120–1; First Clown).

Scripts for Future Performance

Related to performed quotes are a second type of quoted material: scripts for future performance. These consist of forecast words; sometimes meant to be realised, they may also be uttered only hypothetically to imagine what *could* or *might* be said (by oneself and/or by others). If performed quotes were composed in the past for performance in a present, these scripts are composed in the present for performance (sometimes only imaginary) in the future. Early in *Hamlet* there are a significant number of such future scripts in the speech of Hamlet and Polonius, respectively: Hamlet anticipates (in order to forbid) what the soldiers might say at some hypothetical time to come; in the next scene Polonius likewise prepares Reynaldo's investigatory speech regarding Laertes in Paris. After this initial burst, such scripts for future performance occur sporadically and occasion the speech of various characters.

Well, well, we know (i.v.176; Hamlet); *We could, and if we would* (i.v.176; Hamlet); *If we list to speak* (i.v.177; Hamlet); *There be, and if they might* (i.v.177; Hamlet); *I know his father* (ii.i.14–15; Polonius); *And in part him* (ii.i..17; Polonius); *not well* (ii.i.17–19; Polonius); *Good sir* (ii.i.46; Polonius); *friend* (ii.i.46; Polonius); *gentleman* (ii.i.46; Polonius); *closes in the consequence* (ii.i.52; Polonius); *I know the gentleman* (ii.i.53–7; Polonius); *I saw him enter* (ii.i.58; Polonius); *Forgive me my foul murther* (iii.iii.52; Claudius); *Thus didst thou* (iv.vii.57; Laertes); *a grave-maker* (v.i.58–9; First Clown); *Now the King drinks to Hamlet* (v.ii.278; Claudius).

Reading

Certain characters are called upon to read, verbatim, materials that have been written elsewhere, sometimes considerably before the episode of reading. While such reading is arguably a type of performance, what differentiates this form of quotation from songs and performed play speeches is the direct acknowledgement that the words belong to another time and agent. There are five passages of reading marked as quotation, all of them featuring characters reciting something that Hamlet has written.

To the celestial (ii.ii.109–10; Polonius); *In her excellent white bosom* (ii.ii.113; Polonius); *Doubt thou the stars are fire* (ii.ii.116–24; Polonius); *Horatio, when thou shalt have overlook'd this* (iv.vi.13–31; Horatio); *High and mighty* (iv.vii.43–8; Claudius).

Reported Speech

Related to the reading aloud of written material on stage is the direct, neutral reporting of speech uttered elsewhere, or earlier in a scene. This occurs five times, beginning with Hamlet's remembrance of the Ghost's farewell, and including various speakers tasked with expository repetition: Gertrude (in her only quotation), Reynaldo and an anonymous Messenger. Unlike reading as quotation, reported speech draws on sources other than *Hamlet*, and relies on memory rather than manuscript.

Adieu, adieu! remember me (i.v.111; Hamlet, quoting the Ghost); *closes in the consequence* (ii.i.51; Reynaldo, quoting Polonius); *A rat, a rat!* (iv.i.10; Gertrude, quoting Hamlet); *Choose we* (iv.v.107; Messenger quoting people); *Laertes shall be king* (iv.v.109; Messenger quoting people).

Self-quotation

A variety of reported speech occurs when characters quote themselves, either repeating things they have already spoken or (as with Polonius) fictionalising themselves as speaking such lines. There are four such instances of self-quotation.

Lord Hamlet is a prince out of thy star (ii.ii.141–2; Polonius); *'Tis so* (ii.ii.154; Polonius); *Man delights not me* (ii.ii.313–14; Hamlet); *By and by* (iii.ii.387; Hamlet).

Annotation

One of the more memorable types of quotation in *Hamlet* occurs when characters annotate what they have just heard or read. This often involves the critical examination of single words or short phrases, as in Hamlet's initial and entirely characteristic '"seems"' when replying to his mother.

Such annotation reveals the scholarly and/or literary aspect of the play's spoken environment. There are eight such instances.

    seems (I.ii.76; Hamlet, quoting Gertrude); *beautified* (II.ii.III; Polonius, quoting Hamlet); *The mobled queen* (II.ii.503; Hamlet, quoting First Player); *mobled queen* (II.ii.504; Polonius, quoting First Player); *Naked* (IV.vii.51; Claudius, quoting Hamlet); *alone* (IV.vii.52; Claudius, quoting Hamlet); *would* (IV.vii.119; Claudius, quoting himself); *should* (IV.vii.122; Claudius, quoting himself).

Titles, Proverbs and Vatic Speech

This, the most miscellaneous variety of quotation adduced here, includes titles, proverbial wisdom and words imagined to be so generalised that they approach the level of cliché or the sententious. Six such quotations appear in the *Riverside Hamlet*. Titles include the play-within-the-play (named both formally and informally). Hamlet cites a proverb and defines it as such. With Claudius, he engages in a kind of vatic quotation, where the speech is not scripted in relation to particular speakers. Much of Polonius's sententious language has, of course, become quotation over time.

    This must be so (I.ii.106; Claudius); *The Murther of Gonzago* (II.ii.537–8; Hamlet); *The Mouse-trap* (III.ii.237; Hamlet); *While the grass grows* (III.ii.343; Hamlet); *Good morrow, sweet lord* (v.i.82–3; Hamlet); *one* (v.ii.74; Hamlet).

Quotation and Character

These various examples reveal that Shakespeare's major characters are quoters. The metalinguistic nature of quotation allows Shakespeare to highlight their intelligence, verbal dexterity and self-consciousness. To quote, in Shakespeare, is to be. It is no accident, then, that Hamlet quotes almost as soon as we hear him speak: 'Seems, madam? nay, it is, I know not "seems"' (I.ii.76). The prince's repetition of *seems* immediately marks him as intelligent, incisive and rhetorically sophisticated. His dissent (sardonically correcting his mother, the queen's, polite enquiry) is in keeping with the combativeness and dissatisfaction we see in him throughout the play. It is also characteristic of many instances of quotation in *Hamlet*. Indeed, it is tempting to say that Hamlet's agency in quoting the queen's *seems* helps define the relation between quotation and character in Shakespeare: characters who quote display their power over language, and over others, by quoting others' words.

Shakespeare seems to have followed and extended Marlowe's experiments with this technique. Throughout his works, Marlowe's leading characters – including Faustus, Barabas and the Guise – punctuate their restless reach for mastery with quotation. Tamburlaine sets the bar for such linguistic self-assertion early on. When Menaphon promises him that 'Your majesty shall shortly have your wish, / And ride in triumph through Persepolis', Tamburlaine waits for his departure before savouring the words:

> 'And ride in triumph through Persepolis'!
> Is it not brave to be a king, Techelles?
> Usumcasane and Theridamas,
> Is it not passing brave to be a king,
> And ride in triumph through Persepolis?[4]

So delicious to him is Menaphon's image that Tamburlaine repeats his phrase twice (along with 'brave to be a king'). In the terminology of linguistic philosophy, he both *mentions* and *uses* this phrase in a way that leaves little doubt about his will to power. Later he annotates what he has heard in a passage whose quotations have long served to define his character:

> Well said, Theridamas! Speak in that mood,
> For 'will' and 'shall' best fitteth Tamburlaine. (iii.iii.40–1)

To different effect, we hear a structural echo of these lines in Claudius's attention to the twin verbs 'would' and 'should' in his moment of annotation:

> That we would do,
> We should do when we would; for this 'would' changes,
> And hath abatements and delays as many
> As there are tongues, are hands, are accidents,
> And then this 'should' is like a spendthrift's sigh,
> That hurts by easing. (iv.vii.119–22)

Both characters extend themselves via the metalinguistic technique of quotation: first, through the drama's verbal domain, and next – by virtue of their recursive abilities – in our estimation.

At first glance, such verbal domination can seem at the heart of quotation: characters who manipulate others' language strike us as not only verbally sophisticated, but *de facto* figures of the playwright. From the First

---

[4] *Tamburlaine the Great, Part One* in Christopher Marlowe, *The Complete Plays*, ed. Frank Romany and Robert Lindsey (London: Penguin Books, 2003), ii.v.48–54.

Player's speech through to *The Murder of Gonzago* (to which Hamlet famously promises to contribute some lines), various characters in *Hamlet*
imagine speech for others to recite. We could consider, for example, Hamlet's
and Polonius's future scripts: Hamlet anticipating what the soldiers may
say at some future time (giving him away, he fears); and Polonius, for his
part, writing lines for his man, Reynaldo, to use in a Parisian investigation.
Likewise, the First Clown (Gravedigger) provides such a line when he asks
and answers his own riddle: 'say "a grave-maker": the houses he makes
lasts till doomsday' (v.i.58–9). Mastery of others' language also includes
quotation that criticises what it quotes. In addition to Hamlet's *seems*, we
might think of Polonius's remarks on both Hamlet's *beautified* and the
First Player's *mobled queen*, and Claudius's pausing to note that Hamlet
uses both *Naked* and *alone* in his letter. Such instances imply that quotation is at base a gesture of control.

   Yet control describes only part of quotation's range in *Hamlet*. Several
of Claudius's quotations from the preceding section demonstrate that he
is far from dominant in taking up language. His future script in prayer –
'"Forgive me my foul murther"' (iii.iii.52) – testifies to words he feels
unable to say convincingly. So too does the Marlovian structure of his
'would' and 'should' only serve to confirm the distance between these verbs
and Tamburlaine's 'will' and 'shall'. If quoters in *Hamlet* are sometimes
pedantic (and in this way demonstrate a will to mastery), just as frequently
they display a subservient relation to the words they speak. Here chronology may work to lessen, even mock the idea of mastery: to come after
others' words is by definition to be belated, and potentially inferior, to
these words. The structure of decline that dominates the play – 'Hyperion
to a satyr' – maps out a pattern for the secondary, and subsequent, in its
speech. Proverbs by definition precede us, serving not only to steer but
also to correct and judge behaviour: 'Ay, sir, but "While the grass grows" –
the proverb is something musty' (iii.ii.343). Likewise, the First Player's
speech both dazzles Hamlet and leads him to rebuke himself, and the
multiple rhyming lines he pronounces in his antic madness seem similarly barbed, chants that sometimes reek of aggression toward both other
and self. (It is not difficult to read many of his sing-song quotations as
simultaneously manic and self-loathing.) Thus, if performed quotations
can be taken to display an energised and independent agency, in which
such performers as Ophelia may be seen as writing and performing their
own plays-within-the-play, many instances of performed quotation
in *Hamlet* place their speakers in a ministerial position: reciting letters,
singing songs, performing plays on command.

While quotation thickens dramatic speech, it also extends character in multiple directions. Shakespeare uses quotation, in fact, to ground characters in every media and dimension of his industry. In quotation, we see characters acting as playwrights (Hamlet), performers (including the First Player and Ophelia), auditors (including Reynaldo and Claudius) and readers (including Horatio and Claudius). Whether manifesting control or subservience, quotation functions as a metaphor for the full range of acts connected to the theatre: imagining and writing scripts for performance, executing these scripts, hearing them and relaying their words (both from memory and written documents). Collectively, therefore, quotations serve as a *mise-en-abyme* of the entertainment industry as it flourished in and around the early modern playhouses.[5]

Quotation and the Literary

Quotation is one of the secrets to Shakespeare's literary drama, and at the same time asks us to understand that the textures of the literary depend deeply upon the theatrical. The concept of 'literary drama' takes its critical name and definition, of course, from the foundational work of Lukas Erne, whose studies *Shakespeare as Literary Dramatist* and *Shakespeare and the Book Trade* have helped to change how we think of Shakespeare's plays as functioning in his time.[6] Shakespeare's plays, Erne shows, were literary as well as theatrical documents. Because his object of enquiry stretches over many decades, and includes numerous printers, publishers, writers and readers, Erne attends largely to the archival and structural, necessarily stressing the panoramic rather than microscopic.[7] The 'literary' is defined through readership and through Shakespeare's practices as a writer, which are seen to have addressed the marketplace of print. Although he devotes a significant chapter to the differences between 'theatricality' and 'literariness' as they arose between shorter and longer versions of selected Shakespeare plays respectively, Erne cannot dwell on the specific elements of language use that one notes in the work of such scholars as Patricia

---

[5] *Mise-en-abyme*, or roughly 'picture within a picture', is a heraldic term turned into a literary critical tool by André Gide in his *Journals* (1893). Significantly, Gide includes 'the play scene in *Hamlet*' as an example. See André Gide, *Journals i: 1889–1913*, trans. Justin O'Brien (Carbondale: University of Illinois Press, 2000), p. 30. On the concept's application to literary texts, see Lucien Dällenbach, *The Mirror in the Text* (Chicago: University of Chicago Press, 1977), esp. pp. 7ff.

[6] See Lukas Erne, *Shakespeare as Literary Dramatist*, 2nd edn (Cambridge: Cambridge University Press, 2013 (2003)); and *Shakespeare and the Book Trade* (Cambridge: Cambridge University Press, 2013).

[7] On these poles of critical investigation, see Marvin Spevack, 'Shakespeare Microscopic and Panoramic', *Mosaic*, 10:3 (1976), 117–27.

Parker, Frank Kermode and Harry Berger Jr (to name only these).[8] Instead, he cites various 'purple patches' from what appear to be the revised, literary forms of such plays as *Henry V* and *Romeo and Juliet*, asking them as complete units of language to confirm the literariness of these dramatic texts.[9] Yet if Shakespeare's plays were indeed 'literary', we might ask if anything more specific *in* them could help us define that quality.

Among the vast array of forms and devices that characterised early modern drama – including the flowers of rhetoric, blank verse, the bilingual verse/prose system, soliloquies and poetic imagery – quotation seems a key, perhaps *the* key, for defining the multifaceted nature of Shakespeare's achievement as 'literary dramatist'. As we have seen, through quotation Shakespeare effectively stages aspects of writing, reading, performance and listening. Whether through scripting, critique, recitation or song, quotation conveys the activities that made up the composition, performance and consumption of playbooks in early modern England.

While quotation can be seen as encapsulating the theatrical *and* textual aspects of Shakespeare's drama in qualitative ways, its proliferation across certain of his plays marked a distinctive period in his career. A count of quotation marks in the *Riverside* edition of Shakespeare, for example, reveals that *Love's Labour's Lost* contains the most quotations per 1,000 words, followed, in descending order, by *Twelfth Night*, *The Two Gentlemen of Verona*, *Much Ado about Nothing*, *Romeo and Juliet*, *Hamlet* and *The Merchant of Venice*. This array of texts suggests a number of things. To begin with, five of the seven titles are comedies. The relation between quotation and genre seems explained in part by comedy's attraction to wit and to forms such as letters and songs. *Love's Labour's Lost* features multiple instances of the latter, as well as numerous sonnets recited during its action, and performances and instances of verbal annotation, amongst other kinds of quotation.

If comedies are an expected presence in this grouping, however, the presence of *Romeo* and *Hamlet* asks us to look beyond genre. What these plays have in common is that they were written or printed in the late 1590s. Two of the plays (*Two Gentlemen* and *Twelfth Night*) were first published in the First Folio, of course, and the estimated dates of composition for this group range from the spring of 1594 (*Two Gentlemen*) through winter of

---

[8] See, for example, Patricia Parker, *Shakespeare from the Margins: Language, Culture, Context* (Chicago: University of Chicago Press, 1996); Frank Kermode, *Shakespeare's Language* (London: Allen Lane, 2000); and Harry Berger Jr, *Making Trifles of Terrors: Redistributing Complicities in Shakespeare* (Stanford: Stanford University Press, 1997).

[9] See Erne, *Shakespeare as Literary Dramatist*, esp. pp. 250–3.

1600/1 (*Twelfth Night*).[10] But the composition and publication of a number of these quotation-intensive plays falls within a much narrower window. It is possible, for instance, to locate the publication of the 'bad' first quarto of *Romeo and Juliet* in the early months of 1597, and the missing first quarto of *Love's Labour's Lost* during this same year; it was at approximately this same time, in the spring of 1597, that Shakespeare probably composed *The Merchant of Venice* and *Much Ado about Nothing*, followed, within two years, by *Hamlet* in the early months of 1599. Within a twenty-four-month period, then, five of Shakespeare's seven most quotation-intensive plays seem to have made an appearance in print, performance or manuscript.

It seems more than coincidence that this same period also witnessed the emergence of Shakespeare's name on various title pages (the second quarto of *Love's Labour's Lost*, the second quarto of *Richard III* and the second and third quartos of *Richard II*), as well as Francis Meres's mention of Shakespeare – along with citation of fourteen of his titles and the *Sonnets* – in *Palladis Tamia* in 1598.[11] If we extend this window forward by approximately a year, we notice the publication of *Merchant* and *Much Ado* in 1600, and also, that same year, both *Bel-védere; or, The Garden of the Muses* (*STC* 3189–3189.5) and *Englands Parnassus* (*STC* 378–80) (Figures 5 and 6). That these compilations of quotations appeared just as the Shakespeare plays most invested in this linguistic form were composed and/or printed suggests a convergence of wit, quotability and celebrity at the end of the sixteenth century and the beginning of the seventeenth. Some of this energy, though not all (see Chapter 1), coalesced around the person and achievement of William Shakespeare, whose new-found fame was made manifest in both citation and quotation. Quotation, as we have seen, was a means by which linguistic facility was staged in his plays and poems. Significantly, it features not only in *Bel-védere* and *Englands Parnassus*, but also in John Manningham's *Diary*, where (however accurately) Shakespeare is quoted outside the confines of his public writing, although in coy reference to it: 'Then message being brought that Rich. the 3ᵈ. [that is the actor Richard Burbage] was at the dore [for a sexual assignation with a woman Shakespeare was himself busy bedding], Shakespeare caused returne to be made that William the Conquerour was before Rich. the 3.' As Manningham helpfully explains, 'Shakespeares name w̶i̶l̶l̶m'.[12]

---

[10] Dating of Shakespeare's plays in this chapter relies upon Douglas Bruster and Geneviève Smith, 'A New Chronology for Shakespeare's Plays', *Digital Scholarship in the Humanities*, 29 (2014), 1–20.

[11] For discussion of the making of 'Shakespeare' during these years, see Erne's chapter of that title in *Shakespeare as Literary Dramatist*, pp. 80–101.

[12] Quoted from *The Riverside Shakespeare*, p. 1960.

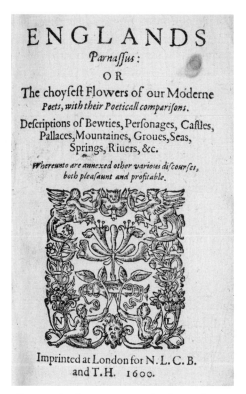

Figure 5   Robert Allott, *Englands Parnassus; or, The choysest flowers of our moderne poets*
(London, 1600), title page.

By the time of this diary entry (13 March 1602), it had perhaps become less necessary to explain the joke, for Shakespeare had quoted himself, and been quoted, into celebrity. Works such as *Love's Labour's Lost* and *Hamlet* are replete with quotation, the kind of language that advertises linguistic proficiency. In contrast to language as USE, quotation's exploitation of a further level of verbal practice (language deployed as MENTION) illustrates a curatorial relation to words, a relation that exceeds while including communication. To communicate well in Shakespeare is one thing; to display the witty acumen necessary for certain kinds of quotation takes characters such as Berowne and Hamlet to a higher level of curation. In this, they, and all of Shakespeare's witty quoters, stand as figures for the playwright. Their success, as speakers, represents in miniature

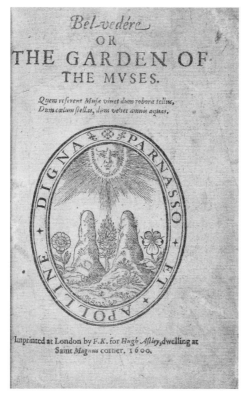

Figure 6   *Bel-vedére, or The Garden of the Muses* (London, 1600), title page.

the very quality and disposition toward language that both produced and confirmed their creator's own achievement.

Conclusion

Hamlet is full of quotation, a complex figure and technique by which Shakespeare combines the skills in composition, performance, audition and reading that subtended the production and consumption of plays in early modern England. Some Shakespearean characters possess a facility with borrowed words closely akin to that of a playwright; as such, quotation can be seen as standing in for the practice of dramatic composition itself. The intensive use of quotation in plays composed and/or printed between 1597 and 1600 corresponds to Shakespeare's new-found prominence as a writer at the end of Elizabeth's reign. More than an accidental marker of this status, the linguistic aptitude behind, and evident in, the quotations of the dramatic works penned and printed during this time were a means by which Shakespeare both described the 'literary' nature of his writing and asserted its claims to literary status.

PART II

Quoting Shakespeare, 1700–2000

Introduction

Kate Rumbold

From Shakespeare's own acts of quotation, we turn to those who quote Shakespeare. The second, and largest, part of this volume spans the years from the beginning of the eighteenth century to the end of the twentieth. What does it mean to quote Shakespeare in this time?

Dr Johnson, writing in 1765, hints that it doesn't mean much at all. In the Preface to his edition of Shakespeare, he praises the 'poet of nature' whose characters 'act and speak by the influence of those general passions and principles by which all minds are agitated, and the whole system of life is continued in motion'. While one *could* extract precepts from the plays, to do so would miss the point. It is in the 'progress of his fable, and the tenor of his dialogue' that Shakespeare's 'power' resides. And so, Johnson says, 'he that tries to recommend him by select quotations, will succeed like the pedant in Hierocles, who, when he offered his house to sale, carried a brick in his pocket as a specimen'.[1]

Quotation, however, has a 'power' of its own. In calling him the 'poet of nature', Johnson praises Shakespeare with a force that would have been remarkable at the beginning of the century, but was, by now, commonplace. Critics have documented the process by which Shakespeare was transformed from a provincial playwright in need of improvement to a national poet and secular deity, amidst the growing valuation of English literary 'classics'.[2] Quotations, we argue, are not by-products of this process, but integral to it. In this brief introduction, I suggest how the practice of quotation shapes, and is shaped by, three broader cultural changes that have a cumulative effect on understanding of 'Shakespeare'.

---

[1] Samuel Johnson, *Johnson on Shakespeare*, vol. VII of *The Yale Edition of the Works of Samuel Johnson*, ed. Arthur Sherbo (New Haven: Yale University Press, 1968), p. 62.

[2] Michael Dobson, *The Making of the National Poet: Shakespeare, Adaptation, and Authorship, 1660–1769* (Oxford: Clarendon Press, 1992); Jean I. Marsden, *The Re-Imagined Text: Shakespeare, Adaptation, and Eighteenth-Century Literary Theory* (Lexington: University Press of Kentucky, 1995); Jonathan Bate, *The Genius of Shakespeare* (London: Picador, 1997).

A Brief History of Quotation (2)

Authority

The early part of this period marks a watershed in the history of quotation. No scholar has articulated this change more acutely than Margreta de Grazia. In 'Shakespeare in Quotation Marks', she observes how typographical marks that, in the seventeenth century, signalled that a line was a 'commonplace' for all to use, came in the eighteenth century to mark off the private property of their author. They became recognisably 'quotation marks'. This change was not instantaneous, but it is indicative of emerging notions of proprietary authorship, shored up by copyright laws.[3] Quotation thus helped establish 'Shakespeare' as an author figure whose own insightful words and phrases were a sign of his authority.[4]

This transformation is visible in the quotation books published in this period. In Part I, we saw that some collections published around 1600 acknowledged the authors of their excerpts with a marginal 'Shakesp.' or 'W. S.'. But their purpose was to facilitate reworking of these well-expressed sentiments, rather than reverence for their authors. In the early eighteenth century, Edward Bysshe's *Art of English Poetry* (1702) marshalled literary quotations as a resource for future writers, but this practice was increasingly denigrated (see Chapter 5). Collections increasingly celebrated individual authors: the first such dedicated collection was William Dodd's *Beauties of Shakespear* (1752). When perpetual copyright ended in 1774, this 'beauties' genre exploded, taking fragments of English literature to a growing domestic audience. The authority Shakespeare accrued in the eighteenth century manifested itself in a new-found advisory role in nineteenth-century collections such as *Sayings from Shakespeare* (1864) and *Shakespeare's Household Words* (1859).

Shakespeare's words themselves were also treated with growing reverence. Adaptations and 'improvements' gave way to more textually faithful reproductions; and conjectural emendation to more historically informed collation. What cemented this reverence was perhaps the acts of quotation – from the admiring conversation of fictional characters to

---

[3] Margreta de Grazia, 'Shakespeare in Quotation Marks', in Jean I. Marsden (ed.), *The Appropriation of Shakespeare: Post-Renaissance Reconstructions of the Works and the Myth* (New York: St Martin's Press, 1992), pp. 57–71.

[4] See also Laura Estill, 'Commonplace Markers and Quotation Marks', *ArchBook: Architectures of the Book*, www.drc.usask.ca/projects/archbook/commonplace.php (7 March 2014; last accessed 17 May 2017).

the illustrative literary quotations in Dr Johnson's *Dictionary* (1755); from periodical essays to House of Commons debates – that, with the words 'as Shakespeare says', repeatedly ascribed authority to the playwright himself.

Education

At the end of the eighteenth century, the quotation books that followed in Dodd's wake took a noticeably didactic turn. Subsequent collections recast Shakespeare's words first as tools for moral improvement, and then as material with which to practise skills in reading, writing and speaking (see Chapter 5). But this elocutionary focus would shift again in the nineteenth century with the expansion of formal education. As classrooms were supplied with collections of extracts from English literature, Shakespeare quotations came to be associated with the highest levels of educational attainment (see Chapter 9).

Shakespeare's role in formal education institutionalised the moral and emotional authority he accrued in the previous century. Indeed, as Gail Marshall finds, the 'Shakespeare' who appeared in school readers was a rather 'admonitory' figure. Growing literacy rates, cheaper print and, eventually, universal access to education created a wider audience for Shakespeare than had existed since his lifetime. The 'Shakespeare' whose lines had been rehearsed by young male readers of *Elegant Extracts* (1784), or mingled palatably with paraphrase by Charles and Mary Lamb for boys to read to their sisters, was increasingly accessible to all kinds of people. But is this only the appearance of accessibility, when Shakespeare's words were aligned with a level of study only few would attain? This tension between the discourses of elite attainment and universality persists in Shakespeare education to the present day.

Audience

If the nineteenth century saw Shakespeare quotation institutionalised in the schoolroom, the twentieth century saw it broadcast far and wide. Shakespeare's global travels began in earnest at the end of the eighteenth century, when multiple European countries claimed him for their national poet and his works travelled to America. In the twentieth century, the new broadcast technology of radio, television and cinema further expanded the reach of Shakespeare's words and phrases.

Makers of film, television and radio could increasingly assume some audience familiarity with Shakespeare from their schooldays. They could use the authority of 'Shakespeare' to legitimate their work, but also creatively deploy quotation, for example, as a trope of learning and intelligence. But twentieth-century media did not just use quotation in the service of entertainment; Shakespeare's words also circulated in propaganda to boost morale in wartime (see Chapter 9). Thus, Shakespeare's authority, established in the eighteenth century, and confirmed by his place in education in the nineteenth, could be deployed for very different audiences in the twentieth and beyond.

In Chapter 5, I reveal the creative use of quotation in eighteenth-century fiction. This is one of several chapters in this part whose focal literary texts not only quote Shakespeare, but depict the act of quotation. Quotations in the novel confer authority on 'Shakespeare' at the same time that Shakespeare helps to underwrite this emerging genre. But this mutual relationship must take account of an overlooked intermediary source: the anthology, or quotation book. Often viewed today with critical suspicion, these collections are a creative resource for novelists – but not merely in the sense of filling gaps in their knowledge. Novelists from Samuel Richardson to Jane Austen show their *characters* in the act of using – and abusing – these sources. They train the reader to distrust these texts, and arguably contribute to the cultural decline of the anthology.

If the quotations in eighteenth-century prose fiction are overt, those in eighteenth-century poetry cannot be so readily marked out and, thanks to the restrictions of the rhyming couplet, are unlikely to be lengthy. In Chapter 6, Brean Hammond examines the uses that Alexander Pope and later poets make of Shakespeare's words. The glancing references in Pope's early work challenge our definitions of 'quotation' and 'allusion'. But as he prepares his edition of Shakespeare, his engagement becomes more sustained, and his quotations begin to recontextualise creatively the playwright's words. Pope's edition itself incorporates quotation: he flagged up 'shining passages' with marginal quotation marks; and his index is organised like a commonplace book, and influenced Dodd's *Beauties of Shakespear*. Hammond traces the influence of Pope's poetic and editorial quotations and reveals, like several chapters in this section, how poetic identity can be forged out of fragments.

By the end of the eighteenth century, bardolatrous quotation had lost some of its freshness. In Chapter 7, Fiona Ritchie and R. S. White show how actors and writers of the Romantic era reignited the power of Shakespeare's phrases: on stage, in skilful performance, and off stage, in sociable exchanges between Romantic poets and writers. White and Ritchie examine the rich and contrasting ways in which quotation is deployed in the performances of Kean, Siddons, Kemble and Jordan, and the letters and conversation of Wordsworth, Byron, Shelley, Blake, Hazlitt and Keats, as well as Helen Maria Williams, Charlotte Smith, Ann Radcliffe and George Crabbe, among others. The chapter celebrates the creative deployment of well-worn phrases in a poetic community of quotation, illuminating a pattern that Balz Engler and Regula Hohl Trillini detect in Chapter 16.

Well-known fragments of Shakespeare find new homes in nineteenth-century fiction, and in Chapter 8, Daniel Pollack-Pelzner shows how writers in the age of Dickens enlist quotation in the construction of narrative voice. As in Chapter 5, these novels not only quote but represent quotation in action by characters. What is striking is how often these quotations by characters are presented as inadequate by comparison to a mode of third-person narration often described as 'Shakespearean'. George Eliot contrasts her characters' quotations with her own narratorial skill; Thomas Hardy distinguishes between his characters' aspirational quotation and the natural, rural language he finds in Shakespeare; and P. G. Wodehouse, by displacing elements of the contemporary practices of quotation on to the figures of Bertie Wooster and Jeeves, explodes the Victorian conventions of quotation.

In Chapter 9, we reach beyond the printed text to sample wider cultural practices of quotation. The chapter incorporates mini-chapters on three important topics: Frans De Bruyn offers a compelling history of political uses of quotation, starting with the rhetorical flights of the eighteenth-century House of Commons in the age of Edmund Burke. Gail Marshall demonstrates the pedagogical role of quotation, memorisation and reading aloud in the nineteenth-century schoolroom, and the effects of conservative extraction on Shakespeare. Ton Hoenselaars examines the ways in which Shakespeare's authority was co-opted by all sides in the First and Second World Wars, his words deployed in settings from propaganda to personal reflection. What happens, he asks, when communities of quotation go to war?

In Chapter 10, poet and critic Craig Raine examines the uses of Shakespeare quotation in twentieth-century drama, fiction and poetry, including that of Tom Stoppard, Samuel Beckett, Rudyard Kipling, W. H. Auden, Louis MacNeice, Saul Bellow, T. S. Eliot, John Berryman and Robert Frost. Quotation inevitably involves the removal of the words' original context: literary quotation, he argues, brings a new, complicating context, and thus new meaning, to the borrowed words. Those new meanings are variously surprising, challenging, moving and revealing of character, and they lead him to observe a paradox. Ironically, Raine argues, quotation is more indirect and less straightforward than allusion, because quotation involves words whose meaning can be distorted by their new literary setting. Allusion, by contrast, invokes a shared topos, which stays closer to the present thought. One might wonder if this is a peculiarly twentieth-century paradox, and whether Pope, for example, writing to a smaller, predominantly gentlemanly readership, might assume recognition of quotation and allusion alike.

If twentieth-century audiences do not always recognise the language of Shakespeare's plays, they will almost certainly recognise the experience of encountering Shakespeare in school. In Chapter 11, Toby Malone shows how a variety of twentieth-century film-makers enlist Shakespeare's language to construct their 'film-worlds'. Initially used to legitimate this emerging medium, Shakespeare's authority would be deployed increasingly playfully on film. Quoting Shakespeare was, and remains, film-character shorthand for brains, even eccentricity; and film-makers frequently evoke audiences' uncomfortable memories of quoting, or failing to quote, Shakespeare in the classroom. Malone shows how film-makers exploit Shakespeare quotations to create film-worlds that are recognisably 'ours', and film-worlds that are distant, alien and yet entirely convincing.

CHAPTER 5

'Shakespeare says ...': The Anthology and the Eighteenth-Century Novel

Kate Rumbold

... much she protested, much she wept, and much she intreated: she was at length permitted to use the little blandishments—and prov'd the truth of *Shakespear*'s observation—

> ———*When maidens sue*
> *Men give like gods, but when they weep and kneel,*
> *All their petitions are as truly theirs*
> *As they themselves wou'd owe them.*
>
> Measure for Measure[1]

Flick through the pages of an eighteenth-century novel and one will quickly see that quoting Shakespeare is common practice. This is quotation at its most visible: not woven into the text, but separated off typographically. So much so that it might look like mere ornamentation. But these Shakespeare quotations are more than flourishes intended to adorn a narrator's musings. What is remarkable about the eighteenth-century novel is just how many of its fictional characters speak his words; what is revealing about their quotations is how they deliver them. From flamboyant speech to earnest repetition, quotation is a major tool for characterisation in the eighteenth-century novel. And since no other author is quoted so widely, nor in such diverse styles, in the novel, none is used more effectively in character-creation than Shakespeare.

This frequent quotation of Shakespeare has implications, however, beyond characterisation: it helps to shape what 'Shakespeare' means outside the novel, too. Shakespeare had been admired since his own lifetime for his skilful representations of the passions, and, in the eighteenth century, his editors increasingly praised his knowledge of human nature.[2] But

---

[1] William Dodd, *The Sisters; or, The History of Lucy and Caroline Sanson, Entrusted to a False Friend*, 2 vols. (London, 1754), vol. II. p. 171.

[2] John Dryden said of Shakespeare that 'All the Images of Nature were still present to him, and he drew them not laboriously, but luckily: when he describes any thing, you more than see it, you feel it too' (*Of Dramatick Poesie, an Essay* (London, 1668), p. 47); Alexander Pope observed that 'The Power

95

through their frequent quotations by fictional characters, novelists have space repeatedly to test Shakespeare's words against new emotional, moral and domestic scenarios, and confirm as never before the insight of 'that grand master of human nature'.[3] Furthermore, by having their characters invoke him directly – 'as our beloved Shakespeare says …'; 'Shakespeare advises well … and that shall be my comfort'; 'as my friend Shakespear has it …' – novelists contribute to the construction of Shakespeare as a knowing author figure.[4] The novel, then, does not simply borrow authority from Shakespeare. Shakespeare and the novel are, in this century, I have recently argued, mutually constructive: the dramatist at once underwrites, and is underwritten by, the novel, and through selective quotation both gain cultural prestige.[5]

But the productive mutual relationship that I revealed in *Shakespeare and the Eighteenth-Century Novel* is not necessarily exclusive, nor direct. Often, it is mediated by an important, but overlooked, source: the anthology, or quotation book. In this chapter, I argue that novelists make highly creative use of anthologised Shakespeare. When critics have, in the past, suggested, for example, that Samuel Richardson gets his Shakespeare via an anthology, it has been to discredit his knowledge. Conversely, since critics assume Jane Austen's direct knowledge of the plays, her uses of anthologised Shakespeare have often been overlooked. To treat anthologies as an index of authorial knowledge is often to miss the point. As this chapter reveals, neither of these authors is necessarily dependent on a quotation book. Rather, they creatively exploit what it means for their *characters* to draw on such a source.

The nature, purpose and reach of quotation books changed drastically in the eighteenth and early nineteenth centuries, and the same Shakespearean extracts were asked to mean different things along the way. Collections designed to support poetic invention gave way to ones that selected the most admired 'beauties' of an author and, in turn, to ones that used those

---

over our *Passions* was never possess'd in a more eminent degree, or display'd in so different instances' (William Shakespeare, *The Works of Shakespear. In Six Volumes. Collated and Corrected by the Former Editions, By Mr. Pope* (London, 1725), vol. I, p. iii).

[3] Sarah Fielding and Jane Collier, *The Cry: A New Dramatic Fable*, 3 vols. (London, 1754), vol. I, p. 112.

[4] Samuel Richardson, *Clarissa; or, The History of a Young Lady*, 2nd edn., 7 vols. (London, 1749), vol. III, p. 49; Samuel Richardson, *Clarissa*, ed. Angus Ross (Harmondsworth: Penguin, 1985), p. 571; Tobias Smollett, *Ferdinand Count Fathom*, ed. Damian Grant (Oxford: Oxford University Press, 1971), p. 183. Subsequent references to *Clarissa* are to Ross's edition, unless otherwise stated, and are given in parentheses in the text.

[5] Kate Rumbold, *Shakespeare and the Eighteenth-Century Novel: Cultures of Quotation from Samuel Richardson to Jane Austen* (Cambridge: Cambridge University Press, 2016).

extracts for moral and educational purposes. This chapter shows characters in three novels, at three different junctures, using – and, importantly, misusing – these collections contrary to their declared purpose. Two of the examples are discussed separately in *Shakespeare and the Eighteenth-Century Novel*; by examining them together, within the history of the evolution of the quotation book, I can show for the first time the longer-term effects of their interaction with this source. For if the anthology is a creative resource for novelists, it is a source that suffers in the creative process. Novelists, this chapter shows, both explicitly and implicitly train their readers to distrust collections of literary extracts, and the kinds of reading they encourage. Consequently, they have helped to obscure not only the wider cultural influence of the collection of quotations, but also its significance as a creative resource for fiction. This chapter looks beyond that critique to reveal the creative uses of the anthologised Shakespeare in the eighteenth-century novel.

Samuel Richardson and Bysshe's *Art of English Poetry*

Edward Bysshe's *The Art of English Poetry* (1702) was a practical handbook for poets. Having asked himself 'what other human Aid could be offer'd to a Poet' alongside a set of '*Rules for making Verses*' and a '*Dictionary of Rhymes*', Bysshe included a collection of literary extracts to furnish aspiring poets with 'Epithets and Synonymes': not alone, but as 'employ'd … by our best Writers'.[6] Bysshe's collection comprised 1,452 quotations from 48 different authors.[7] Its first edition featured little Shakespeare ('Readers of our Age', Bysshe apologised, 'have no ear for' the outmoded 'garb' of such 'ancient' writers as 'Good Shakespeare' and Spenser), but in its most expanded form it included 118 Shakespeare quotations.[8] Yet as new editions of the *Art* continued to appear, the handbook was increasingly disparaged for the unoriginal dependence it represented. That reputation has coloured our understanding of its role.

For some critics, it is to Richardson's shame that many of the literary quotations in his mid-eighteenth-century novels can be traced to Bysshe's *Art*. A. Dwight Culler proposes, somewhat anachronistically perhaps, that Richardson was 'less scrupulous' than other authors, for he

---

[6] Edward Bysshe, *The Art of English Poetry* (London, 1702), Preface, n.p.

[7] A. Dwight Culler, 'Edward Bysshe and the Poet's Handbook', *PMLA*, 63:3 (1948), 858–85 (p. 868).

[8] Compare Dryden (1,201), Pope (155), Cowley (143), Butler (140), Otway (127), Blackmore (125), Shakespeare (118), Milton (117), Rowe (116), Lee (104), Garth (59), Waller (44), plus some minor Restoration poets. Culler, 'Edward Bysshe', p. 868.

borrows from the *Art* at least three times in *Pamela*, 'five in *Sir Charles Grandison*, and forty-three in *Clarissa* – all, of course, with no mention of Bysshe'.[9] Michael E. Connaughton traces two-thirds of the extracts in *Clarissa* to Bysshe's sixth edition, and suggests that Richardson's lack of regard for their original context and his reliance on Bysshe's headings reveals the limits of his literary knowledge.[10] Other scholars, as Leah Price notes, have defended his knowledge by arguing that his quotations are well contextualised.[11] Price herself urges us to regard Bysshe as a meaningful source: a mark of Richardson's interest in fragment and ornament.[12]

But there is more to it: Richardson makes self-conscious, creative use of Bysshe in constructing characters. Culler argues that Richardson's work is 'sprinkled' with 'quotations on love, rape, death, chastity and despair, which the characters call up from their memory on appropriate occasions, but which their creator drew from the *Art of English Poetry*'.[13] Culler distinguishes between characters' 'memory' of literary phrases and the author's own dependence on Bysshe, but Richardson, I suggest, hints that the dependence is not his. Of all the characters in Richardson's *Clarissa*, it is the rakish Robert Lovelace whose quotations can most frequently be traced to Bysshe's *Art*. His very first letter, in which he describes his passion for Clarissa and rails against her indifference, sees him adapt a line from *Othello* – '*Perdition catch my soul, but I do love her*' (p. 146, quoting III. iii.92–3) that has already been conveniently excerpted under 'LOVE' in Bysshe.[14] How would this connection, if it is more than a coincidence, be visible to a reader – and how would they know what to make of it? Sometimes, the connection is proved by misquotation, or misattribution: Bysshe credits Shakespeare, not Dryden, with some lines from the latter's adaptation of *Troilus and Cressida* – beginning 'Oppose not rage, while rage is in its force' – and Lovelace follows suit (p. 800).[15] Other

[9] *Ibid.*, p. 870.
[10] Michael E. Connaughton, 'Richardson's Familiar Quotations: *Clarissa* and Bysshe's *Art of English Poetry*', *Philological Quarterly*, 60:2 (Spring 1981), 183–95.
[11] For example, Jocelyn Harris, 'Richardson: Original or Learned Genius?', in Margaret Anne Doody and Peter Sabor (eds.), *Samuel Richardson: Tercentenary Essays* (Cambridge: Cambridge University Press, 1989), pp. 188–9.
[12] Leah Price, *The Anthology and the Rise of the Novel: From Richardson to George Eliot* (Cambridge: Cambridge University Press, 2000), p. 40.
[13] Culler, 'Edward Bysshe', p. 870.
[14] Edward Bysshe, *The Art of English Poetry*, 8th edn, 2 vols. (London, 1737), vol. II, p. 30.
[15] Bysshe (from the sixth edition onwards) explains that '*To those from* Troilus and Cressida *I have sometimes put* Shakespear, *sometimes* Dryden', ascribing anything not found in Shakespeare's play to the latter author. *Art of English Poetry*, 8th edn, vol. I, preface, sig. A4.

quotations seem to offer visual clues about where he might have found them. In the second edition of *Clarissa*, the abbreviation 'Shakesp.' appears after a quotation from Ferdinand's admiring speech to Miranda, beginning 'Full many a lady / I've eyed with best regard', and evokes the ways in which quotation books attributed their extracts (even though this particular quotation is not from Bysshe).[16] That this attribution style is not applied consistently is probably the result of Richardson making piecemeal adjustments to his text to blacken Lovelace's character after readers professed to admire him. Richardson also has Lovelace's friend Belford lament his (deliberately casual, even gentlemanly) tendency to 'skim the surface' in his reading (p. 1131).

Pick up on any of these fleeting hints, and a reader might detect where Lovelace gets some of his more dangerous ideas. He might have turned to 'PATIENCE' to find ready-adapted lines from *Macbeth* ('Come what come may' (p. 571)) that flattered his sense of his own noble persistence with Clarissa; and to 'REVENGE' to borrow Hamlet's words *the relish of salvation in it* (p. 1184) as his patience wears out.[17] Worse still, the advice to 'Oppose not rage' appears in Bysshe on the same page as 'RAPE'.[18] Richardson gives the impression that Lovelace might have stumbled across the lines with which he defends his worst motives – '*It is* resistance *that inflames desire*' (p. 609) – by skimming a collection of extracts.

Richardson's creativity with Bysshe, then, is to show Lovelace's failure of creativity: this character's virtuosic performance is transcribed from a handbook, and he repeats at length, rather than reinvents, the images he finds there, using Shakespeare not to model well-expressed ideas, but to legitimate his choices ('Shakespeare says … and that shall be my comfort' (p. 571)). But if Lovelace's anthology use is such a helpful guide to his character, why would Richardson not make it more obvious? Crucially, Lovelace's borrowings do not have to be traced specifically to Bysshe to make the point: the contrast with the virtuous Clarissa's quotation style confirms it.[19] Her own quotations are pithier and anti-histrionic, only once corresponding with a (very familiar) extract from *Hamlet* in Bysshe. Lovelace's possible anthology use helps to polarise their characters. His flamboyance is contrasted by her restraint, his performance of old,

16 Richardson, *Clarissa*, 2nd edn, vol. i, p. 203.
17 Bysshe, *Art of English Poetry*, 8th edn, vol. ii, pp. 108, 160.
18 *Ibid.*, vol. ii, p. 151.
19 She prefers diffidence to, 'as Shakespeare says, *the rattling tongue / Of saucy and audacious eloquence*' (p. 397). We might ask if the maxims Clarissa extracts from Shakespeare are ultimately as useful as Lucrece's sententious lines are to her (see Chapter 4).

ready-made knowledge by her careful extractions. Lovelace's style of quotation, in other words, gives Bysshe a bad name.

William Dodd and His *Beauties of Shakespear*

Bysshe's handbook formed the basis of other collections, such as the *Thesaurus dramaticus* (1724). Charles Gildon created a section of 'Shakespeareana' in his *Complete Art of Poetry* (1718) by adding 154 Shakespeare quotations to a selection three-fifths copied from Bysshe. While selections persisted, the declared rationale for collecting them was changing significantly. Anthologies, reflecting an expanding readership, became not tools for writers, but texts for readers. Although Gildon distinguished his collection from Bysshe's mere 'Dictionary of Epithets and Synonymous Words' by adding 'the great *Images* that are to be found in those of our Poets, who are truly great, as well as their Topics and Moral Reflections', his primary purpose remained, like Bysshe's, to enhance readers' 'Poetical Performances'.[20] For the imagined reader of William Dodd's *Beauties of Shakespear* (1752), however, reading the 'finest passages of the finest poet' was an end in itself.[21]

The *Beauties* was the first collection of quotations dedicated entirely to Shakespeare (or indeed to any single author), and Dodd's selections – a mixture of short extracts and longer dialogues, arranged play by play under commonplace headings – were highly influential, perhaps all the more remarkably for a collection compiled in some haste before this former Cambridge student joined the Church. (Dodd went on to become a fashionable preacher who was hanged for forging his employer's signature, a fact that has overshadowed his reputation.) Dodd's selection is not necessarily original: 75 per cent of his passages are listed in Pope's index to his Shakespeare edition, and often under similar headings (see Chapter 6).[22] In turn, some of the passages Pope singles out for admiration may derive from Bysshe.[23] But unlike earlier collections, Dodd frames his collection with the reader's response to Shakespeare prominently in mind. He draws on Longinus, who defines sublimity in terms of the effect on the reader: 'That, on the contrary, is grand and lofty, which the more we consider, the greater ideas we conceive of it; whose force we cannot possibly withstand; which immediately sinks deep, and makes

[20] Charles Gildon, *The Complete Art of Poetry* (London, 1718), Preface, n.p.
[21] William Dodd, *The Beauties of Shakespear*, 2 vols. (London, 1752), vol. I, p. xiii.
[22] Judith M. Kennedy and Richard F. Kennedy (eds.), *Shakespeare: The Critical Tradition*. A Midsummer Night's Dream (London: Athlone Press, 1999), p. 10.
[23] Peter Dixon, 'Edward Bysshe and Pope's "Shakespear"', *Notes and Queries*, 209 (1964), 292–3.

such impression on the mind as cannot easily be worn out or effaced.'[24] Neil Rhodes observes that Dodd's extracts are not mere 'isolated lyric fragments', but 'highlights' of each play, chosen for their 'emotional, moral or imaginative power', and as likely to be 'affective' as aphoristic.[25] Rhodes attributes this new emotional orientation to a growing interest in nature, and to a broader shift from rationality to sensibility. It might, however, owe something to the emotional engagement with Shakespeare modelled by characters in the novel.

Dodd's novelistic redevelopment of the quotation book may also be owed to the fact that he was an aspiring novelist himself. His only novel, *The Sisters; or, The History of Lucy and Caroline Sanson* (1754), was published shortly after the *Beauties*. Unlike the *Beauties*, it was an abject failure. An ostensibly moral tale that travesties the plot of *Clarissa*, it seems to delight in the very salaciousness it warns against when the eponymous sisters are tempted – one successfully – into depravity.[26] *The Sisters* makes frequent reference to Milton and Shakespeare: after Lucy falls into temptation, the 'allusion to *Paradise Lost* is then (unsurprisingly) spelled out with a quotation'.[27] But is the novel's apparently heavy-handed intertextuality mere literary padding, drawing on Dodd's *Beauties* to legitimate the work? Or, since Dodd's Shakespearean knowledge is not in question, might he in fact be making creative use of his own collection in hinting, like Richardson, that it is a source for his *characters*?

Dodd's fictional characters can be seen to engage emotionally with Shakespeare's words in a way that is promoted by his *Beauties*. In the second volume, for example, Mrs Stevens identifies closely with the plight of King Lear:

> Ingratitude from such a child, and to a mother so kind and tender as I have always been to her! Poor miserable *Lear*, I always think of him, and fear I shall go mad like him, provoked as I am by the same cause, and urged by the same ingratitude, well did he say—

> > *Ingratitude, thou marble-hearted fiend,*
> > *More hideous, when thou shew'st thee in a child,*
> > *Than the sea-monster.*

[24] Dodd, *Beauties*, vol. 1, pp. xvi–xvii.
[25] Neil Rhodes, *Shakespeare and the Origins of English* (Oxford: Oxford University Press, 2004), p. 184.
[26] See Adam Rounce, *Fame and Failure 1720–1800: The Unfulfilled Literary Life* (Cambridge: Cambridge University Press, 2013), pp. 77–81.
[27] *Ibid.*, p. 79.

> Mrs *Stevens* was proceeding, when her narrative was interrupted by a letter, which, having first run over, she burst into tears … (Vol. ii, p. 83)

In Mrs Stevens, Dodd performs the kind of relationship with Shakespeare previously displayed by fictional characters such as Clarissa and Lovelace. Her specific source for this emotional identification is likely to have been the *Beauties*: her words, 'Ingratitude from such a child', closely resemble the heading 'Scene xv. *Ingratitude in a Child*', under which this quotation appears in Dodd.[28] There is a hint, though, that her comparison is self-aggrandising: the reader might be amused by her insistence that she and Lear experience 'the same cause', 'the same ingratitude'. As a novelist, then, Dodd uses a quotation economically to construct character; as a character, Mrs Stevens might be seen to enlist an anthology, albeit in a more harmless way than Lovelace, for her own emotional ends.

Shakespeare is invoked for not-so-harmless effect early in the novel when the Sanson sisters' relative, Dookalb (one of several names in the novel that hints in reverse at a real-life target), tries to pander them to two gentlemen. At the end of the evening, the gentlemen pledge their constancy:

> and each clasping his beloved fair one's warm and yielding hand, thus parted with *Shakespeare*'s famed assignation:
>
> > *I swear to thee by* Cupid*'s strongest bow,*
> > *By his best arrow with the golden head,*
> > *By the simplicity of* Venus*' doves,*
> > *By that which knitteth souls and prospers loves;*
> > *By all the vows that ever men have broke,*
> > *In number more than ever woman spoke;*
> > *In that same place thou hast appointed me,*
> > *To-morrow, truly, will I meet with thee.* (vol. i, p. 27)

As in Mrs Stevens's quotation, the preamble – in this case, 'Shakespeare's famed assignation' – strongly recalls the heading that introduces the quotation in Dodd's *Beauties*: 'Assignation'.[29] Dodd places the quotation, albeit indirectly, in the mouths of the gentlemen. Were his readers meant to recognise the insincerity and/or efficacy of borrowing a tender anthology piece for the purposes of seduction? Given the novel's ambiguous morality, were they supposed to approve or disapprove?

The emotional orientation of Dodd's *Beauties* seems be shaped by, and to shape, the novel. If Dodd, like Richardson, attempts to construct character

---

[28] Dodd, *Beauties*, vol. ii, p. 19.
[29] *Ibid.*, vol. i, pp. 76–7.

by evoking their habits of quotation, might he also have his characters use anthologised Shakespeare for particular emotional ends? In a less-than-successful novel, does he nonetheless show creative sophistication in his use of his own collection of quotations?

Jane Austen and Vicesimus Knox's *Elegant Extracts*

Dodd's *Beauties* was not only frequently reprinted, but silently influenced many other collections. At the end of the eighteenth century, though, these collections had rather different rationales: 'this is poetry for moral, not practical, utility'.[30] Dodd had promised the reader 'so much excellent and refin'd morality, and I may venture to say, so much good divinity', but within in a more mixed collection of extracts.[31] By contrast, Elizabeth Griffith set out not to celebrate the beauties of Shakespeare but to 'expound the document of the Moralist';[32] and a collection opportunistically published by George Kearsley distinguished itself from Dodd's *Beauties* by stressing its greater concern with 'impressing on the memory of Youth some of the sublimest and most important lessons of Morality and Religion'.[33] Such collections 'characterize reading literature as a process of moral self-discovery, experienced alone'.[34]

　Thus, an emerging genre of late-eighteenth-century anthologies directed their attention to the improvement of a younger readership. Vicesimus Knox's 1789 *Elegant Extracts* of poetry were subtitled *for the Improvement of Youth, in Speaking, Reading, Thinking, Composing; and in the Conduct of Life*, and William Enfield's *The Speaker* was even more explicitly elocutionary. Such collections taught boys to think, write and speak through excerpts of now 'classic' English literature. Within *Elegant Extracts*, the volume entitled 'DRAMATIC, chiefly from SHAKESPEARE' reproduces Dodd's *Beauties*.[35] As Knox says, 'The best pieces are usually the most popular. They are loudly recommended by the voice of fame, and indeed have been already selected in a variety of volumes of preceding collections.'[36]

[30] Barbara Benedict, *Making the Modern Reader: Cultural Mediation in Early Modern Literary Anthologies* (Princeton: Princeton University Press, 1996), pp. 209–10.

[31] Dodd, *Beauties*, vol. 1, p. xvi. The words 'and I may venture to say, so much good divinity' are excised in the second edition of 1757.

[32] Elizabeth Griffith, *The Morality of Shakespeare's Drama Illustrated* (London, 1775), pp. 525–6.

[33] *The Beauties of Shakespeare* (London: printed for G. Kearsley at No. 46, in Fleet Street, 1783), p. ii.

[34] Benedict, *Making the Modern Reader*, p. 198.

[35] Vicesimus Knox, *Elegant Extracts; or, Useful and Entertaining Pieces of Poetry, Selected for the Improvement of Youth, in Speaking, Reading, Thinking, Composing; and in the Conduct of Life; being Similar in Design to Elegant Extracts in Prose* (London, [1789?]), p. 337.

[36] *Ibid.*, p. iv.

What has Knox to do with Jane Austen? In *Emma*, Harriet misguidedly scorns Robert Martin for reading *Elegant Extracts*. As I have previously suggested, Austen makes a further, less explicit use of the collection for characterisation in *Mansfield Park*. Henry Crawford dazzles the company with an impromptu performance from a copy of *Henry VIII*, which Fanny Price had, moments earlier, been quietly reading to Lady Bertram:

> The King, the Queen, Buckingham, Wolsey, Cromwell, all were given in turn; for with the happiest knack, the happiest power of jumping and guessing, he could always light, at will, on the best scene, or the best speeches of each; and whether it were dignity or pride, or tenderness or remorse, or whatever were to be expressed, he could do it with equal beauty. —It was truly dramatic.[37]

Crawford shrugs off praise of his deep knowledge of Shakespeare: he is not sure if he has seen the play, and 'I do not think I have had a volume of Shakespeare in my hand before, since I was fifteen' (p. 390). Yet critics have admired his 'talent', and suggested, for example, that in catching the characteristic emotions of multiple roles, Crawford performs the eighteenth-century critical and editorial practice of recognising the distinctive individuality of Shakespeare's characters – which seems unlikely given his resolutely casual stance.[38]

The mention of Crawford's youthful reading (or lack of it), and his 'truly dramatic' skill, might point Austen's reader in the direction of Knox's 'DRAMATIC' excerpts. 'The King, the Queen, Buckingham, Wolsey, Cromwell' evokes the headings in both Dodd and Knox (for example, '*Queen* Catherine's *Speech to her Husband*', '*Cardinal* Wolsey's *Speech to* Cromwell'), and, since both anthologists preserve the sequence in which these passages originally appeared, it would be no great challenge for Crawford, even if encountering *Henry VIII* in full for the first time, to map these familiar 'beauties' on to the text by 'jumping and guessing' (p. 390). The connection with Knox is underscored when Edmund Bertram persists in admiring Crawford's skill, and 'The subject of reading aloud was farther discussed' (p. 392). Earlier in the novel, Tom Bertram had tried to assuage Edmund's anger about the planned performance of *The Lover's Vows* by reminding him of the dramatic lines they were encouraged to declaim as children: 'How many a time have we mourned over the dead

---

[37] Jane Austen, *Mansfield Park*, ed. John Wiltshire (Cambridge: Cambridge University Press, 2005), pp. 389–90. Subsequent references are given in parentheses in the text.
[38] Susan Harland, '"Talking" and Reading Shakespeare in Jane Austen's *Mansfield Park*', *Wordsworth Circle*, 39:1/2 (2008), 43–6 (pp. 44–5).

body of Julius Caesar, and to be'd and not to be'd, in this very room, for him amusement!'. But Edmund resists this line of argument: 'It was a very different thing … My father wished us, as school-boys, to speak well, but he would never wish his grown up daughters to be acting plays' (p. 149). Reciting lines from one's schoolboy anthology, he feels, is quite different from involving all the family in a dangerous theatrical event. But Crawford shows that Edmund is naive: his own 'dramatic' reanimation of these elocutionary set-pieces is all the more dangerous for being considered so benignly improving.

If Lovelace has riffled through a poet's handbook, Crawford owes his virtuoso performance to a boys' elocution book. Their impassioned, theatrical quotations are fragmentary, and cribbed.[39] Both misuse their anthology sources – but both, crucially, are challenged by modest women whose virtue is a foil for their histrionic flair. Fanny, though rapt by Crawford's performance, says afterwards that 'I cannot approve his character' (p. 404); Clarissa says of Lovelace that 'he says too many fine things of me' (p. 97). These women's distaste for fine speeches is important, for it is one of the ways in which the novel shapes perceptions of the anthology. The lengthy quotations run counter to advice, oft repeated in eighteenth-century fiction, about extracting utility from one's reading.

These novelists are writing at a time when criticism of quotation books is growing. In Frances Burney's play, *The Witlings* (1779), Bysshe's *Art* is a prop for the hopeless poet, Mr Dabler. In 1789, the American lexicographer and writer Noah Webster considers the 'host of compilers who, in the rage for selecting beauties and abridging the labor of reading, disfigure the works of the purest writers in the nation' a sign of 'the declension of genius in England', and one justification for distancing his nation from the English language: 'America should have her own distinct from all the world.'[40] And in 1799, Hannah More complains that 'brief and disconnected patches of broken and discordant materials', severed from their original source by 'some beauty monger', inflame young readers with the vanity of reciting', but 'neither fill the mind nor form the taste'.[41] What troubles late-century writers is not least the drastic expansion of the form

---

[39] Compare Tiffany Stern and Simon Palfrey's *Shakespeare in Parts* (Oxford: Oxford University Press, 2007) on actors learning only fragments of plays; unlike those early modern performers, who would, one assumes, eventually find out more about the rest of the play, Lovelace and Crawford could continue their solitary performances indefinitely.

[40] Noah Webster, *Dissertations on the English Language* (Boston, 1789), p. 178.

[41] Hannah More, *Strictures on the Modern System of Female Education*, 2 vols. (London, 1799), vol. II, pp. 26–7, quoted in Price, *The Anthology and the Rise of the Novel*, p. 74.

after the end of perpetual copyright in 1774 – and the ease of putting together and selling what Austen called 'some dozen lines of Milton, Pope and Prior, with a paper from the Spectator and a chapter from Sterne'.[42]

Novelists enact this criticism in their fiction by repeatedly connecting the declaiming of extracted speeches with poor reading. In numerous novels of the eighteenth century, the character who appears simply to repeat dramatic or poetic words at length is a figure of mockery or pity. In *David Simple*, Sarah Fielding pictures an unhappy Selimena, who 'walks and struts round the Room, repeating, in an audible voice, all the tragick Strains her memory can furnish, where Women lament their hard Fate, when some dire Mishap has befallen them'; in Fielding and Collier's *The Cry*, the repentant Cylinda laments that she has inhabited the roles of Cleopatra and Hamlet without extracting their wisdom.[43] The novelists take this criticism a step further, however, by suggesting that the novel is the antidote to such poor reading, training its reader through example, and through the critical responses of other characters, to evaluate, extract and apply their reading to their own experience. Amongst thoughtful readers such as Samuel Richardson's Clarissa Harlowe and Harriet Byron, and Sarah Fielding's Cynthia, Camilla and (with Jane Collier) Portia, and Jane Austen's Fanny Price, the performances of Lovelace and Crawford are signalled to the reader as suspect.

Conclusions

What does the treatment of the anthology in the novel mean for the anthology, for the novel and for Shakespeare? By repeatedly holding up his words against their characters' experiences, eighteenth-century novelists help to ascribe moral authority to Shakespeare. This activity is, of course, not unique to the novel, but its frequency, and its literary context, give it a significant cumulative effect. Because their quotations are selective, these fictional experiences invariably 'prove the truth' (in Dodd's words) of his observations (or confirm the insincerity or wrong-headedness of the fictional characters involved). Novelists will continue to use Shakespeare quotations to reveal character, as Daniel Pollack-Pelzner's study of

---

[42] See William St Clair, *The Reading Nation in the Romantic Period* (Cambridge: Cambridge University Press, 2004), pp. 66–83; Jane Austen, *Northanger Abbey*, ed. Barbara M. Benedict and Deirdre Le Faye (Cambridge: Cambridge University Press, 2006), p. 31, quoted in Price, *The Anthology and the Rise of the Novel*, p. 74

[43] Sarah Fielding, *Familiar Letters between the Principal Characters in David Simple, and Some Others*, 2 vols. (London, 1747), vol. I, p. 213; Fielding and Collier, *Cry*, vol. III, pp. 84, 74.

nineteenth-century fiction shows (see Chapter 8). But more than this, as his chapter also suggests, Shakespeare is 'novelised' by these repeated acts of quotation. The frequent ascription of insight to the playwright, in the context of these complex, extended narratives, helps to establish an association between Shakespeare and the detached authority of the narrative voice.

If eighteenth-century novelists collectively constructed 'Shakespeare' as omniscient, insightful, knowing – the qualities, in other words, of a third-person narrator – then they naturally claimed some of these 'Shakespearean' qualities for themselves. Both Richardson and Austen were compared to Shakespeare, and nineteenth-century novelists such as Scott, Eliot, Dickens and Hardy are still regarded as 'great Shakespeareans'.[44]

What about the anthology? The novel shores up its own respectability at the expense of the anthology. It does so not necessarily by overtly criticising the form, but by coupling frequent narratorial commentary about what constitutes a good reader with performances by characters such as Lovelace and Crawford that represent the worst. Novelists train their audience to be suspicious of the abuses of excerpt culture, cautioning against injudicious skimming and the insincere performance of borrowed lines. The rise of the novel has been linked to the decline of the commonplacing tradition, but if the printed collection of quotations continued to flourish in the nineteenth century, its respectability is certainly in question.[45] The anthology, I have shown, is a creative resource for the novel, co-opted directly in the construction of fictional characters, and indirectly in establishing the status of both Shakespeare and the novel. Its poor reputation will obscure its vast influence for centuries to come.

[44] Adrian Poole (ed.), *Great Shakespeareans*, Vol v: *Scott, Dickens, Eliot, Hardy* (London: Continuum, 2011).
[45] David Allan, *Commonplace Books and Reading in Georgian England* (Cambridge: Cambridge University Press, 2010), pp. 255–67.

CHAPTER 6

Pope's Shakespeare and Poetic Quotation in the Early Eighteenth Century

Brean Hammond

Alexander Pope was the most influential poet in the eighteenth century, influencing writers who imitated the models he offered, and writers who rejected them. Analysing the ways in which Pope quotes from and alludes to Shakespeare in his original verse should therefore make a significant contribution to understanding how the century's poets took Shakespeare into creative consideration. An important finding will be that Pope very often recontextualises and resituates Shakespeare in ways that depart from, to the point of diametrically opposing, the original dramatic context. No Shakespearean character, this chapter will suggest, had a greater hold on Pope's imagination than did Falstaff. Nicholas Rowe's pioneering biography of Shakespeare, *Some Account of the Life &c*, which introduced his 1709 edition, expresses the consensus that Falstaff is Shakespeare's greatest character, bearing Warwickshire affinities to the dramatist himself.[1] The way in which Falstaff figures in Pope's verse will therefore be a principal focus here.

Whereas prose writers in the eighteenth century deploy Shakespeare verbatim – whole-cloth excerpts from Shakespeare, often signalled by a change of font, use of quotation marks or announced by introductory phrasing ('as Shakespeare says'; see Chapter 5) – poets in the early eighteenth century seldom use Shakespeare directly. As David Fairer rightly says, what Shakespeare offered was less a source of direct quotation and more a form of experience, emotionally colouring the poets' own composition. He could help to 'create an atmosphere, intensify an emotion, or sharpen an image'.[2] Absence of explicit borrowing results partly from the dominance of the couplet as a poetic form in the eighteenth century. Since Shakespeare wrote in blank verse, any couplet that embodies a quotation

---

[1] See Margreta de Grazia, 'Shakespeare's Anecdotal Character', *Shakespeare Survey*, 68 (2015), 1–14.
[2] David Fairer, 'Shakespeare in Poetry', in Fiona Ritchie and Peter Sabor (eds.), *Shakespeare in the Eighteenth Century* (Cambridge: Cambridge University Press, 2015), pp. 99–117 (p. 108).

will need to be considerably rephrased and is likely to appear as a brief, recognisable fragment, a kind of arc of Shakespearean electricity. Even poets such as James Thomson who write extensively in blank verse do not incline toward the dramatic monologue where direct speech, Shakespearean or otherwise, might be figured.

From the mid-century onward, Shakespeare served poets in an ideological capacity. Poets from Akenside and the Warton brothers to Gray and Collins affix Shakespeare's name to a new poetic manifesto more than they engage directly with his plays. Thomas Warton goes to Shakespeare's tragedies in his 'The Pleasures of Melancholy' (1747) to lubricate his sensibility and enjoy the pleasure of tears. As 'the Moor on Desdemone / Pour[s] the misguided threats of jealous rage', so 'By soft degrees the manly torrent steals' from the poet's swollen eyes.[3] Shakespearean references, in this case to the well-known action of *Othello* and its effect on the reader's sensibility, underwrite a re-energised approach to poetic composition – composition that foregrounds the imagination over public political or ethical writing. Shakespeare is recruited by these mid-century poets for the project of creating an anti-Popean aesthetic.

What, though, of Pope himself, the poet whom these later writers have in their sights – even though they cannot escape him and their writing is still saturated in his verse? What relationship with Shakespeare does his use of quotation suggest that he held? Pope is known to have possessed at least one picture and one bust of Shakespeare, the picture retained in his chamber 'that the constant remembrance of [him] may keep me always humble'.[4] Yet a reading of his original verse might not indicate how important Shakespeare was to him. What Pope says in verse *about* Shakespeare is at best ambivalent. His *Epistle to Augustus*, addressed to King George II, begins by arguing against the prejudice that only authors who have stood the test of time can be valuable – that there can be nothing to celebrate in contemporary poetic achievement. How long dead, though, does a poet have to be to become an 'ancient' and therefore celebrated? A century? And do we appreciate such 'ancients' as Shakespeare justly?

> Shakespear, (whom you and ev'ry Play-house bill
> Style the divine, the matchless, what you will)

[3] Thomas Warton, *The Pleasures of Melancholy: A Poem* (1747), lines 221–4, quoted from David Fairer and Christine Gerrard (eds.), *Eighteenth-Century Poetry: An Annotated Anthology* (Oxford: Blackwell, 1999), p. 372.

[4] Pat Rogers (ed.), *The Alexander Pope Encyclopedia* (London: Greenwood, 2004), p. 267; Alexander Pope, *The Correspondence of Alexander Pope*, ed. George Sherburn, 5 vols. (Oxford: Oxford University Press, 1956), vol. I, p. 120.

> For gain, not glory, wing'd his roving flight,
> And grew Immortal in his own despight.[5]

In paraphrase, Shakespeare was a mercenary playwright who has gained time's accolades in spite of himself. True, we distrust the poet-narrator's voice the more we hear it. 'Pope' would not, we later hear him say, 'damn all Shakespear, like th' affected fool / At Court, who hates whate'er he read at School' (105–6). So he *would* damn *some* Shakespeare! Maybe this narrator's voice is not that of the real Pope but an ironised version of Pope, as critics have suspected? Maybe, but when we come to consider Pope's own edition of Shakespeare published a dozen years earlier, we find that he had no difficulty in damning quite a lot of Shakespeare's writing. One looks in vain for Shakespeare's name in Pope's *The Temple of Fame* (1715) – though admittedly, he includes no modern writers in that poem's pantheon, and as we shall see, Shakespeare is not altogether absent from it.

As attentive readers from John Butt to David Fairer have noted, Pope does not quote Shakespeare extensively in his poetry.[6] Before he began to pursue what he called 'the dull duty' of editing Shakespeare, his poems do show awareness of the plays: awareness taking forms other than deploying Shakespeare's actual words.[7] This is apparent in the choice of the name 'Ariel' for the tutelary spirit in *The Rape of the Lock*, and more generally in the folkloric atmosphere of that poem, previously achieved as successfully, one might judge, only by Shakespeare in *A Midsummer Night's Dream*.[8] Elsewhere, Pope does deploy Shakespeare's words to add cadence to his own lines. He does so, though, in such a way as to problematise the distinction now commonly made between quotation and allusion, and also the nature of allusion itself. At least until the advent of 1980s literary theory, one effect of which was to downgrade any strong conception of authorship, quotation and allusion were both underwritten by authorial intention: if a reference made to another writer was not verbatim, the question of allusion

---

[5] Alexander Pope, *Epistle to Augustus* (*Imitations of Horace*, Epistle II.i), lines 69–73, in *The Poems of Alexander Pope*, ed. John Butt (London: Methuen, 1970 (1963)), p. 638. Subsequent references to Pope's work are to this edition unless otherwise stated and are given in parentheses in the text.

[6] Edwin Abbott's *A Concordance to the Works of Alexander Pope* (New York: Appleton, 1966 (1875)), p. x, cites only ten 'imitations' of Shakespeare in Pope's work. Though Abbott's cases are not all convincing as allusions, this is a significant underestimate. See also John Butt, *Pope's Taste in Shakespeare* (London: Shakespeare Association, 1936), pp. 1–18; and Fairer, 'Shakespeare in Poetry'.

[7] William Shakespeare, *The Works of Shakespear. In six volumes. Collated and corrected by the former editions, By Mr. Pope*, ed. Alexander Pope (London: Jacob Tonson, 1725), vol. I, p. xxii.

[8] For an argument that Pope had a darker allusion in mind in *The Rape of the Lock*, to Henry V's threat of the rape that will await the 'pure maidens' of Harfleur (*Henry V*, III.iii.19ff.), see Catherine Bates, 'Pope's Influence on Shakespeare', *Shakespeare Quarterly*, 42:1 (Spring, 1991), 57–9.

would be determined by probability. How many words do the two passages have in common, and in what order? Since, as we have said, allusion to Shakespeare in eighteenth-century verse seldom takes the form of lengthy collocations, the presence or absence of an allusion may be a matter of judgement, probability and debate. A 'two-word quotation' is easier to identify when it serves as a title, such as William Blake's *Jocund Day*.[9] I would contend that in *Eloisa to Abelard*, Pope does allude to Shakespeare, and uses those allusions to add cadence to his lines. Eloisa's 'Still drink delicious poison from thy eye' (*Eloisa to Abelard*, line 122 (p. 255)) alludes to Cleopatra's 'Now I feed myself / With most delicious poison' (*Antony and Cleopatra*, I.v.27–8). There is the striking oxymoron 'delicious poison' and the metaphor of paradoxical nourishment, albeit Pope transfers food to drink. This, and most of his other borrowings from Shakespeare, would not require a playbook to be open on his desk while composing. It is more likely a phrasal memorial reconstruction, the oxymoron 'delicious poison' recalled because it speaks to the condition of his protagonist. Eloisa, like the protagonists of *Antony and Cleopatra*, is controlled by the emotional double-bind of addiction: the addictive erotic engagement with Abelard that she knows is wholly destructive to her identity and vocation.

Even less clearly an allusion to Shakespeare, because based on a single substantive noun in common, is the passage commencing 'I ought to grieve, but cannot what I ought' (183–94). This surely capitalises on resonances set up in the reader's memory with the soliloquy in *Hamlet*, marked as a 'shining' passage in his edition (discussed later) where Claudius laments the inefficacy of his prayer because he continues to profit from the crime for which he seeks prayer's intercession: 'Oh my offence is rank, it smells to heaven' (III.iii.36–72). Verbally, the two passages come closest when Eloisa tries to pray: 'Now turn'd to heav'n, I weep my past offence, / Now think of thee, and curse my innocence' (187–8). The word 'offence' occurs four times in Claudius's self-scrutiny. For Pope, such lexical repetition would be indecorous, and he permits himself two uses of 'offence', varying the terms with 'crime' and 'sin'. The situational parallel between Pope's character and Shakespeare's cannot be clearer. Both are striving to elude false consciousness, both sensuously desperate to retain the rewards of 'offence' while intellectually convinced that this is impossible. The parallel is indicated not by direct quotation or even by using some of Shakespeare's words reshaped or rearranged to indicate an allusion, as in the earlier *Eloisa* example, but by the deployment of a keyword, 'offence'. That cues us into Claudius's

9 Gary Taylor, *Reinventing Shakespeare* (London: Hogarth Press, 1990), p. 107.

emotional logic and structure of feeling, creating the similarity for a reader who knows *Hamlet*.

Later in his career, however, Pope returned to *Hamlet*, this time deploying near-verbatim quotation as ammunition in his war against his literary enemies. In 1728, James Ralph published his *Night: A Poem in Four Books*, which trades on James Thomson's success with blank verse in *The Seasons* (1726–30). Ralph's Preface defends the use of blank verse over rhyme, and cites Pope's celebrated night-piece from his translation of Book VII of Homer's *Iliad* commencing 'As when the moon, refulgent lamp of night'(line 364). Ralph comments: 'Even here I am afraid, a judicious eye will discern that the Poet (for the sake of *rhime*) has been unhappily led into some inconsistencies.'[10] This, along with the poem *Sawney*, published in the *Monthly Chronicle* on 26 June 1728, which dismisses Pope's Homer and his edition of Shakespeare as lucrative frauds practised against the public, was sufficient to enshrine Ralph in later editions of the *Dunciad*:

> Silence, ye Wolves! while Ralph to Cynthia howls,
> And makes Night hideous – Answer him ye Owls![11]

Lest the reader fail to recognise this as an allusion to *Hamlet*, a footnote gives the reference, under the lemma 'Ralph': 'A name inserted after the first Editions, not known to our Author till he writ a Swearing-piece call'd *Sawney*, very abusive of Dr. *Swift*, Mr. *Gay*, and himself. These lines allude to a thing of his, intituled *Night* a *Poem*. Shakespear, Hamlet: "Visit thus the glimpses of the Moon / Making Night hideous' ".[12] In Shakespearean context, Hamlet is addressing his father's ghost, trying to understand the significance of his reappearance on earth. In Pope's edition, this occurs in Act I, Scene vii (1.iv.51–4 in modern texts), and the lines are as follows:

> What may this mean?
> That thou dead coarse again in complete steel
> Revisit'st thus the glimpses of the moon,
> Making night hideous?[13]

In the *Dunciad* footnote, the change from 'Revisit'st' to 'Visit' is, I think, not a memory slip, but an intentional emendation. Ralph is not revisiting old haunts, like Hamlet's father's ghost. He is visiting for the first time; and

---

[10] James Ralph, *Night: A Poem in Four Books*, 2nd edn (London, 1729), preface, p. viii.
[11] Alexander Pope, *The Poems of Alexander Pope*, Vol. III: *'The Dunciad' (1728) and 'The Dunciad Variorum' (1729)*, ed. Valerie Rumbold (London: Pearson Longman, 2007), pp. 280–1 (III.159–60).
[12] Rumbold notes in the same place that there is perhaps a further allusion in Pope's lines to Waller's 'Of the Paraphrase on the Lord's Prayer, Written by Mrs Wharton'.
[13] Shakespeare, *The Works*, ed. Pope, vol. VI, p. 366.

his vulpine poetry is being *visited upon* Cynthia, the unfortunate moon. Punning on Shakespeare's 'night' and the title of Ralph's poem, Pope gains his revenge for the former's strictures against his own moonlit scene. Edmund Curll is seldom quoted with approval, but he was not wrong when he wrote in *The Curliad* that in *The Dunciad*: 'Poor *Shakespeare* is brought in to patronise this punning Abuse; from this Passage in *Hamlet*. – Visit thus the Glimpses of the Moon / Making Night hideous.'[14] Nevertheless, Curll clearly enjoyed recycling the lines.

Pope's engagement with Shakespeare deepened considerably after he had spent years editing his plays. A greater concentration of allusions can be found in *An Essay on Man* (1733–34), intended to be the prelude to Pope's 'Opus Magnum', an extensive survey of human experience. For a work of such scope, Shakespeare's wisdom was apparently necessary. As for the edition itself, Pope's opening prefatory remarks are, surprisingly, as emphatic on his author's *faults* as on strengths: 'For of all *English* Poets, *Shakespear* must be confessed to be the fairest and fullest subject for Criticism, and to afford the most numerous, as well as the most conspicuous Instances, both of Beauties and Faults' (sig. A2r). Pope finds a broadly sociological explanation for Shakespeare's many deficiencies – those that are not simply the result of poor textual transmission – in the composition of his audience and their poor taste. Overall, he is not reticent about Shakespeare's shortcomings. We are reminded that Shakespeare's reputation in 1725 was only just, if it was at all, *primus inter pares* with Jonson, Fletcher, Beaumont, Massinger and other Jacobethan dramatists.[15] Indeed, one of Pope's prefatory gambits is to set up again the Jonson–Shakespeare comparison not entirely to the latter's credit. We see here Shakespeare's later reputation still being hammered on the anvil of criticism. Pope admired Shakespeare, but certainly did not worship him. Pope's edition, however savagely it was criticised by Lewis Theobald in *Shakespeare Restored* (1726), and however woefully soon the conviction grew in the mind of its publisher, Jacob Tonson Jr, that the job would have to be redone, was nevertheless massively influential. Although at a price of 5 guineas unbound the edition was expensive, Pope's list of subscribers printed in the first volume is not only a Debrett *avant la lettre*, but it includes the names of scores of substantial country gentlemen, and of

---

[14] This was published in the same periodical as Ralph's *Sawney*: the *Monthly Chronicle* for 30 April 1729. It occurs in a section called 'A Key to the New Dunciad', p. 36, where Curll implicitly denies that Ralph wrote *Sawney*.

[15] See, for example, Robert D. Hume, 'Before the Bard: "Shakespeare" in Early Eighteenth-Century London', *ELH*, 64 (1997), 41–75.

many booksellers who would go on to shelve the edition in their libraries
and promote it in their shops. His 'Beauties'-versus-'Faults' approach was
played out in the edition's machinery, much to the cost of his subsequent
editorial reputation: 'some of the most shining passages are distinguish'd by
comma's [*sic*] in the margin; and where the beauty lay not in particulars but
in the whole, a star is prefix'd to the scene' (p. xxiii). Readers of Shakespeare
disliked the incoherence created by Pope's exercise of his personal taste: for
example, reducing the Porter scene in *Macbeth* to a smaller footnote font
and printing *two* Act II, Scenes iv, simply because Pope did not approve of
its low-life bawdy.

   More successful, however distasteful to purist editors, was the technique for pointing out which passages we *should* like. In this regard, Pope
was improving upon pre-existent anthologies of verse quotation. Edward
Bysshe's *Art of English Poetry* (1702) was something of a 'how to' manual,
offering rules for the making of poetry and a handy dictionary of rhymes.
In that context, his 'Collection of the Most Natural, Agreeable, and Noble
Thoughts of the Best English Poets' represents examples of best practice. Bysshe accorded, as Kate Rumbold notes, a relatively low profile to
Shakespeare, the 118 citations placing him below Richard Blackmore and
only a little above Nathaniel Lee (see Chapter 5), thus confirming our
earlier observation that at the turn of the century, Shakespeare had not
yet emerged as a superstar.[16] A notable feature of Pope's edition is its col-
ourful 'Index of the Characters, Sentiments, Speeches and Descriptions
in Shakespear'. This is not an original idea. Nicholas Rowe's edition was
furnished with an alphabetical 'Index of the most beautiful Thoughts,
Descriptions, Speeches &c in Shakespear's *Works*' attached to Volume
VIII; and Charles Gildon's *Complete Art of Poetry* (1718) has an index to its
collection of 'Shakespeariana'. The greater taxonomic complexity of Pope's
index and the prestige of the edition ensured that he would develop even
further the cultural brokerage of his predecessors. Although the compilation of the index is more the work of Fenton than it is of Pope, Pope laid
out its principles in a letter to Tonson and continued to take oversight of
it as the edition was being prepared. 'Whoever you set upon the Index', he
writes to Tonson, 'may proceed upon the Plan of mine to Homer'. This, as
he goes on to illustrate, will involve the master categories of 'Characters' and

---

[16] Edward Bysshe, in his Preface to *The Art of English Poetry* (London, 1702), laments the fact that he
has not been able to provide more citations from Shakespeare, giving as a reason that 'the Garb in
which [he is] Cloath'd, though then Alamode, is now become so out of Fashion, that the Readers of
our Age have no Ear for [him]' (fos. 2r–3v). As Kate Rumbold observes in Chapter 5, even Charles
Gildon's *Complete Art of Poetry* is around 60 per cent based on Bysshe.

'Descriptions', each containing lists of topics alphabetically arranged: for example 'An ambitious man; characterized in Caesar, Act-Sc.-'.[17]

The index that materialised was considerably more complicated than Pope had originally devised. Divided into seven subsections containing 'Characters of Historical Persons', 'Manners, Passions and their External Effects', 'Fictitious Persons, with the Characters ascrib'd to them', 'Thoughts, or Sentiments', 'Speeches' (further defined as 'exhortatory', 'vituperative', 'execrative', 'deliberative', 'narrative', 'pathetic' and 'soliloquies'), 'Descriptions, or Images' (further subdivided into 'persons', 'things', 'places' and 'times and seasons') and finally 'Similies and Allusions', this index provides the reader with a Shakespeare quotation for every occasion. Should you be writing a letter and seeking to embellish your own thoughts on life with something more elevated from Shakespeare, why not go to your shelves and pull down volume VI of Pope's Shakespeare, where you are directed to what is said about the 'shortness and vanity of it' in *Macbeth* or on the 'vicissitudes of it' in *Henry VIII*?

Pope cemented the phenomenon of what we can call 'detachable Shakespeare' – the detachment from their dramatic context of quotable passages, and the transmission of them as 'beauties': self-sufficient statements achieving quasi-proverbial stature, becoming a kind of wisdom literature. The index performs a double duty. It directs the reader back to the play itself. Simultaneously, the very act of detachment gives the anthologised passages a different ontological status from the passages in dramatic context, where the circumstances of utterance and the nature of the utterer must be considered. Soon, William Dodd would collect and publish 'the finest passages of the finest poet' in his *The Beauties of Shakespear* (1752), a publication vastly indebted to Pope's index, providing readers – perhaps despite Dodd's intention, which is more focused on admiration than on utility – with a thesaurus of quotations that would embellish their letters and conversation.[18] This, in turn, would help to form Shakespeare's reputation as a technician of the human heart. Other anthologists would confirm this impression: a *Beauties of Shakespeare* collection printed for George Kearsley in 1783 that takes care to distance itself from that of the unfortunate Dodd, hanged for forgery only six years earlier, assures its readers that 'Shakespeare was one of the greatest Moral Philosophers that ever lived', a 'Universal Genius' who, 'with the most subtle penetration,

---

[17] See Pope, *Correspondence*, vol. II, pp. 213–14: Pope to Jacob Tonson, date uncertain, 1724.
[18] William Dodd, *The Beauties of Shakespear*, 2 vols. (London: T. Waller, 1752), vol. I, preface, p. xiii.

has pierced through the dark developments of the human heart', and whose words teach the 'most important lessons of Morality and Religion'.[19]

After his editorial labours had concluded, Pope began the project that he referred to as his 'Opus Magnum', an elaborate series of poems that would amount to a Horatian ethical system, comprising *An Essay on Man*, the *Moral Essays* and unwritten works including an epic poem having Brutus as its hero.[20] This ambitious masterpiece was never completed, but the *Essay on Man* is the work in which Pope alluded most often to Shakespeare, suggesting that he now conceived of Shakespeare as a philosopher-poet such as he aspired to be. Important imagistic illustrations deployed in the *Essay* originate in Shakespeare. In Epistle IV, for example, Pope uses the analogy of a pebble making circles in a lake to help us understand how love of self can reach out to embrace the whole human race:

> As the small pebble stirs the peaceful lake;
> The centre mov'd, a circle strait succeeds,
> Another still, and still another spreads (IV.364–6).

He is repurposing for his more optimistic purposes Joan La Pucelle's nihilistic words to Charles the Dauphin in *1 Henry VI* (I.iii.133–5), a passage that Pope did mark as 'shining' in the edition:

> Glory is like a circle in the water,
> Which never ceaseth to enlarge itself
> Till by broad spreading it disperse to nought.[21]

Where Pope sees an ever-widening and relatively permanent circle of influence, Shakespeare had seen dispersion and evanescence.

A more local allusion in the *Essay*, however, enables us to demonstrate that Shakespeare was influential on Pope's imagination at a deep level, perhaps even 'in his own despight'. Still bearing in mind the caveat made earlier, that Pope tests any distinction between quotation and allusion, consider Epistle II, lines 53–92. Pope is constructing the basic polarities of the human mind, arguing that a principle of 'self-love', restrained by a contrary principle of 'reason', is what keeps the mechanism working. Self-love makes us want things; reason judges and considers whether it is good for us to have them. There are 'subtle schoolmen' who try to split sense from reason 'With all the rash dexterity of Wit' (84). 'Rash dexterity'! What

---

[19] *The Beauties of Shakespeare: Selected from his plays and poems* (London, 1783), pp. i–ii.

[20] Pope refers to his 'Opus Magnum' in a letter to Swift in 1734. See Pope, *Correspondence*, vol. III, p. 401.

[21] These are Pope's character names. Modern editions have Joan Puzel and Charles the Dolphin.

a brilliantly economical description of wit's *cleverness*, and its disregard for consequences. This near-paradox, holding in tension two quasi-contradictory linguistic elements, is typically Popean, except that Pope found the phrase 'dexterity of wit' in *The Merry Wives of Windsor*. Falstaff uses it to congratulate himself on the device through which he has escaped Ford's clutches when the latter apprehends him making love to Mistress Ford: dressing up as Mother Prat, the witch of Brentford (IV.v.110). This is a passage to which Pope alerts us in the index to his edition: '*escapes undiscover'd, in the disguise of an Old Woman*' (vol. VI, 'back matter', n.p.). *Rash* dexterity at best, since it has cost him a savage beating. Conceivably with that context in mind, Pope has sharpened the phrase with the adjective 'rash'.

The phrase, the character of Falstaff and the play were already present to Pope's imagination when he was writing the *Essay*. The single longest entry in the entire index is dedicated to Falstaff, outperforming all the tragic heroes in containing no fewer than forty-seven items, suggesting that Falstaff stood out for Pope as perhaps Shakespeare's greatest dramatic creation. In the 1728 version of *The Dunciad*, the anti-hero Lewis Theobald is vividly described as 'In a dun night-gown of his own loose skin' (II.22). Disappointingly, perhaps, for Pope enthusiasts, the image originates with Falstaff's self-description in *1 Henry IV*: 'my skin hangs about me like an old lady's loose gown' (III.iii.3). Where Falstaff's claim to having loose skin is the height of implausibility, Pope uses the image of a pellicular nightgown, ungendered, to call attention to Theobald's meagreness – the just desert of an unsuccessful writer unable to secure the comforts of a square meal. Once again we see Pope picking up a striking image from Shakespeare but using it for purposes almost diametrically opposed to those of the host context. At II.247, we are transported to the stinking banks of Fleet Ditch, where the Queen of Dulness issues the challenge to the Dunces to dive into the ditch and prove 'who best can dash thro' thick and thin':

> And who the most in love of dirt excel,
> Or dark dexterity of groping well. (II.255–6)

'Dark' dexterity will give way, as we have seen, to 'rash' in the *Essay*. Images of diving and sinking, allied to conceptions of heaviness and the leaden, are central to Pope's imagination in the late 1720s. They are structural in the early *Dunciad* and in the treatise *Peri bathous; or, The Art of Sinking in Poetry*. They define Pope's comic concept of the bathos outlined in that treatise and supposedly derived from contemporary poetic practice: the anti-sublime, a set of critical canons produced by a new Age of Lead, set up in opposition to the Golden Age prescriptions of Longinus. Pope's imagination was stoked here by his vivid memory of Falstaff in *Merry Wives*, a character possessing the irrepressibility of his own comic creations, the Dunces, and similarly disposed toward a slapstick destiny.

There are two verbatim quotations in Pope's correspondence that invoke the character of Falstaff. In a letter to William Wycherley of 20 May 1709, Pope is coyly disavowing any interest in Fame: 'As for gaining any [reputation], I am as indifferent in the Matter as *Falstaffe* was, and may say of *Fame*, as he did of *Honour, If it comes, it comes unlook'd for; and there's an End on't.'[22] The reference here is to Falstaff's cynical cowardice in *1 Henry IV*, v.iii.61–2, when he says 'Give me life, which if I can save, so: If not, honour comes unlooked for, and there's an end.'

Pope comes as close to quoting Shakespeare verbatim with this reference as he does anywhere in his verse when, in *The Temple of Fame* (1717), he has his first-person narrator express indifference to fame by using Falstaff's formulation:

> Nor Fame I slight, nor for her Favours call;
> She comes unlook'd for, if she comes at all. (lines 513–14 (p. 188))

Again, we catch Pope in the creative act of repurposing his source quotation. Whereas the dramatic context for Falstaff's disavowal of honour makes clear that he wishes to save his own skin and will become a hero only in spite of himself, Pope uses the line to exemplify his stoic indifference to fame. Pope returns to *Merry Wives* in a letter of 1739. Looking for a way to characterise the amiable Dr Richard Cheyne to George Lyttelton, Pope described him as 'so very a child in true Simplicity of Heart, that I love him; as He loves Don Quixote, for the Most Moral and Reasoning Madman in the world … He is … in Shakespear's [language], *as foolish a good kind of Christian Creature* as one shall meet with.' *Merry Wives* still ran in his mind.

And that play continued to be present to his imagination until the end of Pope's writing career. Falstaff describes his discomfiture, following his first attempt on Mistress Ford's virtue, in prose at iii.iv.4ff.:

> Have I lived to be carried in a basket like a barrow of butcher's offal, and to be thrown in the Thames? Well, if I be served such another trick, I'll have my brains ta'en out and buttered, and give them to a dog for a New Year's gift. 'Sblood, the rogues slighted me into the river with as little remorse as they would have drowned a blind bitch's puppies, fifteen i' the litter;

---

[22] Pope, *Correspondence*, vol. i, p. 60.

and you may know by my size that I have a kind of *alacrity in sinking* [my emphasis]: if the bottom were as deep as hell, I should down.

Pope returned to the phrase 'alacrity in sinking' in the *The Dunciad in Four Books* (1743) (IV.20 (p. 767)): 'Soft on her lap her Laureat son reclines.' This line is annotated by Scriblerus and then by 'Bentley'. What is at issue is whether *The Dunciad*'s hero is disqualified for heroic stature by his sheer inertia, his inability to do *anything at all*. Scriblerus's note defends the fact that Colley Cibber, the poem's new anti-hero, does virtually nothing in Book II and sleeps throughout Book III. The note added by 'Bentley' secures a wonderfully Popean opportunity to use Cibber's autobiography as evidence against itself. 'Bentley' observes that Cibber seems to have taken line IV.20 to heart and (in his autobiography)

> appealed to all mankind, 'if he was not as *seldom asleep as any fool?* But it is hoped the Poet hath not injured him, but rather verified his Prophecy (243 of his own Life, 8vo. ch.ix.) where he says '*the Reader will be as much pleased to find me a* Dunce *in my* Old age, *as he was to prove me a* brisk blockhead *in my* Youth'. Wherever there was any room for Briskness, or Alacrity of any sort, *even in sinking*, he hath had it allowed him.[23]

One wonders whether the typographic change here into italics is designed to signal the allusion to Shakespeare, to ensure that the reader does not miss that additional level of intelligence? To the end of his career, then, the figure of Falstaff, and key, memorable phrases in which his character is expressed, stayed with Pope. Hence the parody-annotator's recall of Falstaff's phrase 'alacrity in sinking'. A chain of associations surrounding Falstaff's weight, his brass neck, his feverishly misapplied energy and his propensity to riverbeds seemed to resonate for Pope when he was creating the characters of his dunce-protagonists. Theobald and Cibber were, to Pope, Falstaffian. Shakespeare got under his loosely hanging skin. Pope, in turn, would be a creative irritant to a new generation of poets, such as Mark Akenside and Thomas Gray, who co-opted Shakespeare's increasingly authoritative name rather than quoting his actual words.

---

[23] Colley Cibber, *An Apology for the Life of Mr. Colley Cibber … Written by Himself*, 2nd edn (London, 1740), p. 53.

CHAPTER 7

Shakespeare Quotation in the Romantic Age

Fiona Ritchie and R. S. White

Recognising habits of quotation can guide us toward understanding each individual Romantic writer's attitude toward Shakespeare, while revealing the diverse uses they made of his words. As in the eighteenth century, he was constructed through frequent quotation as object of uncritical admiration, touchstone of literary or theatrical quality, font of wisdom, cultural capital and moral authority. But more than these, he was regarded as friend, teacher, fellow craftsman, creative inspiration and source, moral mentor, therapist, and butt of amiable jokes.

Shakespeare could seem *too* familiar, however. Charles Lamb, in his essay 'On the Tragedies of Shakspeare Considered with Reference to Their Fitness for Stage Representation', rails against the twin practices of quotation and anthologisation because they militate against 'that delightful sensation of freshness' he values in Shakespeare's works. 'How far the very custom of hearing anything *spouted*, withers and blows upon a fine passage, may be seen in those speeches from *Henry the Fifth*, &c. which are current in the mouths of school-boys from their being to be found in *Enfield Speakers*, and such kind of books.'[1] William Enfield's *The Speaker*, first published in 1780, provided passages for elocution lessons, 'with a view to facilitate the improvement of youth'.[2] William Wordsworth owned a copy, and Jonathan Bate guesses that most readers 'would have encountered these books in school or at home'.[3] Lamb pinpoints how this custom of 'spouting' famous passages disconnected from their original contexts impinges on his enjoyment of theatre, and perhaps even of reading:

[1] Charles Lamb, 'On The Tragedies of Shakspeare Considered with Reference to Their Fitness for Stage Representation' (1811), in Jonathan Bate (ed.), *The Romantics on Shakespeare* (Harmondsworth: Penguin, 1992), pp. 111–27 (p. 113).
[2] The quotation is from the full title of Enfield's volume.
[3] Jonathan Bate, *Shakespeare and the English Romantic Imagination* (Oxford: Clarendon Press, 1986), p. 75.

I confess myself utterly unable to appreciate that celebrated soliloquy in *Hamlet*, beginning 'To be or not to be,' or to tell whether it be good, bad, or indifferent, it has been so handled and pawed about by declamatory boys and men, and torn so inhumanly from its living place and principle of continuity in the play, till it is become to me a perfect dead member.[4]

Quotation in the Theatre

In the context of the theatre, Lamb suggests that performance is damaged by the spectator's eagerness to see and hear the delivery of key moments of text delivered woodenly in over-familiar ways. Lamb's critique alludes to the common theatrical practice of 'points', moments of the play in which performers demonstrated virtuosic skill. Actors would often pause at these points to wait for applause, and such moments were frequently depicted in artistic representations of performance: for example, in the image of Edmund Kean as Macbeth in the scene discussed below (Figure 7). This practice created between performers and their appreciative audience the kind of sociable bonding among poets that we shall explore later in the chapter.

Despite Lamb's concerns, theatrical points were widely praised by critics, and quotation is often used to identify these moments. In her prefaces to Longman's *British Theatre* collection, Elizabeth Inchbald highlights moments in which actors excel in their roles, for example in her discussion of John Philip Kemble and Sarah Siddons in *King John*:

> The genius of Kemble gleams terrific through the gloomy John. No auditor can hear him call for his
>> "Kingdom's rivers to take their course
>> "Through his burn'd bosom,"
> and not feel for that moment parched with a scorching fever.

She quotes *King John* (v.vii.38–9) in order to express the emotional impact of Kemble's delivery on the audience. Describing Siddons as Constance she writes that the lines 'Here I and sorrow sit: / This is my throne, bid kings come bow to it' (iii.i.73–4) 'seem like a triumphant reference to her own potent skill in the delineation of woe, as well as to the

---

[4] Lamb, 'On the Tragedies of Shakspeare', p. 113.

agonizing sufferings of the mother of young Arthur'.[5] Inchbald here goes
beyond quotation as identification to reflect both on the actors' powerful
characterisation and also on their acting skill. Siddons's delivery of the
quoted lines develops the character she is playing but the performer is
not totally subsumed by the role at this moment. Rather, the lines self-
consciously assert her skill as a Shakespearean actor. The performers
might also be said to be quoting Shakespeare here, both in the literal
sense of delivering his lines but also in the more abstract sense of calling
attention to his 'beauties' through their self-conscious performance of
such points, which could be separated from the theatrical action, just as
Shakespeare's 'beauties' could be separated from the rest of the text for
readers. For Lamb, Shakespeare's famous speeches, although they may
be expertly delivered by competent actors such as Siddons, Kemble and
Kean, yet appear as 'dead members' because the audience does not pay
sufficient attention to their context in the play.[6] However, such verbal
points remained popular with audiences, who, as Jeffrey Kahan notes,
'concentrated on the emotional magnetism of the lines as set pieces' and
applauded such moments enthusiastically.[7]

Lamb does acknowledge that performance gives him a 'very high
degree of satisfaction',[8] which presumably explains why he was a keen
theatregoer and authored performance reviews, including many of actors in
Shakespearean roles. In these pieces, Lamb's quotations from Shakespeare
often serve as a litmus test of the quality of a performance; the actor sometimes enhances Shakespeare's genius but sometimes falls short. Lamb's
reviews often quote lines of the text that he considers especially beautiful
and moments in the performance that he finds particularly strong, and
sometimes the two converge. His analysis of Dorothy Jordan's Viola is a
good example:

> There is no giving an account how she delivered the disguised story of
> her love for Orsino. It was no set speech, that she had foreseen, so as to
> weave it into an harmonious period, line necessarily following line, to
> make up the music – yet I have heard it so spoken, or rather *read*, not
> without its grace and beauty – but, when she had declared her sister's his-
> tory to be a "blank", and that she "never told her love", there was a pause,

[5] Elizabeth Inchbald, 'Remarks on *King John*', in *The British Theatre*, 25 vols. (London: Longman, Hurst, Rees and Orme, 1808), vol. 1, pp. 3, 4. Each play is paginated individually; *King John* is the third play in this volume.
[6] Lamb, 'On the Tragedies of Shakspeare', p. 113.
[7] Jeffrey Kahan, *The Cult of Kean* (Aldershot: Ashgate, 2006), p. 48.
[8] Lamb, 'On the Tragedies of Shakspeare', p. 113.

as if the story had ended – and then the image of the "worm in the bud" came up as a new suggestion – and the heightened image of "Patience" still followed after that, as by some growing (and not mechanical) process, thought springing up after thought, I would almost say, as they were watered by her tears.[9]

Jordan challenges Lamb's assertion that the famous speeches of Shakespeare no longer have meaning even when given in the context of the play because of the practice of excerpting them for 'spouting'. The power of Jordan's acting, which allows each discrete thought in the speech to develop anew, rather than treating the whole passage as one finished idea, does justice to the complexity of Shakespeare's language and the emotions it expresses. It is only when the brilliance of Shakespeare's lines and of the actor's delivery come together that the emotional resonance of the moment is fully conveyed. Lamb's notion of the unfitness of Shakespeare for stage representation is here fundamentally disturbed.

That theatrical points could be physical as well as verbal is clear from William Hazlitt's discussion of Kean's performance of Macbeth. In the scene following the murder of Duncan (see Figure 7), Kean's 'hesitation, the bewildered look, the coming to himself when he sees his hands bloody; the manner in which his voice clung to his throat, and choaked his utterance; his agony and tears, the force of nature overcome by passion – beggered [*sic*] description. It was a scene, which no one who saw it can ever efface from his recollection'.[10] Hazlitt here describes a sequence of physical expressions of the passions presented by the actor, the series of definite articles creating an impression of known moments that are measures of performance. As Younglim Han writes, 'a sequence of swift changes of emotion in relation to the "points" was the major accepted means of demonstrating the performer's ability'.[11] Hazlitt here uses quotation to evaluate the scene: 'To enquire whether his manner in the latter scene was that of a king who commits a murder, or of a man who commits a murder to become a king, would be "to consider too curiously". But, as a lesson of common humanity, it was heart-rending.'[12] He also points to the dangers of theatrical criticism itself leading to over-analysis. However, the

---

[9] Charles Lamb, 'On Some of the Old Actors', in *Elia: Essays which Have Appeared under that Signature in the London Magazine* (London: Taylor and Hessey, 1823), pp. 302–22 (pp. 303–4).
[10] William Hazlitt, 'From "Mr Kean's Macbeth"', in R. S. White (ed.), *Hazlitt's Criticism of Shakespeare: A Selection* (Lampeter: Edwin Mellen Press, 1996), pp. 217–19 (p. 217).
[11] Younglim Han, *Romantic Shakespeare: From Stage to Page* (Cranbury: Associated University Presses, 2001), p. 39.
[12] Hazlitt, 'Mr Kean's Macbeth', p. 217.

Figure 7   J. Carver, *Mr. Kean, as Macbeth in 'Macbeth'* (London, 1815).

line cited is not from the play under consideration, *Macbeth*, but from a different work (albeit one in which Kean also shone), *Hamlet*. It is spoken by Horatio in response to Hamlet's musing '[t]o what base uses we may return' (v.i.171, 174). The line may simply be a neat turn of phrase that Hazlitt has remembered from Shakespeare but its resonance is transformed in the context of Duncan's murder by Macbeth. Hamlet wonders about the destiny of 'the noble dust of Alexander' and 'Imperious Caesar, dead and turned to clay' (v.i.171, 180). We are, therefore, reminded of Duncan's corporeality, of the reality of his murder. Whether Macbeth is 'a king who commits a murder' or 'a man who commits a murder to become a king' is, as Hazlitt suggests, a moot point, as in either scenario Duncan's fate is the same.

Quotation of Shakespeare out of context – that is, using lines from a different Shakespeare play to elucidate the Shakespeare play being discussed – is found elsewhere in Romantic theatre criticism. In his review of *Twelfth Night* from 1820, Leigh Hunt takes John Emery to task for misunderstanding the character of Sir Toby, 'who is not so much a surly fellow as a mock-heroic one, something between the wit of *Falstaff* and the affected pomposity of "mine host of the Garter" '.[13] Hunt sees a link between the comedy of Sir Toby and that of the characters of *The Merry Wives of Windsor*. He also critiques John Liston as Sir Andrew Aguecheek, although he does praise the actor's performance in the duel scene with Viola as 'ludicrous to perfection. The faintness with which he sinks back on *Sir Toby's* breast is absolute "dissolution and thaw".'[14] By invoking Falstaff cowering in Mistress Page's linen basket in *The Merry Wives of Windsor*, Hunt blurs the line between the character of Sir Andrew and that of Sir Toby, who was also likened to Falstaff in that same play. While this use of quotation might at first seem confusing, the mental link between the characters in fact serves as an implicit form of associationism, a theory derived from John Locke and developed by David Hartley that was much discussed in the period and applied to Shakespeare following Walter Whiter's *A Specimen of a Commentary on Shakespeare* (1794). Hunt's evocation of Falstaff in his review can therefore be read as inspired lateral thinking, drawing connections between different characters and plays in order better to elucidate the nature of comedy in *Twelfth Night*. This associationism is aided by the culture of points, which facilitates the comparison of moments excerpted from various plays. Not only were Shakespeare's plays put in dialogue with each other through the use of quotation in criticism, Romantic writers also used quotation in their conversations with each other about Shakespeare, as we shall now see.

Quotation and Sociability

Collections such as Dodd's *Beauties of Shakespear* (1752) (see Chapters 5 and 6) ensured the widespread recognisability of quotations. Phrases from Shakespeare peppered speeches in Parliament (see Chapter 9), and the rhetorical effectiveness suggests not only recognition of the source but even

---

[13] Leigh Hunt, '*Twelfth Night*', in Lawrence Huston Houtchens and Carolyn Washburn Houtchens (eds.), *Leigh Hunt's Dramatic Criticism 1808–1831* (New York: Columbia University Press, 1949), pp. 227–31 (p. 228).
[14] *Ibid.*, p. 229.

its dramatic context. Edmund Burke, for example, won a parliamentary debate by bringing tears to the eyes of many by quoting Macduff's 'he had no children' (*Macbeth*, IV.iii.218) in order to reveal the heartlessness of his opponent.[15] Christopher Reid coined the phrase 'quotation community' to describe the eighteenth-century House of Commons, and the phrase could apply also to writers.[16] They genially assimilate Shakespeare's words into their communication, playfully requoting and responding in a spirit of creative interaction. Recent critics assert the centrality of sociability among poetic circles and friendship networks. The titles of Coleridge's journal *The Friend* (1809–10) and Hazlitt's collection of essays *Table-Talk* (1821), alongside 'conversation poems', all indicate what Lucy Newlyn has termed 'companionable forms: conversation as a poetic ideal'.[17] Felicity James notes that even the barest of quotations could make a personal point between friends, suggesting that, in a letter to Coleridge, Charles Lamb uses as a subtle reproach for betrayal in friendship Hamlet's phrase to Horatio, 'I will wear him / In my heart's core, ay, *in my heart of heart* / as I do thee' (III.ii.62–4) (Lamb wrote 'in my heart of hearts').[18] We see in action the easy trading of quotations between Shelley and Byron as they argue about *Hamlet*, justifying general points by reference to the text in a conversation reputedly transcribed by Mary Shelley.[19] John Keats frequently hits the note of conversational intimacy, never more movingly than when he was desperately ill and wrote to Rice 'Like poor Falstaff, though I do not babble, I think of green fields'.[20] Writing to his brother and sister-in-law in America, he could imagine Shakespeare's shared presence as glue that holds friends together in 'a direct communication of spirit' dissolving separation: 'I shall read a passage of Shakespeare every Sunday at ten o Clock – you read one {a}t the same time and we shall be as near each other as blind bodies can be in the same room' (Vol. II, p. 5), This prompts him to transcribe his own

---

[15] David Dwan and Christopher J. Insole (eds.), *The Cambridge Companion to Edmund Burke* (Cambridge: Cambridge University Press, 2012), p. 47.

[16] Christopher Reid, *Imprison'd Wranglers: The Rhetorical Culture of the House of Commons 1760–1800* (Oxford: Oxford University Press, 2012), p. 219.

[17] Lucy Newlyn, *Reading, Writing, and Romanticism: The Anxiety of Reception* (Oxford: Oxford University Press, 2000), p. 72.

[18] Letter to Coleridge in early 1797, reprinted in Edwin W. Marrs (ed.), *The Letters of Charles and Mary Lamb*, 3 vols. (Ithaca: Cornell University Press, 1975), vol. I, p. 92; quoted in Felicity James, *Charles Lamb, Coleridge and Wordsworth: Reading Friendship in the 1790s* (Basingstoke: Palgrave Macmillan, 2008), p. 172.

[19] Reprinted in Bate, *The Romantics on Shakespeare*, pp. 335–49.

[20] John Keats, *The Letters of John Keats 1814–1821*, ed. Hyder Edward Rollins, 2 vols. (Cambridge: Harvard University Press, 1958), vol. II, p. 260, quoting *Henry V*, II.iii.16. Subsequent references to Keats's letters are to this edition and are given in parentheses in the text.

poem musing on the companionship of poets, dead and alive, 'Bards of Passion and of Mirth / Ye have left your souls on earth—' (Vol. II, pp. 25–6), whimsically suggesting that the 'quotation community' is not divided by death. Shakespeare is one among the 'old poets' who, as Hazlitt was to say, 'sit with me at breakfast … walk with me before dinner … and seated round, discourse the silent hours away'.[21]

Quotation seems irresistible even when resisting the temptation. Wordsworth, in the Preface to *Lyrical Ballads*, repeatedly extols the virtues of 'the real language of men' (or 'of nature'), warning against poetic diction learned from the 'phrases and figures of speech which from father to son have long been regarded as the common inheritance of Poets'. However, almost inadvertently he drops in a quotation from Milton's *Paradise Lost* (1667, 1674) – 'Some natural tears they dropped' – and *Measure for Measure*, to make his point against quotation: 'Poetry sheds no tears "such as Angels weep", but natural and human tears'.[22] Later, adapting a quotation from *Hamlet* – 'Sure he that made us with such large discourse, / Looking before and after' (IV.iv.36–7) – he extols the power of Shakespeare's words in a famous passage that begins 'Emphatically may it be said of the Poet, As Shakespeare hath said of man, "that he looks before and after"' (p. 259). Thomas Festa suggests that the inexact quotation implies Wordsworth is recollecting *Hamlet* from memory and not especially aptly, but Wordsworth really has in his sights his next, adulatory sentence: '[Shakespeare] is the rock of defence of human nature; and upholder and preserver, carrying everywhere with him relationship and love.'[23] By implication, the process of transmission involves judicious allusiveness and memorial quotation as a responsibility of modern poets, to ensure the influence will not die. In his own poetry, however, Wordsworth is relatively true to his creed of avoiding poeticisms, and generally avoids direct literary quotation. Even amongst veiled quotations in *The Prelude* there are hundreds more allusions to Milton's words than Shakespeare's, and these are discreetly embedded in a phrase or two rather than 'pointed': in 'Simon Lee, the Old Huntsman',

[21] Quoted in *Literary Remains of the Late William Hazlitt … By His Son* (London: Saunders and Otley, 1836), p. xxi.
[22] John Milton, *Paradise Lost*, Book XII, line 645, in *Milton: Poetical Works*, ed. Douglas Bush (London: Oxford University Press, 1966), p. 459; *Measure for Measure*, II.ii.126. *Wordsworth and Coleridge: Lyrical Ballads*, ed. R. L. Brett and A. R. Jones, rev. edn (London: Methuen, 1965), p. 254. Subsequent references are to this edition and are given in parentheses in the text.
[23] Thomas Festa, 'The State of Unfeigned Nature: Poetic Imagination from Shakespeare to Wordsworth', in Joseph M. Ortiz (ed.), *Shakespeare and the Culture of Romanticism* (Farnham: Ashgate, 2013), pp. 77–98 (p. 85).

Wordsworth interpolates unobtrusive Shakespearean quotations, from
Sonnet 30, line 1, and *As You Like It*, II.I.15–17:

> Oh reader! had you in your mind
> Such stores as *silent thought* can bring,
> Oh gentle reader! you would find
> *A tale in every thing.* (p. 62, lines 73–6; our italics)

The quotations shift attention away from the narrative and toward the
reading process, from the tale to the teller, who is as conscious a craftsman
as Shakespeare.

Byron used Shakespeare's words more playfully. True to his self-
fashioning of effortless superiority, he was never seen to be reading and he
frequently disparaged Shakespeare's skill as a writer, preferring Pope. In the
conversation with Shelley mentioned above, he criticises *Hamlet* as lacking
unity, a charge that Shelley refutes by reading from an essay he has written
on the subject, at such length that Byron falls asleep. However, Byron
elsewhere quotes from every work except *The Comedy of Errors* and *Venus
and Adonis*, paying scant attention to either genre or context by distancing
words borrowed from a tragedy in a tone of mockery. Despite his anti-
scholasticism and anti-bardolatry, more often than not he uses quotation
marks and sometimes even supplies full references. The emphasis thus falls
on Byron's own trademark tone of ironic self-dramatisation, humorously
reversed in his Oscar Wilde-like aphorism 'I think it great affectation not
to quote oneself.'[24] There is a sense in which Byron is aggressively appropriating Shakespeare's words for his own use.[25] In a letter to Thomas Moore
in 1814 declaring he is to be married, Byron describes his paramour as
'invested with "golden opinions of all sorts of men", and as full of "most
blest conditions", as Desdemona herself', quoting from first *Macbeth*
(I.vii.33) and then *Othello* (I.i.236).[26] In his journal of the same year, he
uses words from *3 Henry VI* (V.vi.84) and *Hamlet* (II.ii.291) to describe
himself as 'a solitary hobgoblin': 'True,—"*I am myself alone.*" … do I regret
it?—um—"*Man delights not me*", and only one woman—at a time' (p. 188;
our italics). There follow what may be a reference to *The Tempest* ('would
I were in my island!'; compare Caliban, 'This island's mine', I.ii.331) and a

---

[24] 'Byron and Shelley on the Character of Hamlet', *The New Monthly Magazine and Literary Journal*,
    n.s. Vol. 29 (London: Henry Colburn and Richard Bentley, [1830]), 327–36 (p. 328).
[25] Bate, *The Romantics on Shakespeare*, p. 336.
[26] Lord Byron to Thomas Moore, 20 September 1814, in *Byron's Poetry and Prose*, ed. Alice Levine
    (New York: W. W. Norton, 2010), p. 188. Subsequent references are to this edition and are given in
    parentheses in the text.

barrage of quotations from *Richard III*, *King Lear* and *Macbeth*: 'At times, I fear, "I am not in my perfect mind" [*The Tragedy of King Lear*, IV.vi.63] … "Prithee undo this button—Why should a cat, a rat, a dog, have life— and *thou* no life at all?" [misquoted from v.iii.280–3] … "I 'gin to be a- weary of the sun" [*Macbeth*, v.v.48)]' (pp. 184–5). In *Don Juan* (1809–24), Shakespeare is not spared Byron's characteristically strained rhymes and half-rhyming for comic effect: ' "To be, or not to be? that is the question", / Says Shakespeare, who just now is much in fashion', and 'Her wish was but to "kill, kill, kill", like Lear's, / And then her thirst of blood was quenched in tears.'[27] By contrast with some of his contemporaries, there is a per- vading impression that Byron feels quoting Shakespeare is a superficial activity and in *Don Juan* he says as much:

> … though I am a simple noddy,
> I think one Shakespeare puts the same thought in
> The mouth of some one in his plays so doting,
> Which many people pass for wits by quoting. (VII.21)

In the body of his extraordinary mock-epic, Byron accommodates Shakespeare into his own distinctively conversational, digressively anec- dotal and debunking voice, quoting from over twenty plays with virtuoso ingenuity and often incongruity. Through his persona he distinguishes his context from Shakespeare's dramatic moment, mocking readers' preten- tiousness while inviting the *cognoscenti* to share his clever levity.

Claire Claremont wrote in her journal that Shelley always had in his pocket 'three small volumes of Shakespeare and carries them about every- where with him'.[28] He quoted Shakespeare as much as, if not more than, any of his contemporaries, but woven into the seams of his poetry rather than blazoned as overt quotation. This in itself opened him up to criti- cism that *The Cenci* (1819) contained 'perhaps the most numerous and fla- grant plagiarisms, especially from Shakespeare, to be found in his poems'.[29] Although a cruel misjudgement that stung the poet, it is a revealing accus- ation. Shelley's quotations might often *look* like plagiarisms because, unlike Byron, he does use exact or near-exact phrases in his own work with no distancing signals to indicate they are not his own. It is just possible they

---

[27] Lord Byron, *Don Juan*, ed. Leslie A. Marchand (Boston: Houghton Mifflin, 1958), IX.xiv, v.cxxxvi. Subsequent references are to this edition and are given in parentheses in the text.
[28] K. N. Cameron and D. H. Reiman (eds.), *Shelley and His Circle 1773–1822*, 6 vols. (Cambridge: Harvard University Press, 1961–73), vol. III, p. 346.
[29] J. S. Baynes writing anonymously, quoted in Beach Langston, 'Shelley's Use of Shakespeare', *Huntington Library Quarterly*, 12 (1949): 163–90 (p. 168).

are sometimes unconscious borrowings, but, for such a studied craftsman as Shelley, this is unlikely. More plausibly, he is unobtrusively invoking a suggestive Shakespearean context to enrich his own poetic effect or imply an attitude. Often it seems that association of ideas brings a specific quotation to mind, which in its turn informs, illuminates and clarifies Shelley's tone and meaning. Alongside dozens of occurrences that can be described as simple 'echoes' there are also repetitions of phrases such as 'azure veins' in *Queen Mab* (1813), significantly from *The Rape of Lucrece* (418–20); and 'curtain of sleep' in *Prometheus Unbound* (1820) and 'To curtain her sleeping world' in *Queen Mab*, both ominously recalling 'The curtained sleep' in *Macbeth* (II.i.49–51).[30] As we might expect, references to Shakespeare's words, as well as overall structural and thematic parallels, are most evident in Shelley's dramatic works, *The Cenci* and *Prometheus Unbound*.[31] However, he would certainly have been indignant to hear such borrowings called 'plagiarism', since it is clear that a part of his creative process involves an intertextual engagement with Shakespeare's drama, where subliminal associations enhance his own circumstantially different poetic contexts. The quotations are intended as artistically functional and integrated, unlike the differentiating strategies characteristic of Byron.

William Blake was steeped in Shakespeare, not only as a reader but more unexpectedly as a theatregoer.[32] Lacking a close network of literary figures (rather, he socialised with artists and publishers), his use of Shakespeare, and even more so Milton, resembled less a conversation than an internalised dialectic, working out his own creative ideas in a spirit of inner argument perhaps influenced by what he saw on stage. Supernatural elements appealed to the visionary poet: the ghosts in *Hamlet*, *Richard III* and *Julius Caesar*; the fairies in *A Midsummer Night's Dream*; the witches (whom he regarded as 'Goddesses of Destiny') and Hecate in *Macbeth*. References are used as part of Blake's ongoing celebration of the imagination over reason.[33] For example, in *Milton* (1804–10) he quotes Theseus's

[30] P. B. Shelley, *Shelley's Poetry and Prose*, ed. Donald H. Reiman and Neil Fraistat (New York: W. W. Norton, 2002), pp. 17, 271, 36.

[31] For others, see David Lee Clark, 'Shelley and Shakespeare', *Publications of the Modern Language Association*, 54 (1939), 261–87; and Bate, *Shakespeare and the English Romantic Imagination*, Chapter 10. See also Bernard Beatty, 'Shelley, Shakespeare, and Theatre', in Michael O'Neill and Anthony Howe (eds.), *The Oxford Handbook of Percy Bysshe Shelley* (Oxford: Oxford University Press, 2013), pp. 546–60.

[32] Chantelle L. MacPhee, '"All the World's a Stage": William Blake and William Shakespeare', unpublished Ph.D. thesis, Glasgow University (2002), Chapter 1.

[33] William Blake, *A Descriptive Catalogue* (1809), reprinted in *The Complete Writings of William Blake*, ed. Geoffrey Keynes (Oxford: Oxford University Press, 1966), Plate 28, lines 1–5 (p. 569).

dismissal of the poet's imagination (*A Midsummer Night's Dream*, v.i.2–22) in a way that paradoxically extols the faculty:

> Creating form & beauty around the dark regions of sorrow,
> *Giving to airy nothing a name & a habitation*
> Delightful – with bounds to the infinite putting off the indefinite
> Into most holy forms of thought (such is the power of inspiration).[34]

Blake's enigmatic print named *Pity* (see cover) is an attempt to represent visually the dense complexity of imagery in the Shakespearean 'naked new-born babe' quotation from *Macbeth* (i.vii.21). Other artists of the period, such as Fuseli and Barrie, provide similar visual quotations of passages from Shakespeare, in ways that often suggest critical readings and new understandings.[35]

While 'Enfield Speakers' were aimed at schoolboys rather than their sisters, Shakespeare's status as a vernacular author meant that women had greater access to his words than to those of classical literary models, and they were just as enthusiastic about Shakespeare as their male counterparts. Helen Maria Williams weaves quotations into 'An Address to Poetry' (1790):

> Where shall I pursue gay Ariel's flight,
> Or wander where those hags of night
> With deeds unnamed shall freeze my trembling soul?[36]

Her eulogy is based on a patchwork of quotations, referring in particular to Shakespeare's female characters Cordelia, Desdemona and Ophelia. Titania is a particular favourite of Mary Robinson ('Oberon's Invitation to Titania' followed by 'Titania's Answer to Oberon' (1806)) and Ann Radcliffe ('Titania to her Love' in *Romance of the Forest* (1791)).[37] Charlotte Smith is one of her age's most frequent quoters of Shakespeare. She sometimes seems conscious of avoiding the charge of plagiarism by using punctuation to acknowledge quotations, for example in her sonnet 'On the Departure of the Nightingale' (1790), where line 4 reads 'And pour thy music on the

---

[34] William Blake, *Blake: The Complete Poems*, ed. W. H. Stevenson and David V. Erdman (London: Longman, 1971), p. 536.

[35] See Stuart Sillars, *Painting Shakespeare: The Artist as Critic, 1720–1820* (Cambridge: Cambridge University Press, 2006).

[36] Quoted in Andrew Ashfield (ed.), *Romantic Women Poets, 1770–1838: An Anthology* (Manchester: Manchester University Press, 1995), p. xv in1.

[37] Mary Robinson, *Selected Poems*, ed. Judith Pascoe (Ontario: Broadview Press, 2000), p. 344; Ann Radcliffe, *The Romance of the Forest*, ed. Chloe Chard (Oxford: Oxford University Press, 1999 [1986]), p. 284.

"night's dull ear"' (*Henry V*, iv.Chorus.11).[38] In 'The Emigrants' (1793) she even provides the source in a footnote once again quoting the Chorus in *Henry V* (Prologue.7–8): 'And, in the ranks, "Famine, and Sword, and Fire, Crouch for employment." '[39] Joy Currie summarises a variety of functions of quotation in Charlotte Smith's works in this way:

> Through allusions and quotations, [Smith] creates moments of shared emotion between her speakers, Shakespeare, and herself; appropriates his language and metaphors; claims authority for her use of natural history; claims equality with male writers; claims authority for her expression of political views; and develops extended analogies between Shakespeare's themes and characters and her own.[40]

The description might apply with individual variations to other Romantic writers' multiple functions of quotation.

Quotation as Interpretation

Romantic writers not only used Shakespeare quotations in their creative works but also in some cases anticipated the medium of modern literary analysis. Hazlitt pioneered the kind of commentary that unearths political significances in Shakespeare, as Uttara Natarajan has shown at work in his purposeful quotations from the 'illegitimate' Edmund in *Lear,* where class is the issue. Contemporaries noticed and responded. Indignantly replying to Gifford's arch-conservative attack on Hazlitt's overuse of Shakespearean quotation, Hazlitt ripostes 'I can only answer that "I would not change that vice for your best virtue." '[41] Coleridge, in Volume II, Chapter 15 of *Biographia literaria*, exemplifies what he calls 'practical criticism', in particular using imagery study to illuminate the style of 'myriad-minded Shakespeare'.[42] The choice of texts for critical analysis – *Venus and Adonis, The Rape of Lucrece* and the Sonnets – was unusual since the poems were not valued as highly as the plays by his contemporaries. Coleridge argues that in these early works we see signs that Shakespeare was 'a natural

[38] *British Women Poets of the Romantic Era: An Anthology*, ed. Paula R. Feldman (Baltimore: Johns Hopkins University Press: 1997), p. 685.

[39] Charlotte Turner Smith, *The Emigrants: A poem, in two books* (London: printed for T. Cadell, 1793), p. 44.

[40] Joy Currie, ' "Mature Poets Steal": Charlotte Smith's Appropriations of Shakespeare', in Ortiz, *Shakespeare and the Culture of Romanticism*, pp. 99–120 (p. 100).

[41] Adrian Poole (ed.), *Great Shakespeareans*, Vol. IV: *Lamb, Hazlitt, Keats* (London: Continuum, 2010), pp.102–4.

[42] Samuel Taylor Coleridge, *Biographia literaria*, ed. George Watson (London: Everyman's Library, 1956), pp. 175–80. Subsequent references are to this edition and are given in parentheses in the text.

poetic genius', 'born not made' as a poet of 'intuitive' imagination who could reach further than even the most industrious and learned craftsman working 'as a trade' (p. 176). He did so by 'reducing multitude into a unity of effect' through 'intertexture' (p. 176). Coleridge is anticipating and even creating the critical vocabulary to be used over 100 years later by exponents of New Criticism. Through quotation, he illustrates the visual immediacy of Shakespeare's poetry operating 'through a series and never broken chain of imagery, always vivid and, because unbroken, often minute'. Pictorial images become poetry only when 'they are modified by a dominant passion', writes Coleridge, 'or by associated thoughts or images awakened by that passion', coalescing into a unified instant infused with emotion. He quotes Sonnet 33 ('Full many a glorious morning have I seen') to illustrate the operation of imagery that 'moulds and colours itself to the circumstances, passion, or character, present and foremost in the mind' (pp. 178–9). He follows with quotations from *King Lear*, *Othello* and Sonnet 98 quoted in full ('*From you have I been absent in the spring*'); then *Venus and Adonis*, most notably the lines 'Look! how a bright star shooteth from the sky, / So glides he in the night from Venus' eye' (lines 815–16), to illustrate 'the liveliest image of succession with the feeling of simultaneousness' (p. 179) as an effect that poetry can achieve but that eludes the painter. Coleridge writes as a fellow practitioner eager to crack the master's secret of loading imagery with passion and emotional unity. His own poetry, as J. L. Lowes brilliantly showed, is an intensely personal, focused synthesis of diverse sources, quotations, allusions, echoes and borrowings.[43]

Keats is also one of the great, creative readers of Shakespeare, but in different ways from the obsessional Coleridge, writing in letters rather than discursive criticism and pervasively indebted to Hazlitt.[44] He famously described Shakespeare in his letters as a poet of 'negative capability', a faculty allowing the poet to be a non-judgemental 'thoroughfare' for contrasting feelings and thoughts, and in such a spirit he himself uses quotations to subtly inform his own poetry (Keats, *Letters*, Vol. 1, pp. 193–4, 386–7). In the markings and annotations on his texts of Shakespeare's works we can trace his initial, excited responses, such as those that inspired his sonnet 'On Sitting Down to Read *King Lear* Once Again'. Whole letters become admiring, mini-anthologies of quotations offered in the enthusiast's spirit

---

[43] John Livingstone Lowes, *The Road to Xanadu: A Study in the Ways of the Imagination*, 2nd edn (Princeton: Princeton University Press, 1964), p. 311.

[44] For a longer account, see R. S. White, *Keats as a Reader of Shakespeare* (London: Athlone Press, 1987); and Beth Lau, 'John Keats', in Poole, *Lamb, Hazlitt, Keats*, pp. 109–59.

of 'I look upon fine Phrases like a Lover' but also often offer astute commentary (Vol. II, p. 139). In an early letter to the artist Benjamin Haydon, Keats, evidently with text in front of him, quotes the first seven lines of *Love's Labour's Lost*, knowing that the subject of future 'fame' for them both is what the egotistical Haydon wants to hear (Vol. I, pp. 140–1). He then turns to his own poetic failings and ambitions, quoting Edgar in the Dover Cliff scene in *King Lear* (IV.v.15) to express his feelings: 'I have been in such a state of Mind as to read over my Lines and hate them. I am one that "gathers Samphire, dreadful trade" – the Cliff of Poesy towers above me' (Vol. I, p. 141). Shakespeare, he hopes, will be the 'good Genius' and 'Presider' looking over both: 'I never quite despair and I read Shakspeare – indeed I shall I think never read any other Book much' (Vol. I, p. 142). From object of enthusiastic veneration and conduit for sociability, Shakespeare's words now become emotional therapy for Keats's 'horrid Morbidity of Temperament' and antidote to his 'disappointment' (Vol. I, p. 142). In a rapid association of ideas carried through Shakespearean quotations, Keats develops the subject of fame, turning to Hazlitt, who sees Shakespeare as providing contemporary political insight. He then quotes from *Antony and Cleopatra* to illuminate ways in which lives of public figures such as the waning Napoleon and Antony are 'as common in particulars as other Men's' (Vol. I, p. 144) and are inadvertently revealed in a casual, spontaneous gesture like Antony's display of petulance: 'He's walking in the garden – thus, *and spurns – The rush that lies* before him' (III.v.14–15, Keats' emphasis (Vol. I, p. 144). Beth Lau highlights Keats's preference for striking momentary pictorial effects of imagery while showing scant consideration for the Shakespearean contexts, but in a letter such as this, one can trace an associative meditation on 'fame', uncovering unexpected links and subtexts between quoted passages, moving from poetry to politics. In Keats's poetry, we generally find echoes rather than identifiable quotations, transmuted into 'unheard' melodies that are 'sweeter' than the heard, distant half-recollections and semi-unconscious allusions.[45]

Epigraphs

Novelists customarily used quotations, often from Shakespeare, as headpieces to chapters, to comment thematically on the action or as a shorthand

[45] John Keats, 'Ode on a Grecian Urn', in John Barnard (ed.) *John Keats: The Complete Poems*, 2nd edn (Harmondsworth: Penguin, 1977), p. 344. See R. S. White, 'Shakespearean Music in Keats' "Ode to a Nightingale"', *English*, 30 (1981), 217–29.

way to create an effect. Ann Radcliffe, in *The Mysteries of Udolpho: A Romance*, uses her chapter epigraphs as reminders of dramatic contexts from *Hamlet* and *Macbeth* to establish a gothic *grand guignol*: 'I could a tale unfold, whose lightest word / Would harrow up thy soul [SHAKSPEARE]'; later, Titania's words from *A Midsummer Night's Dream* prepare Radcliffe's readers for the supernatural.[46] Sometimes poets did the same in prefacing and framing their longer works with quotations. George Crabbe uses between three and five quotations from Shakespeare as epigraphs to each of his *Tales* (1812) mainly to shed light on his characters. Byron almost compulsively did the same, but usually to signal an ironic perspective. *English Bards and Scotch Reviewers* (1809) is headed satirically with

> 'I had rather be a kitten, and cry mew!
> Than one of these same metre ballad-mongers.'
> SHAKESPEARE (*1 Henry IV*, 3.1.125–6)

Cantos VI, VII and VIII of *Don Juan* were printed in 1823 as a single volume, and on its title page the ribald and irreverent tone of the work is signalled by Sir Toby's 'cakes and ale' speech from *Twelfth Night* (II.iii.99). Anna Barbauld begins her brief, spirited poem of domestic observation, 'Washing-Day', with an epigraph from Jacques's 'All the world's a stage' speech (*As You Like It*, II.vii.161–3): '… and their voice, / Turning again towards childish treble, pipes / And whistles in its sound.–'[47]

One thing that seems conspicuously missing from Romantic tendencies of quotation is 'the anxiety of influence', the sense of being inhibited by Shakespeare, unlike the Latin and Greek classical writers who, as Edward Young had written, '*intimidate* us with the splendor of their renown, and thus under diffidence bury our strength'.[48] By contrast, Shakespeare was regarded in the Romantic period as empowering and inspiring poets, and as the kind of 'affable familiar ghost' he himself refers to in Sonnet 86. His omnipresence as facilitator of conversational sociability in the theatre and in literature embodies the nexus between familiarity and novelty and highlights tensions between well-worn, even hackneyed, quotation and original creativity that partly characterise Romanticism.

---

[46] Ann Radcliffe, *The Mysteries of Udolpho*, 2 vols. (London: G. G. and J. Robinson, 1795), vol. I, chapter 2, p. 52; vol. II, chapter 2, p. 25. See also Kate Rumbold, 'Ann Radcliffe's Gothic epigraphs', in *Shakespeare and the Eighteenth-Century Novel: Cultures of Quotation from Samuel Richardson to Jane Austen* (Cambridge: Cambridge University Press, 2016), pp. 133–56.

[47] Anna Barbauld, 'Washing-Day', in *British Women Poets of the Romantic Era*, ed. Feldman, p. 67.

[48] Harold Bloom, *The Anxiety of Influence: A Theory of Poetry* (Oxford: Oxford University Press, 1973); Edward Young, *Conjectures on Original Composition* (1759), ed. Edith J. Morley (Manchester: Manchester University Press, 1918), p. 9.

CHAPTER 8

Quoting Shakespeare in the British Novel from Dickens to Wodehouse

Daniel Pollack-Pelzner

Hem! Shakspeare

Toward the beginning of the nineteenth century, Jane Austen could have a character in *Mansfield Park* remark offhandedly 'We all talk Shakespeare, use his similes, and describe with his descriptions.'[1] By the end of the century, '[w]e all' encompassed a far broader set than Austen's leisured gentry. Expanded access to Shakespeare on stage and page arose from the end of the patent theatres' monopoly on straight Shakespeare performance; the rise of touring and regional productions outside London; the publication of cheap editions of the complete works, often illustrated; and the circulation of Shakespeare in periodicals and proverb books.[2] Talking Shakespeare became widespread through organisations both voluntary (working men's institutes, women's study clubs) and compulsory: the 1870 Education Act required English schoolchildren to recite Shakespeare passages for their exams, establishing Shakespeare quotation as a form of nationally socialised identity (see Chapter 9).[3] As the cult that George Bernard Shaw – half sceptically, half enviously – dubbed 'Bardolatry' gained converts, talking Shakespeare diffused through space and time: outward, under the worrisome banner of the British Empire Shakespeare Society ('Using no other weapon but his name'), and backward, thanks to the historical project of the *Oxford English Dictionary*, whose editors told researchers that if they found a word in the Shakespeare concordance, they

---

[1] Jane Austen, *Mansfield Park*, ed. John Wiltshire (Cambridge: Cambridge University Press, 2005), pp. 190–1.

[2] For an overview of these changes, see Gail Marshall (ed.), *Shakespeare in the Nineteenth Century* (Cambridge: Cambridge University Press, 2012); and Kathryn Prince, *Shakespeare in the Victorian Periodicals* (New York: Routledge, 2008).

[3] Andrew Murphy, *Shakespeare for the People: Working-Class Readers, 1800–1900* (Cambridge: Cambridge University Press, 2008); Katherine West Scheil, *She Hath Been Reading: Women and Shakespeare Study Clubs in America* (Ithaca: Cornell University Press, 2012); Catherine Robson, *Heart Beats: Everyday Life and the Memorized Poem* (Princeton: Princeton University Press, 2012).

need not look for an earlier source – effectively turning the act of speaking English into the practice of quoting Shakespeare.[4]

If everyone was quoting Shakespeare, could everyone claim his burgeoning authority? For British novelists, this social question had a formal corollary in the distribution of Shakespearean speech between character and narrator, between quoted dialogue and authorial discourse. The critic Peter Bayne invoked a commonplace conjecture in an essay on Shakespeare and George Eliot: 'It has been said that if Shakespeare had lived in the Victorian age, he would have written novels.'[5] Yet the absence of a narrator from Shakespeare's plays puzzled Victorian critics who tried to imagine Shakespeare as a novelist. What would a narrative voice sound like for an author whose plays only give the voices of his characters?[6] And how could quoting Shakespeare help to establish that voice?[7]

Novelists heralded as Victorian Shakespeares frequently navigated the varied nineteenth-century practices of Shakespeare quotation (in the classroom, in compilation books, in stage spoofs) to construct the relationship between narrator and character, and to negotiate the dialogue between Shakespeare's voice and the voice of the novel. This chapter looks at three novelists whose practices intersect and contrast: George Eliot, who resists the Bardolatrous imputation of a Shakespearean character's wisdom to its author by distinguishing her own characters' inept Shakespeare quotations from her narrative voice; Thomas Hardy, who claims the authority of Shakespearean pastoral, regional language against the glib quotations of his more cosmopolitan characters; and a latter-day Victorian, P. G. Wodehouse, who plays the irreverent, defamiliarising gambits of Victorian Shakespeare burlesques against the educational and commonplace authority that Shakespeare quotations accrue.

As novelists developed a contemporary narrative voice, they also negotiated the distance between Shakespeare quotation as a relic of literary history and as a force of everyday speech. Charles Dickens, for

---

[4] George Bernard Shaw, 'Better than Shakespear?', in Edwin Wilson (ed.) *Shaw on Shakespeare*, (New York: Applause, 1961), p. 217; British Empire Shakespeare Society quoted in William Greenslade, 'Shakespeare and Politics', in Marshall, *Shakespeare in the Nineteenth Century*, pp. 229–50 (p. 244); John Willinsky, *Empire of Words: The Reign of the OED* (Princeton: Princeton University Press, 1994), pp. 57, 72.

[5] [Peter Bayne], 'Shakespeare and George Eliot', *Blackwood's Magazine* 133:810 (1883), 524–38 (p. 524).

[6] Adrian Poole discusses this question in his introduction to Adrian Poole (ed.), *Great Shakespeareans*, Vol. v: *Scott, Dickens, Eliot, Hardy* (London: Continuum, 2011), pp. 1–9.

[7] See Kate Rumbold's conclusion to her *Shakespeare and the Eighteenth-Century Novel: Cultures of Quotation from Samuel Richardson to Jane Austen* (Cambridge: Cambridge University Press, 2016), pp. 181–3.

instance, saturates his novels with Shakespeare quotations and with his characters' self-referential speech tags, so that his phrases would circulate as Shakespearean 'household words', in the quotation from *Henry V* that he chose for the masthead of his weekly journal (iv.iii.52).[8] Yet Dickens also mocks the nineteenth-century ideal that anyone could claim Shakespeare's quoted authority, or that anyone's words could boast a Shakespearean pedigree, through his use of a curious interjection, 'Hem! Shakspeare'.

The phrase pops up oddly in *The Pickwick Papers* (1836–7) when Mr Pickwick's roguish cell-mate in the Fleet Prison notices him waking up: ' "Why, bless the gentleman's honest heart and soul!" said the Zephyr, turning round and affecting the extremity of surprise; "the gentleman *is* awake. Hem; Shakspeare. How do you do, Sir? How is Mary and Sarah, Sir? and the dear lady at home, Sir – eh, Sir?" '[9] The Zephyr is mocking Pickwick with this excessively solicitous display, but it's not clear how Shakespeare plays into the joke. Is Shakespeare here in the vocative, a playfully honorific term of address for Pickwick parallel to 'Sir', or in the nominative, a faux citation for some unidentified quotation preceding? The perplexity recurs in *Bleak House* (1853), when the out-of-work Jobling is about to interrupt a job proposal from his friend Guppy, but their mutual friend 'the sagacious Smallweed checks him with a dry cough, and the words, "Hem! Shakspeare!" '.[10] Again, no obvious quotation has occurred to elicit this attribution; instead, it seems almost as if 'Shakspeare', with its guttural, plosive consonants, is the continuation of a cough.

When this phrase occurs in other Victorian writers, it's clearly an attributive tag for a preceding quotation. Gustave Louis Maurice Strauss, in his *Reminiscences of an Old Bohemian* (1883), explains that: '[i]n the olden days which I am now writing about, a kind of mania seemed to have taken possession of many of our set to deal in Shakespeare quotations on every occasion, in and out of season, always tacking to the tail, "hem – Shakspeare" '.[11] Whether Smallweed – a legal apprentice – or the Zephyr – a prison inmate – would have fallen into Strauss's bohemian set seems improbable; part of the humour of their citational coughs consists in the class pretension of their purporting to cite Shakespeare at all. The comic

---

[8] For an account of how Dickens's narrative strategies trade on Shakespeare, see Daniel Pollack-Pelzner, 'Dickens and Shakespeare's Household Words', *ELH*, 78:3 (Fall, 2011), 533–56. Valerie L. Gager catalogues and analyses hundreds of Shakespeare quotations in *Shakespeare and Dickens: The Dynamics of Influence* (Cambridge: Cambridge University Press, 1996).

[9] Charles Dickens, *The Pickwick Papers*, ed. Mark Wormald (London: Penguin, 1999), p. 553.

[10] Charles Dickens, *Bleak House*, ed. Nicola Bradbury (London: Penguin, 1996), p. 325.

[11] Gustave Louis Maurice Strauss, *Reminiscences of an Old Bohemian*, rev. edn (London: Downey, 1895), p. 285.

potential of tacking the abbreviated 'ahem' where no quotation exists seems also to have occurred to Dickens's contemporaries. In *Punch*, in author Francis Cowley Burnand's 'More Happy Thoughts' (1870), one Captain Dyngwell mocks a German professor researching the etymology of the word *Cockalorum*: 'it's "Whatever you please, my little dear, only blow your nose and don't breathe upon the glasses." To which he gives an air of authority, very confusing to the Professor, by adding, "hem! Shakspeare", which causes the good Herr another sleepless night in his library.'[12]

Dickens's joke seems to be casting his characters as Captain Dyngwells to their interlocutors' (or to the reader's) Professor, trading on Shakespeare's authority by hemming Shakespeare without, in fact, quoting him. But even if there's no Shakespearean quotation to cite, the form of the citation itself might bear a Shakespearean pedigree. In *As You Like It*, Celia tries to comfort her lovesick cousin Rosalind, who mourns that amorous woes have caught burs in her heart. 'Hem them away', Celia counsels, and Rosalind replies in kind: 'I would try, if I could cry "hem" and have him' (1.iii.14–15). Rosalind's longing cough becomes a punning speech-act, if a throat-clearing 'hem' could become a heart-filling summons for Orlando, the homophonic partner 'him'. Perhaps 'Hem; Shakspeare' sometimes echoes Rosalind's wish to possess the absent figure, willing Will into everyday speech. Eliot, Hardy and Wodehouse all work through the desire that Dickens summons to settle – or unsettle – who can speak in Shakespeare's voice.

The Shakespearean Narrator

In nineteenth-century reviews, George Eliot's narrative voice was often evaluated in relation to Shakespeare's, exemplifying that curious counter-factual assumption that Shakespeare would have been a Victorian novelist. That narrative comparison, in turn, conditioned Eliot's own use of Shakespeare quotations, which test the limits of commonplacing practices to represent authentic emotion. In a review of *Daniel Deronda* (1876), Edwin Whipple, a leading Boston critic, raised the common concern that Eliot's narrative voice interrupts the action of her novels; she 'ever appears on the scene as a looker-on', Whipple wrote, 'pouring forth a stream of remarks, wittily wise or tenderly wise'.[13] This riff on the title of Alexander Main's anthology, *Wise, Witty, and Tender Sayings in Prose and Verse Selected*

[12] Francis Cowley Burnand, 'More Happy Thoughts', *Punch*, 58 (5 March 1870), 89.
[13] Edwin P. Whipple, 'Review: *Daniel Deronda*', *North American Review*, 124:254 (1877), 31–52 (p. 34).

from the Works of George Eliot (1871), suggests the extent to which, as Leah Price has argued, the process of excerpting sayings from Eliot's works made her write further novels with an eye toward what could be excerpted.[14] (See Chapters 2 and 4 for Shakespeare's own use of this practice.) For Whipple, the adjectives with which Main describes Eliot's work, 'witty' and 'tender', have become adverbial modes of practice for Eliot herself. And in *Daniel Deronda*, Whipple sees this practice run amok: the novel 'so overflows with thoughts that an ordinary novel-reader, dazzled by the blaze which is intended to enlighten him, is tempted to complain that he is impeded rather than assisted by the subtle meditation which is brought in to reinforce clear representation'. The 'blaze' of Eliot's narration risks blinding her reader.

By what standard, then, should Whipple assess Eliot's voice? The answer may not be surprising: 'A reference to the greatest creator and delineator of human character that the world has ever seen is always in point.'[15] A familiar figure comes to Eliot's defence, transformed from a dramatist to a novelist:

> Shakespeare is open to the objection that, considered strictly from the point of view of the dramatist, he laid upon his characters a heavy burden of superfluous thought, which retarded the action of the play, and at the same time added nothing to our knowledge of the *dramatis personae*. Whatever violation of the rules of dramatic art Shakespeare may have committed, and however superfluous much of his thinking may appear to dramatic critics, the great body of his readers could ill spare the undramatic thinking he so profusely poured into his dramas; but if we could imagine Shakespeare as a writer of novels after the modern fashion, it is easy to conjecture that he would have retrenched some of the maxims of general wisdom which he put into the mouths of his characters to be spoken from the stage, and used them in commenting on his personages and on the incidents in which they appeared.[16]

Like Eliot, Shakespeare slowed down action with non-narrative thought, and just as *Daniel Deronda* 'overflows with thoughts', so many characters' thoughts in Shakespeare's plays could appear 'superfluous', 'profusely poured'. Yet, Whipple contends, most readers would not sacrifice those thoughts for a more streamlined plot, perhaps because they furnish the beauties for which Shakespeare and Eliot alike were cherished. Thus, 'if we

[14] Leah Price, *The Anthology and the Rise of the Novel* (Cambridge: Cambridge University Press, 2000), pp. 105–56.
[15] Whipple, 'Review: *Daniel Deronda*', p. 34.
[16] *Ibid.*, pp. 34–5.

could imagine Shakespeare as a writer of novels after the modern fashion', he would sound a lot like George Eliot. Whipple adds an orthodox caveat, 'George Eliot is no Shakespeare', but in going on to compare *Daniel Deronda* to *Hamlet*, Whipple establishes that the maxims that adorn Eliot's narrative possess Shakespearean pedigree.[17]

When Shakespearean maxims themselves appear in Eliot's novels, however, their status is much more conflicted. A central way that Bardolatry affected reading practices was in the frequent reattribution of maxims from Shakespeare's characters to Shakespeare himself, recasting characters' speech as authorial wisdom. That shift, which Whipple imagined as transforming Shakespeare into a novelist, characterised most nineteenth-century collections of Shakespeare quotations and proverbs, from Mary Cowden Clarke's to John Bartlett's.[18] George Eliot, who shared G. H. Lewes's scepticism toward the cult of Shakespeare worship, distanced herself from the Bardolatrous conflation of author and character by carefully distinguishing her narrator's speech from that of her characters. In particular, like her precursor Henry Fielding in the previous century, she reserved the power to quote Shakespeare persuasively for herself, exposing the aridity or absurdity of her characters' attempts.[19]

In *Middlemarch* (1871), for instance, Eliot reveals the hollowness of characters who supply Shakespeare commonplaces in lieu of authentic expression. When Dorothea Brooke, the heroine of *Middlemarch*, is described as a 'beauty', the term evokes those admirable literary extracts that appeared in collections of 'beauties' from the end of the eighteenth century (see Chapter 5). It also evokes the more quotidian ways in which archaic quotations circulated in contemporary prose: her plain attire threw her appearance into relief and 'gave her the impressiveness of a fine quotation from the Bible,—or from one of our elder poets,—in a paragraph of to-day's newspaper'.[20] So described, she becomes disturbingly collectable by one such as Mr Casaubon, who frequently substitutes fine quotations

[17] *Ibid.*, p. 35. Eliot, of course, famously questioned the ethical and social authority of 'men of maxims' in Book VII, Chapter 2 of *The Mill on the Floss* (ed. A. S. Byatt (London: Penguin, 1979)).

[18] On this practice, see Margreta de Grazia, 'Shakespeare in Quotation Marks', in Jean I. Marsden (ed.), *Appropriating Shakespeare: Post Renaissance Reconstructions of the Works and the Myth* (New York: Harvester Wheatsheaf, 1991), pp. 57–72; and Marjorie Garber, 'Bartlett's Familiar Shakespeare', in Marjorie Garber (ed.), *Profiling Shakespeare* (New York: Routledge, 2008).

[19] For more general accounts of Eliot denying her characters the maturity and breadth of vision her narrator attains, see J. Hillis Miller, *Victorian Subjects* (Durham: Duke University Press, 1991), p. 82; and Franco Moretti, *The Way of the World: The 'Bildungsroman' in European Culture*, 2nd edn, trans. Albert Sbragia (London: Verso, 2000), p. 222.

[20] George Eliot, *Middlemarch*, ed. Rosemary Ashton (London: Penguin, 1994), p. 7. Subsequent references are to this edition and are given in parentheses in the text.

for emotional disclosure. When, in their courtship, Dorothea offers 'expressions of devout feeling', Casaubon assents, 'usually with an appropriate quotation' (p. 33), just as he offers quoted judgements of the art of Rome in lieu of the personal preferences Dorothea seeks. Perhaps his most distressing appropriation of a beauty comes when Dorothea begs him to forgive her for questioning his working methods: ' "My dear Dorothea— 'who with repentance is not satisfied, is not of heaven nor earth'.—You do not think me worthy to be banished by that severe sentence", said Mr Casaubon, exerting himself to make a strong statement, and also to smile faintly' (p. 210). Casaubon's quoted sentence is 'severe' not only in the absoluteness of its edict but in its impersonal, negative construction. Rather than deliver the personal utterance 'I forgive you', Casaubon offers an extract that defines the abstract pronoun 'who' would not accept repentance. Worse, this quotation comes from the troubling conclusion to Shakespeare's *Two Gentlemen of Verona*, when Valentine finds his beloved Silvia being raped by his friend Proteus, and then abruptly forgives his apologetic friend with these words and, shockingly, offers to relinquish Silvia to him (v.iv.79–83). This passage prompted Eliot to write in her journal: 'That play disgusted me more than ever in the final scene where Valentine, on Proteus' mere begging pardon when he has no longer any hope of gaining his ends, says: "All that was mine in Silvia I give thee"!— Sylvia standing by.'[21] Casaubon is no Valentine – he is most unwilling to relinquish his bride to any rival lover – but his use of Valentine's line conveys a similar indifference to his bride's emotional state. The beauties of Shakespeare fade when they stand in place of real feeling, the product of exertion and a faint smile rather than Dorothea's 'quick sob' (p. 210).

Eliot brings out this tension between lived experience and citational emotion in other characters, too. For a young woman like Mary Garth, Shakespeare might well furnish the emotional experience of love, as in her playful catalogue of her 'experience' deflected into literary examples from *Romeo and Juliet* through *Waverley* (p. 138). The gradual replacement of literary commonplace with lived experience forms a classic novelistic education, from Don Quixote through Catherine Morland to Emma Bovary – a shift, as well, from romance to realism. What makes Casaubon disturbing is that he continues to take refuge in quotation even after he is married; he has become, in the narrator's own phrase, 'a lifeless embalmment of knowledge' (p. 196). Whereas Eliot as a narrator can draw animating mottoes from *Troilus and Cressida* (Chapter 26), *The Tempest* (Chapter 32), *2 Henry*

---

[21] Quoted in Gordon Haight, *George Eliot* (London: Penguin, 1986 (1968)), p. 178.

VI (Chapter 33), *Twelfth Night* (Chapter 41), *Henry VIII* (Chapter 42), *2 Henry IV* (Chapter 60), *Measure for Measure* (Chapters 66 and 71) and *Henry V* (Chapter 77), Casaubon's sense of quotation filters out life:

> If [Dorothea] spoke with any keenness of interest to Mr Casaubon, he heard her with an air of patience as if she had given a quotation from the Delectus familiar to him from his tender years, and sometimes mentioned curtly what ancient sects or personages had held similar ideas, as if there were too much of that sort in stock already. (p. 361)

Critics have associated Shakespeare with feminine sympathy in Eliot's novels, but the sympathy that Eliot frequently elicits for Casaubon does not extend to his practice of quotation.[22] Even Shakespeare's Sonnets, which Eliot cites as mottoes for Chapters 24, 58 and 82, only emphasise Casaubon's sterility when he derives his ideas of masculinity from their conventional reproductive imperative: 'no sonneteer had insisted on Mr Casaubon's leaving a copy of himself' (p. 278).

Eliot's anti-Bardolatrous demarcation between author's and characters' quotations extends, in certain cases, to the mottoes themselves.[23] Whereas Walter Scott, Eliot's precedent for reviving the practice of chapter epigraphs, attributes his Shakespearean epigraphs in *Waverley* directly to 'Shakespeare', in keeping with the search for authorial wisdom common to quotation books, Eliot attributes her motto for Chapter 60 of *Middlemarch* to the character from *2 Henry IV* who speaks it, Justice Shallow.[24] This particular epigraph serves up the pretensions of any character to authorial quotability: 'Good phrases are surely, and ever were, very commendable.' That ostensible praise is rapidly deflated by its source – Shakespeare's verbose Justice, appraising a rather pedestrian expression of one of Falstaff's henchmen – as well as its apparent target within the chapter: Eliot's equally grandiloquent auctioneer, Borthrop Trumbull, 'an amateur of superior phrases' (p. 310) like Justice Shallow, who inflates the value of mediocre merchandise with lofty language, jumbled poetic allusions and pretentious pronunciations. Sustaining the Shakespearean foolery, Eliot has Trumbull sell a motley lot to 'a young Slender of the neighbourhood' (p. 607) – alluding to Justice Shallow's dim-witted nephew in *The Merry Wives of*

---

[22] Marianne Novy, *Engaging with Shakespeare: Responses of George Eliot and Other Women Novelists* (Athens: University of Georgia Press, 1994); Robert Sawyer, *Victorian Appropriations of Shakespeare* (Madison: Fairleigh Dickinson University Press, 2003).

[23] For an overview of the varied functions of Eliot's mottoes, see David Leon Higdon, 'George Eliot and the Art of the Epigraph', *Nineteenth-Century Fiction*, 25:2 (1970), 127–51.

[24] See, for example, the epigraphs to Chapters 66 and 68 of Walter Scott, *Waverley*, ed. Andrew Hook (London: Penguin, 2004).

Windsor – after he has articulated his oratorical method: 'It what we call a figure of speech – speech at a high figure, as one may say' (p. 311). Shallow's limited profundity, excerpted as a motto, not only jabs at Trumbull's rhetorical economy, but also undermines the activity of commending 'good phrases' that characters like him aspire to practise. Even if part of Eliot's novelistic project is to extend Shakespearean sympathy to figures such as Trumbull and Casaubon, whose blinkered language impedes their human relationships, she questions the expanding nineteenth-century practice of bolstering dubious speech with a Shakespearean attribution. The power to quote and be quoted successfully is Eliot's alone.

Return of the Native Tongue

Thomas Hardy shared Eliot's scepticism toward glib Shakespeare quotation, yet he constructed a different kind of Shakespearean narrative voice: one that rooted Shakespeare's authority less in the proper application of commonplace mottoes than in regional, sylvan speech, and that negotiated the tension between Shakespeare as a signifier of linguistic urbanity and Shakespeare as the common tongue. For Hardy, Shakespeare's language seemed closely akin to nature and its traditional inhabitants. When Hardy began to read Shakespeare intensively at the age of twenty-three (in the same edition, by Samuel Weller Singer, that Dickens had first consulted thirty years earlier), he seemed particularly excited to find correspondences between archaic phrases in the plays and idioms from his native Dorset. The marginal notes in his edition become more copious when Hardy encounters an odd phrase that has an equivalent in Dorset dialect: Hamlet's expression 'miching mallecho' (III.ii.124), for instance, which Hardy noted was still in Dorset parlance, or Ophelia's 'dupped the chamber door' (IV. ii.53) as a match to the Dorset idiom 'do the door'.[25] It was as though he were discovering that his native lexicon, which he had thought an impediment to his untutored literary ambitions, might turn out to be his way in; he'd unwittingly been talking Shakespeare all along. And in his early works, particularly *Under the Greenwood Tree* (1872), the sylvan world of Dorset labourers talks Shakespeare as well. Patricia Ingham has argued that the language of nature for Hardy is Darwinian, and were it to reflect a poetic tradition, one might expect Hardy to align his archaic Wessex with Old English verse, as his contemporary Gerard Manley Hopkins does, or,

[25] Dennis Taylor reproduces Hardy's marginal annotations in 'Hardy's Copy of *Hamlet*', *Thomas Hardy Journal*, 20:3 (2004), 87–112.

if in a pastoral mode, then to the classical model of Virgil's Eclogues.[26] Hardy, however, marks his pastoral as distinctly Shakespearean. *Under the Greenwood Tree* takes its title from the song in *As You Like It* that beseeches any willing courtier who wishes to 'turn his merry note / Unto the sweet bird's throat' to 'come hither, come hither, come hither' to the Forest of Arden (II.v.4–5); and the nightingale that serenades the wedded couple at the end of the novel sings: 'Tippiwit! swe-e-et! ki-ki-ki! Come hither, come hither, come hither!'.[27] Shakespeare's language has become interfused with the sounds of Hardy's native land.

Yet talking Shakespeare for Hardy also meant to participate in the world of literary ambition, sophisticated education and linguistic manipulation that threatened his sylvan ideal. Mastering Shakespeare's language was key to Hardy's own self-imposed programme of literary apprenticeship: he copied out many passages from the plays in his notebooks, glossing unfamiliar words and playing with distinctive phrases. But the characters in Hardy's novels who demonstrate the greatest facility with Shakespearean quotations, as Adrian Poole has argued, are often the least to be trusted.[28] Alec d'Urberville, for example, encounters Tess 'sitting like Im-patience on a monument' (a twist on *Twelfth Night*, II.iv.III), 'suited the action to the word' (Hamlet's advice to the players, III.ii.16) 'and whistled a line of "Take O take those lips away"' (*Measure for Measure*'s song of a lover's perfidy, IV.i.I).[29] Hardy tells us that 'the allusion was lost on Tess', ensuring that it won't be on the reader, but also marking the gap between Durbeyfield innocence of literary conceits and d'Urberville dexterity. Even as Hardy courts a readership that will recognise his own quotational facility, he exposes the danger of those who wield that skill too well.

Hardy's challenge, then, was to develop a narrative voice that could deploy the sophistication of Shakespearean quotation without losing its grounding in native speech. *The Woodlanders* (1887), written in his major period between *The Mayor of Casterbridge* (1886) and *Tess of the d'Urbervilles* (1891), brings the conflict between Shakespeare as traditional woodland knowledge and Shakespeare as threatening literary sophistication into dramatic focus. The novel's moral stalwarts, the woodsman Giles

[26] Patricia Ingham, 'Introduction', in Thomas Hardy, *The Woodlanders*, ed. Patricia Ingham (London: Penguin, 1998), pp. xvi–xxxiv; subsequent references are to this edition and are given in parentheses in the text. See also Jonathan Wike, 'The World as Text in Hardy's Fiction', *Nineteenth-Century Literature*, 47:4 (1993), 455–71.

[27] Thomas Hardy, *Under the Greenwood Tree*, ed. Tim Dolin (London: Penguin, 1998), p. 159.

[28] Adrian Poole, *Shakespeare and the Victorians* (London: Arden Shakespeare, 2004), p. 147.

[29] Thomas Hardy, *Tess of the d'Urbervilles*, ed. Scott Elledge, 3rd edn (New York: Norton, 1991), p. 45.

Winterborne and his unrequited admirer, Marty South, are distinguished by their ability to decipher the 'wondrous world of sap and leaves'; they can 'read its hieroglyphs as ordinary writing'. As Giles's beloved, Grace Melbury, consoles Marty: 'You and he could speak in a tongue that nobody else knew— … the tongue of the trees and fruits and flowers themselves' (pp. 330–1). That tongue is also Shakespeare's. The banished Duke in *As You Like It* fantasises that, in the Forest of Arden, he will gain something like the capacity of Marty and Giles to find 'tongues in trees' and 'books in the running brooks' (ii.i.16). And as Marty's and Giles's tongues echo Shakespeare's, the narrator speaks about them in Shakespearean terms. Realising that she has wronged Giles by breaking their engagement, Grace, the narrator tells us, pities him as:

> one who, notwithstanding these things, had, like Hamlet's friend, borne himself throughout his scathing
> 'As one, in suffering all, that suffers nothing',
> investing himself thereby with a real touch of sublimity. (p. 219)

In his copy of *Hamlet*, Hardy had written his own father's name next to these lines in praise of Horatio (iii.ii.64); Grace's appreciation gives Giles a touch of both Horatio and Hardy senior. But this brush with literary pedigree doesn't tarnish Giles's virtue; on the contrary, he is to Grace an exemplar of 'nature unadorned', of 'undiluted manliness', and the best of 'unvarnished men' (pp. 206, 219).

Marty, too, receives a painful touch of Shakespeare. In Sonnet 111 – a Hardyesque lament that his lowly profession as a public playwright makes him ill-suited to genteel life – the speaker says 'my nature is subdued / To what it works in, like the dyer's hand' (lines 6–7). An early review picked up the phrase: Havelock Ellis, who also praised Hardy for having created Shakespearean comic peasants, thought the intimate connection between his rustics and their environment deserved particular mention. They 'have grown to have something of the contours of the things among which they live', Ellis wrote; their 'nature is subdued to what it works in, like the dyer's hand'.[30] But when Marty helps her ailing father split wood into spars, the narrator reveals that her palm 'was red and blistering, as if this present occupation were not frequent enough with her to subdue it to what it worked in' (p. 10). Marty's plight punningly echoes Shakespeare's simile: the dye that casts its worker's hand becomes 'a cast of the die of

---

[30] Havelock Ellis, 'Thomas Hardy's Novels', *Westminster Review*, 119 (April 1883), 334–64.

destiny [that] had decided that the girl should handle the tool' (p. 10). Giles is ultimately subdued to the woods he works in: though Grace becomes drawn to his earthy appearance in 'leggings dyed with fruit-stains' (p. 206), her appearance at his cabin in a storm forces him outside to die under the inhospitable branches.

Hardy contrasts these steadfast Shakespearean rustics with the fickleness of Edred Fitzpiers, the newly arrived county doctor, who reads poetry assiduously but lacks the woodlanders' knowledge of tongues in trees. 'Casting a die by impulse' leads him to woo Grace away from Giles (p. 163); after he forsakes her for a former actress, he attempts to win back her heart with a smooth tongue, claiming his love has deepened since his infidelity.

> 'It is a different kind of love altogether', said he. 'Less passionate; more profound. It has nothing to do with the material conditions of the object at all; much to do with her character and goodness, as revealed by closer observation. "Love talks with better knowledge, and knowledge with dearer love."'
> 'That's out of *Measure for Measure*', said she slily.
> 'Oh yes – I meant it as a citation', blandly replied Fitzpiers. 'Well then, why not give me a very little bit of your heart again?'
> The crash of a felled tree in the remote depths of the wood recalled the past at that moment, and all the homely faithfulness of Winterborne. 'Don't ask it! My heart is in the grave with Giles', she replied staunchly.[31] (p. 340)

It's a risky business to prove your wiser affections by quoting the Duke in *Measure for Measure*, who has abdicated his office and disguised himself as a friar and is now reproving a lecher for his ill-informed protestations (III.ii.152–3); it's riskier still to pass off the Duke's glib chiasmus ('Love … knowledge … knowledge … love') as your own. Hardy's quotation marks suggest that he meant his readers to detect Fitzpiers's citation, but the blandness of Fitzpiers's reply hints that he did not intend to be as forthcoming with his source. The 'crash of a felled tree' that brings Grace back to Giles's fidelity overwhelms Fitzpiers's literary language with the language of the woods. Yet Grace, whose expensive education has equipped her to recognise a Shakespearean line – perhaps even better than Fitzpiers, who may take it as a commonplace – ends up returning to the doctor, leaving Marty to pine alone over Giles's grave. Though a country girl by birth, Grace is no Tess; the allusion – in fact, quotation – is not lost on her, and the novel permits her the possibility of a respectable middle-class future, perhaps with a copy of Samuel Weller Singer's ten-volume edition on her bookshelf.

---

[31] I am indebted to Heather Brink-Roby for drawing my attention to this passage.

Yet the crash of the tree also resounds with 'the crash of broken commandments' that Hardy later contended was 'as necessary an accompaniment to the catastrophe of a tragedy as the noise of drum and cymbals to a triumphal march'.[32] For a novel that longs for the pastoral comedy of *As You Like It* while recognising the stoic tragedy of *Hamlet* (in addition to several references to the self-destructive jealousy of *Othello* and the disturbed ambition of *Macbeth*), the uneasy comedy of *Measure for Measure* (or of 'All's well that ends well', as an old woodlander assures Grace after her husband's departure (p. 211)) may best match the novel's complex tone and genre.[33] And like Eliot's uniquely authoritative narrator, it may be only Hardy the narrator who can achieve the blend of education and empathy to wield Shakespearean quotations without abusing his audience. Toward the end of a century anxious about the power to speak through the Bard's voice, Shakespeare quotation helps Hardy negotiate the challenge of gaining literary sophistication without losing the language of nature.

Shakespeare Burlesque

While Hardy attempts to naturalise Shakespeare's voice, P. G. Wodehouse brings out the defamiliarising comedy of warbling native wood-notes wild. Jumbled allusions, misattributed quotations, high verse cuddled up to street slang – the conventions of Victorian novelists crack open in Wodehouse's frothy novels, especially those narrated in what Richard Usborne has dubbed the 'magpie babble' of Wodehouse's effervescently dim bachelor Bertie Wooster.[34] As if in parody of a Victorian recitation curriculum, his mash-up sentences play Shakespeare quotation against half-remembered Victorian schoolboy verse, newspaper lingo and Boy Scout hokum: 'Beneath the thingummies of what-d'you-call-it', Bertie says of his own indomitability, 'his head, wind and weather permitting, is as a rule bloody but unbowed, and if the slings and arrows of outrageous fortune want to crush his proud spirit, they have to pull their socks up and make a special effort'.[35] Wodehouse implies that if the 'To be or not to be'

[32] Thomas Hardy, 'Candour in English Fiction', *New Review*, 2:8 (January 1890), 15–21.
[33] Frederick S. Boas, *Shakspere and His Predecessors* (New York: Charles Scribner's Sons, 1896), pp. 344–5.
[34] Richard Usborne, *Plum Sauce: A P. G. Wodehouse Companion* (New York: Overlook, 2003), p. 60.
[35] P. G. Wodehouse, *Jeeves and the Feudal Spirit* (New York: Scribner, 2000 (1954)), p. 219. Subsequent references are to this edition and are given in parentheses in the text.

soliloquy wants pride of place in Bertie's patois, it'll have to take up arms to get it.

Wodehouse is seldom placed among British novelistic royalty with Dickens, Eliot and Hardy, but focusing on the role that Shakespeare quotation plays in constructing a narrative voice helps to reveal Wodehouse's role as a jester in that court. Shakespeare suffers slings and arrows in the Jeeves and Wooster novels (as Bertie's accounts of his adventures with his gentleman's personal gentleman are known), arising frequently from Bertie's inability to recognise Shakespeare when he appears, an Eliotic gap between knowing author and clueless character. 'There is a method by means of which Mrs. Travers can be extricated from her sea of troubles. Shakespeare', Jeeves informs Bertie in *Jeeves and the Feudal Spirit* (1954), attributing his brief *Hamlet* quotation, but Bertie mistakes the nominative for the vocative: 'I didn't know why he was addressing me as Shakespeare, but I motioned him to continue' (p. 126). (Were Dickens's Zephyr to accost him with a 'Hem! Shakspeare', Bertie would probably offer to shake hands.) When the phrase next surfaces in a conversation with said Mrs Travers, Bertie attributes it to Jeeves: 'We've got to get you out of your sea of troubles, as Jeeves calls it. Everything else is relatively unimportant. My thoughts of self are merely in about the proportion of the vermouth to the gin in a strongish dry martini' (pp. 148–9). This alcoholic definition of self-consciousness could account for Bertie's sloshed appropriation of Shakespeare for his better half, were it not so pervasive. The joke presumes the reader's greater literacy, but literature itself comes under redefinition. Pondering the course ahead, Bertie again summons his Bartlett's Familiar Jeeves:

> 'If it were … what's that expression of yours?'
> 'If it were done when 'tis done, then 'twere well it were done quickly, sir.'
> 'That's right. No sense in standing humming and hawing.'
> 'No, sir. There is a tide in the affairs of men which, taken at the flood, leads on to fortune.'
> 'Exactly', I said.
> I couldn't have put it better myself. (pp. 128–9)

Jeeves adroitly channels Macbeth and Brutus to Bertie's horseback cliché, but the effect is less of dramatic poetry entering the novel than of companion adages holding a conversation.

Wodehouse's fictions play on all sorts of Shakespeare quotation practices, from half-remembered touchstones ('sleep which does something which has slipped my mind to the something sleeve of care') to misattributed catchphrases ('Did [Archimedes] say Eureka? I thought it was Shakespeare') to maxims reassigned from the Bard to the butler. (A pal's vacillation is 'rather like that of the cat in the adage, which, according to Jeeves, and I suppose he knows, let "I dare not" wait upon "I would."')[36] In *Joy in the Morning* (1947), Jeeves functions explicitly as an index of Shakespeare quotations, supplying thematically grouped beauties on demand. 'What did Shakespeare say about ingratitude?', an angry Boko Fittleworth asks Jeeves after being spurned for a well-intentioned deed. ' "Blow, blow, thou winter wind", sir', Jeeves replies, ' "thou art not so unkind as man's ingratitude". He also alludes to the quality as "thou marble-hearted fiend"' (p. 121). This is AskJeeves.com *avant la lettre*; it's also an enactment of the compilations, from the seventeenth century through Thomas Dolby's *The Shakespearean Dictionary* (1832), that list extracts under alphabetised topic headings. (Dolby includes both Amiens's song from *As You Like It* and Lear's curse at Goneril under 'Ingratitude'.)[37] Bertie applies Matthew Arnold's famous praise of Shakespeare to Jeeves – 'Others abide our question. Thou art free' – but the effect is less to cast Jeeves as Shakespeare the poet than to frame him as the Victorian Shakespeare-function: the embodiment of wisdom, captured in iterable phrases.[38]

Why such relentless riffs on the cultural sanctity of Shakespearean quotation? Wodehouse brings the Shakespearean negotiations of Dickens, Eliot and Hardy to a head: his narrative voice summons the authority of Bardolatrous quotation while also spoofing the reverential practice of attributing everyday speech to the Bard. It's a dialectic common to nineteenth-century Shakespeare burlesques, which irreverently dug up the now-hallowed ground of Shakespeare's language. In his study of these popular Victorian entertainments, Richard Schoch proposes that 'burlesque continually shifts its focus from Shakespeare's texts as dramatic masterpieces to Shakespeare's texts as objects of canonization' – echoing Eliot's scepticism toward Bardolatry.[39] Wodehouse acted in at least one such burlesque during his last year at Dulwich School – W. S. Gilbert's

[36] These three examples come, respectively, from P. G. Wodehouse, *The Code of the Woosters* (New York: Vintage, 1975 (1938)), pp. 222 and 199; and P. G. Wodehouse, *Joy in the Morning* (New York: Perennial, 1983 (1947)), p. 19. Subsequent references are to these editions and are given in parentheses in the text.

[37] Thomas Dolby, *The Shakespearean Dictionary* (London: Smith, Elder, 1832), pp. 154–5.

[38] P. G. Wodehouse, *Thank You, Jeeves* (New York: Overlook Press, 2000 (1934)), p. 144. Subsequent references are to this edition and are given in parentheses in the text.

[39] Richard W. Schoch, *Not Shakespeare: Bardolatry and Burlesque in the Nineteenth Century* (Cambridge: Cambridge University Press, 2002), p. 67.

Rosencrantz and Guildenstern (1874) – and his own Shakespeare games could be read in the Victorian burlesque tradition.[40] The school paper singled out for praise a scene from Gilbert's burlesque in which Wodehouse, as Guildenstern, partnered with Rosencrantz to frustrate Hamlet's 'To be or not to be' soliloquy by taking his rhetorical questions literally.[41]

HAM: For who would bear the whips and scorns of time –
ROS: (*as guessing a riddle*) *Who'd* bear the whips and scorns? Now, let me see.
  Who'd *bear* them, eh?
GUIL: (*same business*) Who'd bear the *scorns* of time?
ROS: (*correcting him*) The *whips* and scorns.
GUIL: The whips and scorns, of course.

(HAMLET *about to protest.*)

Don't tell us – let us guess – the *whips* of time?[42]

Victorian Shakespeare burlesques point out the gap between reverent Shakespeare quotation and commonplace speech, a gap Wodehouse never fails to mind. Rosencrantz and Guildenstern's quizzical repetition of Hamlet's culturally enshrined words ('the *whips* of time?') echoes throughout Bertie's dialogues with Jeeves, Shakespearean soliloquy turned to contemporary banter. A speech from *Twelfth Night*, for instance, gets teased in *Thank You, Jeeves* (1934), when Bertie explains a hitch in an American heiress's prospects for marrying his friend Chuffy:

> 'And what is worrying her is that he does not tell his love, but lets conceal-ment like … like what, Jeeves?'
>   'A worm i' the bud, sir.'
>   'Feed on his something …'
>   'Damask cheek, sir.'
>   'Damask? You're sure?'
>   'Quite sure, sir.' (pp. 50–1)

A set-piece description from the eighteenth-century novel onward, Viola's account of unexpressed love is defamiliarised as a line Bertie feels he ought to know but can neither quite remember nor quite credit.[43] A few pages

---

[40] For an account of this tradition, which turns to Dickens instead of Wodehouse, see Daniel Pollack-Pelzner, 'Shakespeare Burlesque and the Performing Self', *Victorian Studies*, 54:3 (Spring, 2012), 401–9.

[41] Robert McCrum, *Wodehouse: A Life* (London: Viking, 2004), p. 36n427.

[42] W. S. Gilbert, *Rosencrantz and Guildenstern* (1891), in W. S. Gilbert, *Original Plays* (London: Chatto & Windus, 1924), pp. 81–2.

[43] See Rumbold, *Shakespeare and the Eighteenth-Century Novel*.

later, he has absorbed the Shakespearean diction into his personal slang, but remains skeptical:

> 'But suppose the sale of the house does not go through?'
>   'In that case, I fear, sir ...'
> 'The damask cheek will continue to do business at the old stand indefinitely?'
>   'Exactly, sir.'
>   'You really are sure it is "damask"?'
>   'Yes, sir.'
> 'But it doesn't seem to mean anything.'
>   'An archaic adjective, sir. I fancy it is intended to signify a healthy complexion.'
>   'Well, Chuffy's got that.'
>   'Yes, sir.'
> 'But what good's a healthy complexion if you don't get the girl?'
>   'Very true, sir.' (pp. 54–5)

Wodehouse as Guildenstern worried over 'whips' and 'scorns'; here, through Bertie, he challenges the damask Elizabethan lexicon that we accept as natural in applying Shakespearean wisdom to our own situation. While Dickens spoofed the 'Hem! Shakspeare' tag as an empty signifier of cultural authority, an invocation of Shakespeare's status for meaningless speech, Wodehouse's burlesque patter asks if Shakespearean language itself has become meaningless, a set of adages devoid of any specific referent. When we all talk Shakespeare, as Austen's Edmund Bertram posited, are we really saying anything?

'Shakespeare's stuff is different from mine', Wodehouse once remarked, 'but that is not to say that it is inferior'.[44] Wodehouse loved Shakespeare; *Love's Labour's Lost*, the most verbally pyrotechnic of the comedies, was his favourite play, and when he was briefly interned by the Nazis in 1940, the first book he packed for captivity was *The Complete Works of Shakespeare*.[45] It's easy, then, to read the narrator Bertie's frequent dismissal of Shakespeare as one more ironic feature of his miseducated outlook, even if his narration ultimately provides more canny quotations than the savvy author/duped character dyad might imply.

The novel Wodehouse was drafting when the Nazis captured him, *Joy in the Morning*, lets Bertie loose at Shakespeare's expense. Bertie takes Shakespeare as the paradigmatic writer, but makes him the lunatic, rather than the poet: 'One has, of course, to make allowances for writers, all of

---

[44] P. G. Wodehouse, 'Kind Words for Shakespeare', *Punch*, 230 (1956), 328.
[45] McCrum, *Wodehouse*, pp. 211, 276.

them being more or less loony. Look at Shakespeare, for instance. Very unbalanced. Used to go about stealing ducks' (p. 55; 'deer' according to legend, but 'ducks' sounds funnier and points to Bertie's misperception). When one particularly loony writer, Boko Fittleworth, recently dumped by his fiancée, asks Bertie 'what construction you place on the words "I never want to see or speak to you again in this world or the next, you miserable fathead"', Bertie comforts him: 'You can't go by what a girl says, when she's giving you the devil for making a chump of yourself. It's like Shakespeare. Sounds well, but doesn't mean anything' (pp. 127–8). This principle guides Bertie's discussion with Jeeves of the Ghost's words to Hamlet (prompted by a request from Boko to insult his Uncle Percy, who objects to his marriage):

> 'I shall be shortly telling Uncle Percy things about himself which will do something to his knotted and combined locks which at the moment has slipped my memory.'
> 'Make his knotted and combined locks to part and each particular hair to stand on end like quills upon the fretful porpentine, sir.'
> 'Porpentine?'
> 'Yes, sir.'
> 'That can't be right. There isn't such a thing.' (p. 158)

A moment later, 'porpentine' again receives the 'damask' treatment:

> 'If I could show you that list Boko drafted out of the things he wants me to say – I unfortunately left it in my room, where it fell from my nerveless fingers – your knotted and combined locks would part all right, believe me. You're sure it's porpentine?'
> 'Yes, sir.'
> 'Very odd. But I suppose half the time Shakespeare just shoved down anything that came into his head.' (p. 160)

Yet just as the high–low gag has run its course, Bertie finds the Shakespearean archaism literalised:

> It was not immediately that the tired eyelids closed in sleep, for some hidden hand had placed a hedgehog between the sheets – practically, you might say, a fretful porpentine. Assuming this to be Boko's handiwork, I was strongly inclined to transfer it to his couch. Reflecting, however, that while this would teach him a much needed lesson it would be a bit tough on the porpentine, I took the latter into the garden and loosed it into the grass. (p. 224)

One way to read this omnipresent 'porpentine' would be as a kind of schoolboy currency, like Boko's hedgehog: a curio swapped between Oxford and Eton alumni in memory of erstwhile classroom pranks. For Bertie, 'the old *in statu pupillari* days' justify any fumbled literary quotations that don't get attributed to Jeeves. This is from *The Code of the Woosters* (1938), when a stolen policeman's helmet turns up in Bertie's room, to the shock of all present:

> Pop Bassett, like the chap in the poem which I had to write out fifty times at school for introducing a white mouse into the English Literature hour, was plainly feeling like some watcher of the skies when a new planet swims into his ken, while Aunt Dahlia and Constable Oates resembled respectively stout Cortez staring at the Pacific and all his men looking at each other with a wild surmise, silent upon a peak in Darien. (p. 204)

Between Bertie's chipper slang ('Pop', 'chap') and Keats's lyricism ('wild surmise'), there's a delinquent spin to the allusion: Bertie can quote Keats's sonnet 'On First Looking into Chapman's Homer', not because he paid attention in English Literature hour, but because he was punished for trying to subvert it. When Bertie needles Shakespeare's 'porpentine', he can tip his cap to the English prep school curriculum and, in the spirit of Gilbert's burlesque, thumb his nose at the same time.

It's tempting to read this polysemous porpentine as a figure of fugitive language itself. When Bertie tries to turn a prosaic 'hedgehog' into a poetic 'porpentine' out of *Hamlet*, the figural slips away from the literal, inevitably 'loosed' from the constraints of individual usage. In the mode of Victorian Shakespeare burlesque, Wodehouse tests the relationship between Shakespearean phrases and vernacular speech. Earlier in *The Code of the Woosters*, when Bertie expresses doubt over whether to steal a particular silver cow creamer that his aunt has asked him to pinch, Jeeves expresses solidarity through Hamlet's soliloquy:

> 'I quite understand, sir, and thus the native hue of resolution is sicklied o'er with the pale cast of thought, and enterprises of great pith and moment with this regard their currents turn awry and lose the name of action.'
> 'Exactly! You take the words out of my mouth.' (p. 33)

Of course, the chance that Hamlet's words could ever come unfiltered out of Bertie's magpie mouth is slightly lower than the odds on monkeys with a typewriter. But there's the rub: Wodehouse establishes Shakespeare quotations as the voice of omniscience even as he spoofs them as hackneyed archaisms. We're far enough from Shakespeare that his sayings have entered the curriculum but too far for them to pass as the word on the street. A narrating self that speaks Shakespeare is a self always in quotation marks. Put another way, Wodehouse authorises Shakespeare quotations without ever naturalising them. Bertie's favourite attribution for a poetic line, besides Jeeves, is the genial, general 'as the fellow said', but Wodehouse invites us to question whether Shakespeare could plausibly pass as anyone's contemporary fellow.

If the Victorian cult of Shakespeare established both his singularity and his universality, unique among all writers for being uniquely applicable to everyone, novelists from Dickens to Wodehouse interrogated that cult, even as they traded on its currency. Shakespeare quotation conveyed an authority that could all too easily be traduced or travestied. Although Eliot was regarded as Shakespearean because of the quotable maxims that distinguished her narrative voice, she questioned her characters' impulse to substitute quotation for authentic expression. Hardy found that expression in a narrative language that seemed to quote Shakespeare naturally, in contrast to his characters' manipulative seduction-by-quotation, but Wodehouse channelled the burlesque tradition to ask whether the archaisms of Shakespearean speech could ever sound natural three centuries later, even as they amassed an authoritative force. It may be true that, in a British novel, characters all talk Shakespeare, but not without a higher narrative authority to take the words out of their mouth.

CHAPTER 9

Pedagogy and Propaganda
The Uses of Quotation, 1750–1945

Frans De Bruyn; Gail Marshall; Ton Hoenselaars

QUOTING SHAKESPEARE IN POLITICAL CONTEXTS
FROM THE MID-EIGHTEENTH CENTURY TO
THE VICTORIANS

Frans De Bruyn

As Shakespeare acquired the status of national poet in the second half of the eighteenth century, the very act of quoting him became, culturally speaking, a political gesture: an implicit invocation of the bard's authority on behalf of one's argument and a validation of one's intellectual credentials. But this is to define the political in the most general terms. The following case study confines itself, therefore, to specifically defined political contexts: parliamentary discourse, newspaper editorialising, pamphlet polemics – and it touches on a range of political communities: political actors and politicians, journalists and commentators, and working class and revolutionary radicals.

In order to grasp the political import of acts of citation, it is important to recognise that practices of quotation, both in written texts and in political oratory, underwent a significant evolution in the eighteenth and nineteenth centuries, occasioning much self-conscious questioning. 'I scarcely ever quote; the reason is, I always think', asserted the political radical Thomas Paine in 1776, rejecting the habit of quotation as 'a sign of a diffident and derivative mind'.[1] In an essay on quotation, James Boswell similarly acknowledges that his readers are likely to regard the practice as 'downright pedantry', and for Thomas De Quincey, direct quotations 'always express a mind not fully possessed by its subject, and abate the tone of earnestness which ought to preside either in very passionate or in very

---

[1] Thomas Paine, *The Writings of Thomas Paine*, 2 vols. (New York: G. P. Putnam's Sons, 1906), Vol. 1, p. 235.

severe composition'.[2] In the context of political persuasion, these disparaging views can be linked to the historical roots of political quotation in the ancient rhetorical traditions of topoi and commonplaces – the topics, rhetorical strategies, passages and illustrations that a speaker would find useful in developing different kinds of arguments (such as a legal defence, eulogy or political debate).[3] The rhetorical study of such commonplaces was in decline during the eighteenth century. Citing an over-familiar passage by Shakespeare to illustrate an argument could, by the early 1800s, prompt charges of unoriginality or insincerity. Indeed, as Fiona Ritchie and R. S. White point out in Chapter 7, the use of Shakespeare for elocutionary training was disparaged by Charles Lamb and others.

But other culturally significant uses of quotation, displacing the commonplace tradition, emerged. A notable instance is British parliamentary debate, in which speakers habitually cited classical authors and English poets and dramatists in the course of their speeches. A memorable instance, recorded by Nathaniel Wraxall, a political memoirist who served as a Member of Parliament in the 1780s and 1790s, was the debate in late 1783 on the East India Bill, in which 'History, antient and modern, Poetry, Scripture, all were successively pressed into the service … of the contending parties'. Shakespeare featured prominently: he and other vernacular poets were by this time displacing classical authors as prime sources for public quotation. During the debate, 'Some of the finest Passages of Shakespeare, taken from his "Julius Caesar", were applied by [John] Scott and [Richard] Arden to [Charles James] Fox', including a line from a soliloquy (ii.i.10–34) in which Brutus weighs the risks of empowering Caesar by crowning him: 'It is the bright day that brings forth the adder.' An appeal by one MP to delay final passage of the Bill was underscored with the plea 'of Desdemona to Othello, "Kill me not to-night, my Lord! let me live but one day!"' (v.ii.78, 80, misquoted).[4]

In the relatively closed sphere of formal political participation in late-eighteenth- and early-nineteenth-century Britain, quotation was a badge of identity denoting one's membership in the community of the

---

[2]   James Boswell, 'The Hypochondriack', no. xxi, *London Magazine* (June 1779), 244; Thomas De Quincey, *The Collected Writings of Thomas De Quincey*, ed. David Masson, 14 vols. (Edinburgh: Adam and Charles Black, 1890), vol. v, p. 100.

[3]   See Christopher Reid, *Imprison'd Wranglers: The Rhetorical Culture of the House of Commons, 1760–1800* (Oxford: Oxford University Press, 2012), pp. 214–39. See also David Allan, *Commonplace Books and Reading in Georgian England* (Cambridge: Cambridge University Press, 2010).

[4]   Nathaniel Wraxall, *The Historical and the Posthumous Memoirs of Sir Nathaniel William Wraxall 1772–1784*, ed. Henry B. Wheatley, 5 vols. (London, 1884), vol. iii, pp. 181–5.

enfranchised: 'the ability to cite an approved authority at once signified one's right to belong to an élite group and solicited the cultural sympathies of its members ... Within the Commons Chamber contemporary speakers saw that to quote accurately and, more to the point, appositely, was to wield a certain kind of power.'[5] Wraxall identifies Edmund Burke and Richard Brinsley Sheridan as especially resourceful in their use of literary quotation. Sheridan's speech on 8 December 1783 was by all accounts a tour de force.[6] He repeatedly capped or contested the quotations of his opponents. According to the report of the debate in Sheridan's published *Speeches*, he 'took up the several quotations from Shakespeare, Milton, and the book of Revelations [*sic*]; of Mr. Wilberforce, Mr. Arden, and Mr. Scott, foiling them each with their own weapons, and citing, with the most happy ease and correctness, passages from almost the same pages that controverted their quotations, and told strongly for the bill'.[7]

It was deemed even more skilful to use a quotation that called to mind the context of the source text and applied it aptly to its new circumstances. In 1794, Sheridan praised Fox for standing alone in his opposition to war with revolutionary France by quoting Shakespeare's aloof Roman hero Coriolanus, whose words prognosticating his son's future greatness are applied by Sheridan to Fox's political future: 'To him [Fox], in the stormy hour, the nation would turn, and they would find him, "Like a great sea-mark, standing every flaw, / And saving those that eye him"' (v.iii.74–5). These parliamentary habits of quotation continued into the Victorian period, abetted by an education system that stressed recitation of passages from 'classical authors' such as Shakespeare, as Vicesimus Knox advised in his pedagogical manual *Liberal Education* (1781), or as William Enfield prescribed for the dissenting academy at Warrington.[8] The great Victorian Prime Ministers – Lord Melbourne, Benjamin Disraeli and William Gladstone – all possessed a formidable knowledge of Shakespeare and deployed it repeatedly in their speeches and writings.[9] In a parliamentary tribute upon the death of the Liberal statesman John Bright, Gladstone attested to the political weight of quotations from Shakespeare:

[5] Christopher Reid, 'Foiling the Rival: Argument and Identity in Sheridan's Speeches', in James Morwood and David Crane (ed.), *Sheridan Studies*, (Cambridge: Cambridge University Press, 1995), pp. 114–30 (p. 119).
[6] *Ibid.*, p. 120.
[7] Richard Brinsley Sheridan, *Speeches of the Late Right Honourable Richard Brinsley Sheridan*, 5 vols. (London, 1816), vol. I, p. 72.
[8] William Enfield, *The Speaker* (London, 1774).
[9] See William Greenslade, 'Shakespeare and Politics', in Gail Marshall (ed.), *Shakespeare in the Nineteenth Century* (Cambridge: Cambridge University Press, 2012), pp. 239–41.

Mr. Bright was … one of the chief guardians among us of the purity of the
English tongue. He knew how the character of the nation is associated with
its language … so the tongue of his people was to him almost an object of
worship; and in the long course of his speeches it would be difficult … to
find a single case in which that noble language, the language of Shakespeare
and of Milton, did not receive an illustration from his Parliamentary
eloquence.[10]

Effective quotation was much more than a game of one-upmanship.
Samuel Johnson insisted that quotation bespeaks 'a community of
mind': 'Classical quotation is the *parole* of literary men all over the world.'[11]
By the time Johnson made this remark, Shakespeare was, as Johnson himself had affirmed in the Preface to his edition, a classic author whose words
constituted a page in the passport by which 'literary men' identify themselves.[12] In Gladstone's eulogy to Bright, the act of quoting Shakespeare is
represented as a means of calling into being a national political community, forging allegiance in the broadest sense. But the protean Shakespeare
was also appropriated to foster more partisan commitments, both conservative and radical, creating communities, to adapt Johnson's phrase, of
political mind.

A prime instance of the loyalist appropriation of Shakespeare is
Edmund Burke's frequent citation of Shakespeare's great tragedies, especially *Macbeth*, in his writings on the French Revolution in order to present the revolution as a narrative of regicidal usurpation. Beginning with
his account in *Reflections on the Revolution in France* (1790) of the assault
upon Louis XVI and Marie Antoinette at Versailles, which he presents as
a harrowing tragic episode, Burke invokes Shakespeare repeatedly. When
he was advised to tone down his version of events, Burke defended himself
with a quotation from *Hamlet* (II.ii.541–2): ' "Whats Hecuba to him or he
to Hecuba that he should weep for her?" Why because she was Hecuba,
the Queen of Troy, the wife of Priam, and sufferd in the close of Life
a thousand Calamities.'[13] Like Hamlet, Burke recoils at the thought that
he could weep over the fate of a fictitious character in a play but then be
left indifferent by real-life events. By invoking Shakespearean tragedy, he
strives to create a loyalist political community through a shared experience

[10] *Hansard*, vol. 334 (29 March 1889), col. 1171, www.hansard.millbanksystems.com/commons/1889/
mar/29/the-late-mr-john-bright (last accessed 8 May 2017).
[11] James Boswell, *The Life of Samuel Johnson* [8 May 1781], 2 vols. (London, 1791), vol. II, p. 390.
[12] See Marjorie Garber, *Quotation Marks* (London: Routledge, 2003), pp. 1, 15–16.
[13] Edmund Burke, *The Correspondence of Edmund Burke*, ed. Thomas W. Copeland, 10 vols.
(Cambridge: Cambridge University Press, 1958–78), vol. VI, p. 90.

of powerful feelings: 'when kings are hurled from their thrones … [w]e are alarmed into reflection; our minds (as it has long since been observed) are purified by terror and pity'.[14]

The scene Burke describes – the king and queen's 'troubled, melancholy repose' interrupted by a revolutionary rabble – is prepared for, as Jonathan Bate notes, by a quotation from Macbeth's invocation of sleep, after murdering Duncan, as a 'Balm of hurt minds' (II.ii.38).[15] This is the first of many such associations by quotation in Burke's polemics; his subsequent *A Letter to a Noble Lord* (1796) underscores the heartlessness of the French *philosophes* by citing Lady Macbeth's prayer that no 'compunctious visitings of nature' be permitted to shake her from her fell purpose (I.v.44).[16] Quotations from Shakespeare's key tragedies focus attention on themes of hereditary succession, usurpation and regicide – precisely those principles that opponents of the revolution believed to be fundamentally at issue. And *Macbeth* confronts the most terrifying question of all: what drives men and women to become regicides?[17]

More often, as the loyalist newspaper *The Anti-Jacobin; or, Weekly Examiner* illustrates, quotations from Shakespeare in debates over the French Revolution are drawn from the history plays. The first issue (20 November 1797) cites the Chorus in *Henry V*:

> O England! Model to thy inward greatness,
> Like little body with a mighty heart,—
> What might'st thou do, that honour would thee do,
> Were all thy children kind and natural. (II.0.16–19)

The epigraphs sometimes comment on other news of the day but mostly they exhort Britain to stand up to French bellicosity, as the epigraph to number 20 (26 March 1798) illustrates:

> This England never did, nor never shall,
> Lie at the proud foot of a Conqueror:
> Come the three Corners of the World in arms,
> And we shall shock them. (*King John*, v.vii.112–13, 116–17)

---

[14] Edmund Burke, *The Writings and Speeches of Edmund Burke*, ed. Paul Langford, 9 vols. (Oxford: Clarendon Press, 1981–91), vol. VIII, pp. 131–2.

[15] *Ibid.*, vol. VIII, p. 121.

[16] *Ibid.*, vol. IX, p. 176.

[17] Jonathan Bate, *Shakespearean Constitutions* (Oxford: Clarendon Press, 1989), pp. 88–9. See also Frans De Bruyn, 'William Shakespeare and Edmund Burke: Literary Allusion in Eighteenth-Century British Political Rhetoric', in Peter Sabor and Paul Yachnin (eds.), *Shakespeare and the Eighteenth Century* (London: Ashgate, 2008), pp. 85–102; and Frans De Bruyn, 'Shakespeare and the French Revolution', in Peter Sabor and Fiona Ritchie (eds.), *Shakespeare in the Eighteenth Century* (Cambridge: Cambridge University Press, 2012), pp. 297–313.

Unlike quotations in political speeches, these journalistic citations tend not to be contextualised; they are chosen primarily for their patriotic sentiments.

Shakespeare could also be quoted in a bid to forge radical political allegiances. In the Victorian period, with the emergence of working-class political movements, reformers stressed Shakespeare's humble origins and argued that he was not, as William Hazlitt famously asserted, a poet of power, exalting 'the one above the infinite many, might before right', but an egalitarian.[18] The Chartist movement was especially vocal in opposing the high-cultural tendency to place Shakespeare above politics. 'The gentleman critics complain that the union of poetry with politics is always hurtful to the politics, and fatal to the poetry', observes a writer in the *Chartist Circular*.[19] Nothing could be further from the truth: 'What is poetry but impassioned truth – philosophy is its essence … Are there no politics in "Hamlet"?'. If Shakespeare is truly the great exemplar of the English language, he belongs as much to working people as to the gentlemen.[20] The columnist drives his point home with speeches by Henry IV and Prince Henry on the burdens of kingship, which he quotes as 'the Radical teaching of two of the greatest of men'.[21] In this very spirit, the *Northern Star*, a Chartist newspaper, ran a column called 'Chartism from Shakespeare', in which Shakespeare's Roman and historical plays are mined for quotations that comment on the state of the nation and offer Shakespearean precedents for the political reforms demanded by the Chartists. One especially pointed citation is taken from *Coriolanus* (a favourite source). A hungry plebeian declares, 'We are accounted *poor* citizens; the patricians *good*. What authority surfeits on, would relieve us … [B]ut they think we are too dear; the leanness that afflicts us, the object of our misery, is as an inventory to particularize their abundance' (1.1.12–17).[22]

---

[18] William Hazlitt, *Characters of Shakespear's Plays*, vol. IV of *The Complete Works of William Hazlitt*, ed. P. P. Howe, 21 vols. (London: J. M. Dent and Sons, 1930–4), p. 214.

[19] 'The Politics of Poets', *Chartist Circular* [Glasgow], 42 (11 July 1840).

[20] See Greenslade, 'Shakespeare and Politics', pp. 229–32; see also Peter Holbrook, 'Shakespeare, "The Cause of the People", and *The Chartist Circular* 1839–1842', *Textual Practice*, 20 (2006), 203–29; Andrew Murphy, *Shakespeare for the People* (Cambridge: Cambridge University Press, 2008), pp. 135–61; Kathryn Prince, *Shakespeare in the Victorian Periodicals* (New York: Routledge, 2008), pp. 16–36; and Anthony Taylor, 'Shakespeare and Radicalism', *Historical Journal*, 45 (2002), 357–79.

[21] The speeches are taken from *1* and *2 Henry IV*, and a third, misattributed passage comes from *3 Henry VI*.

[22] Quoted in 'Chartism from Shakespeare, No. 2', *Northern Star and Leeds General Advertiser*, 129 (2 May 1840).

The instances outlined here are only a sample of the range and diversity of political uses of Shakespeare quotation during the period in which modern political institutions emerged in Great Britain. The striking thing about them all, despite the divergence in political views on which Shakespeare is invoked, is, as Jonathan Bate notes, the premise that 'his plays matter, that they are to be valued'. Bate underscores this point with a mordant quotation from Hazlitt: 'We shall have a thousand Political Economists, before we have another Shakespear.'[23]

SHAKESPEARE IN VICTORIAN EDUCATION

Gail Marshall

In the nineteenth century, Shakespeare became an intrinsic part of the culture not just of the middle and upper classes, but of the population of Britain as a whole, thanks to the increasingly systematised development of a national education system. In the classroom, Shakespeare's words were repurposed for pedagogical ends. This educational orientation was not, of course, new: collections of quotations, intended at the beginning of the eighteenth century to act as raw materials for aspiring poets, had been transformed by the century's close into resources for didactic and moral improvement (see Chapter 5). But where a handful of late-century guides such as *Elegant Extracts* and the *Speaker* had supported the development of (primarily) boys in reading, writing and speaking, in both home and classroom, the rapidly growing market created by the expansion of formal education in the nineteenth century saw the production of quotation books and anthologies on a mass scale. This mini-chapter looks closely at the ways in which Shakespeare's words are extracted in a number of Victorian school readers, and at the values and purposes his quotations are asked to fulfil. Packaged for memorisation, recitation and transcription, and often framed as morally valuable, Shakespeare's quotations in this period were wrested from their original contexts and co-opted to conservative ends.

According to Francis Barker, the first time that students faced formally public exams in their knowledge of Shakespeare was in the qualifying examinations for the Indian Civil Service.[24] *The India List and India Office*

---

[23] William Hazlitt, 'The New School of Reform', in *Complete Works*, vol. XII, p. 187, quoted in Bate, *Shakespearean Constitutions*, p. 9.

[24] Francis Barker, 'Nationalism, Nomadism and Belonging in Europe: *Coriolanus*', in John J. Joughin (ed.), *Shakespeare and National Culture* (Manchester: Manchester University Press, 1997), pp. 233–66 (p. 262 n12).

List for 1905 specifies that candidates for these exams, as well as those for Class I Clerkships in the Home Civil Service, will sit a paper on English language and literature in which they 'will be expected to show a general acquaintance with the course of English Literature, as represented (mainly) by the following writers in verse and prose, between the reign of Edward III and the accession of Queen Victoria'. Shakespeare appears amongst a list of poets that also included Chaucer, Langland, Spenser, Milton, Dryden, Pope, Gray, Collins, Johnson, Goldsmith, Crabbe, Cowper, Campbell, Wordsworth, Scott, Byron, Coleridge, Shelley and Keats. Candidates are assured that '[a] minute knowledge of the works of these authors will not be looked for in this part of the Examination', which will rather 'test how far the Candidates have studied the chief productions of the greatest English writers *in themselves*, and are acquainted with the leading characteristics of their thought and style. And with the place which each of them occupies in the history of English Literature'.[25] In the second part of the exam, however, which was based in more specific, though still ambitiously long periods, more detailed knowledge of specific texts was required. The Shakespeare texts for 1905 were *The Tempest* and *Henry VIII*, which make for an intriguing insight into leadership for would-be administrators, particularly in India.

Realistically, the level of in-depth knowledge of Shakespeare envisaged here was only available to those who were educated either at the leading public schools or by private tutors. Liberal politician and four-times Prime Minister W. E. Gladstone, who left Eton in 1827 (and spent his first night after leaving school watching Charles Kemble's Falstaff in *1 Henry IV* at Covent Garden), was equipped by his schooling not only with a substantial knowledge of Shakespeare, but also, through having had to recite Shakespeare at length in the classroom, with performative abilities that would stand him in good stead in Parliament, where he had observed that 'success in legislative affairs depended directly upon the skills of seasoned orators'.[26]

But Shakespeare was far from being the preserve of the ruling and upper classes in Victorian Britain; rather, he represented a demotic and democratic force that was available to all but that was not necessarily initially achieved through formal education. In *Shakespeare for the People: Working-Class*

---

[25] *The India List and India Office List for 1905* (London: Harrison, 1905), p. 199.
[26] Glynne Wickham, 'Gladstone, Oratory and the Theatre', in P. J. Jagger (ed.), *Gladstone* (London: Hambledon Press, 1998), pp. 1–32 (p. 9). See also William Greenslade, 'Shakespeare and Politics', in Marshall (ed.), *Shakespeare in the Nineteenth Century*, pp. 229–50 (pp. 239–40).

Readers, 1800–1900, Andrew Murphy shows how, against the backdrop of a very gradual increase in the availability of formal education for children in Britain, working-class readers did come to be formally educated about Shakespeare. The formalisation of education provision took a significant step forward with the creation of the Committee of Council on Education in 1858, and with a body of school inspectors, the best-known of whom was poet and critic, Matthew Arnold. New guidelines as to expected levels of reading competency, enforced by the visits of school inspectors and the requirement that they test children annually, coupled with the 1861 Newcastle Commission's recommendation that schools be paid by results, led to the birth of a publishing industry that supplied the needs of schools now embedded in formalised structures of expectation and finance.[27]

The government began to lay down 'guidelines for what children at each one of the defined set of "standards" should be capable of reading', and publishers supplied texts that provided reading appropriate to each level of attainment.[28] Within these works, Shakespeare was available as a set of quotations, rather than whole plays. Initially, provision was patchy: Arnold notes in his report of schools in 1860 that he has

> seen school-books belonging to the cheapest, and therefore most popular series in use in our primary schools, in which far more than half of the poetical extracts were the composition either of the anonymous compilers themselves, or of American writers of the second or third order; and these books were to be some poor child's Anthology of a literature so varied and so powerful as the English![29]

As the century progressed, however, publishers came to meet schools' needs with carefully calibrated readers and text books, such as *Laurie's Graduated Series of Reading Lesson Books*, Charles Bilton's *The Class and Standard Series of Reading Books; adapted to the requirements of the revised code*, and the *Nelson Royal Readers*.

Shakespeare appeared in these collections along with a range of other writers from the Renaissance to the present day, chief amongst whom tended to be Milton, the major Romantic poets, James Thomson and Walter Scott. A closer look at a couple of texts will give a flavour of the ways in which Shakespeare quotations might be encountered. In Bilton's Preface

[27] Andrew Murphy, *Shakespeare for the People: Working-Class Readers, 1800–1900* (Cambridge: Cambridge University Press, 2008), pp. 40ff.
[28] *Ibid.*, p. 48.
[29] Matthew Arnold, 'General Report for the Year 1860', in Francis Sandford (ed.), *Reports on Elementary Schools, 1852–1882* (London: Macmillan, 1889), quoted in Murphy, *Shakespeare for the People*, p. 48.

to *Book v, A Poetical Reader* (1868), he notes that 'All experienced teachers know and appreciate the great utility of good poetry as a means of forming the taste, cultivating the moral perceptions, exercising the imagination, and awakening and stimulating the desire for the acquisition of know-ledge.'[30] Bilton goes on: 'This selection is intended for the use of children in whom the teacher is endeavouring to implant a love of reading for the sake of its uses and pleasures' (p. v), but clearly other more personal and ideological values, concerning the formation of correct taste and appro-priate morality, are implied here too. What is clear is that the reading and learning of poetry are being put at the heart of the curriculum, providing the 'groundwork of lessons, in Geography, grammar, History, etc.' (p. vii), as well as 'helping to secure a good style of reading and strengthening the memory of the learners, and expanding their minds, by means of the store of words and ideas thus acquired' in the practice of reciting pieces learned by heart (p. viii).

Shakespeare quotations are usefully versatile in Bilton and appear in a number of forms: as brief quotations, grouped with other writers under themed headings; in more substantial sections from the plays and in extracts from the Lambs' *Tales from Shakespeare* (1807), where quotations are mediated by paraphrase and third-person narration. Smaller snippets, or 'gobbets', of writers including Shakespeare form the predominant con-tent of this text, despite some commentators' opinion that the use of such extracts ran counter to the cultivation of proper reading habits.[31]

In a section of poetry extracts entitled 'Day and Night', Shakespeare, referred to as 'our greatest poet' (p. 136), is represented by a series of extended quotations:

> the gentle lark, weary of rest,
> From his moist cabinet mounts up on high,
> And wakes the morning, from whose silver breast
> The sun ariseth in his majesty
> Who doth the world so gloriously behold,
> That cedar-tops and hills seem burnish'd gold.
> (p. 156, quoting *Venus and Adonis*, lines 853–7)

> Full many a glorious morning have I seen
> Flatter the mountain-tops with sovereign eye,

---

[30] Charles Bilton, 'Preface' to *The Class and Standard Series of Reading Books; adapted to the requirements of the revised code. Book v. A Poetical Reader* (London: Longmans, Green, 1868), pp. v–viii (p. v). Subsequent references are given in parentheses in the text.

[31] See, for instance, Lucy H. M. Soulsby, *Stray Thoughts on Reading* (London: Longmans, Green, 1897), p. 28.

> Kissing with golden face the meadows green,
> Gilding pale streams with heavenly alchemy.
> (p. 156, quoting Sonnet 33, lines 1–4)

> Look! the world's comforter, with weary gait
> His day's hot task hath ended in the west;
> The owl, night's herald, shrieks, 'tis very late;
> The sheep are gone to fold, birds to their nest,
>   And coal-black clouds that shadow heaven's light
> Do summon us to part, and bid good night.
> (p. 139, quoting *Venus and Adonis*, lines 529–34)

These lines from *Venus and Adonis* and Sonnet 33 are given with no attribution apart from Shakespeare's name, no source text details, and no context beyond the heading of 'Day and Night'. The choice of Sonnet 33 is particularly intriguing given the nineteenth century's broadly held suspicion of the Sonnets' potentially homosexual content. Bilton excludes the sonnet's ending, whose pun on 'son' and 'suns' embeds its meaning in a wistful invocation of male–male love:

> Even so my sun one early morn did shine
> With all triumphant splendor on my brow;
> But out! alack! he was but one hour mine,
> The region cloud hath mask'd him from me now.
> Yet him for this my love no whit disdaineth;
> Suns of the world may stain when heaven's sun staineth.
> (Sonnet 33, lines 9–14)

Lifted from this context, however, just as images of sun and darkness are lifted from the sensually explicit narrative of *Venus and Adonis*, Bilton's choice of lines seems to close down any possibility of radical interpretation. Instead, selective quotation turns them into innocuous descriptions.

Shakespeare also supplies Bilton with seemingly innocuous images of nature. In a section on 'Favourite Flowers', Bilton says that 'The great Shakespeare writes of the time'

> When daisies pied and violets blue
>   And lady-smocks all silver-white
> And cuckoo-buds of yellow hue
>   Do paint the meadows with delight.
> (p. 172, quoting *Love's Labour's Lost*, v.ii.902–5)

'And again he says':

> I know a bank where the wild thyme blows,
> Where oxlips and the nodding violet grows,

> Quite over-canopied with luscious woodbine,
> With sweet musk-roses and with eglantine.
> (p. 172, quoting *A Midsummer Night's Dream*, ii.i.249–52)

But while these images of nature seem to be extracted for their lush descriptiveness, others have a more political edge. In a last image from nature, Bilton gives us the Archbishop of Canterbury's speech from *Henry V*, i.ii, or 'the famous passage on the honey bees' in which they teach 'the act of order to a peopled kingdom':

> They have a king and officers of sorts;
> Where some, like magistrates, correct at home,
> Others, like merchants, venture trade abroad,
> Others, like soldiers, armed in their stings,
> Make boot upon the summer's velvet buds,
> Which pillage they with merry march bring home
> To the tent-royal of their emperor;
> Who, busied in his majesty, surveys
> The singing masons building roofs of gold,
> The civil citizens kneading up the honey,
> The poor mechanic porters crowding in
> Their heavy burdens at his narrow gate,
> The sad-eyed justice, with his surly hum,
> Delivering o'er to executors pale
> The lazy yawning drone. (p. 188, quoting *Henry V*, i.ii.190–204)

The extract, describing an organic eco-system of effort, collaboration and expediency, works curiously against the impulse of the Archbishop's speech, which is to persuade Henry to go to war with France, at the end of which the King declares 'Call in the messengers sent from the Dauphin' (i. ii.221), thus opening the tennis-ball scene, which presages his declaration of war. Under the apparent pre-eminence of his ubiquity, and in the apparently neutral context of an educational textbook, Shakespeare's words can be appropriated or co-opted for ideological ends, his very availability enabling his enforced collaboration.

Elsewhere in Bilton's book, dramatic scenes of political complexity become a training ground for speakers and politicians of the future. Shakespeare appears in more substantial form in twelve pages of extracts from *Richard II* – the 'Quarrel between Henry Bolingbroke and the Duke of Norfolk' (pp. 119–23; *Richard II*, i.i) and the 'Banishment of Bolingbroke and Norfolk' (pp. 124–33; *Richard II*, i.iii) – and in Charles and Mary Lamb's chapter on *The Merchant of Venice*, which includes a significant portion of the trial scene (pp. 104–18). These are all selections that would have been read aloud in classrooms and provided opportunity for eloquent declamation and rhetorical persuasion (the practices of memorisation and recitation peaked in the British schoolroom between 1875 and 1900).[32]

In Nelson's *Royal Readers*, quotation from Shakespeare provides opportunities for pathos in classroom recitation. In *The Royal School Series. Royal Poetical Readers: No. iii for Standards 5 and 6* (1882), Shakespeare is represented by two scenes from *King John* (iv.1–2), which see Prince Arthur poignantly begging Hubert to spare him from having his eyes burnt in their sockets, Hubert's determination to lie to King John that Arthur is dead and noblemen pleading for Arthur's release from imprisonment.[33] The other extended extract is from *Henry VIII*, iii.ii.351–458 (pp. 61–5), where Cardinal Wolsey bemoans his fall from the King's favour, and hears from Cromwell of Thomas More's ascendancy and Anne Boleyn's secret marriage to the King. The key tone again is pathos, with some injunctions that Cromwell act better and more wisely than Wolsey himself had done:

> fling away ambition:
> By that sin fell the angels; how can man then,
> The image of his Maker, hope to win by't?
> Love thyself last: cherish those hearts that hate thee;
> Corruption wins not more than honesty. (p. 64; iii.ii.441–5)

And

> O Cromwell, Cromwell!
> Had I but serv'd my God with half the zeal
> I serv'd my king, he would not in mine age
> Have left me to mine enemies (p. 64; iii.ii.455–8)

Ideologically, these extracts are very much in line with the extracts from Shakespeare found in another Nelson publication of that year: *The Royal School Series. No. v: The Royal Readers*. Shakespeare is conspicuously absent from the longer passages that are given for class reading, but appears in a selection of 'CHOICE QUOTATIONS. To be written from memory', the aims of which are pedagogic in a broad sense, as the extracts' headings suggest. Nelson's Shakespeare is a rather admonitory moral figure, and these headings include: 'True Nobility', 'Fear God', 'Human Life' (three entries), 'Content', 'Good for Evil, Life', 'Conscience' (four entries),

[32] Catherine Robson, *Heart Beats: Everyday Life and the Memorized Poem* (Princeton: Princeton University Press, 2012), p. 5.
[33] *The Royal School Series. Royal Poetical Readers: No. iii for Standards 5 and 6* (London: Nelson, 1882), pp. 53–60. Subsequent references are given in parentheses in the text.

'Industry' and 'The Blessings of a Low Station'. For the latter, Anne Boleyn provides the chastening thought that ''tis better to be lowly born, / And range with humble livers in content, / Than to be perk'd up in a glistering grief, / And wear a golden sorrow' (*Henry VIII*, ii.iii.19–22).[34] The author of Wolsey's woes has herself been cast down. On 'Character', we read:

> Good name in man and woman, dear my lord,
> Is the immediate jewel of their souls.
> Who steals my purse steals trash. 'Tis something, nothing:
> 'Twas mine, 'tis his, and has been slave to thousands.
> But he that filches from me my good name
> Robs me of that which not enriches him
> And makes me poor indeed. (p. 358)

Coming from Iago's lips in *Othello*, iii.iii.155–60, the words can only be heard with foreboding and cynicism, but out of the play's context, they seem to operate as a simple assertion that a good name is above price. However, in the context of a late-Victorian schoolbook, the mercantile flavour of the financial metaphor speaks of the economic value of a good name to a generation being educated to take their part in the country's business.

Despite the inclusion of many quotations in formal education, though, it is not certain that this Shakespearean training really was for all. Shakespeare quotations first appear in Nelson's *Royal Readers* at Standards 5 and 6; and in the school syllabus, Shakespeare is first mentioned at Standard 6, where the requirement is '[t]o recite 150 lines from Shakespeare or Milton, or some other standard author, and to explain the words and allusions'.[35] But as Murphy notes, of the 3.5 million children presenting for inspection in 1882, only 1.9 per cent passed the reading requirement at Standard 6.[36]

Familiarity with Shakespeare was, however, also garnered in other venues in the nineteenth century, in local and West End theatres; in abridged versions; in domestic settings and vernacular expressions; and as part of the rhetoric of other writers, for some of whom Shakespeare was almost a second language, most vividly acquired by auto-didactic channels. In an educational setting, however, during most of the nineteenth century, Shakespeare's excellence – he is frequently cited in school readers as 'the greatest of dramatic poets' – is stymied.[37] Later writers might make creative,

---

[34] *The Royal School Series. No. v: The Royal Readers* (London: Nelson, 1882), p. 357.
[35] Robson, *Heart Beats*, p. 62.
[36] Murphy, *Shakespeare for the People*, p. 50.
[37] *Royal Poetical Readers: No. iii*(London:, p. 80.

even subversive, use of the very experience of encountering Shakespeare in the classroom, for ironic or comedic effect (see, for example, the work of Victorian-educated P. G. Wodehouse in Chapter 8, and numerous examples from twentieth-century film in Chapter 11). But the vitality, richness, variety and subversive energy of his works seem ill-served by the practice of quoting him in educational texts of the nineteenth century.

QUOTATIONS AT WAR: THE FIRST AND SECOND WORLD WARS

Ton Hoenselaars

In the summer of 1914, the German emperor, Wilhelm II, and the chief of the Austro-Hungarian General Staff, Conrad von Hötzendorff, perceived the Balkan crisis, occasioned by the terrorist attack in Sarajevo, as an existential crisis. In the latter's words, it was 'a matter of "to be or not to be" '.[38] Hötzendorff's claim – possibly building on Ferdinand Freiligrath's mid-nineteenth-century observation 'Germany is Hamlet' – set the tone of the debate for years to come. Soon after the outbreak of the Great War, the German propaganda machine started to market postcards, depicting Wilhelm II and the Austrian emperor, Franz Josef I, spreading the same philosophy: 'Um sein oder nicht sein handelt es sich' ('To be or not to be, that's what it's all about').[39]

The German emperor's persona, not of a procrastinating but of a decisive Hamlet, invited a sharp response from the French enemy. On 11 August 1914 – barely more than a week into the war – the right-wing newspaper *La Croix* devoted a short article to the Germans, quoting 'Être ou ne pas être'. Apparently, the paper commented, the German emperor, 'taking up arms against a world of enemies', had found it necessary to quote from Shakespeare's *Hamlet*. But should he not, instead, have quoted something from the same play such as: 'There's something rotten in Germany; it is the German himself who has committed horror and barbarism'?[40] This early French response to the emperor's personal brand of Hamletism in 1914 was not to be the last. Throughout the war, Wilhelm II cited the words of Shakespeare to emphasise the urgency of events. As a consequence, whenever the German army suffered any significant losses, the

---

[38] Fritz Fischer, *War of Illusions: German Policies from 1911 to 1914* (New York: W. W. Norton, 1975), p. 395.

[39] See www.bildpostkarten.uni-osnabrueck.de/displayimage.php?pos=-1592 (last accessed 10 May 2017).

[40] *La Croix*, 11 August 1914, p. 3.

French media made the emperor eat his Shakespearean words. Wilhelm II was shown as Hamlet, addressing a skull in a typical Prussian spike helmet, with the words: 'Être ou ne plus être …' ('To be or no longer to be …'). The illustration originally appeared on the front page of the *Echo de Paris* on 20 August 1915, and was soon given wider and more lasting circulation by the popular reader's digest journal, *Messidor*.[41] Its popularity in the German and French presses at the time may explain the corrective cartoon and quotation by the Stratford-based cartoonist and *ancien combatant*, Bruce Bairnsfather. Following the significant British capture of the German salient at Fricourt (during the Battle of the Somme in July 1916), Bairnsfather depicted a Tommy addressing not a skull, nor a helmet, but a typical German flatcap, with the words: 'Alas! Poor Herr Von Yorick!'.[42]

As the war progressed and anti-war sentiment grew, quotations from *Hamlet* also came to be used to convey personal grief. This is illustrated by the *Offertoire*, a collection of illustrated sketches written by Fernand Pignatel, who spent time in the French trenches in 1918. One of the engravings, entitled 'Hamlet', depicts a *poilu* (as the French 'Tommy' was called) interrupting his manual digging of a war grave by studying one of the skulls that he has found. The image is accompanied by the familiar text 'To be or not to be'.[43]

Together, these examples, and a host of others, suggest that much of the history of the First World War may be reconstructed in terms of quotations from Shakespeare's work. In part, this can be explained by the existence of complex and conscious cultures of Shakespearean quotation. At the time the Great War broke out, for example, English newspapers too were already in the habit of printing columns of literary quotations that seemed apt as a comment on the news of the day.

The Great War did not interrupt this culture of quotation but strengthened it, and when in the middle of the war the tercentenary of Shakespeare's death was commemorated, the event occasioned book-length anthologies of such applied quotations, now combining the English nation's affinity with Shakespeare and its inevitable concern with the continuing hostilities beyond the Channel. One of these anthologies is Francis Colmer's *Shakespeare in Time of War* of 1916. It presents quotations from

---

[41] *L'Echo de Paris*, 20 August 1915, p. 1; *La Grande Guerre par les grands écrivains*, *Messidor*, 22 (5 December 1915), p. 704.

[42] Captain Bruce Bairnsfather, *Fragments from France* (New York: G. P. Putnam's Sons and The Knickerbocker Press, [*c.* 1917]), p. 115.

[43] Fernand Pignatel, *L'Offertoire: Trente scènes du calvaire du poilu*, illustrated by Pierre Gerbaud (Paris: Etienne Chiron, 1921), pp. 13–14.

Shakespeare, thematically arranged, so the reader who might, say, be eager
to know Shakespeare's comments on Wilhelm II, could turn to the section
entitled 'Imperious Caesar'.[44] But the opinionated Bard also had a view
on the 'Torpedoing of the *Lusitania*' (p. 91), the 'Gallipoli Campaign and
Allies at Salonika' (p. 94), the 'Defeat of the German Fleet off Falkland
Islands' (p. 102) and many other topics. Literary historians neglect to interpret this valuable source of the people's Shakespeare at their own peril. The
countless applications produce a veritable sense of amazement, even today,
and suggest how much the very merger of the Bard's quotations with the
news of the day aimed to nurture the Englishman's constitution.

Rarer than Colmer's *Shakespeare in Time of War* – with its educational
agenda serving to inform an ignorant reader – was the Revd Frederick
Askew's *Shakespeare Tercentenary Souvenir* (1916). Askew took unspecified quotations from Shakespeare, as the Prelude informs us, 'almost at
random', in order to seek 'some verbal expression for the nation's soul in
its hour of agony'.[45] The anthology thus defines the nation's psychology
in wartime through quotations, thereby suggesting that, faced with the
horrors of the Great War, Shakespeare would have been as outraged as the
twentieth-century Englishman. A case in point is the Easter Rising of 1916
and the role of Sir Roger Casement. Casement is compared to Macbeth's
predecessor as Thane of Cawdor, who was justly punished for his political
treason with a foreign nation and his commerce with insurgent rebels:

> ROGER CASEMENT HANGED AT PENTONVILLE.
> He labour'd in his country's wreck …
> But treasons capital, confess'd and proved,
> Have overthrown him. (p. 5)

Elsewhere, Casement is given the voice of the disgruntled Caliban (p. 7).
Significantly, the Revd Askew not only draws on Shakespeare's words and
applies them to the present; he actually takes the art of citation one step
further than others, by using the complete works to predict the future,
although he modestly limits himself to the war year ahead (1916–17).[46]

---

[44] Francis Colmer, *Shakespeare in Time of War: Excerpts from the Plays Arranged with Topical Allusion* (New York: E. P. Dutton, 1916), pp. 49–58. Subsequent references are given in parentheses in the text.

[45] Fred[erick] Askew, *Shakespeare Tercentenary Souvenir: England's Thoughts in Shakespeare's Words* (Lowestoft: Flood & Son, 1916), p. 3. Subsequent references are given in parentheses in the text.

[46] 'Shakespearean Prophecies for the Third Year of War', in Askew, *Shakespeare Tercentenary Souvenir*, pp. 78–9.

The tradition of citing Shakespeare for the war cause was so popular that listeners actually identified Shakespeare as the author even when he was, perhaps, not even cited. The Second World War provides a telling example. In August 1940, Winston Churchill spoke the unforgettable words: 'Never in the field of human conflict has so much been owed to so few.' These words have been widely quoted since, and many believe that Shakespeare's *Henry V* is 'the ultimate source'.[47] However, as Jonathan Rose has recently noted, a 'more likely source' was Sir Thomas Gower's comment on the Battle of Bannockburn. On this occasion, the English were routed by a Scottish army, inviting the comment: 'Never so many ran from so few in less ado.'[48] Rather than quoting Shakespeare's *Henry V*, Churchill would have transformed the memory of an English defeat into a battle cry for a new victory.

When studying Shakespearean quotations in wartime, it is ill advised to focus exclusively on the immediate political and military spheres. The new total war of the twentieth century, with armed conflict also involving innocent civilians, created new and private practices of quotation. Countless civilian internees behind the barbed wire of their camps developed survival cultures that included reading, writing and citing Shakespeare. A case in point is the Polish Countess Karolina Lanckorońska, who was originally imprisoned for her Second World War resistance activities in Lemberg (Lvov) and later held at Ravensbrück. In September 1942, at Lemberg prison, she started her diary with a full quotation of Richard II's prison soliloquy: 'I have been studying how I may compare / This prison where I live unto the world' (v.v.1–2).[49] Several days later, in another diary entry, Lanckorońska spoke to herself in a stern voice, reminding herself of the words of Edgar in *King Lear* (v.ii.9–11):

> What, in ill thoughts again? Men must endure
> Their going hence, even as their coming hither:
> Ripeness is all. (p. 167)

---

[47] Jonathan Rose, *The Literary Churchill: Author, Reader, Actor* (New Haven: Yale University Press, 2014), pp. 333–4.

[48] *Ibid.*, p. 334.

[49] Karolina Lanckorońska, *Those who Trespass against Us: One Woman's War against the Nazis*, trans. Noel Clark (London: Pimlico, 2005), pp. 161–2. Subsequent references are given in parentheses in the text.

It is an insight that prepares us for the next quotation, from *Julius Caesar* (II.ii.34–7), where the stoic worldview of *King Lear* is expressed even more explicitly:

> Of all the wonders that I yet have heard
> It seems to me most strange that men should fear
> Seeing that death, a necessary end
> Will come when it will come. (p. 168)

On a personal level, these Shakespearean quotations enable one to reconstruct a psychological crisis that is warded off by engaging in dialogue with Shakespeare. In broader terms, we witness the countess countering the barbarism of the day with daily quotations from a deified author. Finally, given Lanckorońska's Polish roots, we identify a mode of Shakespearean citation practised across borders, which transforms it, as in the case of the German emperor in the First World War, into a transnational, European phenomenon.

As 'Shakespeare' was read and quoted in the many camps of the two world wars, the meaning of these cultures of quotation was significantly different from those prevailing in the political arena beyond the perimeter fence. In order to appreciate the disparity between these practices, it seems worth comparing the way in which the same Shakespearean quotation might circulate in both spheres. Shortly after the outbreak of the First World War, the British government sought to enlist civilians for the military cause, and commissioned a Parliamentary Recruiting Committee to issue a series of posters. One of these posters, published in January 1915 – incidentally, the same year that witnessed the publication of the 'Women of England say: "Go"!' poster – quotes Lady Macbeth's words to Ross at the end of the failed banquet, where she wants all guests gone: 'Stand not upon the order of your going, / But go at once' (III.iv.121–2).[50] Understandably, the words are ascribed to 'Shakespeare, *Macbeth*' rather than his character.

The same quotation mobilised on the public poster for propaganda purposes in Britain also appeared in the *Ruhleben Camp Magazine*, the journal of the British civilian internees at Ruhleben Camp, Berlin (1914–18). It was part of a familiar list of passages from the so-called 'Ruhleben Shakespeare', and produced with the same conviction as Askew and Colmer's anthologies, namely that, as Colmer says, '[n]o other book

---

[50] Respectively Imperial War Museum, PST 2763, at www.iwm.org.uk/collections/item/object/14592; and Imperial War Museum, PST 5154, at www.iwm.org.uk/collections/item/object/28444 (both last accessed 18 May 2017).

presents such a boundless scope', and that 'from none can the *sortes* with such propriety be cast' (p. xxxv). Under the heading of 'Shakespeare, KG' (*Kriegsgefangener* [prisoner of war] or 'Kaiser's Guest'), the internees listed a number of themes relating to their appalling internment ('Our Universal Prayer', 'The Pessimist' and 'After Many Days'), and playfully set these off with apt quotations from Shakespeare. The last theme on the page, 'The Day of Days', focuses the quotation from *Macbeth*, 'Stand not upon the order of your going, But go at once! – Macbeth, Act 3, sc. 5'.[51] From a cultural-historical point of view, there is great irony in the fact that within the space of approximately one year, the same citation from Shakespeare should be used both to persuade the English to join up for the war abroad, *and* to give expression to a civilian desire to return to Blighty.

Beyond the obvious irony, however, we should learn to recognise the citation practice of the British internees as a distress call for freedom via Shakespeare. Within the then current cultures of quotation, 'Shakespeare' became the spokesman for those unused to writing poetry or keeping a diary, and he still speaks to us on behalf of those war victims who have themselves remained proverbially silent about their experience. Perhaps the clearest evidence of this at Ruhleben is the notebook of George Beringer, which contains complete sequences of quotations from Shakespeare with no comment. They tell us more about his own state of mind than that of the Bard. Take Beringer's use of Hamlet's first soliloquy ('O that this too too solid flesh would melt', 1.ii.129), or his last, which really captures the despondency of a prisoner after three years in a horsebox at a German racecourse that has been converted into an internment camp:

> What is a man,
> If his chief good and market of his time
> Be but to sleep and feed? – a beast, no more.
> Sure, he that made us with such large discourse,
> Looking before and after, gave us not
> That capability and god-like reason
> To fust in us unused.[52]

Internees such as Beringer support Askew's conviction that the language of Shakespeare was 'far too sublime and telling to be ignored by those … seeking verbal expression for the nation's soul in its hour of agony' (p. 3).

[51] *Ruhleben Camp Magazine*, 3 (May 1916), p. 41.
[52] *Hamlet*, IV.iv.33–9. See George Beringer, in Liddle Collection, Brotherton Library, Leeds, RUH 04.

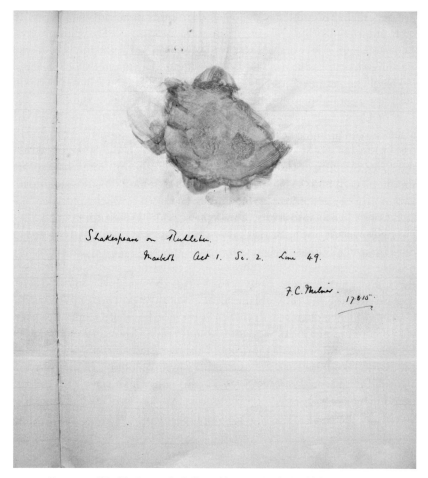

Shakespeare on Ruhleben.
        Macbeth   Act 1. Sc. 2. Line 49.

                                F. C. Milner.
                                    17.8.15.

Figure 8   ' "Stable Jottings": Collected by Eric Swale (Ruhleben 1914–15)'.

Clearly, it was not simply any essential value of Shakespeare's text that attracted the internees to draw on the man from Stratford and his work. For British internees in Germany, where the conviction persisted that Shakespeare was really German, to quote Shakespeare was also a patriotic act of claiming or reclaiming the Bard. On numerous occasions, then, capitalising on his broader cultural value by quoting from his work seems to have been more important than any principle of interpretation. This may be demonstrated with reference to the *Macbeth* quotation that Ruhleben internee F. C. Milner recorded in the *liber amicorum* of his friend, W. E. Swale. The quotation is a drop of real blood (turned rusty and brown over the years), spread across the upper half of the page, with, under it, the reference '*Macbeth*. Act 1. Sc. 2. Line 49' (Figure 8).

For all its seeming precision, this reference takes the reader to a line in Shakespeare that is less than apposite: 'What bloody man is that?' (*Macbeth*, I.ii.i). Milner adopts the persona of the academic who acknowledges the authority of the poet and the text, but only so that the inexactness of the practice will redirect attention to his own anger and frustration after years of captivity. Ruhleben Camp, Milner states, was pure misery, an absolute disaster, or, in terms that Lady Macbeth could have used (see V.i.31–67), a bloody spot.[53] As he distances himself from the written work and its quotability, Milner begins to speak for himself and achieves something of great poetic originality.

---

[53] W. E. Swale in Beringer, RUH 52.

CHAPTER 10

The Impossibility of Quotation: Twentieth-Century Literature

Craig Raine

In his life of Dickens (1872–4), John Forster, charting the movement in Dickens from fairy tale to social criticism, drops in a quotation from *Othello*: 'What were now to be conquered were the more formidable dragons and giants that had their places at our own hearths, and the weapons to be used were of a finer than the "ice brook's temper".'[1] The context has *nothing* to do with the second weapon that Othello uses to kill himself, the first having been taken by Montano. The quotation is a tic. It is an accessory, a bit of intellectual chic, a flashing of credentials, name-checking, part of the belletrist's armoury in the nineteenth century. In P. P. Howe's monumental edition of Hazlitt, the two final volumes are given over to citing and sourcing Hazlitt's quotations. The intention behind Forster's quotation is to show how cultivated the writer is. The quotation is from Shakespeare, but is fundamentally interchangeable with Milton, or any other sufficiently canonical author. It is not germane. It is a well-connected, well-bred, well-read flourish.

Preceding chapters have traced the history of books of quotations – sometimes eclectic, sometimes selections from particular authors. Laurence Sterne, for example, after his death, was refashioned in *The Beauties of Sterne* (1782), his innuendoes expunged, his comedy muted, until he appeared a writer of high-minded sentiment.[2] It is part of my thesis that *all* literary quotation is selective and inevitably involves a degree of misrepresentation. It loses context and acquires another. It is an import whose import is changed. My examples are drawn from Rudyard Kipling to Tom Stoppard, representatively rather than chronologically. They demonstrate two unexpected paradoxes in action. First, quotation can be original. Second, apparently straightforward quotation tends to function, in

[1] John Forster, *The Life of Dickens*, ed. J. W. T. Ley (London: Cecil Palmer, 1928), pp. 316–18.
[2] Laurence Sterne, *The Beauties of Sterne Including All His Pathetic Tales, and Most Distinguished Observations on Life Selected for the Heart of Sensibility*, ed. W. H. (London, 1788).

twentieth-century literature, *more* indirectly than an allusion can. It typically accrues so much new, complicating meaning that quotation, as we usually think of it, may even be impossible in literature.

The Originality of Modern Quotation: Borges and Duchamp

There is an apocryphal story – told by Isaac Asimov, among others – about the old lady who sees a performance of *Hamlet* for the first time at the age of eighty.[3] She is enthusiastic about the play but astonished that it should contain so much quotation. Implicit here is the popularity of Shakespeare as a *point de répère* and source for moral aphorism. The primrose path ('of dalliance'; *Hamlet*, 1.iii.50) hardly needs inverted commas. It now has another life, a life on its own. It has fled the nest. It is independent of Shakespeare and his play. The old lady – Mrs Barthes, I believe – has encountered it, and other phrases, out there in the wide world. For her, it exists before the play. This is a parable of transmission.

Two seminal, non-Shakespearean examples. In his story 'Pierre Menard, Author of the *Quixote*' (1934), Jorge Luis Borges argues that a work of art exists in its historical moment and cannot escape it. So, were *Madame Bovary* written now, it would mean something very different from Flaubert's text. It would be an historical novel, a genre exercise, a pastiche – word perfect but still a pastiche. Context is crucial. Borges supports this proposition by inverting it. His protagonist hopes to write 'a few pages which would coincide – word for word and line for line with those of Miguel de Cervantes'. Without copying. And he succeeds in writing an exact replica of the ninth and thirty-eighth chapters of the first part, and a fragment of Chapter 22. But of course, Menard's text is also fundamentally different from Cervantes's text – because it is written in 1934. The cleverness, the joke, is that Borges finds Menard's identical words not belated but 'more subtle', 'almost infinitely richer' – though Menard's style 'suffers from a certain affectation' that in Cervantes seems natural.[4]

We need a figure for this skew. In 1919, Marcel Duchamp drew a moustache and beard on a reproduction of the Mona Lisa and called his composition *LHOOQ*. His title is a pun: the letters when pronounced in French sound like 'elle a chaud au cul', meaning 'she is hot in the arse'. So, a desecration as well as a recomposition. Dada. No longer the enigma

---

[3] Isaac Asimov, *Asimov's Guide to Shakespeare* (New Jersey: Avenel Books, 1970), p. vii.
[4] Jorge Luis Borges, *Labyrinths: Selected Stories and other Writings*, ed. Donald A. Yates and James E. Irby (London: Penguin, 1970), pp. 62–71.

of legend, but a goer, a slapper. (Actually, not so different from Walter Pater's famously rhapsodical paragraph that inflects her mystery with the vampiric.[5]) Eventually, Duchamp reverted to the original. However, the original was no longer Leonardo's original. It was now entitled *LHOOQ Shaved*. He was quoting the original exactly but now it meant something different – a different original, supplanting that of Leonardo.

Obviously it is possible to quote Shakespeare in critical discourse without altering Shakespeare's meaning. Might it be impossible, though, to quote Shakespeare in literature? Is quotation illusory? Do quotations from Shakespeare inevitably change their meaning in their new context? Are even direct quotations cognate with variants, versions, retreads?

Stoppard and Beckett

'Rosencrantz and Guildenstern are dead' (*Hamlet*, v.ii.354) is spoken by the Ambassador in Act v of Shakespeare's play. The Ambassador is looking for thanks, having faithfully carried out Hamlet's commission, but he is too late. Hamlet is dead. Now, the exact words *Rosencrantz and Guildenstern Are Dead* refer to Tom Stoppard's 1966 play; and thus to the idea that these minor characters are fated to die – are in fact effectively dead even as they fret about their status, for example, as characters without the proper dimensions of memory. They are literary constructs. They have no past. Their ontological status is determined: Stoppard's figure for this is the boat that is carrying them to England and their deaths. They can walk about, have the illusion of freedom, but they are actually circumscribed by the boat and its destination. Shakespeare's exact words are not only quoted. They are usurped. In practice, primacy isn't simply chronological.

Beckett's *Happy Days* (1961) antedates and possibly inspires *Rosencrantz and Guildenstern*. *Waiting for Godot* (1956) and its two loquacious tramps are certainly a pronounced influence on the Stoppard. In *Happy Days*, Winnie, buried 'up to her diddies', quotes Shakespeare – *Romeo and Juliet*, *Hamlet*, *Twelfth Night* and *Cymbeline*.[6] As she applies her lippy, Winnie inspects her mouth in the hand-mirror and says: 'Ensign crimson', followed by 'Pale flag' (p. 14). We are being referred to *Romeo and Juliet*, v.iii.94–6. Romeo is contemplating, as he wrongly thinks, the dead Juliet: 'Thou art not conquered. Beauty's ensign yet / Is crimson in thy lips and in thy cheeks, / And death's

[5] Walter Pater, *The Renaissance: Studies in Art and Poetry* (London: Macmillan, 1924), p. 130.
[6] Samuel Beckett, *Happy Days* (London: Faber, 1963), p. 14. Subsequent references are given in parentheses in the text.

pale flag is not advanced there.' We are being shown the futility of keeping up appearances when Winnie is effectively dead, buried alive.

More importantly, the quotation references Winnie's acting career. *Happy Days* is about the stage construct, a fiction with no life off stage – the very conceit that Stoppard is exploring in *Rosencrantz and Guildenstern Are Dead*. Winnie dries at one point: 'Words fail, there are times when even they fail' (p. 20). 'What is that unforgettable line?' (p. 37) she asks at the beginning of Act II – when we see the parasol that burnt in the first act has been replaced, like a prop. The stage performance is implicit in the bell at the beginning of the play, ushering the audience into the auditorium. It is also 'the bell for sleep' (p. 37), to signal the end of the interval, during which she sleeps. Beckett's bleak joke is that her performance is so tedious, so repetitive, that the audience nods off, too: 'Strange feeling that someone is looking at me. I am clear, then dim, then gone, then dim again, then clear again, and so on, back and forth, in and out of someone's eye' (p. 31).

Winnie's quotation from *Romeo and Juliet* becomes, in its new context, not a poignant misprision, but rather a *Verfremdungseffekt*, a glazed encouragement to apathy when faced with Winnie's liminal ontology. The 'unforgettable' quotation from *Cymbeline* is, of course, 'Fear no more the heat o'th'sun' (IV.ii.257) – another instance of an illusory death, like Juliet's, which is here pressed into service for something different. Namely, the half-life of the stage construct 'literally' feeling the heat of the sun or the lighting effect that creates the illusion.

Kipling and Auden

'The rest is silence' will do as an epitomising instance of my argument. It is quoted both in Kipling's story 'Mrs Bathhurst' (1904) and the opening poem of W. H. Auden's commentary on *The Tempest*, *The Sea and the Mirror* (1942–4). Hamlet's last words are:

> O, I die, Horatio!
> The potent poison quite o'ercrows my spirit.
> I cannot live to hear the news from England,
> But I do prophesy th'election lights
> On Fortinbras; he has my dying voice.
> So tell him, with th'occurrents more and less,
> Which have solicited – the rest is silence. [*Dies*] (v.ii.331–7)

The metaphor of the crowing cock takes us back to the beginning of the play, when the Ghost disappears ('It faded on the crowing of the cock'; I.i.157) – as Hamlet is about to disappear. But what does the half line 'the rest is silence' mean? It means there is nothing more to tell. It is a full-stop, a period. It also refers to Hamlet's finally bidding adieu to speech, after so many words, so many soliloquies. It is his quietus. Horatio adds: 'Good night sweet prince, / And flights of angels sing thee to thy rest' (v.ii.338–9). The repetition of 'rest' effects a change – a shift from 'remainder' (what is left) to 'repose'. Horatio is clear about the possibility of heaven, Hamlet less so: 'the rest [in both senses] is silence'.

In 'Mrs Bathurst', the erratic Vickery in Cape Town compulsively watches silent biograph film of Mrs Bathurst arriving on the Western Mail at Paddington Station, at the end of her journey from New Zealand. Vickery volunteers a certain amount of information to his companion Pyecroft. The information: 'remember. That I am *not* a murderer, because my lawful wife died in childbed six weeks after I came out [to South Africa]. That much at least I am clear of'. Pyecroft, baffled, asks, 'Then what have you done that signifies? What's the rest of it?'. Pyecroft, a cockney, reports Vickery's response: ' "The rest", 'e says, "is silence".'[7] Whereupon Vickery disappears from the narrative – reappearing, perhaps, as a charred corpse, beside a railway line up-country. Pyecroft has no idea Vickery is quoting Hamlet. So the quotation establishes a cultural difference between the two men. (Very different from the difference in emphasis between Hamlet and Horatio.) Vickery is a warrant officer. Pyecroft is an Able Seaman. The Shakespeare represents the enigma of broken narrative, the crimp of snapped thread. As in *Hamlet*, this is a conclusion that is not a conclusion. But it is a different kind of inconclusiveness – not metaphysical, but physical. Vickery simply vanishes.

Pyecroft is telling the story to Hooper, a railway inspector, who seems on several occasions to be about to produce Vickery's false teeth from his waistcoat pocket – a grisly memento from the charred corpse that would identify it as Vickery. But Hooper never does show us the teeth: 'Mr Hooper brought his hand away from his waistcoat pocket – empty' (p. 364). The four words of Shakespeare bring with them the antecedent words – 'th'occurrents more and less', by which Hamlet means the circumstances that have led to this grisly denouement. Readers of 'Mrs Bathurst' are in the position of Fortinbras *before* Horatio has explained how the corpse-littered finale came about. 'Mrs Bathurst' is *Hamlet* without the synopsis, without sequentiality. So 'the rest is silence' is exactly reproduced in Kipling's story but it means differently. In *Hamlet*, it is the sense of an ending. In 'Mrs Bathurst', it is a cover-up.

Now for the Auden. Auden's 'Preface' to *The Sea and the Mirror* is spoken by 'the Stage Manager to the Critics'. It isn't an easy poem to understand. There are four stanzas and the quotation from Shakespeare is in the last. What the quotation means depends on the three preceding verses.

> … the nonchalant couple go
> Waltzing across the tightrope
> As if there were no death
> Or hope of falling down;
> The wounded cry as the clown
> Doubles his meaning, and O
> How the dear little children laugh
> When the drums roll and the lovely
> Lady is sawn in half.[8]

So the poem begins with an extended circus metaphor, where the circus is equivalent to the romance world of the late plays – in which death is redeemed (Imogen, Perdita, Marina). The tightrope walkers 'demonstrate' there is no possibility of death, nor *hope* of death – a twist that is authentic Auden, who is wedded to complication. 'The wounded cry as the clown / Doubles his meaning'. This needs some unpacking. First, there is the counter-intuitive idea that double entendre provokes sadness rather than mirth. But the clown repertory is founded on non-violent, consequenceless slapstick – the pratfall, the custard pie, violence deprived of telos. In other words, the clown stands for invulnerability – and in this way he doubles his meaning.

With the 'Lady … sawn in half', Auden's rhyme and topos is borrowed from the song 'Friendship' by Cole Porter (1939; performed by Ethel Merman and Bert Lahr): 'if you're ever sawn in half, / I won't laugh'. Here the children laugh because, again, there is no death. The circus is a pastoral world, a romance world.

> O what authority gives
> Existence its surprise?
> Science is happy to answer
> That the ghosts who haunt our lives
> Are handy with mirrors and wire,
> That song and sugar and fire,

[8] W. H. Auden, *For the Time Being* (London: Faber, 1945), p. 7, lines 1–10. Subsequent references to Auden are to this edition and are given in parentheses in the text.

Courage and come-hither eyes
Have a genius for taking pains.
But how does one think up a habit?
Our wonder, our terror remains. (lines 11–20)

'O what authority gives / Existence its surprise?' Auden doesn't mean an
eternal freshness. He means a further dimension – death and what comes
after death – and the lack of reliable 'authority' to quote on the subject.
Science's rational answer is that the spiritual dimension is fake, a manipulation, a contrivance – 'mirrors and wire'. The sexual/love/alcohol impulses
are temporarily transcendent: 'a genius for taking pains', which is a variant
on the aphorism that genius is a gift for taking infinite pains. Here it
means the removal of pain.

But what, asks Auden, makes us *habitually* fear death and speculate that
we will survive it? The third stanza involves the dramatisation of death
in art:

Art opens the fishiest eye
To the Flesh and the Devil who heat
The Chamber of Temptation
Where heroes roar and die.
We are wet with sympathy now;
Thanks for the evening; but how
Shall we satisfy when we meet,
Between Shall-I and I-will,
The lion's mouth whose hunger
No metaphors can fill? (lines 21–30)

Auden references but rewrites Meshach, Shadrach and Abednego in the
fiery furnace, and Daniel in the lions' den. In the Bible, the young men
survive. Here, we see instead a simulacrum of death. And the temptation
is desire, the heat of desire. This, like the circus, is a romance, but what
will happen when we confront not a metaphor but the actual lion – death
itself?

Well, who in his own backyard
Has not opened his heart to the smiling
Secret he cannot quote?
Which goes to show that the Bard
Was sober when he wrote
That this world of fact we love
Is unsubstantial stuff:
All the rest is silence
On the other side of the wall;

And the silence ripeness,
And the ripeness all. (lines 31–41)

'Well, who in his own backyard / Has not opened his heart to the smiling / Secret he cannot quote?' This means that in private we harbour a conviction of survival after death, but we can't be specific, can't 'quote' an authority.

We know the world of fact will disappear. And after that? 'All the rest is silence / On the other side of the wall; / And the silence ripeness, / And the ripeness all.' Following his paraphrase of what Shakespeare 'wrote' in *The Tempest* of the 'insubstantial pageant' (IV.i.155), Auden conflates two plays, *Hamlet* and *King Lear*: 'Men must endure / Their going hence, even as their coming hither: / Ripeness is all.' (V.ii.10). In each case, Shakespeare is continent and reserved. 'The readiness is all' in *Hamlet* (V.ii.194–5). But Auden's fusion implies not stoicism but fruition. Again, the words are almost exactly as they are in Shakespeare, but their import is transfigured.

The idea of quotation is central in this final stanza of Auden's. He begins by invoking the 'authority' of quotation – as a source outside the self – which is inoperative. And then proceeds to quote not once but twice – using the authority of Shakespeare, while at the same time working his actual words until they mean something different from the original.

Kipling versus MacNeice

In Kipling's story 'Love o' Women' (1893) a womanising gentleman ranker called Larry Tighe is dying of syphilis. In the late stages, his locomotor ataxia, his wrecked nervous system, is so bad he can't walk and is carried on a litter. He is carried to meet his old forsaken love, who now works in a whorehouse – a fate he is responsible for – and there he declares, like the wounded Antony outside Cleopatra's Monument in Shakespeare's play, 'I am dying, Egypt, dying' (*Antony and Cleopatra*, IV.xv.43). By 'Egypt', he means, of course, Cleopatra.

But there is a crucial difference. The difference is this. Larry Tighe's story is narrated by Terence Mulvaney, an Irish soldier who has had his own problems with women. So what Tighe, in Mulvaney's accent, actually says is not the dulcet Shakespearean delivery we are used to from Gielgud. But instead, 'I am dyin', Aigypt, dyin'.'[9] Mulvaney of course has no idea

---

[9] Kipling, 'Love o' Women', in *Many Inventions* (London: Macmillan, 1893), pp. 247–78 (p. 275).

that Larry Tighe is quoting from Shakespeare. (Anymore than Pyecroft knew Vickery was quoting from *Hamlet*.)

The effect is at once elevated – that Shakespearean afflatus borrowed – and radically, riskily remade, still as a tragedy, but a tragedy below the salt. Kipling is a great democratic writer, who believed that the colonel's lady and Judy O'Grady are sisters under their skins. You can't underestimate the work the dialect is doing here to re-present the familiar Shakespearean plangency. The familiar words are defamiliarised. It *feels* completely different because it sounds different. It could sound comic. It might sound comic if Kipling had chosen a Midlands accent, a Birmingham accent. As it is, it sounds new. As if the anonymous people, people who don't get a mention in Plutarch, are granted the poetry of their own lives.

The same Shakespearean quotation would be a lot less effective without the dialect. We can check this statement, as it happens, because Louis MacNeice, the Ulster poet, used the very same quotation, without an Irish accent, in his poem 'The Sunlight on the Garden' (1936–8). This is the first stanza:

> The sunlight on the garden
> Hardens and grows cold,
> We cannot cage the minute
> Within its nets of gold,
> When all is told
> We cannot beg for pardon.[10]

Let's skip to the third stanza:

> The sky was good for flying
> Defying the church bells
> And every evil iron
> Siren and what it tells:
> The earth compels,
> We are dying, Egypt, dying
>
> And not expecting pardon[.] (p. 105)

So, there is no reprieve from the death sentence we all have to live with.

It is Shakespeare straight. Or very nearly straight. '*We* are dying, Egypt, dying.' No monkeying around with the voicing. And it is little more than a short-cut for MacNeice – a quick way of telling us that time flies and that we are dying all the time, if not at this particular moment. In Kipling

---

[10] Louis MacNeice, *Collected Poems 1925–1948* (London: Faber, 1949), p. 104. Subsequent references to MacNeice are to this edition.

and Shakespeare, the phrase speaks out of the moment of crisis. In the MacNeice poem, dying is a chronic condition, not a critical one. And it doesn't mean what it means in Shakespeare's play. It is a *memento mori* in MacNeice. So, the same words, but radically different in meaning. 'Egypt' means absolutely nothing in the MacNeice.

I once talked to the great sculptor Ron Mueck. When he is stuck with a piece – he mainly does people – he turns his back on the piece and spins round, or looks over his shoulder – because he's trying to take the over-familiar by surprise, to catch it off its guard. Kipling's dialect is a way of catching Shakespeare by surprise – and us, too. And it means that the quotation is both exact and very different. In Shakespeare's play, Antony is employing the highest register. He addresses not Cleopatra but Egypt, whose destiny is embodied in Cleopatra. Larry Tighe is aspiring to the highest register – to poetry – as he dies ignobly, eaten away by syphilis.

Bellow

Antony and Cleopatra is also crucial to Saul Bellow's 1975 novel, *Humboldt's Gift*. Charlie Citrine is an ageing writer infatuated with a woman 'going on thirty', Renata.[11] He boasts about his cholesterol levels and the healthy condition of his prostate. He isn't in his first youth. Nor is Antony. But Shakespeare gives us little of Antony's medical records, his blood pressure readings. The parallel works in favour of Antony. Citrine is diminished by the template. He claims kin but he is the comic version:

> Suddenly I got the idea. I went into what I called an Antony and Cleopatra mood. Let Rome in Tiber melt. Let the world know that such a mutual pair could wheel through Chicago in a silver Mercedes, the engine ticking like wizard-made toy millipedes and subtler than a Swiss Accutron – no, an Audemars Piguet with jewelled Peruvian butterfly wings! (p. 39)

The Mercedes is a luxury item, referred to constantly. It is the equivalent of Cleopatra's opulent barge. 'The great captain Citrine who had once burst the buckles of his armour in heroic scuffles now cooled gypsy Renata's lust and in his dotage had bought a luxury Mercedes-Benz' (p. 59). Citrine's identification is indiscriminate. He seems not to realise that Philo's characterisation of Antony is a criticism, not a compliment.

---

[11] Saul Bellow, *Humboldt's Gift* (London: Penguin, 1975), p. 189. Subsequent references are given in parentheses in the text.

He is 'a strumpet's fool' (I.i.13). Citrine glories in his dotage. He embraces the erotic foolishness.

In Shakespeare's play, of course, the principals are ordinary, bad-tempered, slightly ludicrous, volatile, temperamental, off-duty from their historic selves, pyjama-clad in Peter Brook's famous production. There is an ironic fissure between the Cleopatra who wants to go fishing and her status as a monarch. Antony has a distinguished military past and even in his decline is capable of noble acts – sending Enobarbus's treasure after him when he has deserted Antony's side, breaking Enobarbus's heart by the gesture. Whereas all the heartbreak in *Humboldt's Gift* is comic, mock-heroic, an old man chasing tail. Over-ripeness is all in Bellow's great comedy.

Insofar as the novel touches on tragedy, it is through Von Humboldt Fleisher, a comic, pill-popping, deranged genius figure who dies tragically. He is a poet – unequal to America's coarse pragmatism but someone who is nearly the business, just not Big Business, the industrial complex: 'I remember the shine in his eyes when he dropped his voice to pronounce the word "relume" spoken by a fellow about to commit a murder, or when he spoke Cleopatra's words "I have immortal longings in me". The man loved art deeply' (p. 235). Shakespeare in the novel is a synecdoche for poetry, the possibility of poetry, and Shakespeare is everywhere: *Hamlet*, *The Winter's Tale*, *Julius Caesar*, *Macbeth*.

Citrine doesn't have classic jealousy. He makes terms. He climbs down. Whereas Humboldt quotes Leontes (*The Winter's Tale*, I.ii.108) and inhabits the space: 'I have tremor cordis on me: my heart dances; but not for joy, not joy' (p. 402). But even Humboldt's disfiguring jealousy differs from Leontes's in its sordid particulars: he drags his wife Kathleen by the hair; she leaves behind her high heels, resistant, rooted in the earth. The new context for Shakespeare's brilliantly ironic words is unsparing. Citrine is lower down the scale: 'I tried quoting Shakespeare to myself – words to the effect that Caesar and Danger were two lions whelped on the same day, and Caesar the elder and more terrible. [Citrine is trying for gravitas as he imagines the unfaithful Renata and Flonzaley in bed: 'the other fellow's toes'! (p. 401)] But that was aiming too high and it didn't work.' (pp. 401–2)

What we have here isn't simply the quotation of Shakespeare. It is essentially the discrepancy between grubby, black farcical reality and the reach of Shakespeare's language. When Citrine visits Humboldt and Kathleen in their run-down house in 'the Jersey back country' (p. 25), Humboldt quotes *Macbeth*, I.vi.1, 5–6: 'This castle hath a pleasant seat. Also, The heaven's breath smells wooingly here' (p. 26). The actuality, however, is different: 'The acid smell of the gas refineries went into your lungs like a spur. The rushes were as brown as onion soup' (p. 25). For all the irony of 'heaven's breath' in Shakespeare's play, the same lines set the standard here from which reality falls catastrophically short. Shakespeare in quotation represents not only itself but 'the longing for passionate speech', Humboldt's 'Shakespearean longing' (p. 227).

In *Mr Sammler's Planet* (1970), *Antony and Cleopatra* reappears. Mr Sammler is worrying about his unstable daughter Shula and thinking how she needs the stabilising, healing, consoling, assuaging powers of a man. He himself is not up to the job: 'For one thing, *he* never bestrode the world like a Colossus with armies and navies, dropping coronets from his pockets. He was only an old Jew whom they had hacked at, shot at, but missed killing somehow.' *Antony and Cleopatra* is again the benchmark for Eros: 'As, Antony dying, Cleopatra cried she wouldn't abide in this dull world which "in thy absence is No better than a sty". And? A sty, and? He now remembered the end, fit for this night. "There is nothing left remarkable Beneath the visiting moon."' Mr Sammler may not remember the precise words, but he is conscious of their import – the possibility of a relationship so rich that its end leaves the world itself impoverished. The evocation of the moon means something additional in the context of this novel where the moon is envisaged as a refuge from 'this glorious planet', the earth currently being poisoned: 'But wasn't everything being done to make it intolerable to abide here, an unconscious collaboration of all souls spreading madness and poison?'.[12] Not ecology then, but psychology – damage to the soul. Again, the quotation accrues to itself meaning not present in the original.

T. S. Eliot

Sometimes, a quotation accrues an extra author. Eliot's use of Shakespeare in *The Waste Land* (1922) is open and occluded. The notes to the poem assiduously identify all the citations of Shakespeare. Except for one. The quotation from *Hamlet* at the end of 'A Game of Chess' is not identified. It is the moment where the drinkers at the pub say good night when Time is called. (*The Waste Land* is a poem predicated on the idea of the simultaneity of time. Hence, too, that 'Shakespeherian Rag' with its ragged time.[13]) One line is a direct quotation from the deranged Ophelia (*Hamlet*,

---

[12] Saul Bellow, *Mr Sammler's Planet* (London: Penguin, 1970), pp. 157–8.
[13] T. S. Eliot, *Collected Poems 1909–1962* (London: Faber and Faber, 1963), p. 67, line 128. Subsequent references are to this edition and are given in parentheses in the text.

IV.v.71–2): 'Good night ladies, good night sweet ladies, good night, good night'. But Eliot wraps it up with extra good nights:

> Goonight Bill. Goonight Lou. Goonight May. Goonight.
> Ta ta. Goonight. Goonight.
> Good night, ladies, good night, sweet ladies, good night, good
> night. (p. 68, lines 170–2)

As the passage now stands, it quotes Shakespeare but it also alludes to the great, definitive good night in James Joyce's story, 'The Dead' (1914). As Gabriel Conroy leaves the house of his two maiden aunts, Joyce tells us, in a sentence, that 'Good night was said.' It would be enough. But Joyce is a genius of thoroughness, so we get the good nights in all their amplitude:

> —Well, good night, Aunt Kate, and thanks for the pleasant evening.
> —Good night, Gabriel. Good night, Gretta!
> —Good night, Aunt Kate, and thanks ever so much. Good night,
> Aunt Julia.
> —O, good night, Gretta, I didn't see you.
> —Good night, Mr D'Arcy. Good night, Miss O'Callaghan.
> —Good night, Miss Morkan.
> —Good night, again.
> —Good night, all. Safe home.
> —Good night. Good night.[14]

Brilliant. Why does Eliot allude to Joyce *and* quote Ophelia? Because in *The Waste Land*, everyone has a previous life: 'Stetson! / You who were with me in the ships at Mylae!' (p. 65, lines 69–70). The Battle of Mylae: 260 BC. Stetson: a hat, product of the John B. Stetson Co., founded in 1865. Eliot, with his own thoroughness, wants to add that words, even ordinary words, have a bit of previous.

Perhaps I can end by referencing one of my own poems, 'City Gent' (1984).[15] It quotes *Richard III*. I am describing office life:

> [I] trap the telephone
> awkwardly under my chin
>
> like Richard Crookback,
> crying A Horse! A Horse!
> My kingdom for a horse!
> But only to myself,
>
> ironically[.]

---

[14] James Joyce, *Dubliners* (1914) (London: Penguin, 2000), pp. 209–10.
[15] Craig Raine, *Rich* (London: Faber and Faber, 1984), p. 24.

So, first, there is the visual pun, the parallel between the hunchback and the awkward posture involved in wedging the phone between chin and shoulder to keep the hands free. But Richard's anguished call for a mount at the Battle of Bosworth Field (v.iv.7) is now, in 1984, part of a larger pattern of nostalgia, a plea for more nature in the office and city environment. I was working at Faber and Faber in Queen Square, London WC1 at the heart of Bloomsbury. I would rather have been somewhere else. I was discontented, writing little, and barely compensated by the power I allegedly wielded as Poetry Editor, my so-called 'kingdom'. All of which is a long way from Shakespeare's original intention though my import from the play is accurately worded.

In the opening of *Ash-Wednesday* (1930), Eliot quotes Shakespeare's Sonnet 29: 'Desiring this man's gift and that man's scope' (p. 95, line 4). In the Shakespeare, it is 'Desiring this man's art, and that man's scope' (Sonnet 29, line 7). There is a one-word difference – 'gift' for 'art'. Is Eliot simply removing a possible ambiguity (the idea that 'art' might refer to a *collection* rather than a skill)? For a moment, it might appear that the meaning, as opposed to the exact words, is for once unchanged. But it is not so. In Sonnet 29, the poet lists discontents, admits to envy of others' achievements. In *Ash-Wednesday*, the speaker has gone beyond envy. 'I no longer strive to strive towards such things' (line 5). QED.

Coda: Quotation versus Allusion

The focus of this chapter (and volume) is direct quotation – allusion having already been covered extensively in Shakespeare criticism. The relationship of literary quotation *to* allusion needs rethinking, however. There is an elegant theoretical paradox to be uncovered.

John Berryman's Dream Song 29 (in *77 Dream Songs* (1964)) owes a debt to Shakespeare that is crucial to its meaning. The Dream Songs feature a version of Berryman called Henry. Berryman generally denied the confessional aspect of his poetry. 'I am not Henry', he said more than once.[16] He *was* Henry. Henry is a poet, a drunk, an irascible comic chronicler of his suicidal and murderous tendencies. Berryman committed suicide by jumping off the Washington Avenue Bridge in Minneapolis, Minnesota, in January 1972. Dream Song 29 is his great poem of irrational guilt, of the hangover that dreams sometimes leave us with:

[16] Note to John Berryman, *His Toy, His Dream, His Rest* (London: Faber and Faber, 1969), p. ix.

There sat down, once, a thing on Henry's heart
so heavy, if he had a hundred years
& more, & weeping, sleepless, in all them time
Henry could not make good.
Starts again always in Henry's ears
the little cough somewhere, an odour, a chime …

But never did Henry, as he thought he did,
end anyone and hacks her body up
and hide the pieces, where they may be found.
He knows: he went over everyone, & nobody's missing.
Often he reckons, in the dawn, them up.
Nobody is ever missing.[17]

Don't be fooled by the drunken syntax, be charmed by it. It is an idio-
lect, a singular way of speaking that Berryman invented for his alter ego,
Henry – a man intimate with his murderous interior and his unsleeping
remorse. Berryman was also a great Shakespeare scholar who spent decades
editing the several versions of *King Lear*. But the play that is relevant
here isn't *King Lear*. The play we need to hear, to *overhear*, in Berryman's
first line is *Richard III*. Just before the Battle of Bosworth Field, Richard
Crookback spends a troubled night. His dreams are visited by his many
victims, wishing their murderer ill. The ghost of Clarence comes. And
he says: 'Let me sit heavy in thy soul tomorrow' (v.iii.134). This is what
Berryman-Henry alludes to in his opening line: 'There sat down, once, a
thing on Henry's heart / so heavy'.

It isn't often that poets choose their analogues from the annals of villainy.
Richard III: it might as well be Hitler. Modernism has accustomed us to
self-irony but this is something new – self-exposure. Self-exposure that
means identifying with the bad guys.

This reference to Shakespeare's play is hidden. Commentators haven't
picked up on it. But though the mechanism is occluded and not at all
straightforward, its import is quite direct. We are being referred to the
villainous Richard III as an example of moral equivalence. The meaning of
Shakespeare's words doesn't change. They remain a curse.

Another example: Robert Frost's poem 'The Gum Gatherer' (*Mountain
Interval* (1916)) is a bucolic vignette of a country worker pursuing his
livelihood – and additionally a figure for the poet. This identification
brings into focus and resolves certain velleities, certain uncertainties, in
the text of Frost's poem – aspects of Frost's portrait that seem faintly at

---

[17] John Berryman, *77 Dream Songs* (London: Faber and Faber, 1964), p. 33.

odds, an imperfect fit, with the country occupation. We only know that Frost intends his gum-gatherer to be an image for the poet if we know our Shakespeare. The poem as a whole alludes to two lines of *Timon of Athens* (I.i.22–3): 'Our poesy is as a gum which oozes / From whence 'tis nourished.' The Poet is speaking.

These two examples, from Berryman and Frost, use cite-specific verbal triggers to guide the reader. They do not advertise themselves. They are there for the expert. And they work like sophisticated crossword puzzle clues – involving a high degree of difficulty – to take us to a clear and simple destination.

Whereas, my argument has been that the direct quotation is open about its provenance yet takes the reader into a new, complicating literary context. There is inevitably a degree of distortion as the new context inflects the meaning, though the words are exact and true to the source. What seems direct proves to be the opposite – indirect in differing degrees.

Paradoxically, allusion – the indirect, oblique and sometimes hidden invocation – leads the reader more directly than 'exact' quotation to a straightforward destination. How and why? Because what is summoned by the allusion is a topos rather than the particular phrase. The particular phrase is only the means, the door, with its intricate Chubb lock, that opens onto the lucid topos – the evil of Richard III, Shakespeare's idea of poetry as spontaneous expression. In fact, not even the idea of poetry as spontaneous expression – just the idea of 'poetry'. Simple.

CHAPTER II

Quoting Shakespeare in Twentieth-Century Film

Toby Malone

Introduction

In the twentieth century, Shakespeare's words began to be quoted in a new way: to create film-worlds. Cinema is itself a re-creation of worlds, which feature details for film-makers' probing camera lenses to explore, minutely textured to a scale not feasible in the live theatre. Without restrictive laws of man or nature as logistical impediments, film-worlds can take on any form imaginable. Familiar landmarks, accents, fashions and brands might tie film-worlds to our own reality, but there is no risk of an audience mistaking the contents for real life. The phrase 'In a world' is so ubiquitous in movie trailers as to invite parody or pastiche, but it points to the truism that films create and re-create worlds, which audiences are invited to interpret. Film-makers position limitless interpretive signifiers to achieve world completion for the audience's benefit, and 'in a world' where Shakespeare is among the most cited figures in the history of cinema – a claim easily verified through Douglas Lanier's exhaustive 'Film Spin-Offs and Citations' – the volume of filmic Shakespearean signifiers in the form of references and quotations bears deeper consideration than it has been given in previous scholarship.[1]

This chapter deduces the rationale behind using Shakespeare's words in this way. It explores the multiple facets of creation through quotation in the cinema – from proverbial Shakespeare to musical and flashback quotation – and the device's usefulness in signalling information about characters, relationships and expected audience reactions. It argues that the early history of Shakespeare on film is relevant to our understanding of cinematic Shakespeare quotation much later in the century. Film-makers have long

---

[1] Douglas Lanier, 'Film Spin-Offs and Citations. Introduction, "On the Virtues of Illegitimacy: Free Shakespeare on Film"', and 'Entries Play by Play', in Richard Burt (ed.), *Shakespeares after Shakespeare: An Encyclopedia of the Bard in Mass Media and Popular Culture*, Vol. 1 (Westport: Greenwood, 2007), pp. 132–7 and 138–364 respectively.

exploited productively a perception of Shakespeare's cultural status. In particular, Shakespeare is typically quoted in film-world depictions of cultural issues, classroom education and personal intelligence.

Quotation in Film-World Creation

Rarely do films claim to depict reality or real life: many are 'based on' true stories, where liberties are taken for the sake of narrative clarity or entertainment value.[2] Almost always, film-worlds are fictional, where catastrophic violence can rain down on familiar-looking New York City streetscapes with no fear the actual city is under siege. Products, politicians, news reports – are all fictionalised, but retain enough of 'our' world to register as recognisable touchstones. As Nelson Goodman suggests, fictional worlds are made from 'other older worlds', in a process of 're-making' what is already held by an audience into something familiar yet new.[3] In order to populate these film-worlds, film-makers might fill them with elements new to the audience but common in the fictional setting (a brand of breakfast cereal invented by the studio's art department rather than using product placement, perhaps), or elements the audience use in their own lives (such as the iconic Coca-Cola billboard that recurs through Baz Luhrmann's *Red Curtain Trilogy*), or elements that invoke the 'real world' but with a fictional spin (such as the McDonald's-style 'Golden Arches' restaurant founded by Pat and Mac Macbeth in Billy Morrissette's 2001 *Scotland, Pa.*). These choices, of course, do not merely sit with set and prop designers: screenwriters tread a fine line between the familiar (assuming audiences will work to make connections for themselves) and the fictive (jarring the audience from the illusive reality film often approaches). Along this spectrum, the words of Shakespeare come into play. Quotation is not simply a further example of cinematic 're-making' of new from old. It is also a synecdoche for the entire process: in creative uses of quotation, commonly shared words and sayings can be revitalised.

A figure as frequently quoted as Shakespeare in the modern vernacular would seem an inevitable candidate to emerge in screenplays of films: after all, if the photo-realism of twentieth-century film sought to skirt so close

---

[2] 'Real life' in the cinema is rare outside the documentary form: the sensational response to the supposedly 'found footage' *Blair Witch Project* (1999) abated precipitously once it was established it was not real footage at all, and the 'actors' were alive and well. The notable failure of the film's sequel (2000) in part reflects that some of the success of the first film came from its unusual supposed 'realness'.

[3] Nelson Goodman, *Ways of Worldmaking* (Indianapolis: Hackett, 1978), pp. 6–7.

to the meticulous re-creation of a familiar real-world, then it follows the population of film-worlds will include elements familiar to the audience. Many of his more common phrases have, of course, passed into casual usage as idiom or adage, without reference to the Shakespeare, and appear accordingly in film. For example, it is unlikely *Julius Caesar*, I.ii.272 was on screenwriter Nia Vardalos's mind when, in *My Big Fat Greek Wedding* (2002), one Greek-American wedding guest comments 'It's all Greek to me'; the humour is in applying a general saying to a specifically Greek setting. But when rock band Letters to Cleo perform a cover of Nick Lowe's 1978 song 'Cruel to be Kind' in *10 Things I Hate about You* (1999), a teen adaptation of *The Taming of the Shrew*, the quotation of Hamlet's 'I must be cruel only to be kind' (III.iv.179) seems a deliberate reappropriation of a Shakespearean phrase now in popular usage, rounding out the adaptation's film-world that, from the Stratford family to Padua High School, is tinged with Shakespeare-related language.

At other times, the use (conscious or not) of heightened Shakespearean language offers a sophisticated air to the speaker: scam artist Harold Hill, of *The Music Man* (1962), paraphrases *Julius Caesar*, II.ii.32 when he says that 'Cowards die a thousand deaths, the brave man ... only five hundred.' Hill's deliberate misquotation demonstrates – to a knowing film audience – his low opinion of the credulous townsfolk who heed him. Ronald Harwood's *The Dresser* (1983) – which features the on- and off-stage life of Sir, an aging actor, and includes the 'speaking-backstage-in-quotations' habit familiar to any long-standing theatre troupe – also appears to anticipate an audience with some shorthand knowledge of the works. At one point Sir's dresser, Norman, proclaims the health of his employer by joyously quoting 'King Richard's himself again!', an amusingly non-Shakespearean line from Colley Cibber's 1600 adaptation that suggests Sir's link to august early theatrical traditions, when fragments of Cibber still found themselves performed alongside Shakespeare. A very sophisticated touch indeed.

The audience, then, is key to this exchange. As Daniel Yacavone suggests, 'non-diegetic elements of a film, ones with no discernible source in its fictional reality, belong as inseparably to the world it creates and that is experienced by the viewer, as do its settings or characters'.[4] When characters on film listen to, hum or are accompanied by soundtrack music extant prior to the film's creation, the audience is encouraged not only to

---

[4] Daniel Yacavone, *Film Worlds: A Philosophical Aesthetics of Cinema* (New York: Columbia University Press), p. 84.

believe these characters inhabit a world in which that music exists (a sort of parallel-world scenario), but also to make positive associations between their previous experience of that music and this new setting. The cross-dressing Mercutio's energetic, drug-influenced cover of Candi Staton's 1976 *Young Hearts Run Free* in Baz Luhrmann's *William Shakespeare's Romeo + Juliet* (1996) appeals to the audience's familiarity with the disco song, and recontextualises the Capulet Ball scene.

In the same way, film-makers frequently exploit their audience's familiarity with Shakespeare. Characters who quote Shakespeare – from low-brow to high, from those who quote unwittingly to those who do so for effect – establish a real-world link to the words' original source. (Compare Chapter 3, where Beatrice Groves discusses how quotation and allusion can function diegetically and extradiegetically.) As the following section will demonstrate, the interpretive onus for these quotations often shifts: sometimes quotations exist to signal information about the speaker; sometimes to embellish interaction between characters (where the characters either acknowledge or disregard the citation, to effect); sometimes they exist as unwitting adages; sometimes openly to 'nudge' the audience with their cleverness.

Quotation as Cultural Prestige

How, though, do we reconcile elevated theatrical language in a medium that values naturalistic speech? Steve Martin's 1991 *L.A. Story* skewers the vapidity of Hollywood and points comically to this discrepancy. In his opening voice-over, Martin invokes Shakespeare to describe Los Angeles:[5]

> I have a favourite quote about L.A. by Shakespeare:
>
> *This other Eden …*
> *Demi-paradise …*
> *This precious stone …*
> *Set in the silver sea of this earth,*
> *This ground … this Los Angeles.*

By concluding the famous 'this scept'red isle' speech (*Richard II*, II.i.40–50) with a resounding 'this Los Angeles', Martin satirises the city's short-sighted self-regard. Later, Martin invokes *Macbeth* as part of the same voice-over:

[5] *L.A. Story*, dir. Mick Jackson (Carolco Pictures, 1992).

Sitting there at that moment, I thought of Shakespeare again. He said,

Hey, life is pretty stupid.
Lots of hubbub to keep you busy
But really not amounting to much.

Of course I'm paraphrasing.

Martin's humorous reinterpretation of the 'tale / Told by an idiot' (*Macbeth*, v.v.23–27) goes beyond misquotation to full vernacular paraphrase, but he presents it as direct quotation ('Shakespeare … said') to claim for his statement some of the cultural authority of that name, as film has done since its earliest days.

The dilemmas of mixing heightened language with technologically implied cinematic verisimilitude has been debated persuasively elsewhere, but Shakespeare has been a mainstay of cinema since Herbert Beerbohm Tree's 1899 *King John* excerpt.[6] In the early days of the nickelodeon theatres, cinema was viewed as theatre's unworthy bastard cousin, and, as Kenneth Rothwell points out, it was through the 1908 innovation of impresario J. Stuart Blackton and his Vitagraph Company that Shakespeare moved into the film mainstream:

> Seeing a compelling need for 'quality' motion pictures to attract 'classier' audiences … Blackton made public domain Shakespeare a pawn in a bid for higher social status. 'Class', 'classy', and 'classier' became the mantras of the early film makers as they fought to gain respectability, envisioning a mythical audience for high-mimetic Shakespeare made up of Margaret Dumont types out of the Marx Brothers movies.[7]

To Judith Buchanan, the Vitagraph films sought 'to be known not just as entertaining but as pictures simultaneously able to perform a socially edifying function – to inform, educate, and inspire'.[8] These early acknowledgements of Shakespeare as an agent of 'class' and education were a harbinger to the coming cinematic deployment of the texts, and the tension between 'low-class' cinema and 'high-class' Shakespeare affirmed culture as attainable by the everyman. As cinema became better established and more reputable, film-makers used Shakespeare less to garner cultural

---

[6] See Douglas Lanier, *Shakespeare and Modern Popular Culture* (Oxford: Oxford University Press, 2002); and Kenneth Rothwell, *A History of Shakespeare on Screen* (Cambridge: Cambridge University Press, 2004), for two outstanding approaches.
[7] Rothwell, *A History of Shakespeare on Screen*, p. 6.
[8] Judith Buchanan, *Shakespeare on Silent Film: An Excellent Dumb Discourse* (Cambridge: Cambridge University Press, 2009), p. 108.

approval for their medium, and more for deliberate contrast with the popular form. It's difficult to see any other purpose for Sam Spade's (mis) quotation of *The Tempest* ('The, uh, stuff dreams are made of') in *The Maltese Falcon* (1941) but as a deliberate juxtaposition between the medium and the content, one so apparently impactful that in 2005 the American Film Institute voted it the fourteenth best film quote of the century.[9]

Shakespeare is present throughout the history of mainstream cinema, from the silent era to the rise of the studio system and on into the predominance of the star system, television and the blockbuster industry. Michael Anderegg notes that the presence of Shakespeare within these film-worlds (where, arguably, no quotation is ever really necessary) promotes Shakespeare as a paragon of high culture through the position of his works within popular culture; and Lanier suggests the deliberate contrasting of Shakespeare to a new lowbrow context is acknowledgement of the playwright's 'cultural prestige'.[10] In the ribald film *Porky's II: The Next Day* (1983), a religious group denounces a performance of *A Midsummer Night's Dream* as 'vile, blasphemous, [and] intolerable'. The protesting reverend quotes an exchange between Petruchio and Kate as evidence of Shakespeare's distasteful language; the school principal rebuts his criticism with graphic biblical verses. The fact that the reverend's response, 'the devil can cite scripture to his purpose', is from *The Merchant of Venice* (I.iii.90) is not underlined, but the irony is apparent to any audience member with knowledge of the source. Shakespeare is championed throughout the film as an example of high culture in need of defence from the parodic depiction of a Bible-belt mob bent on justice; after negative reviews of their first, rather raunchier *Porky's* film, it was perhaps hoped he would validate the sequel.

Since citations rarely disappear organically into a modern-language scene (excepting, perhaps, as adages), quotations of Shakespeare can appear in film as self-reflective, overt displays of 'brains': sometimes to impress a character on screen, or to intimate deeper nuance to an audience. On the other hand, unwitting or unskilful use of Shakespeare sends a different signal: the audience is expected to check the phrase against their own mental catalogue, and pass judgement on what may be at best a malapropism and at worst a display of ignorant hubris. In the 1988 animated feature *An American Tail*, refugee mouse Fievel Mousekewitz meets Warren

---

[9] www.afi.com/100Years/quotes.aspx (last accessed 18 May 2017).

[10] Michael Anderegg, *Cinematic Shakespeare* (Lanham: Rowman and Littlefield, 2004), p. 201; Lanier, 'Film Spin-Offs and Citations', p. 134.

T. Rat, a pretentious rodent who self-consciously (mis)quotes poetry. At one point Warren histrionically declaims 'Taken at the tide, 'twill lead to fortune. If denied, 'twill never return', a clear attempt to reference Brutus's 'There is a tide in the affairs of men. / Which, taken at the flood, leads on to fortune; / Omitted, all the voyage of their life / Is bound in shallows and in miseries' (*Julius Caesar*, IV.iii.218–21). To the target demographic of young children, this heightened, antiquated speech might be as grand and impressive as it is to Fievel. To a moderately aware adult viewer, this may land as Shakespearean, but its status as a quotation from deep in the canon may conceal the exact phrasing error. To a Shakespeare buff, the humour may lie in the misquotation. We may argue this error is a deliberate variant adapted to the situation; regardless of intention, we learn a great deal about Warren in a few short phrases. Whether he is well educated or has illusions of education, his decision to declaim for the effect on those around him suggests his pompousness and even, to more knowing viewers, his hubris.

Warren T. Rat's example is, of course, not isolated: like characters in fiction, film characters often use Shakespearean quotation to validate their cultural knowledge, or at least to communicate its illusion. In the horrific adaptation *Tromeo and Juliet* (1996), the Lord Capulet figure ('Cappy') calls a Montague ('Monty Que') 'Thou villainous, abominable kidnapper of youth', only to turn immediately to the camera to cite his 'source': '*Henry Four*, Act Four, Scene Two'. Suffice to say, this is not actual Shakespearean text, but an audience might take his word for it. As noted, *The Music Man*'s Harold Hill prefaces his misquotations (as Steve Martin did in *L.A. Story*) with the authoritative-sounding 'What did Shakespeare say?', to defy disagreement. An amusingly hubristic recitation of 'To be or not to be' features in both Jerry Lewis's *The Nutty Professor* (1963) and Charles Chaplin's *A King in New York* (1971).

Thus the appearance of quotations on film speaks to a wide array of viewers. A viewer well versed in Shakespeare may contextualise the phrase in relation to the original works; another, less familiar viewer may be aware *something* is being quoted; and a viewer with no knowledge of the works can accept the quotation at face value, which Tony Howard suggests might 'guarantee "interest and excitement" because of the source material's proven strength'.[11]

[11] Tony Howard, 'Shakespeare's Cinematic Offshoots', in Russell Jackson (ed.), *The Cambridge Companion to Shakespeare on Film* (Cambridge: Cambridge University Press, 2000), pp. 295–313 (p. 297).

Quoting Shakespeare in the Cinematic Classroom

Films play on an audience familiarity with Shakespeare most probably gained in the school classroom, and they frequently return creatively to that setting, evoking youthful experiences of being challenged, moved or utterly bored by Shakespeare.

In the romantic comedy *In & Out* (1997), self-absorbed movie star Cameron Drake (Matt Dillon) is brought back to his roots by Shakespeare quotation: he recalls a romantic recitation of *Romeo and Juliet* in his high school days, and haltingly exchanges lines from the balcony scene with his former teacher. By contrast, the very mention of Shakespeare in John Keating's (Robin Williams) English Literature classroom in *Dead Poets Society* (1990) is enough to elicit a groan, which Keating indulges by likening Shakespeare to root canal surgery. It is not until Keating makes Shakespeare 'interesting' by faux-quoting Shakespearean-sounding text in impersonation of film stars Marlon Brando and John Wayne that the mood shifts, and the boys roar with laughter.

Shakespeare is often represented in film as a challenging obstacle, and mastering quotation symbolises educational progress. In the comedy *Renaissance Man* (1994), the supposedly 'dumbest' recruits at an army base go from struggling with verse to creating a rap-battle version of *Hamlet*. After they pass their final exam, the soldiers' progress is demonstrated in an impromptu, initially halting but gradually heartfelt, recitation of the St Crispin's Day speech (*Henry V*, IV.ii.41–67) during a training exercise, now meaningfully applied to their own experience. In Michael Hoffman's *The Emperor's Club* (2002), a classroom exercise sees *Julius Caesar* read aloud and interrogated by intelligent schoolboys, whose intellectual rivalries are closely reflected in their extended quotation. In *Billy Madison* (1995), twenty-seven-year-old Madison (Adam Sandler) competes in an 'education decathlon' to win back his family business; one event is recitation of 'To be or not to be' (*Hamlet*, III.i.56–90). His rival Eric (Bradley Whitford), reading from a paperback edition of the play, is upstaged by Sandler, ridiculously clad in Elizabethan doublet, lines memorised, clutching a skull. His costume and by-heart quotation are rewarded with a standing ovation.

This recurring trope of Shakespeare's difficulty means when a student expresses interest, enthusiasm or even comprehension, they are regarded as unusual. In *Twilight: New Moon* (2009), a teacher accuses century-old vampire Edward Cullen of not paying attention to an in-class screening of Franco Zeffirelli's *Romeo and Juliet* (which others conspicuously doze through), and is unnerved when Cullen recites Romeo's 'O, here will I set up my everlasting rest' speech (v.iii.109–15). For Edward, knowledge of Shakespeare, demonstrated through quotation, underlines his advanced age and experience; he is a worldly figure deserving of young audiences' sighs.

Indeed, Shakespeare appears in film-world classrooms expressly to interact with film audiences' own understanding of the cultural figure of 'Shakespeare'. Shakespeare in a film classroom typically involves quotation of iconic phrases perhaps familiar enough to the audience, often aided by the prominent appearance of the word 'Shakespeare' or 'Hamlet' on the blackboard behind the teacher. His quotation is a film-world synecdoche for education and intelligence: those who speak it well are generally regarded as somehow 'better' than those who don't, but in some films (*Renaissance Man*) characters strive to become 'better', while in others (*Billy Madison*), the 'betters' are ridiculed.

This extends to quotations that occur during the performance of Shakespeare within film-worlds (rather than full adaptations or realisations of Shakespearean plays on film). Performed Shakespeare can imply cultural superiority in film-worlds, placed in relief against the simpler desires of the protagonists. The teen comedy *Get Over It!* (2001) centres on a high school production of *A Midsummer Night's Dream*, in which the protagonist is reluctantly cast as Lysander so he can woo the girl who plays Hermia. In this case, much is made of the impenetrability of Shakespeare's words, the intelligence of those who 'get' it, and the ridiculousness of the play's director, who retains memories of his 'salad days' as a bewigged, Yorick-clutching one-man *Hamlet*.

The point that binds filmic quotation of Shakespeare in classrooms or on stage is the high stakes: an exam, a performance, love. Shakespeare is a poetic figure easily connected to higher stakes: an obstacle, an achievement, a means of impressing someone. Shakespeare becomes a way in, to indicate the role the film-makers intend the audience to fulfil, either as ally or opponent to those who quote the texts.

The romantic comedy *Shakespeare in Love* (1998) imagines how *Romeo and Juliet* was conceived, written and first performed, and Shakespeare himself is depicted as playing for high stakes, both professionally and personally. Along this emotional learning curve, the film imagines the genesis of many of Shakespeare's iconic phrases. Here, quotations are not yet quotations, or stale words to weary schoolboys, but fodder for Shakespeare's fertile mind. A street preacher bellows 'the Rose smells thusly rank by any name! I say a plague on both their houses!', and a passing Shakespeare (Joseph Fiennes) files the lines away for *Romeo and Juliet*. Tom Stoppard and Marc Norman's depiction of Shakespeare as an artist who appropriates others' text speaks knowingly (and accurately – see the chapters in Part I) to Greene's 'upstart crow' criticism. Their Shakespeare also carelessly tosses off proto-quotes when he visits his apothecary ('Words, words, words'), when he despairs over the love of a woman ('I am fortune's fool') and when he negotiates with his producer ('Doubt that the stars are fire, doubt that the sun doth move'). For the film audience, these now-familiar quotations suggest Shakespeare's genius is a product of the world as much as it is an inherent quality waiting to be drawn out. In this romantic narrative, at least, early borrowings are driven by writer's block and urgent deadlines; upon meeting his muse, Viola de Lesseps, he finds inspiration for *Romeo and Juliet* and, later, *Twelfth Night*. He no longer needs to quote those he overhears but creates quotable lines of his own: a simple lesson that invites the audience to feel comfortably close-up to the workings of genius. On the other hand, as we'll now see, there are many ways in which quotation can function as a distancing technique.

Quotation as a Distancing Technique

Just as Stoppard and Norman use Shakespearean language to construct a richly evocative Elizabethan world, film-makers often use Shakespearean quotation to remind us the created film-world is not necessarily 'our' world. Whether used glancingly (as when a Hogwarts choir sings 'Double, double, toil and trouble' (*Macbeth*, IV.i.35) in *Harry Potter and the Prisoner of Azkaban* (2004)), or systematically, as in *Star Trek VI: The Undiscovered Country* (1991) or *Willy Wonka and the Chocolate Factory* (1971, both discussed below), Shakespeare quotation, for all its familiarity from a film audience's real-world experience, can create distinctly other-worldly effects. Since quotation lends itself to use as a distancing technique (see Chapter 4), it is a particularly useful device for this cinematic purpose.

From the *Hamlet*-inspired title, *Star Trek VI: The Undiscovered Country* immediately owes a great deal to Shakespeare, and features the Klingons, an antagonist race who idolise his words. The effect of allying Klingons with Shakespeare immediately textures them as a cultured race and affirms Shakespeare as a writer of inter-galactic status. When General Gorkon (RSC veteran David Warner) claims 'You have never experienced Shakespeare until you have read him in the original Klingon', it is clear the many quotations throughout the film ('To be or not to be? That is the question that preoccupies our people'; 'Once more into the breach dear friends'; 'Cry havoc and let slip the dogs of war'; 'Well, most kind … parting is such sweet sorrow. Captain, have we not heard the chimes at midnight?') are not incidental, as Lanier's analysis suggests.[12] Indeed, one character's use of Shakespearean text is so frequent he is chided for the repetition: a gesture toward cultural superiority and appropriation. In the context of the Klingon race, Shakespeare is positioned as more than a mere playwright: quotations are talismans common to all, an indication of cultural strength and progress. Since political quotation of Shakespeare is also well known to us on planet Earth, such appropriation aids the series's verisimilitude, encouraging belief in a world of political complexity parallel to our own, but at the same time emphasising its distant, alien nature.

The fantastical film-world of *Willy Wonka and the Chocolate Factory* also features a surprising amount of Shakespeare, all spoken by Gene Wilder's eccentric Wonka. Wonka's use of quotations in response to ordinary enquiries indicates an unforeseen character depth, but those quotations are never overt or referenced. In a crowded elevator, Wonka remarks 'Is it my soul that calls upon my name?' (*Romeo and Juliet*, II.ii.164); as he pedals to mix confectionery, he hums 'In spring time, the only pretty ring time' (*As You Like It*, v.iii.19); in contemplation, he asks 'Where is fancy bred, in the heart or in the head?' (*The Merchant of Venice*, III.ii.63). As a family is evicted from his factory tour, he calls 'adieu, adieu, parting is such sweet sorrow' (*Romeo and Juliet*, II.ii.184), and finally, when he tests Charlie's faith, he notes 'So shines a good deed in a weary world' (adapting *The Merchant of Venice*, v.i.89). Each quotation establishes the heightened, cerebral character of Wonka, and adds to his secretive mystique. These quotations – and others from authors such as Edison, Ogden Nash and Keats – were a deliberate addition to Roald Dahl's 1964 novel-world by screenwriter David Seltzer. They contribute verbally to the heightened, dream-like visual world of Wonka's factory, and underscore its distance from the gritty London landscape, back to which most of the 'ordinary' golden ticket holders will be abruptly, even savagely, returned.

Sometimes, full-length film adaptations of Shakespeare plays borrow other Shakespearean – or pseudo-Shakespearean – lines to sustain their created film-world. Tasked with writing a new linking line in *Henry V* (1989), textual advisor Russell Jackson suggested 'So constant and unspotted didst thou seem', adapted from *A Midsummer Night's Dream*, I.i.110.[13] And while Zeffirelli's *Romeo and Juliet* (1968) featured a number of improvised and jarringly modern phrases (such as 'baby's dropped his sword' and 'cut his hair') in its fight scenes, it also incorporated more

---

[12] Lanier, *Shakespeare and Modern Popular Culture*, pp. 1–3.
[13] Russell Jackson, 'Working with Shakespeare: Confessions of an Advisor', *Cineaste*, 24:1 (1999), 42–4.

Shakespearean-sounding threats. Tybalt tells Benvolio 'Hie thee home, fragment', which strongly suggests *Coriolanus*, I.i.206 ('Go get you home, you fragments'). The Nurse calls Mercutio a 'punk rampant', an epithet with no precedent in Shakespeare, but twice used as a term of derision in Marston's *The Dutch Courtesan* (1605).[14]

Sometimes, these world-creating borrowings are musical. Tchaikovsky's *Romeo and Juliet* suite appears extradiegetically in George Cukor's 1936 *Romeo and Juliet*, but the same film's diegetic musical citations include lyrics from *Twelfth Night* ('O Mistress Mine' (II.ii.33), 'Come away, come away death' (II.iv.49) and *The Tempest* ('Honour, Riches, Marriage, Blessing' (IV.i.106)). Similarly, Richard Eyre's *Richard III* (1995) begins with a jazz arrangement of Marlowe's 'Come Live with Me and Be My Love', while Tim Blake-Nelson's *Othello* adaptation, *O* (2000), is bookended with arias from Verdi's *Otello*. At other times, interpolated quotations fill in back-story for audience members for whom the world is new and unfamiliar. Laurence Olivier interpolates lines and scenes from *3 Henry VI* in his *Richard III* (1955), a gesture repeated in Richard Eyre's 1996 adaptation. Kenneth Branagh similarly inserts several flashback moments in *Henry V* (1989) of happier days in the Boar's Head Tavern, particularly as Hal prepares to execute Bardolph. The juxtaposition of the remembered, fresh-faced boy with the stony-faced king, accompanied with 'Do not thou, when thou art king, hang a thief. / No, thou shalt' (*1 Henry IV*, I.ii.49–50), is a particularly effective interpolation.

But in no other film adaptation of Shakespeare are interpolated quotations from other plays used to such dazzling and comprehensive effect as in Baz Luhrmann's *William Shakespeare's Romeo + Juliet*. All artistic departments were tasked with creating Verona Beach, a no-place setting where all elements, from advertising slogans to food wrappers to graffiti, are quotationally related to Shakespeare. This extends, too, to spoken text. The first words a character speaks after the film's Chorus is a fragmentary citation: 'Pedlar's excrement!' ('Let me pocket up my pedlar's excrement'; *The Winter's Tale*, IV.iv.680), 'King Urinal!' ('Thou art a Castilian-King-urinal!'; *The Merry Wives of Windsor*, II.iii.26), 'Go Rot!' ('Make that thy question, and go rot'; *The Winter's Tale*, I.ii.321), a bespoke exclamation

---

[14] Michael York (Tybalt) and Pat Heywood (Nurse) are both classically trained performers, so it is possible that actors suggested the interpolations. Heywood worked extensively with the National Theatre in the 1960s, which produced *The Dutch Courtesan* at the 1964 Chichester Festival. Heywood was not a member of that Chichester company, but John Stride (Zeffirelli's Romeo at the Old Vic in 1960) played Young Freevill, who speaks the phrase 'Go, y'are grown a punk rampant'.

invented on set.[15] Throughout Luhrmann's filming process, every effort was made to ensure all incidental text was appropriately Shakespearean, so lines from across Shakespeare's canon were incorporated where possible. This approach works to develop a uniquely unfamiliar world (to return to Goodman's 'familiar but new' construct) built of constituent parts known individually but newly united in an unusually rich film-world.

Conclusion

While Shakespeare quotation finds an obviously natural home in films such as Luhrmann's, it is also, as we have seen, a contributory element in the creation of many other kinds of film-world. It has been a means of sustaining cinematic illusion, as well as playing with the audience's inevitable distance from it. In sum, then, Shakespeare quotation has been a surprisingly versatile and enduring tool for twentieth-century film-makers. With Shakespeare traditionally employed to assert the form's respectability, the quotation of his words has continued to play a role in film-world creation in general – and in addressing audience perceptions of culture, education and intelligence in particular. Regardless of audience knowledge, Shakespeare quotation means *something* on film; and when placed in tension with the rest of a film-world, it becomes an invaluable shorthand not far from the Vitagraph Company aims – to educate, inspire and reassure.

---

[15] For more, see Toby Malone, 'Beyond the Red Curtain of Verona Beach: Baz Luhrmann's *William Shakespeare's Romeo + Juliet*', *Shakespeare Survey*, 65 (2012), 398–412.

PART III

Quoting Shakespeare Now

Introduction

Julie Maxwell and Kate Rumbold

How is Shakespeare now being quoted?

If we consult recent books of Shakespeare quotations, we may get an impression of a now-marginal cultural activity from a bygone era. Though these collections continue to proliferate in the twenty-first century, they are contemporary incarnations of much older publishing ventures we have previously met in this study. So their tone is often nostalgic, sentimental, whimsical or kitsch. Some proffer Shakespeare's insights on the biggest subjects – love, life, nature, death and the seven ages of man, as in Arden Shakespeare's 2001 series of quotation books. Others exploit Shakespeare's verbal agility for the reader's personal gain: in *Shakespeare for Lawyers: A Practical Guide to Quoting the Bard*, light-heartedly published by the American Bar Association in 2011, quotation is a means to best your colleagues in groan-worthy repartee; in *Shakespeare and the Art of Verbal Seduction* (2003) quoting 'the Bard's best seducing lines' can 'cajole, charm or even proposition the object of your desire'.[1] Others playfully unite Shakespeare's phrases with unlikely contexts, positioning him as an ironic authority in realms from child-rearing (*Shakespeare's Guide to Parenting* (2015)) to golf (*Shakespeare: The Golfer's Companion* (2005)).[2] The classic literary status that Shakespeare and his printers once sought to gain, via quotation, for his writing is now implicit (and maintained) even in these unserious examples.

The market for the quotation book is, however, only fractionally representative. Shakespeare quotation is vividly present across contemporary cultural forms, sometimes in ways that have only become possible or popular in this century. The e-book, for example, facilitates new means to

---

[1] Margaret Graham Tebo, *Shakespeare for Lawyers: A Practical Guide to Quoting the Bard* (Chicago: American Bar Association, 2011); Wayne F. Hill and Cynthia Öttchen, *Shakespeare and the Art of Verbal Seduction* (New York: Three Rivers Press, 2003).
[2] James Andrews, *Shakespeare's Guide to Parenting* (London: Penguin, 2015); Syd Pritchard, *Shakespeare: The Golfer's Companion* (Oxford: Trafford, 2005).

identify and share quotations among a global readership. Quotation books are increasingly marginal to the ways in which Shakespeare circulates in the twenty-first century; and yet, in their reverence and resource-making, they embody the often contradictory creative practices of quoting his words today. This section enables us to take a long view of the evolving and remarkably persistent cultural practice of Shakespeare quotation, and, to compare quotation *in* Shakespeare's writing with quotation *of* Shakespeare in the present day.

A Brief History of Quotation (3)

As we saw in Part I, Shakespeare's own habits as a quoter developed in relation to such factors as educational and compositional practice, humanist theories of history, and the technology and trade of the early modern book. How, then, might contemporary pedagogy, literary theory, digital publication and social media bear on how writers are now quoting Shakespeare?

Douglas Lanier's *Shakespeare and Modern Popular Culture* (2002) paid attention to the role of Shakespeare in cultural forms such as films, comics, television, novels and advertising that, he argued, powerfully shape our understanding of 'Shakespeare'.[3] In the decade and a half since then, Shakespeare continues to be quoted in these popular forms. But his phrases have also appeared in spaces beyond those imagined in Lanier's inclusive study, including Facebook and Vimeo (launched 2004), YouTube (2005), Twitter (2006), Tumblr (2007) and Pinterest (2010).

These new media platforms have expanded the range of places in which Shakespeare is routinely quoted today. They also promise to alter the dynamics of his relationship to modern culture. First, the 'Shakespeare' that circulates online in quotations, memes and video clips is not simply offered up to consumers by film-makers, broadcasters, advertisers and novelists, but created and/or circulated by users themselves. Second, then, Shakespeare's new-media presence might qualify Lanier's observation that 'the "and" in Shakespeare and popular culture marks not just a link but a distinction'.[4] Does what Lanier calls the 'ambivalence' of that 'and' – the 'simultaneous attraction and tension between Shakespeare and popular culture' – disappear, or become more complex, when the boundaries of culture and commerce, high and low, are blurred by acts of everyday creativity?[5]

---

[3] Douglas Lanier, *Shakespeare and Modern Popular Culture* (Oxford: Oxford University Press, 2002).
[4] *Ibid.*, p. 3.
[5] *Ibid.*, p. 4.

There is nothing new, of course, about Shakespeare quotation and user-generated creativity: alongside writers and artists, 'ordinary' readers have been making extracts personally meaningful since Shakespeare's lifetime.[6] Perhaps what has changed is the iterability, and influence, of these idiosyncratic borrowings. Social media platforms rehabituate practices of formal quotation by encouraging readers to 'share' a post on Facebook or 'retweet' or 'quote tweet' on Twitter. Such platforms can give the impression of a global community of quotation, rather than the more localised and class-determined communities of earlier centuries (see Chapter 9).

But this impression might be idealistic at best and dangerous at worst. Critics are ruefully aware in early 2017 that the 'radical connectivity' of social media platforms can underpin not just global communities, but narrow interest groups. Since the 2016 US election, much newspaper copy has been devoted to examining how social media platforms function as 'echo chambers', offering up to users the kind of materials they have previously 'liked', skewing the 'news' they read and polarising ideologies.[7] Political quotation of Shakespeare in the twenty-first century is not only a case, then, of copy-writers comparing world players to his characters (as in Chapter 9) – or the actor Bryan Cranston's recent description of Donald Trump as 'a classic tragic Shakespearean character'.[8] Nor is it limited to the transparent appropriation of Shakespeare's words, as when Trump of Trump Tower placed himself up there with Shakespeare: 'When I remember the line from *Romeo and Juliet* – "what's in a name?" – I have to laugh. What's in a name could be far more than the Bard or I ever could have imagined.'[9] (The Bard or I!) It's billions of dollars, then, that are not dreamt of in Horatio's philosophy! Quotation is built into the very fabric of social media, affecting what we see as well as what we say. Knowing this, we may well wonder, what are the ethics of quotation?

Clearly, the ambivalent 'and' of 'Shakespeare and popular culture' does not completely disappear in these contemporary platforms. 'Shakespeare' must function, at least residually, as an authority figure for the Twitter hashtag game #RuinShakespeare, in which users compete to make bathetic

[6] See, for example, Sasha Roberts, *Reading Shakespeare's Poems in Early Modern England* (Basingstoke: Palgrave Macmillan, 2003); and David Allan, *Commonplace Books and Reading in Georgian England* (Cambridge: Cambridge University Press, 2010).

[7] Issie Lapowsky, 'Facebook Alone Didn't Create Trump – the Click Economy Did' (12 November 2016), www.wired.com/2016/11/facebook-alone-didnt-create-trump-click-economy/ (last accessed 19 May 2017).

[8] www.bbc.co.uk/news/election-us-2016-37829018 (last accessed 23 January 2017).

[9] www.publicseminar.org/2015/12/shakespeare-and-trump-whats-in-a-name/#.WIYH3YXXKUk (last accessed 23 January 2017).

misquotations, to work. It certainly persists in other forms. In the professional creative writing contexts that are the focus of the first three chapters of this part, more conventionally reverent discourses of quotation operate in fascinating tension with the practice of creative reuse.

At first sight, the contemporary politics of quotation would seem to have nothing in common with the methods or the products of university creative writing courses, the subject of Chapter 12. However, Julie Maxwell shows how quoting Shakespeare functions, first, in a relatively narrow sphere of academic politics, and second, in fictional depictions of international political issues by writers either trained or teaching on such programmes. While some of the pedagogic functions for quotation remain identical to their sixteenth-century usage – as authoritative precedent, technical illustration and creative raw material – they are more typically inflected or affected by the intervening centuries of Shakespeare quotation. The chapter also gives an unexpected twist to one of the historical developments this volume has been tracing. The use of Shakespeare quotation in education was previously decried by Romantic writers, in positively dull decline by the Victorian period, and the character note of swots or show-offs in late-twentieth-century film (see Chapters 7, 9 and 11). Quoting Shakespeare is having a new lease of life, however, not only in Creative Writing teaching, but in a wider redefinition of university English Literature departments and an excitingly emergent school of Creative Criticism.

The following two chapters, by Christy Desmet and Peter Kirwan, discuss examples of Shakespeare quotation in new writing. Desmet is the co-founder and co-general editor of *Borrowers and Lenders: The Journal of Shakespeare and Appropriation.* Her account in Chapter 13 of quoting Shakespeare in contemporary poetry and prose takes us along a full spectrum – from sonnets composed entirely from Shakespeare's words, to novels that use Shakespearean plots or titles loudly, but then disrupt the very expectation they set up by extremely *in*frequent quotation. Like Maxwell, Desmet is concerned with the relations between theory and practice when writers quote their 'artistic predecessor' Shakespeare. If writers themselves sometimes describe the act of quotation too simplistically – as a matter of theft or deference – how might other theoretical models shed light on the complexity of the practice? Desmet also shows us how consciously some writers do reflect on their creative processes, using paratextual materials to draw them to readers' attention. (Compare Shakespeare's own use of the paratext for generating quotations from the first edition of *The Rape of Lucrece* discussed in Chapter 2. A contemporary technological equivalent would be an author inserting Kindle highlighters into their own text.) Desmet distinguishes between dominant quotation habits in contemporary prose versus poetry, as well as in literary versus popular novels. These paradigms can be tested by the reader on examples in other chapters.

In Chapter 14, Kirwan looks closely at some of the most extreme cases of quoting Shakespeare and, like Desmet, finds that it is not a simple case of deference but one of highly sophisticated play. Paul Griffiths's 2008 novel *let me tell you* is written entirely in 'Ophelian' – a restricted corpus of under 500 words spoken by Ophelia in Shakespeare's *Hamlet*. Ben Power's play of the following year, *A Tender Thing*, rearranges the text of *Romeo and Juliet* to tell the story of the ageing couple. This 'constrained' writing is echoed in Kirwan's own critical decision to focus on these two examples in particular. Detailed analysis of these experiments is used, however, to pinpoint what is at work in quotation more generally – as a creative negotiation between restriction and free expression (compare Shakespeare's own experiments with this quotation effect in *Hamlet*, discussed in Chapter 4). Quotation, as both Bruster and Kirwan show us, is importantly connected to control. And the creative tension of now quoting Shakespeare can be productive of new works that are at once ingenious, moving and thought-provoking.

In Chapter 15, Graham Holderness revisits the publication moment of his paradigm-shifting collection *The Shakespeare Myth* (1988). This volume challenged anti-capitalist, Leavisite critique of mass culture by taking seriously cultural products such as advertising. But as Holderness now acknowledges, the book's Marxist framework ironically reinforced this culture/commerce divide, and this persists in criticism today. Where Lanier vowed to 'respect' the ambivalence of the 'and' in 'Shakespeare and popular culture', Holderness urges us to move on. Rather than lament advertising's commercial appropriation of Shakespeare, we should understand its creativity. In a sustained reading of an H&M jeans advert – itself an extended quotation of *West Side Story* and Baz Luhrmann's *Romeo + Juliet* – Holderness takes critics to task for over-reading the film's possible allusions (for example, to US foreign policy) at the expense of its creative quotation.

The *HyperHamlet* database tracks four centuries of creative quotation, and, in a mini-chapter in Chapter 16, its makers, Balz Engler and Regula Hohl Trillini, enthuse about the ways in which digital technology can illuminate the history of quotation. Digital tools can both amass vast corpora of verbal parallels and notice patterns that might escape the human eye. Engler and Hohl Trillini dub one such pattern the 'Romantic routine': a combination of reverence for, and frequent casual reference to, Shakespeare that characterises Romantic-era writing. Databases, they remind us, are not the 'cornucopia' we might imagine. But if there are limitations, there are also opportunities. The prospect of tracing 'rhizomatic' connections between intermediary texts means we might one day understand more fully how quotations travel.

Perhaps the greatest challenge facing such a database would be to keep up with the 'quotidian flow' of references generated by literary and non-literary users in the digital sphere. Stephen O'Neill is an authoritative guide to this ever-expanding digital universe, and in the first mini-chapter in Chapter 16 he examines its continuities with the long history of quotation. As a useful corrective to the trope of user-generated content, he reminds us that digital Shakespeare quotation happens in a combination of human agency, Shakespeare and the technology that shapes such activity. Yet if digital culture renders quotation easy through such affordances as cut and paste, that is not to diminish the creative agency of the users. O'Neill observes how the fragmentation of Shakespeare contributes to the impression of his valency. His dispersal is not to be mourned: it tethers Shakespeare's language to the future. But what does this mean for future researchers?

This final part of the volume, then, examines different kinds of creative quotation, from the increasingly formalised products of creative-writing education and the Oulipian constraints of experimental drama, to the everyday digital constraints of the tweet. What emerges is a sense of the increasing open-endedness of Shakespeare quotation. Lanier described the mutuality of Shakespeare and modern culture; Marjorie Garber argued that 'Shakespeare makes modern culture and modern culture makes Shakespeare'.[10] But in the 'unlimited archive' of the internet, is it possible to capture the 'Shakespeare' that is being created? Looking backward, would a more exhaustive database of quotations consolidate, or shatter, our understanding of what 'Shakespeare' meant in previous centuries? Looking forward, what might 'Shakespeare' turn out to be if we could keep up with the boundless uses of his words today?

[10] Marjorie Garber, *Shakespeare and Modern Culture* (New York: Pantheon Books, 2008), p. xiii.

CHAPTER 12

Creative Writing: Quoting Shakespeare in Theory and in Practice

Julie Maxwell

In late 2014, an advertisement from Her Majesty's Government was aired on British television: 'Now's the Time for Superfast Broadband'.[1] The voice-over boasted 'A kingdom connected by creativity – that's us'. Shots of the white cliffs of Dover (that well-known work of British art) were presented in support of the thesis. So were the quintessentially English cultural activities of fish-and-chip-eating and tea-drinking. And, significantly for us, a royal blue, ribbon-bookmarked, gilt-edged edition of *Shakespeare Quotations*. Why this quaint quotation book rather than, say, a shot of Olivier playing Hamlet? A synecdoche for all the other synecdoches in the ad, the famously quoted bits stood for the nation as a whole, for the best of British in the heavily edited version. Those past achievements were imagined to be somehow distilled into collective urban brains across contemporary Britain: as the voice-over put it, 'from midnight oil-burning dreamers to tech city innovators', the latter represented by a screen shot of a Harry Potter novel on Kindle.

But if Britain as 'a kingdom connected by creativity' (or even by reliable broadband) is an optimistic oversimplification, then what should or can we know about Shakespeare quotation and contemporary creativity? This chapter focuses on how Shakespeare is now being quoted in Creative Writing pedagogy and practice – especially in British universities, where there is a drive to establish the credibility of this apparently new discipline, sometimes against considerable scepticism or even hostility. 'There remains in circulation a myth that writing can't be taught.'[2] '[A]nd its corollary, *should it be taught?*'[3] We know that quotation played a key role in Shakespeare's *own* education and training as a writer. The gathering of

---

[1] www.gov.uk/gosuperfast (last accessed 27 April 2017).
[2] Julia Bell and Paul Magyrs (eds.), *The Creative Writing Coursebook* (London: Pan Macmillan, 2001), p. xi.
[3] Paul Dawson, *Creative Writing and the New Humanities* (London: Routledge, 2005), p. 1.

quotations into commonplace books, for later creative use, was standard practice. The sometimes unexpected effects on Shakespeare's writing have been receiving attention in recent scholarship, both in this volume and elsewhere (see Part I).[4] Practice did not necessarily correspond to theory. A thriving culture of quotation evolved, with rich results. What role(s), though, is Shakespeare quotation playing in contemporary Creative Writing, including Creative Criticism? How and why do creative writers, both in theory and in practice, now endeavour to connect their words to Shakespeare's? How does practice correlate *to* theory here?

As we'll see, there are comparably rich relationships to explore in the contemporary context, ranging from matters of academic politics to major issues in global politics. The first half of this chapter will show how university teachers of Creative Writing tend to quote Shakespeare – with its aura of authority – in an effort to legitimate the discipline and/or particular approaches to teaching it. This is notably the case when their pedagogic theories are in conflict with long-existent literary theories. The second half of the chapter will look at examples of Creative Writing in practice, by contemporary novelists who have graduated from or teach such programmes. Here, the functions of quoting Shakespeare are far more diverse, unpredictable and inventive. They draw on – even renovate – literary theory in sometimes surprising ways, to depict national and international problems. In other words, Shakespeare as an authority and writing model is in productive tension with Shakespeare quotation as a limitless creative resource.

This range attests, not only to the interests and skills of individual quoters, or even the long-standing multiplicity of Shakespeare's cultural uses, but to the nature of quotation itself. The numerous possible characteristics of quotation – its invocation of an authority, its association-creation, recognisability, linguistic playfulness, extracted nature, high portability, shared status or sometimes elite credentials – make it a versatile tool.

Quoting Shakespeare in Creative Writing Pedagogy

In the UK, quoting Shakespeare in Creative Writing education emerges from a particular complex of institutional histories, disciplinary developments and bad press. Such factors help to explain why some

---

[4] Neil Rhodes, *Shakespeare and the Origins of English* (Oxford: Oxford University Press, 2004), pp. 45–84; Julie Maxwell, 'How the Renaissance (Mis)Used Sources: Shakespeare and the Art of Misquotation', in Laurie Maguire (ed.), *How to Do Things with Shakespeare* (Oxford: Blackwell, 2008), pp. 54–76.

practitioners of Creative Writing co-opt Shakespeare's words to promote and defend their discipline: a usage that this section will discuss in detail, with examples taken from leading textbooks, manuals and reflective pedagogic essays associated with British degree programmes. Unlike, say, the USA, where Creative Writing courses have been part of higher education since the end of the nineteenth century, in British universities there has been a twenty-first-century renaissance of Creative Writing teaching.[5] Previously, it was typically offered at MA level in specialist centres such as the University of East Anglia (UEA, from 1970 onward). Within the past fifteen years, however, the majority of British universities have begun to offer degrees in Creative Writing (often combined with English Literature) at undergraduate and doctoral levels too.[6] Many former 'English Literature' departments are therefore now describing themselves as schools of 'English and Creative Writing'. Literary scholars not necessarily involved in the teaching of Creative Writing themselves are *also* embracing creativity as never before in their own work. There is currently a movement to erase unduly rigid distinctions between creative and critical forms of writing, in a new school of Creative Criticism.[7]

Despite – and alongside – such positive developments, the perceived novelty of the discipline in Britain has contributed to the scepticism about whether Creative Writing can actually be taught. In defence of Creative Writing, the venerable historical example of Shakespeare (from the British 'kingdom connected by creativity') is therefore sometimes cited. Proponents point out that even the nation's Bard needed input from others to develop as a writer. In support of the general parallel, specific quotations from Shakespeare are co-opted. This is, in other words, Shakespeare quotation as a debating tactic, a practice that goes back to eighteenth-century British parliamentary politics (see Chapter 9). Here, for example, is David Morley, co-founder and Director of the highly regarded University of Warwick Writing Programme. Arguing that Creative Writing could play a central role in the academy and feed into all disciplines (not just, then, Creative Criticism), he quotes from *Henry VIII*, 1.iv.26. 'The school of wildness', as he dubs Creative Writing, 'is on the prowl; it has new purposes and

[5] D. G. Myers, *The Elephants Teach: Creative Writing since 1880* (Chicago: University of Chicago Press, 1996).

[6] Heather Beck (ed.), *Teaching Creative Writing* (Basingstoke: Palgrave Macmillan, 2012), esp. 'Part I: History', 'Part III: Undergraduate Creative Writing' and 'Part IV: Postgraduate Creative Writing'.

[7] See, for example, Graham Holderness, *Nine Lives of William Shakespeare* (London: Bloomsbury, 2011), p. 9; Graham Holderness, *Tales from Shakespeare: Creative Collisions* (Cambridge: Cambridge University Press, 2014).

territories and a motto of its own: "If I chance to talk a little wild, forgive me" – Shakespeare'.[8]

Why does this quotation appear in this way? There's nothing new, as previous chapters have shown, about quoting a character's line from a play as the authorial statement of Shakespeare himself. (Compare Blake's vehement disagreement with the practice: 'Thus Fools quote Shakespeare The above is Theseus' opinion Not Shakespeares You might as well quote Satan's blasphemies from Milton & give them as Miltons Opinions' (*sic*)).[9] In this case, the inconvenient fact of the play's co-authorship with John Fletcher goes unmentioned. This quotation is partly a form of retort. 'Creative writing has been looked upon with intellectual suspicion, or dismissed as a school for amateurism and wildness.'[10] So the Shakespearean motto owns the insult instead. Creative Writing is implicitly associated with a long critical tradition in which the Bard has been seen as the child of nature, warbling his woodnotes wild. At first sight, this may look like a counter-productive paradox: utilising the original genius trope in defence of *training* Creative Writers. The point, though, is that even geniuses can be helped. This is Shakespeare regarded as a writer of instinctive creative talent who benefited from a measure of rhetorical training (the 'ancient discipline' of 'teaching … writing') but was not overly learned or restricted by his education.[11] Some of Morley's student or academic readers will already be acquainted with this much-reiterated picture: Shakespeare as a man of small Latin and less Greek, praised by Dryden (and long thereafter) for his natural genius. Regardless, the Shakespeare connection is a legitimating move in this particular argument for Creative Writing. Claims such as 'A good writer can scent creative wildness' connect to and amplify the quotation.[12]

As in the HM Government ad, quoting Shakespeare's cultural brand name is key here – to marketing as well as to teaching Creative Writing, and advancing its position within the academy. This differs from, say, free-floating phrases and tags in media usage that do not directly involve invocation of Shakespearean authority. Quoting or misquoting familiar lines from Shakespeare is a media tic that may be mildly enjoyable to readers. By

---

[8] David Morley, *The Cambridge Introduction to Creative Writing* (Cambridge: Cambridge University Press, 2007), p. 20; see also p. 109.

[9] William Blake, *The Complete Poetry and Prose of William Blake*, ed. David V. Erdman, new edn (Berkeley: University of California Press, 2008), p. 601.

[10] Morley, *Cambridge Introduction to Creative Writing*, p. 20.

[11] *Ibid.*

[12] *Ibid.*

contrast, Morley selects from a relatively unknown part of the Shakespeare canon. The freshness of the quotation also functions to highlight his own relatively 'wild' and unfamiliar way of writing in the stylistically conservative context of academic publishing. Morley instead offers a mode closer to the self-help manual, with frequent use of second-person address and the first-person plural. 'Talk[ing] a little wild' is a faintly threatening approach ('on the prowl') indicative of the central problem: Creative Writing's struggle to position itself as a credible discipline of independent standing in academia.

It is not only, of course, Creative Writing's emergent status in the UK that is an obstacle to gaining such respectability. The cliché or 'myth that writing can't be taught' is an opinion often gleefully sustained by the British media, with reports of even Creative Writing teachers themselves denouncing the enterprise. 'Creative writing courses are a "waste of time", according to the novelist – and creative writing teacher – Hanif Kureishi', the *Guardian* reported in 2014.[13] Respected writers on the British literary scene (in addition to those, like Kureishi, directly involved in teaching Creative Writing) have cast doubt on its pedagogic value.

Creative Writing has featured, often as an object of comical derision, in twenty-first-century British novels from Muriel Spark's *The Finishing School* (2004) to Howard Jacobson's *Zoo Time* (2012). In this context, Shakespeare is as likely to be quoted against the Creative Writing programme as for it. Guy Ableman, the hero of *Zoo Time*, is a struggling novelist who studied 'creative fucking writing' at the 'University of the Fenlands' (read: the University of East Anglia, where Ian McEwan, Kazuo Ishiguro and other well-known contemporary British novelists took the MA).[14] Jacobson read English Literature under F. R. Leavis at Cambridge, and later taught there. Perceiving the present-day state of letters to be parlous (to wit: Guy Ableman's own novels are not as appreciated as he'd like), the hero peppers the story with exasperated quotations from Shakespeare. Goats and monkeys! goes without quotation marks (or any form of attribution to Shakespeare): those in the know will know what he means (p. 216; *Othello*, iv.i.254). To everyone else he is – he's well aware – just ranting. Goodnight, sweet prince (p. 54; *Hamlet*, v.ii.338). Shakespeare quotation serves here as the language of the literati (or literate), just as it did in earlier

---

[13] www.theguardian.com/books/2014/mar/04/creative-writing-courses-waste-of-time-hanif-kureishi (last accessed 27 April 2017).

[14] Howard Jacobson, *Zoo Time* (London: Bloomsbury, 2012), pp. 150–1. Subsequent references are to this edition and are given in parentheses in the text.

centuries. By contrast, quotations from Milton are identified. 'Milton was describing Hell when he coined the phrase "darkness visible". "Region of sorrow", "torture without end". I knew the very place he had in mind – Chipping Norton' (an Oxfordshire village) (p. 72). Whereas recognition of *Paradise Lost* could once be assumed from an educated readership too, shared Shakespeare quotation is here the last bastion of culture. Of another Oxfordshire village ('Whichever-over-Shitheap') the hero says, 'I'll count myself a king of infinite space there after bloody London' (p. 330; *Hamlet*, II.ii.244).

Quoting Shakespeare both for and against Creative Writing is, then, a broad debating tactic in contemporary cultural contexts. But the proponents of Creative Writing also use Shakespeare quotations more specifically – to endorse particular pedagogic methods and exercises. This co-option of Shakespeare in Creative Writing's service is closely related to the university and departmental milieux in which the new programmes are appearing. As Neil Rhodes points out: 'Since almost everybody agrees, from connoisseurs of Renaissance rhetoric to post-colonialist critics, that Shakespeare has to appear on the menu, whatever else your Department of English might be serving up, it would be reasonable to ask whether Shakespeare himself studied creative writing.'[15] The idea that he did is implicit if not explicit in the championing of some of these specific approaches to Creative Writing. Fiona Sampson, for example, a Professor of Poetry at the University of Roehampton, argues for the importance of trialling creative translation. She quotes as an epigraph, 'Why Bottom, thou art translated!' (adapted from *A Midsummer Night's Dream*, III.i.98: 'Bless thee, Bottom, bless thee! Thou art translated!').[16] At first sight this creative misquotation looks decorative. Shakespeare's use of the verb ('translated' = 'transformed') has a different primary semantic connotation from ours. Sampson explains, however, that '[a] translation "carries something across": but, as this chapter's Shakespearean epigraph reminds us, there is always a degree of *transformation* in that process'.[17] Translation, then, is creative. The context is a discussion of the deep roots of anglophone literary culture in translated traditions – especially the classics and the Bible, which have influenced the development of many writers including Shakespeare himself (see Part I). Instead, therefore, of seeming like a side-line ('Why should the emerging

---

[15] Rhodes, *Origins*, p. 45.
[16] Fiona Sampson, 'Creative Translation', in David Morley and Philip Neilsen (eds.), *The Cambridge Companion to Creative Writing* (Cambridge: Cambridge University Press, 2012), pp. 118–32 (p. 120).
[17] *Ibid.*

creative writer bother with translation?'), the transformed Shakespeare quotation is designed to clinch the claim that this area of Creative Writing training is fundamental.[18]

We might compare and contrast the way that quotations from *As You Like It* have recently functioned to 'authenticate' other Creative Writing methods. In a chapter in *The Cambridge Companion to Creative Writing* (2012), Bronwyn Lea utilises an age-old tradition of quoting an exemplary author for the purposes of technical illustration:

> The music of poetry, to state things simply, privileges stressed syllables and aims for as few unstressed syllables as possible. Take, for example, the famous line from Shakespeare's *As You Like It*: '**All** the **world's** a **stage**', which is composed of three stressed and only two unstressed syllables. Without the contraction – **All** the **world** is a **stage**' – we get an additional unstressed syllable, which breaks Shakespeare's rhythmic pattern. While both lines mean the same thing, Shakespeare's version is more dynamic.[19]

This is a rudimentary comment on metre illustrated by a quotation from Shakespeare for perfectly straightforward reasons. Because the line is familiar, it may be easier for an uninitiated ear to hear the stresses. But because it is Shakespeare, there is an inevitably heartening sense that one is learning a craft with examples from a demonstrable expert, not just reputable, but a supreme success story as a writer. Although some teachers of Creative Writing insist that the goal is not publication, those who quote Shakespeare's example are appealing to the desire for success – an entirely natural aspiration for fee-paying student-customers, and a shaping influence on both the existence and the nature of Creative Writing courses. Morley also quotes from *As You Like It*, to endorse a writing game ('Shakespeare's Field Trip') that might otherwise sound touchy-feely. He advises:

> … hang [your writing] from the branch of a tree … By placing your poem or story in the 'publication' of a natural space, you are echoing a moment in Shakespeare's *As You Like It*, when the lover hangs sonnets from the trees of the Forest of Arden:
>> these trees shall be my books
>> And in their barks my thoughts I'll character
>> That every eye which in this forest looks
>> Shall see thy virtue witnessed everywhere.

[18] *Ibid.*, p. 118.
[19] Bronwyn Lea, 'Poetics and Poetry', in Morley and Neilsen, *Cambridge Companion to Creative Writing*, pp. 67–86 (p. 73).

(For your interest, this workshop was pioneered in a remnant of the ancient Forest of Arden in Warwickshire, England.)[20]

Does it matter that Orlando's poems are dire, and that Shakespeare is getting comedy from his character's eccentric inscription of trees rather than recommending it as a writing exercise that he had, say, tried and tested himself before going on to *Hamlet* and the Sonnets? Would it be comparable to modelling a drama workshop on the mechanicals in *A Midsummer Night's Dream*? For Morley, a former ecologist and naturalist 'known for his pioneering ecological poetry installations within natural landscapes', the example from *As You Like It* has an obvious personal attraction.[21] But quoting Shakespeare to underwrite a programme or particular exercise is also characteristic of the university approach to Creative Writing. The parenthetical comment about the Forest of Arden adds a seal of authenticity, a creative writer's equivalent to primary research in the archives.

Another key reason for quoting Shakespeare is Creative Writing's uneasy relationship to English Literature teaching. In particular, the literary-theoretical approaches that have dominated in the university for decades. In the Preface to his pioneering study of the American field, *The Elephants Teach: Creative Writing since 1880*, D. G. Myers quoted *Hamlet*. Again, Shakespeare's words were used as a bulwark against opposing approaches. Myers explained that he wanted to tell the history of Creative Writing's rise without subscribing, as was the norm, to 'some currently dominant figure's system of thought'. 'These days', Myers wrote (it was 1996), 'much scholarship in English is sicklied o'er with the pale cast of "theory"'.[22] It was only the word 'theory' that needed to be placed in dubious inverted commas. An educated American readership could be expected (like Howard Jacobson's ideal reader) to recognise a line from *Hamlet* (III.i.85) when they saw it. And to recognise its implications: the appeal to an ancient expression, from the world's most famous soliloquy, rather than 'some' passing academic vogue. Except: theory is far from passé. Although a post-theoretical age has been hailed, and literary-historical approaches such as Myers's can be read as an intermediary development, in practice Creative Writing's relationship to literary theory is a continuing and difficult negotiation.[23] The novelist A. L. Kennedy, who also teaches Creative Writing at Warwick,

[20] Morley, *Cambridge Introduction to Creative Writing*, p. 138.
[21] Morley and Neilsen, *Cambridge Companion to Creative Writing*, p. xi.
[22] Myers, *The Elephants Teach*, pp. xi–xii.
[23] Jonathan Bate, 'Foreword: On Criticism and Creativity', in Morley and Neilsen, *Cambridge Companion to Creative Writing*, pp. xv–xviii (pp. xvii–xviii); Mike Harris, 'Shakespeare Was More Creative When He Was Dead: Is Creativity Theory a Better Fit on Creative Writing than Literary

quotes Shakespeare in her book *On Writing* (2013). Giving the passage from *King Lear* beginning 'Sir I love you more than words can wield the matter' (I.i.50) she briskly remarks: 'let's not get into that stuff about Shakespeare being a dead white male, so we don't get to play with his stuff – his words aren't'.[24] Quotation is used to extricate Shakespeare from the irritations of Theory, and to express a writer's living relationship with words.

Other teachers of Creative Writing advocate a pragmatic approach with roots in creative quotation. Andrew Cowan, for example, the Director of the Creative Writing programme at UEA, has described the glaring discrepancy between his university training in literary theory and his own first creative efforts. He soon discovered he simply didn't have the skills for the job, that he had learned a set of theories that bore no obvious resemblance to the practice it purported to analyse. Ironically, he then found himself required to teach a similar, literary-theory-based approach to undergraduates. What he therefore advises in his *Art of Writing Fiction* (2011) is an approach not dissimilar, in one important respect, to Shakespeare's own training. With almost all Creative Writing guidance, the writer's notebook comes first. Cowan's description sounds much like a modern incarnation of the early modern commonplace book: an 'all-inclusive compendium of observations, reflections, quotations, other people's recommendations, memos-to-self' in which the writer may 'accumulate a bank of words and phrases, descriptive paragraphs and character sketches, snatches of dialogue and (perhaps) quotations from other writers that will act as ... the basis from which you can begin a new work'.[25] In short: do as writers do, or have done, for centuries.

Quoting Shakespeare's example and even his words as authoritative is, then, characteristic of the university approach. It is not, of course, inevitable or intrinsic to the experience of a new writer. This may be seen by contrast with Creative Writing in other educational contexts. In the school classroom, Shakespeare quotation is deployed as a stimulus to creativity, and to engage young school students with Shakespeare, rather than as an authorising precedent. Teaching resource books suggest that pupils make 'an eye-catching poster with an intriguing quotation', or 'select a character and choose five quotations as part of your presentation when you

---

Theory?', *New Writing*, 8:2 (2011), 171–82. For a positive view, however, see Kim Lasky, 'Couplings, Matings, Hybridizations: What Writers Can Gain from Critical Theory', in Beck, *Teaching Creative Writing*, pp. 143–8.

[24] A. L. Kennedy, *On Writing* (London; Jonathan Cape, 2013), p. 356.

[25] Andrew Cowan, *The Art of Writing Fiction* (London: Routledge, 2011), pp. 23, 14.

introduce yourself, in role, to the rest of the class'.[26] The whole endeavour in the classroom is, after all, to make Shakespeare excitingly approachable, not to impress his example as (forbiddingly) pre-eminent. Similarly, in *Creative Writing for Dummies* (2009), 'To be or not to be' is quoted in a down-to-earth discussion of voice-over – while, in a self-published and non-university-affiliated handbook, Shakespeare is dispensed with altogether.[27]

What happens, though, when Shakespeare is quoted in practice by writers? How, if at all, do their practices relate the foregoing theories?

Quoting Shakespeare in Creative Writing Practice: Two Case Studies

The preceding section argued that university teachers of Creative Writing tend to quote Shakespeare defensively, and/or in illustration and promotion of particular approaches to their discipline. Compared to these relatively finite usages, the quotation of Shakespeare in Creative Writing practice is, in a word, creative. Richly original, varied and rewarding our attention, it could therefore be taken as one particular justification of the Creative Writing endeavour. This section will look at two examples by authors associated with Creative Writing in the academy: Gail Jones's novel *Sorry* (2007) and Ian McEwan's *Saturday* (2011). McEwan was once upon a time the inaugural student of Creative Writing at UEA, and is frequently claimed as the discipline's best British success story. Gail Jones is a multi-prize-winning novelist and Professor in Writing at the University of Western Sydney, where she teaches a combination of creative and critical studies.[28] Both write, then, from a position of highly informed familiarity with university approaches to literature and creativity. The exceptionally creative quotation that marks their two novels cannot necessarily be attributed, of course, to this professional training or experience. Writers from very different backgrounds quote Shakespeare ingeniously too. But Jones's and McEwan's narratives certainly engage consciously with this area of study.

---

[26] Rex Gibson, *Teaching Shakespeare: A Handbook for Teachers* (Cambridge: Cambridge University Press, 1998), p. 244; James Stredder, *The North Face of Shakespeare: Activities for Teaching the Plays* (Cambridge: Cambridge University Press, 2009), p. 17.

[27] Maggie Hamand, *Creative Writing for Dummies* (Chichester: John Wiley, 2009), p. 78; Cathie Hartigan and Margaret James, *The Creative Writing Student's Handbook* (North Charleston: CreateSpace Independent Publishing Platform, 2014), pp. 13–14.

[28] www.westernsydney.edu.au/writing_and_society/postgraduate_study/ma_in_cultural_and_creative_Practice (last accessed 17 January 2016).

Jones's novel *Sorry* extensively quotes passages from Shakespeare, in order to reflect on a topic more typical of postcolonial literary criticism – how the Bard has been misused by the British overseas. It is also Jones's ambition to reinvigorate literary theory itself, in an assertion of fiction's intellectual equality. 'All our forms of writing', she has argued, 'resource us as profoundly as theoretical disquisition and philosophical inquiry'.[29]

Before turning to the novel itself, it is worth noting a related critical essay on 're-imagining critical paradigms' that Jones published the preceding year. There, she quotes Derrida quoting *Hamlet*. The 'logic of haunting' (that is, the appearance of the Ghost) is said to be 'the destruction of the opposition "to be or not to be"'. A ghost is the perfect illustration of to be and not to be. At the moment of this deconstructive rupture, 'the ghost requires us not to forget the wrongs of history and to work for reparation in the future'. Such 'justice claims' are similarly at the heart of *Sorry*'s quotation of Shakespeare.[30] The novel is about the historic mistreatment of Aboriginal Australians and the title refers specifically to the Australian Prime Minister John Howard's failure to apologise, especially on National Sorry Day, for past government policies.

The novel begins, in a tradition that may be traced back to the eighteenth-century English novel, with an epigraph from *The Winter's Tale* that hints at what is to come: 'thy mother / Appeared to me last night'.[31] The novel's narrator, Perdita, is a girl struggling to grow up with a mother who goes around making 'fierce, lunatic quotations' from Shakespeare (p. 13). A typical example: 'When Mrs Trevor asked how she felt, an innocent enough enquiry, Stella replied, '*You do me wrong to take me out o' the grave*' (p. 25; *King Lear*, iv.vii.45). Quoting Shakespeare is a persistent mode of emotional self-dramatisation for this neglectful and unhinged parent.

But quotation is not just a tool for individual self-expression. Like the narrator's anthropologist father, Nicholas Keene, Stella is English. The dysfunctional family have emigrated to Australia, so Nicholas can study the native, and the British heritage they bring with them is depicted as oppressive. *Sorry*, which Jones has described as a political allegory, involves a postcolonial theory of Shakespeare as the tool of the oppressor. Quotation is the form that facilitates this oppression, because it is how 'the words of William Shakespeare' may be 'wrenched out of theatrical decorum to service a personal fury' (p. 34).

---

[29] Gail Jones, 'A Dreaming, A Sauntering: Re-Imagining Critical Paradigms', *JASAL*, 5 (2006), 11–24 (p. 11).
[30] *Ibid.*, p. 16.
[31] Gail Jones, *Sorry* (London: Harvill Secker, 2007), p. 1, quoting *The Winter's Tale*, iii.iii.307–8. Subsequent references are to this edition and are given in parentheses in the text.

Or anything else, for that matter. Quoting Shakespeare is here akin to quoting the Bible: used and abused for every purpose.

Quotations also provide Perdita, however, with the means to argue back – and Jones with a means to correct the squint that reduces 'Shakespeare' to his worst users, and unjustly damns *him* for it. The restrictive theory Stella imposes on Perdita – that 'everything one needed to know about life was in a volume of Shakespeare' – is impaired by the very fact that his words can be quoted (p. 37). Broken up, that is, into bits that are of an inevitably 'partial' nature and not the whole picture, particularly her own experience of the physicality of the Australian outback (p. 65). At the narrative climax, Stella is 'calmly reciting *Macbeth*' (the passage beginning 'Infirm of purpose! Give me the daggers' (II.ii.55–6)) while her husband is dying of a stab wound to the neck (p. 124). The shock of this event causes Perdita to develop speech problems. To treat her, Dr Oblov develops a Shakespearean method: encouraging her to speak in iambic pentameter, or Shakespearean pastiche. Finally, one day, when she lights on the same passage from *Macbeth* in the doctor's Collected Works of Shakespeare, the quotation triggers her memory of 'the complete, recovered scene of her father's death' (p. 192). Total recall from the complete works.

The novel offers us, then, a move beyond what are now familiar (if not thoroughly hackneyed) deconstructive and postcolonial positions. It makes a sympathetic attempt to exonerate Shakespeare's words from kneejerk theoretical finger-pointing, rather like A. L. Kennedy's comment in the preceding section. And quotations, which typically function in literary criticism as the evidence to be analysed – so conventional a practice that we hardly pause to think about it – suddenly seem startlingly fresh here. The novel has methods of persuasion and enticement not available to the critical article. Abstract ideas can be made sensuous and emotionally engaging. From this position, Jones finds a creative way to redeem a postcolonially despised Shakespeare – to generate new words from Shakespeare's necessarily fixed ones. And it's apt that she draws especially on his own late drama of redemption (*The Winter's Tale*) to do so.

Sorry's Creative Criticism approach to quoting Shakespeare may be compared with other attempts to move beyond existent theories. In *Shakespeare after Theory* (1999), David Scott Kastan argued that 'Theory can complicate and contest the categories of analysis, but the clarification and correction of those categories … can come only through historical scholarship.'[32] In other words, with theory we go around in repetitive

[32] David Scott Kastan, *Shakespeare after Theory* (New York: Routledge, 1999), p. 28.

circles, ever finding the fault, whereas literary history endeavours to add to knowledge and find some answers. But it is not 'only' historical scholarship (then in the ascendant in literary studies) that can advance beyond theory. Creative Writing also offers to 're-imagine critical paradigms', in Jones's phrase, in this case via Shakespeare quotation.

Since then, a new school of Creative Criticism has begun to emerge more noticeably. In Graham Holderness's *Nine Lives of Shakespeare* (2011), for example, short stories about Shakespeare and Shakespeareans appear alongside non-fictional discussions of the facts and traditions of Shakespeare biography. Within this larger project, quotations function locally as a deliberately hybrid tool. As Holderness explains, his story 'Best for Winter' is a stream-of-consciousness depiction of Shakespeare at the time he was writing *The Winter's Tale*: 'Quotations from *The Winter's Tale* and other plays are mingled with imagined memories of Shakespeare's rural childhood, extracts from the documents detailing his commercial transactions, and everyday detail from his London biography. The "hybridity" explicitly discussed in the play is shown to be the very essence of both writing and life.'[33] It is also the essence of Holderness's genre-breaking approach to writing Shakespeare's life. In previous critical biographies, quotations from the works have been used in expected ways – to argue for particular connections between the life and the art, or in passages of literary criticism, or in comments on Shakespeare's enrichment of the English language and metaphor stock. In common with these other biographies, *Nine Lives* features a variant on the domestic-row trope – the quotation of one's own words against oneself. A quote from *Lear*, for example, appears to rap Shakespeare over the knuckles for not doing enough personally for the poor and oppressed.[34] But thereafter, the possibilities are boundless. In a story that fuses bibliographic scholarship with Dan Brown-esque thriller, another quote from *Lear* spooks a grave-robbing Edward Malone ('The Shakespeare Code'). In 'The Adventure of Shakespeare's Ring', Sherlock Holmes's favourite Shakespeare quotations prove instrumental to a tale that encourages us to deduce for ourselves the affinity 'between the methods of the famous fictional detective and those of the literary biographer'.[35] Here are Shakespeare's words entering and energising a work of literary scholarship in ways that would have been unthinkable (quite literally) not so long ago.

[33] Holderness, *Nine Lives*, p. 90.
[34] *Ibid.*, p. 87.
[35] *Ibid.*, p. 122.

One last, and particularly rich, extended example of how quoting Shakespeare creatively may reimagine and rejuvenate old literary theories: Ian McEwan's novel *Saturday*. *Saturday*'s characters include an emerging poet, a newly successful creative writer who studied English Literature at Oxford and learned, even earlier than that, to quote by heart long passages from Shakespeare and other authors. So she has a recall like Perdita's. The novel has allegorical dimensions, too, stemming from the political concerns of the 'kingdom connected by creativity' (to borrow the words of the advertisement mentioned at the beginning of this chapter). *Saturday* is a post-9/11 novel set on the eve of the Iraq War. Many state-of-the-nation novels, of course, tackle big issues in the contemporary world. Shakespeare's global familiarity and eminence are sometimes used by contemporary novelists to do so, in a manner analogous to Shakespeare's wartime quotation (see Chapter 9). The precocious ten-year-old hero of Jonathan Safran Foer's *Extremely Loud & Incredibly Close* (2005), for example, quotes and even comically rewrites a scene of *Hamlet* after his own father's death in the 9/11 attacks. In Emily Mandel St John's *Station Eleven* (2014), meanwhile, the quotation of lines from *King Lear* in the wrong order is the beginning of the end of the world as we know it (compare the discussion of this novel in Chapter 13). After the apocalypse, what will survive of us is Shakespeare (and *Star Trek*). And what will connect us to the past is quotation, which serves this time as a synecdoche for an almost entirely lost way of living.

But *Saturday* is one of the most elegantly achieved examples of quoting Shakespeare in the contemporary novel. If Jones's *Sorry* uses strangely flagrant quotations to force us to think, in *Saturday* the mode steals upon us. And unlike Holderness's *Nine Lives*, there is, of course, no guiding authorial explanation. Instead we perceive everything, including these quotations, through the consciousness of the British neurosurgeon Henry Perowne. He is highly intelligent, introspective and informed but, unlike his daughter Daisy, has no literary training or aptitude. He reads novels only to please her, which is an ingeniously counter-intuitive (and latently comical) way of making him fascinating to the novel-reader. Parking in central London, Perowne hears on the radio a rallying call to an anti-Iraq-War demonstration: 'Those who stay in their beds this Saturday morning', a famous actor raises her voice to say, 'will curse themselves they are not here'.[36] We are told that 'the

---

[36] Ian McEwan, *Saturday* (London: Jonathan Cape, 2011), p. 125. Subsequent references are to this edition and are given in parentheses in the text.

allusion is lost on Perowne', but once the source of the Shakespearean reference is clearly identified by an 'earnest reporter', it starts to come clearly into view – as a quotation (from *Henry V*, iv.iii.64–5) (p. 125). '[W]hy should a peace demonstrator want to quote a warrior king?', Perowne wonders to himself (p. 125). Implicitly, the reader is prompted to wonder why quotations (from Shakespeare, Darwin, Medawar, medical textbooks, personal conversations) keep recurring throughout Perowne's day. As the central plot develops, he finds himself menaced by a gangster in a car park. Perowne soon realises that the gangster, Baxter, suffers from an incurable genetic syndrome. 'The misfortune lies within a single gene, in an excessive repeat of a single sequence – CAG. Here's biological determinism in its purest form' (p. 93). And here's one important reason for the novel's use of quotations. As the trained reader can spot, it's a neatly formal equivalent to this particular medical condition. 'The longer the repeat, the earlier and more severe the onset' (p. 94). (Compare the nice equivalence in the title of McEwan's more recent novel *Nutshell* (2016) – an embryonic one-word quotation from *Hamlet* (ii.ii.243) perfectly suited to the story's foetal narrator.)

As the plot draws to its climax, however, a converse and more positive possibility develops. What if quotations suggest unpredictability rather than determinism? If the 'repeat' or the quotation is brief and not excessive? Perowne's immediate family members have gathered in his London home to celebrate his daughter Daisy's return from Paris, and the publication of her first volume of poetry, entitled *My Saucy Bark*. The short titular quotation from Sonnet 80 (lines 7–8) is interpreted by her grandfather (another poet) as a compliment to himself:

> He drinks again, and quotes in a curious singsong.
> > My saucy bark, inferior far to his
> > On your broad main doth bravely appear.
> He's twinkly, and teasing her the way he used to. 'Now. Be honest. Who is the other poet with talent the size of a galleon?'

> (p. 199)

But Daisy irritates him by pointing out his slight misquotation instead. 'Granddad, it's not "doth bravely appear" … how can the line scan with "bravely"?'(p. 199). The correct word is '*wilfully*' (p. 199). The narrative significance of this quotation lies in their very near future – when Baxter and his criminal crony get into the house and threaten sexual violence. '*My Saucy Bark*. By Saucy Daisy Perowne' (p. 219). Their misinterpretation of Shakespeare's archaic language ('saucy' means 'impertinent') is analogous to the fact that they don't, in fact, find Daisy saucy (because she's pregnant).

It also anticipates the unpredictable narrative resolution: Daisy unexpectedly effects a mood swing in Baxter by reciting a Matthew Arnold poem
that is, like Shakespeare's sonnet, '*wilfully* archaic' (my italics) (p. 220).

All this quoting is more than a demonstration of formal ingenuity reminiscent of the last century's school of New Criticism. Tellingly, as Perowne
thinks over the day's events, he feels a shared social responsibility for Baxter.
Britain is, in this analysis, a kingdom connected by a duty of care to all
its citizens. The quotations now represent the cultural resources that are
imagined to hold the nation together – or at least to have the potential to
do so. As another fictional character muses, in Alexander McCall Smith's
novel *Love over Scotland* (2006):

> We were held together by our common culture, by our shared experience of
> literature and the arts, by scraps of song that we all knew, by bits of history
> half-remembered and half-understood but still making up what it was that
> we thought we were. If that was taken away, we were diminished, cut off
> from one another because we had nothing to share.[37]

It's like a national scrapbook gluing everyone together – until it's removed.
And there is a further worry. Just as quotations can be used in ways never
anticipated by their writer (witness the abuse of Shakespeare's works in *Sorry*),
so too Perowne fears the unpredictable consequences of the impending Iraq
War. Consequences with which, as *Shakespeare and Quotation* goes to press
over a decade later, the world is very much still living – and dying.

Conclusion

How Shakespeare is quoted critically in Creative Writing textbooks
is indicative of the discipline's status problems in the academy. As new
programmes endeavour to provide fledgling writers with authoritative
approaches on which they can rely, the Shakespeare connection is often
invoked as a legitimating move.

When writers quote Shakespeare in creative practice, however, even old
theoretical paradigms can be used in surprisingly refreshing and formally
elegant ways. Trained novelists are now quoting Shakespeare to address
the global problems that connect us all: 9/11, the collectiveness of moral
responsibility for criminal actions, the unforeseeable consequences of the
Iraq War, the apocalypse still on the horizon. Meantime, a new school of
Creative Criticism is also quoting Shakespeare to tell its own stories.

---

[37] Alexander McCall Smith, *Love over Scotland* (Edinburgh: Polygon, 2006), p. 173.

CHAPTER 13

Quoting Shakespeare in Contemporary Poetry and Prose

Christy Desmet

Contemporary poetry and prose that quote Shakespeare engage, implicitly or explicitly, in theoretical discussion about the nature of Shakespearean appropriation. The works discussed here are concerned with the dynamics of semantic possession: which words belong to Shakespeare, what happens when others lay claim to Shakespeare's words, and how that transaction modifies the writer's relationship with Shakespeare as artistic predecessor. With two exceptions – David Foster Wallace's influential postmodern novel *Infinite Jest* (1996) and Stephen Ratcliffe's original sonnet remix (1989), which spawned a series of such rewritings – all of the works considered have been published since the advent of the twenty-first century. As self-conscious students of their craft, the authors share a tendency to reflect on the identity of literature as at once oral production, written script and print artefact. Frequently, they reflect on these differences in paratexual commentary that supplements their literary products.

As appropriators of Shakespeare, the writers discussed in this chapter often describe their relation to their source texts through the simple binary between literary deference and insouciant theft, or 'taking what I like', in Linda Bamber's title phrase.[1] The products of their literary practice, however, demonstrate a substantially richer dynamic between quoter and quoted. Three theoretical models that map out the inherent tension between source and citation in these texts are quotation as *écriture* (graphical marking as deferred signification), ventriloquism (two bodies vying for possession of the same words) and dialogics (double-voiced discourse saturated with multiple meanings).

Quotation as a form of *écriture* focuses on the paradoxes of verbal replication as a dialectic between the arbitrary marks of print convention and the aural illusion of ventriloquism. In modern print culture,

---

[1] Linda Bamber, *Taking What I Like: Short Stories* (Boston: David R. Godine, 2013). Subsequent references are given in parentheses in the text.

the simplest way to signal quotation as the verbatim copy of another's words is through the conventional signs of quotation marks or inverted commas. In her well-known study of this rhetorical practice, Marjorie Garber analyses how the simplicity of quotation *marks* belies the doubly uncanny nature of quotation. First, there is the slippery nature of writing itself. Quotation in writing demonstrates the Derridean lesson that the stable relation between signifier and referent promised by the presence of quotation marks is eternally deferred. Considered as speech, the (parasitic) Derridean complement to writing, quotation is no more stable and proper as a rhetorical practice. In her study of *Hamlet*, Garber proposes that a quotation may be considered 'a kind of cultural ventriloquism, a throwing of the voice that is also an appropriation of authority'.[2] From this perspective, one speech act becomes the contested property of two different speakers. Thus, Hamlet, both writing down in his tables and internalising the Ghost's command, 'Remember me' (i.v.91), becomes a conduit for the Ghost's words rather than a speaker in his own right. While the ventriloquist appropriates to himself the source's words, the power of the dead to speak (through quotation) raises as well the opposite possibility, that when the dead (*Hamlet*'s Ghost) speak, the living (Hamlet) are rendered speechless.[3] In this model, two speakers cannot share the same words amicably; one or the other must be suppressed. Thus, while quotation marks are the topographic signs of deference, quotation as ventriloquism is an aggressive act of appropriation that can put under erasure, so to speak, both the quoter and the quoted.

Dialogics offers an alternative to the two-body/one voice dilemma of (oral) ventriloquism and the equally slippery dynamics of quotation as the eternally deferred signification of (graphic) *écriture*. Gary Saul Morson puts forward a model of quotation as 'double-voiced discourse', a conversation that occurs at once between speakers and within words themselves. He begins by acknowledging Mikhail Bakhtin's well-known premise that 'the word is always half someone else's', 'shaped in dialogic interaction with an alien word that is already in an object'.[4] On the syntactic level, within every quotation as double-voiced discourse there are two speakers: 'A quotation has its own shadowy *second speaker*, who is not identical to

[2] Marjorie Garber, *Quotation Marks* (London: Routledge, 2002), p. 16.
[3] Marjorie Garber, *Shakespeare's Ghost Writers: Literature as Uncanny Causality* (London: Methuen, 1987), p. 138.
[4] M. M. Bakhtin, *The Dialogic Imagination: Four Essays*, ed. Michael Holquist, trans. Caryl Emerson and Michael Holquist (Austin: University of Texas Press, 1981), p. 279.

the speaker of the source. Recognising the role of the quotation's second speaker is essential to understanding the life of the quotation.'[5] The original author's sovereignty is widely recognised in law and social practice, but in Morson's formulation, both first and second speakers have 'rights'.[6] Accordingly, he defines a spectrum of relationships between two engaged but separate speakers: you can speak as yourself, mark cited material carefully with quotation marks, paraphrase, or produce indirect discourse to interject a greater or lesser degree of separation between source and quotation. In this way, the two-body/one-voice problem created by quotation as ventriloquism/*écriture* is reconceived as two voices engaged dialogically with one another along a relational spectrum.

The remainder of this chapter examines the dynamics of Shakespearean quotation in a mixture of contemporary poetry and prose – organised not by literary genre, but according to the ways in which these artists play with Shakespearean texts as artistic material available for appropriation. The first two sections of the chapter focus on reworkings of Shakespearean texts as meditations on artistic craft, ranged along a continuum from free-wheeling, even raucous remixing of Shakespeare's words to, less frequently but powerfully, a tightly controlled, parsimonious quotation. The third section considers the ethics of quotation as appropriation, ranging from an act of theft to a saving gift. The fourth explores more extreme visions of the literary politics of quotation through the limit cases of a thoroughly irreverent riffing on Shakespeare's text and an imagined dystopia in which Shakespearean quotation becomes a poetic way of experiencing life as something more than mere survival.

Remixing Shakespeare

Among Shakespeare's works, contemporary poets have perhaps engaged most intensively with the Sonnets. Selective quotation takes place against the broader background of 'rewriting' or translating the poems, in the terms used by Sharmila Cohen and Paul Legault. In their 2012 anthology, Cohen and Legault assigned each sonnet to a different poet and charged them to 'translate' the sonnet 'from English to English'. The resulting acts of appropriation aim variously to 'inhabit', 'put [a] mark on', 'break

[5] Gary Saul Morson, *The Words of Others: From Quotation to Culture* (New Haven: Yale University Press, 2011), p. 96 (emphasis in original).
[6] *Ibid.*, p. 99.

down' and 'steal' from Shakespeare's poems.[7] Parody, the most traditional form of rewriting Shakespeare demonstrated in the anthology, involves no quotation beyond citation of those words required to signal syntactic imitation. See, for instance, the insouciantly homely inversion of Sonnet 130 by Harryette Mullen, which begins: 'My honeybunch's peppers are nothing like neon. Today's special at Red Lobster is redder than her kisser' (p. 204, lines 1–2). One strain of stylistic translation that engages more theoretically with quotation as a rhetorical practice involves typographical manipulation. Daniel Tiffany quotes Sonnet 43 verbatim, simply reversing the figure/ground relationship of the page to offer an X-ray version of the poem, white print on a black background (p. 63). Through the typographical manipulation, Shakespeare's sonnet becomes a ghostly version of itself.

Another form of translation that involves quotation of Shakespeare through purely typographical means are mirror poems, which reverse the word order of the Shakespearean original while maintaining its fourteen-line structure. Within the Cohen–Legault anthology, Sina Queyras produces four mirror poems from Sonnet 85, first selecting words in bold from Shakespeare's version; then reversing the poem from last word to first, striking through words that disrupt the emerging sense of this new poem; then omitting the stricken words to leave empty spaces within the poetic line; and, in the fourth and final iteration, bringing the dispersed words together in regular syntactic formation to create a wholly new verse (pp. 129–30). Maureen Owen does something similar with Sonnet 147, reversing the poem's order line by line and word by word, and then pulling out into the margins extraneous words that would mar the sense of the new sonnet when the lines are read traditionally, from top to bottom and left to right (p. 225). The result is a dialogue between the new poem (left) and leftover words (right) (Figure 9). Finally, for Sonnet 51, which she reworks in three different ways, Martha Ronk focuses on single words and combinations of words, coupling them to form new syntactic strings. The second version is a rhetorical tour de force, composed entirely from prepositions; first-person pronouns; and the poem's logical backbone, the 'when–then' proposition (pp. 77–8).

Another form of Shakespearean rewriting is the erasure poem. Stephen Ratcliffe's *[where late the sweet] BIRDS SANG* (1989) offers an entire chapbook of erasure poems based on Shakespeare's Sonnets. While the

---

[7] Sharmila Cohen and Paul Legault (eds.), *The Sonnets: Translating and Rewriting Shakespeare* (Callicoon: Telephone/Nightboat Books, 2012), p. i. Subsequent references to this collection are given in parentheses in the text.

Maureen Owen   SONNET **147**

night as dark as hell as black as art	who
bright thee thought and fair thee sworn have I	for
express'd vainly truth the from random	at
are madmen's as discourse my and thoughts	my
unrest evermore with mad-frantic	and
care past is reason now am I cure	past
except did physic which death is	desire
approve now desperate I and me left	hath
kept not are prescriptions his that	angry
love my to physician the reason my	
please to appetite sickly uncertain	the
ill the preserve doth which that on	feeding
disease the nurseth longer which that	for
still longing fever a as is love my	

Figure 9   Maureen Owen's rewriting of Shakespeare's Sonnet 147.

book's back cover demonstrates the process of erasure with Sonnet 73, circling some words and scribbling over others, within the body of the chapbook the Shakespearean substratum disappears entirely, leaving *in situ* within the fourteen-line format only those words that have not been erased. Confronted with a series of clean pattern poems, even the Shakespeare-savvy reader is hard-pressed to find the original Sonnets within Ratcliffe's offerings. Transcribed below, without the spaces created in the printed version by erasure of text, is Ratcliffe's reconstitution of Shakespeare's poem by a selective quotation of words, and even parts of words:

in
one, or
which
birds sang
after sun
a
second
glowing
a
-bed where
was
makes

leave
makes[8]

Writing is revealed as *écriture* by way of typography rather than in spite of it, so that Radcliffe's largely obliterated Shakespeare sonnets demonstrate the erasure of both quoter and quotee as Shakespeare's voice is appropriated and then reproduced through disjointed words.[9]

Ratcliffe's tendency to break up words is extended and mechanised in K. Silem Mohammad's chapbook, *Sonnagrams 1–20* (2009). As the author's note explains, he fed the first twenty sonnets of the 1609 sequence, line by line and poem by poem, into an anagram generator, so that each line offered a new group of words. He moved this altered text to a word-processed document, and then clicked-and-dragged the text of each line, letter by letter, to make a new poem in iambic pentameter with an English sonnet rhyme scheme. (Leftover letters were used to construct the nonsensical titles.) Collectively, the sonnets read as a Shakespearean 'Jabberwocky'. Take, for instance, the familiar opening lines of Sonnet 3: 'Look in thy glass and tell the face thou viewest / Now is the time that face should form another.' Courtesy of the anagram machine, Mohammad's version comes out this way:

> Go softly to the Disneyland Hotel,
> Its simulacral threshold grown sublime:
> The bedrooms all emit that new car smell,
> Like nothing else in bourgie Anaheim.[10]

Thanks to the careful crafting of rhythm and rhyme, the new version sounds eerily Shakespearean, even as its parodic content can hold together only for the length of four lines, to be supplanted by further nonsense in the next quatrain. *Sonnagrams* quotes Shakespeare (on the level of the letter) without quoting his poetry (on the level of the word), presenting poetry as *écriture*. The careful maintenance of Shakespearean rhyme and rhythm also makes Mohammad's poetry a species of garbled ventriloquism.

Within Cohen and Legault's anthology, Dana Wier performs a similar kind of Shakespearean ventriloquism by simply repeating each line of Sonnet 106 to produce an echo effect through graphical repetition, as if the poem were the product of a printer malfunction (p. 174). While one voice does not obliterate the other, the second speaker is limited to

[8] Stephen Ratcliffe, *[where late the sweet] BIRDS SANG* (Berkeley: O Books, 1989), n.p.
[9] On the way in which quotation marks call into question the authority of both 'quotation and quotee' and put both 'under erasure', in the phrase of Jacques Derrida, see Garber, *Quotation Marks*, p. 11.
[10] K. Silem Mohammad, *Sonnagrams 1–20* (Cincinnati: Slack Buddha Press, 2009), lines 1–4.

subservient repetition. In a more elaborate dramatisation of this echo effect, repeated at the four corners of the Whispering Gallery in Grand Central Station, Marcella Durand and Betsy Fagin 'took turns reading' Sonnet 47 to one another while 'train announcements, rush-hour ambient noise and tourists using the gallery simultaneously disrupted and enriched the translation' (p. 68, authors' note). Each iteration of the sonnet begins with the familiar words 'Betwixt mine eye', and then moves, through the haphazard pattern of verbal traffic around the two poets, in a different direction. The transcribed discourse creates graphic representations of many voices coalescing at random. This poetry is chaotic, but genuinely dialogic.

The most interesting sonnet remix, from a theoretical perspective, is poet and visual artist Jen Bervin's *Nets* (2004). First published as an art book, then a mass-produced paperback by Ugly Duckling Press, *Nets* is an octavo-sized pocket-book with pleasing typeface and a tan cover of rough rag, adorned only with a black graphic of a net. Each cream-coloured page contains one sonnet: Shakespeare's lines are rendered in pale grey, with only those words singled out to create Bervin's own poems floating above the Shakespearean lines in bold black type. As her 'Working Note' states: 'I stripped Shakespeare's sonnets bare to the "nets" to make the space of the poem open, porous, possible – a divergent elsewhere. When we write poems, the history of poetry is with us, pre-inscribed in the white of the page; when we read or write poems, we do it with or against this palimpsest.'[11] Bervin's palimpsest poems enjoy an ambivalent relationship with the Shakespeare poems they overlie. As double-voiced discourse, the palimpsest of *Nets* puts Bervin's sense into conversation with Shakespeare's. For instance, the 'tattered weed of small worth' of Sonnet 2 (line 4), an admonitory metaphor of the future fate of the young man's youth, becomes the protagonist of its own drama: in Bervin's poem, 'A weed of small worth asked to be new made' (line 4). Abstract nouns are often the subjects, even the agents, of Bervin's poems. So are natural entities. In Sonnet 12, Shakespeare gives us the image of 'lofty trees, barren of leaves' (line 5). In the layered revision by Bervin, 'count the trees green, girded up in sheaves' (line 7), the trees have been rejuvenated and newly adorned. It is possible to see Bervin's poems as parasitic on or deferring to Shakespeare. But because of the aesthetic qualities of the material book, where both bold and faded print have texture and tone, the viewer's oscillation between

[11] Jen Bervin, *Nets* (Berkeley: Ugly Duckling Press, 2004), n.p. Subsequent references are given in parentheses in the text.

looking at and looking through the page makes the palimpsest sonnets vibrantly dialogic.

A self-published dramatic remix from Nigeria-born British artist and blogger Ben Arogundade, *The Shakespeare Mashup* (2011), also attempts to use the computer to produce Shakespearean fragments that can be recombined into a new narrative. Arogundade downloaded *Romeo and Juliet* and *Othello* from online sources into a Word document and excised the stage directions and dialogue from all characters but the principal four lovers.[12] With the help of an unidentified computer program, he randomised the remaining text, then began selecting and arranging textual bits to make conversational exchanges that largely make sense within the new plot, but provide knowledgeable readers with the amusement of recognising the marriage of disparate sources and dramatic situations. (Compare Chapter 14, on quotation in Oulipian texts.) For Arogundade, as for some of the poets discussed here, sharing understanding of the process of remix seems crucial to the artistic experience. Like Bervin, he uses textile metaphors for the final product, calling the artistic process 'a kind of digital crochet' (p. 73). This mash-up has a complicated plot line in which Othello, convinced that Desdemona has been unfaithful, begins an affair with Juliet. Desdemona, in revenge, arranges a gay tryst between Othello and Romeo. One sample of dramatic exchange between Othello and Juliet in bed illustrates the mash-up's method and comic effect. Juliet criticises: 'You kiss by the book', to which Othello replies 'An unauthorised kiss', and Juliet concurs cheerfully: 'Amen'. To Othello's next gambit, 'Are you not a strumpet?', Juliet demurs 'It is an honour I dream not of' (p. 146). With nothing more complicated than direct quotations, Arogundade successfully transforms Juliet at her most demure, acknowledging her parents' authority in matters of the heart, into a ribald ironist.

But while mash-up artists play with Shakespeare's verse as plentiful and plastic material for new art, a few writers, almost perversely, turn parsimonious quotation into an art form. The greatest tour de force of this type has to be David Foster Wallace's monumental novel *Infinite Jest* (1996). While the book's title suggests correctly that it can be read profitably as an appropriation of *Hamlet*, readers are hard-pressed to find any Shakespearean phrases in the 1,100-page book beyond its title and the endnote references to Poor Yorick Entertainment Unlimited. *Infinite Jest* is also the name

---

[12] Ben Arogundade, *The Shakespeare Mashup: Shakespeare Plays 'Othello' and 'Romeo and Juliet' Remixed*, e-book (Conwy: Arogundade Limited, 2011), pp. 54–6. Subsequent references are given in parentheses in the text.

of James O. Incandenza's infamous film, the deadly 'entertainment' that reduces spectators to infants who are so absorbed in it that they soil themselves and starve to death.[13] The broad outlines of the plot have little to do with *Hamlet*. Hamlet's 'feigned madness' becomes an overt object of the protagonist Hal Incandenza's scattered musings only very late in the novel, where he considers that it has 'always seemed a little preposterous that Hamlet, for all his paralyzing doubt about everything, never once doubts the reality of the ghost. Never questions whether his own madness might not in fact be unfeigned … That is, whether Hamlet might only be *feigning* feigning' (pp. 900–1). Perhaps there is some covert quotation of relatively common words from *Hamlet* – 'doubt', 'madness' and even 'ghost' – but these are not marked by Wallace to prompt recognition of phrases from the play. At the same time, thematic connections with *Hamlet* may be reinforced by external evidence. Stephen J. Burn notes that Wallace often abbreviated his book title as '*In. Jest*, a homophone, of course, for *ingest*'.[14] In a particularly clever way, these homophonic puns take us away from Shakespeare as strong precursor – the book openly mocks Harold Bloom's theories of literary filiation – but takes us back to another, more corporeal and territorial source, *Hamlet's* Gravedigger scene and the skull and bodies turned to earth that populate it. Wallace's lines of literary ancestry are porous, contaminated and as full of holes as Bervin's nets. As a rewriting of Shakespeare's *Hamlet*, *Infinite Jest* is a pocky corpse that is not simply parasitic on its source, but dissolves into it as bodies into ground in an elaborate alimentary metaphor. Any dialogic interaction with Shakespeare's plays can take place only after reading the novel – a Herculean labour – and in the reader's own thinking.

Quotation as Theft and Salvation

While David Foster Wallace is cagey about his Shakespeare connections, critic-writer Linda Bamber takes on with zeal the cultural politics of Shakespearean quotation. *Taking What I Like: Short Stories* (2013) works with a venerable definition of appropriation as 'seizure for one's own purposes'.[15] Her collected stories, most of which deal with Shakespearean plots, work

[13] David Foster Wallace, *Infinite Jest* (New York: Back Bay Books/Little, Brown, 1996), pp. 990–3.
[14] Stephen J. Burn, '"Webs of Nerves Pulsing and Firing": *Infinite Jest* and the Science of Mind', in Marshall Boswell and Stephen J. Burn (eds.), *A Companion to David Foster Wallace Studies* (New York: Palgrave Macmillan, 2013), pp. 59–85 (p. 65).
[15] Jean I. Marsden (ed.), *The Appropriation of Shakespeare: Post-Renaissance Reconstructions of the Works and the Myth* (New York: St Martin's Press, 1991), p. 1.

through a puckish rewriting of the plays in contemporary terms, peppered with selected Shakespearean quotations that acknowledge faithfully their origin through the author's use of italics. (Compare Chapter 12.) The result is conceptually a mix of appropriation as theft – 'taking what I like' – and literary deference. 'Casting Call' is a wild send-up of *Othello* in which an academic Desdemona is murdered by Othello in a nearly all-white English department, but finds happiness after that 'death' working at a historically black college. In this radical reworking of Shakespeare's tragedy, we find sprinkled through Desdemona's musings all of the famous lines and phrases that academics might have underlined in their *Cambridge Shakespeare* for teaching the text to undergraduates: for instance, an 'extravagant and wheeling stranger' (p. 12); 'Keep up your bright swords, for the dew will rust them' (p. 16); 'Even now an old black ram is tupping your white ewe' (p. 15); 'To be now a sensible man, by and by a fool, and presently a beast' (p. 31); and finally, 'Put out the light and then put out the light' (p. 33).

'In the Forest' hews closely to the plot of *As You Like It*, providing metadramatic commentary on its implausibility through interpolated snatches of conversation between fictional observers named A and Q, and some witty banter about the artificiality of the play's language by the characters of *As You Like It*:

> 'I'd help you if I could', says Corin. '*But I am shepherd to another man and do not shear the fleeces that I graze*'.[16]
> 'Huh?' says Touchstone.
> 'He means he's a hired hand', guesses Celia. Corin nods.
> 'I don't own my own sheep', he says. 'I don't even have my own place'. (p. 95)

In general, the texts incorporate Shakespearean lines smoothly into Bamber's own prose, demonstrating the Renaissance practice of *imitatio*, a topic upon which the narrator offers readers a mini-lecture. Renaissance students populated purloined forms with new content, or vice versa: 'If new art arose from the process, so much the better; but the real point was to get the student thoroughly soaked in the past' (p. 103). The author-narrator notes that 'I myself am practicing imitation, taking what I like from *As You Like It*' and concludes with a meditation of the opposed fates of Thomas Lodge's *Rosalynde* and Shakespeare's appropriation of it: 'As always, it's the execution, not the material, that counts' (p. 103).

---

[16] This is a direct quotation of *As You Like It*, IV.ii.72.

Within Bamber's critical framework, a successful 'execution' seems to lie in the plot rather than in the incorporated Shakespearean quotes, for the story ends with Phoebe, apparently married happily to Sylvius, complaining to Corin that she had known 'all along' that ' "Ganymede" was a woman' (p. 119) and that it was the woman to whom she was attracted. 'Cleopatra and Antony' continues the discussion of story retelling as appropriation, with special attention to the give-and-take between Shakespeare and Plutarch as source in Philo and Demetrius's reworking of the barge speech, with reflection on Shakespeare's trenchant diction. In the end, however, the words of Shakespeare and Bamber-as-narrator remain distinct from one another. There is no ghosting, no drifting signification, no intense dialogism within the word. Shakespeare, feminist characters and scholarly narrator all get their say, but the conversation remains merely polite.

The penultimate story in the collection does offer a more theoretical and extended meditation on the social uses of performing (and therefore of quoting) Shakespeare. 'An Incarceration of Hamlets', a dramatic meditation on prison Shakespeare, considers the two-body/one-voice paradox of ventriloquism and its potential for dialogical engagement. The incarcerated actors discuss their varied relations to their characters, whether one can or should fill the part of Hamlet or Horatio with the prisoner's own story, and whether one can understand one's own crime or achieve redemption by playing Shakespeare's revenge tragedy. The most striking icons of performance, however, are not cheering. The first is the multiple actors who play Hamlet in Act v, all gathered in the prison yard and practising their lines alone, while spectators ranged on benches along the track watch them. This small gang of Hamlets, in performance, yields a more docile, orderly delivery of those lines. More horrifying is the scene of men from solitary confinement discussing Shakespeare with their teacher. With arms handcuffed behind them and led by a leather leash, they line up in separate cells and, kneeling, discuss Shakespeare through opened ports in the steel doors that separate them (p. 184). Nevertheless, for all this Bamber ends on an upbeat note: 'Borrowing Shakespeare's linguistic beauty to describe one's own experience is empowering for us all. For men in prison, mastering his work can be a veritable claim to transformation' (p. 163). The redemptive narrative in accounts of prison Shakespeare has been critiqued, but while Bamber calls into question her own cheerful assertion of Shakespeare's power to heal by recording the horrific underside of this institutionalised performance, her implied criticism of the virtues of mouthing Shakespeare's words never reaches a theoretical level.[17]

Riffing on Shakespeare

While the theoretical spectrum from writerly quotation (*écriture*) to speech (ventriloquism) and dialogism represents a dominant paradigm for Shakespearean quotation in contemporary poetry and literary prose, some – largely popular – writers challenge altogether this paradigm, in terms of its ability to make sense of quotation as a rhetorical practice. Christopher Moore's popular novel *Fool* (2009) disrupts the paradigm by championing, and practising, 'Shakespearean' linguistic practice as a vagrant art. *Fool*, which retells the story of *King Lear* from the perspective of the Fool-as-hero, sticks to the basic plotlines of Shakespeare's play, but adds extra characters – largely castle help, but also the three witches from *Macbeth* and a female ghost – and embroiders the story with seemingly endless sexual encounters between Pocket (the Fool) and a host of willing females, including Lear's two eldest daughters. Equally baroque is the Fool's way with language: as one reviewer puts it, 'Pocket spiels like a music-hall comedian, with a relentless spate of winking and blatant sexual banter and a constant patter of quips, japes and backtalk.'[18] He is especially prone to profane neologisms and phrases, such as 'fuckstockings' or 'heinous fuckery').[19] Buried within all the ribaldry, however, there is some consideration of quotation as a practice. Pocket himself is a phraseological machine, engaging in an implicit battle of wit with Shakespeare himself. By contrast, the 'nitwit' (loc. 2600) Drool is a master ventriloquist, echoing perfectly the words and even intonation of others. Direct quoting, it seems, is a Fool's game. At the same time, the novel mocks both Shakespeare's verbal riffing and its own semantic promiscuousness. The Shakespearean character who spews forth nonsense with complete ease is Edgar as Poor Tom, whose ranting about the 'foul fiend' (loc. 3302) can be as wearing as Pocket's relentless bawdy.

Both Shakespeare and the novelist who riffs on him, Moore seems to say, are capable of idiocy. Moore 'immersed' himself for two years in Shakespeare on stage, page and DVD, and declares that, having 'watched

---

[17] See, for instance, Matt Kozusko, 'Monstrous! Actors, Audiences, Inmates, and the Politics of Reading Shakespeare', *Shakespeare Bulletin*, 28 (2010), 235–51.
[18] Michael Dirda, 'Michael Dirda on *Fool* by Christopher Moore', *Washington Post*, 8 February 2009.
[19] Christopher Moore, *Fool: A Novel*, e-book (New York: William Morrow, 2009), pp. 146, 281. Subsequent references are given in parentheses in the text.

thirty different performances of *King Lear*' and listened 'to a dozen different Lears rage at the storm and lament what complete nitwits they had been', 'I wanted to leap onstage and kill the old man myself' (Afterword, locs. 4759–62). There is much to be appreciated in his verbal manipulation of Shakespeare for comic effect. In the trial scene, for instance, Goneril largely sticks to her text, until she finally runs out of hyperboles: 'Sir I love you more than words can say. I love you more than eyesight, space, and liberty. I love you beyond anything that can be valued, rich or rare. No less than life itself, with grace, health, beauty, and honor. I love you above all things, even pie' (loc. 697). Moore thematises the difficulty of inventing new curses on Goneril, and ones different from Shakespeare's, when he has Lear sputter: 'Thou detested viper. Thou ungrateful fiend' (loc. 2030). This effort combines key words from different utterances by Shakespeare's king ('*Detested* kite, thou liest' (I.iv.218) and 'Ingratitude, thou marble-hearted *fiend*, / More hideous when thou show'st thee in a child / Than the sea monster!' (I.iv.213, emphasis added) with the word 'viper', which appears in a number of Shakespeare plays, but not *King Lear*. Pocket continues Lear's cursing: ' "Slag", I offered, "Thou piteous prick-pull. Thou vainglorious virago … Do jump in Albany, I can't go on forever, no matter how inspired" ' (loc. 2040). Pocket's propensity for semantic generation, as natural and unrelenting as his sexual activity, wears its artistic legacy lightly.

Moore, while engaged with the simpler dialectic between deference and defiance that is found in discussion of Shakespearean appropriation, skirts the more theoretical issues involved in postmodern quotation of Shakespeare. Neither Shakespeare's ghost nor a murdering ventriloquist, Moore also avoids to a large extent any intensely dialogic engagement with his source. His response to the dilemma of quotation as appropriation is to riff on the Shakespearean text, engaging with Shakespeare as cultural icon through semantic excess. This return to quotation as *écriture* in the wild becomes a comic antidote to the two-body/one-voice dilemma inherent in the practice.

Dystopian Quotation: 'Because Survival is Insufficient'

Finally, Emily St John Mandel's novel *Station Eleven* (2015) offers a philosophical perspective on the social function of others' words. This novel begins with the premise that the world's population has been decimated overnight by a wildly contagious Georgian flu. Within a few days, everything that is familiar from the contemporary world is gone: 'No more diving into pools of chlorinated water lit green from below. No more ball games played out under floodlights. No more porch lights with moths fluttering on summer nights. No more trains running under the surface of cities on the dazzling power of the electric third rail. No more cities. No more films, except rarely, except with a generator drowning out half the dialogue'.[20] The entire social infrastructure and media landscape have vanished.

What remain of culture, as provided by an itinerant band of performers called the Travelling Symphony, are music and Shakespeare. Although Shakespeare is a nostalgic remnant of the pre-apocalyptic world, the novel demonstrates repeatedly that knowledge of the plays has no real social efficacy. In the opening scene, during a performance of *King Lear* in Toronto, we are introduced to aspiring emergency medical technician (EMT) Jeevan Chaudhary, and a child actress, Kirsten, whom he befriends when the collapse of Lear on stage is swiftly followed by the disaster of Georgian flu. At the moment when the novel commences, ageing actor Arthur Leander, becoming ill and disoriented, gets King Lear's lines out of order. Jeevan, 'who knew the play very well, realised that the actor had skipped back twelve lines', following 'Down from the waist they are centaurs' with a muttered rendition of 'the wren goes to't' (p. 1). He rushes on stage to administer aid, but is too late to save the actor from a fatal heart attack. Arthur's mangling of the Shakespearean lines and subsequent collapse presage the imminent collapse of society world-wide. Knowledge of Shakespeare temporarily gives Jeevan purpose – after his heroic attempt, he feels certain that becoming an EMT is his vocation – but the fatal flu prevents his career, and Jeevan disappears for most of the narrative.

In the post-apocalypse, Kirsten grows up as part of the Travelling Symphony, who quote Shakespeare daily on the road as they haul their meagre belongings and walk point to forestall attacks:

> 'But who comes here?' the man learning the part of Edgar said. His name was August, and he had only recently taken to acting. He was the second violin and a secret poet, which is to say no one in the company except Kirsten knew he wrote poetry, and the seventh guitar. 'The safer sense will ne'er accommodate ... will ne'er accommodate ... line?'
> 'His master thus', Kirsten said.
> 'Cheers. The safer sense will ne'er accommodate his master thus.' (p. 37)

[20] Emily St John Mandel, *Station Eleven: A Novel* (New York: Vintage, 2015), p. 31. Subsequent references are given in parentheses in the text.

The role of Shakespeare in preserving the Symphony is unclear. Shakespeare certainly keeps them going down the road, but the group's motto, 'because survival is insufficient' (p. 58), is lifted from *Star Trek: Voyager*. Similarly, we are given no particular insight into the effect Shakespeare has on the audiences who attend the Travelling Symphony's performances. Somehow, Shakespeare seems important. In the beginning, the Symphony had performed some modern plays, 'but what was startling, what no one would have anticipated, was that audiences seemed to prefer Shakespeare' (p. 38). Shakespeare seems important, but he does not necessarily have any ethical impact. When the frightening Prophet (who turns out to be Arthur's only son, Tyler) pursues the Symphony to reclaim his intended child bride, who has escaped as a stowaway in their caravan, he and Kirsten negotiate in lines from an improbable common text – not Shakespeare, nor the thickly annotated New Testament the Prophet carries, but the visionary comic book *Dr Eleven*, created by Arthur Leander's long-dead first wife, the two extant copies of which are in the possession of the Prophet and Kirsten, respectively. Shakespeare is irrelevant to the private language of this chance diplomacy. As the Prophet prepares to execute Kirsten, a boy soldier impulsively kills the Prophet and then himself. Did Shakespeare, which he had watched in performance the previous evening, make him save Kirsten? We never know.

Shakespearean quotations, uttered largely in rehearsal and performance but occasionally finding their way into the daily discourse of *Station Eleven's* characters, are in the end nothing more than portable aphorisms, on a par with similar utterances from *Star Trek*, *Dr Eleven*, the New Testament and even sayings remembered from the internet. These quotations circulate among the players and their audiences, moving along their route with the itinerant company. To this extent, they are like other objects in this complicated narrative that move, apparently at random, from person to person, such as the snowflake paperweight that is carried as a talisman for years, then quietly drops out of sight, indicating that such signifiers no longer have social value. Similarly, *Station Eleven* leaves us in doubt about the cultural value of Shakespeare. When the Travelling Symphony leaves the airport after a musical concert and Shakespearean performance, the denizens are humming Bach and murmuring Shakespeare, but their Shakespeare seems to be a musical sign of lifted spirits, a catchy saying more than anything else. Here, we have gone beyond even dialogism as a model for successful communication through shared language, for it is sound rather than sense that provides the social cement that keeps people going after the apocalypse.

Methodological Coda

The Introduction to Gary Saul Morson's *The Words of Others* (2011) opens with an amusing anecdote, in which a university graduation speaker, with a string of wise, mostly unattributed quotations, exhorts his young audience to serve others. The audience responds variously with angst, acknowledgement and annoyance, depending on their relationship to each quotation in question. One listener, however, takes out her iPhone to search for a phrase. In the age of the internet, we can track down Shakespearean quotations with ease, and I have used liberally both Google and the Folger Digital Texts to nail down and confirm quotations in my given texts. It is unclear exactly how contemporary authors access their Shakespearean quotations. Certainly, the sonnet remixers begin with a material text, even if the edition is unspecified. Linda Bamber's identity as an academic predisposes the reader to treat her italicised quotations as coming from a printed Shakespeare text or her teaching memory. But David Foster Wallace need not have reread *Hamlet* closely to come up with *Infinite Jest* for a title, even though commentators are confident that the novel resonates with *Hamlet*. Perhaps, in the end, it does not matter – particularly if we, like the denizens of Mandel's *Station Eleven*, draw our greatest comfort and pleasure from the sound (and surrounding cultural ambiance) rather than the sense of Shakespeare. The act of quotation, as the theoretical models with which this chapter began intimate, engages persons, texts and words in tangled webs of relations. What those works that probe most insistently the social function of quotation reveal, however, is the reality that quotation is a deeply embodied and powerfully affective act that has within it something beyond language.

CHAPTER 14

Mis/Quotation in Constrained Writing

Peter Kirwan

> So now I come to speak. At last. I will tell you all I know. I was deceived to
> think I could not do this. I have the powers; I take them here. I have the
> right. I have the means. My words may be poor, but they will have to do.[1]

I begin with a quotation about words, a quotation that is itself an amalgamation of other quotations; it is made up entirely of words spoken by
Ophelia in *Hamlet*. It is a statement of the ability and right to speak, a
reappropriation of words already spoken in order to say something new – or
something old that needs to be heard in a new way. Yet this quotation also
admits the limitations of the speaker's 'poor' words, words that 'will have
to do'. This chapter's concern is the creative negotiation of the restrictions
implicit in quotation, the extent to which free expression is curtailed or
enabled by the use of another's words. As the speaker of the above extract
articulates her own self-awareness and agency, she also expresses metafic-
tional cognisance of her limited vocabulary: a limitation that this chapter
argues is endemic to the very act of quotation.[2]

Quotation is, at its core, an act of creative appropriation. This might
initially seem counterintuitive; the introduction into a new work of a
pre-existing source might be read as a restriction of potential meaning,
stymieing originality by defaulting to another's words. But a quotation's
meaning is not intrinsic or fixed but dependent entirely on the strategic
resituation of words in each new context; while the quoted words may be
presented as having authority, this authority is shaped by the one deploying
it in service of a new agenda. In this view, the creative act is not the writing
of new words, but the skilful arrangement of pre-existing words to a new
purpose. The texts I discuss here take this to an extreme in quoting strategies that, rather than deploy discrete Shakespearean soundbites, instead

[1] Paul Griffiths, *let me tell you* (Hastings: Reality St. Editions, 2008), p. 8. Subsequent references are
given in parentheses in the text.
[2] See also Chapter 4 in this collection.

247

draw their entire vocabulary from limited Shakespearean corpora. Ben
Power's play *A Tender Thing* (2009) reorganises the text of *Romeo and Juliet*
to tell the story of an elderly couple dealing with their mortality, while
Paul Griffiths's Oulipian novel *let me tell you* (2008) narrows its focus further to create an imaginative prequel to *Hamlet* using only words spoken
in the play by Ophelia. Both texts deploy the *confinement* articulated in
Margreta de Grazia's reading of Barthes: 'Affixing a quotation to a speaker
is motivated by the same impulse as affiliating a work to an author: both
work to limit the generativity of language, confining it to the perimeters of
a single consciousness (and its complementary unconscious), ordinary or
extraordinary.'[3] While the two works are both new, they confine themselves
to the perimeters of a single consciousness – Shakespeare's – by restricting
themselves to his words. If Shakespearean quotations carry authority, then
that authority theoretically underpins every word.

Both texts adhere (with different degrees of rigidity) to self-imposed
rules that seek liberation through confinement, exploiting the creative
tension offered by a limited vocabulary and the 'ghosting' presence of
two Shakespearean ur-texts that are among Shakespeare's most widely
disseminated and adapted plays.[4] *Romeo and Juliet* and *Hamlet* exert
powerful interpretive force on texts that appropriate their stories, characters
and words, yet these histories of appropriation allow Power and Griffiths
to enter a space of confinement that nonetheless is semantically and culturally rich in proliferating meanings. Both texts are influenced by the
Oulipian school, described thus by Daniel Becker:

> Since its creation in 1960 … oulipian inquiry has yielded novels without
> certain vowels, love stories without gender, poems without words, books
> that never end, books that do nothing but end, books that would tech-
> nically take longer to read than most geological eras have lasted … These
> works, all of them governed in some way by strict technical constraints or
> elaborate architectural designs, are attempts to prove the hypothesis that the
> most arbitrary structural mandates can be the most creatively liberating.[5]

Part of the pleasure of reading Oulipian literature is becoming conscious
of the authorial ingenuity required in adhering to the work's rules of

---

[3] Margreta de Grazia, 'Shakespeare in Quotation Marks', in Jean I. Marsden (ed.), *The Appropriation of Shakespeare: Post-Renaissance Reconstructions of the Works and the Myth* (New York: Harvester Wheatsheaf, 1991), pp. 57–71 (p. 68).

[4] On 'ghosting', see Marvin Carlson, *The Haunted Stage* (Ann Arbor: University of Michigan Press, 2001).

[5] Daniel Levin Becker, *Any Subtle Channels: In Praise of Potential Literature* (Cambridge: Harvard University Press, 2012), p. 6.

creation. These rules allow both authors simultaneously to subordinate themselves to Shakespeare (both texts proclaim on their back covers their deference to Shakespeare's words) and to foreground more subtly their own agency in redistributing Shakespeare's words to new purpose. The reader or audience familiar with *Romeo and Juliet* and *Hamlet* should, theoretically, be able to recognise every word as Shakespearean, and yet the works are rather *mis*quotations on a massive scale, juxtaposing Shakespearean words and lines in unfamiliar ways. As such, the texts demand a more active, even creative, form of participation and recognition from their audiences.

A Tender Thing

The RSC production of Ben Power's *A Tender Thing* premiered in Newcastle-upon-Tyne in 2009 and was revived in 2012 in Stratford-upon-Avon as the closing production of the World Shakespeare Festival. The play is a two-hander, with an intimate, domestic focus following an elderly couple reflecting on their life together while their health deteriorates. Most of *Romeo and Juliet* is discarded in favour of those lines that best fit this narrative. The following, from the opening scene, is indicative of Power's adaptive strategies. Romeo enters carrying a small bottle while Juliet sleeps in bed. Following a long opening speech that draws from Romeo's final lines in *Romeo and Juliet*, v.iii, Juliet awakes and the two engage in the following dialogue (I mark the original speaker and corresponding line reference in the right hand column):

JULIET: Good even to my ghostly confessor.	**Juliet (II.vi.21)**
Either my eyesight fails or thou lookst pale.	**Juliet (III.v.57)**
ROMEO: And trust me, love, in my eye so do you.	**Romeo (III.v.58)**
Is there no pity sitting in the clouds	
That sees into the bottom of our grief?	**Juliet (III.v.196–7)**
Eyes, look your last. Arms, take your last embrace.	
And lips …	**Romeo (v.iii.112–13)**
JULIET: Sssh.	**(original)**
I do remember well where we should be	
And here we are. Where is my Romeo?	**Juliet (v.iii.149–50)**
ROMEO: Call me but love and I'll be new baptis'd:	
Henceforth I'll never be thy Romeo.	**Romeo (II.ii.50–1)**
JULIET: Did my heart love till now? Forswear it, sight.	
For I ne'er saw true beauty till this night.	**Romeo (I.v.51–2)**

Give me thy hand.[6]   **Friar Laurence (III.iii.172);**
                                             Romeo (V.iii.81); Capulet (V.iii.296)

In performance the audience hears a sequence of recognisable lines, most
of which are spoken in *Romeo and Juliet* by the correlating characters. Yet
Power's text rearranges the play and reverses the arc of Shakespeare's. The
tomb-like setting of the bed that will become their deathbed is introduced
with words taken from Romeo's dying speech (V.ii), but then the dialogue
moves backwards through their parting (III.v), then their first declarations
of love (II.ii), then first sight (I.v). The effect is twofold. First, this is a
microcosm for the narrative circularity of Power's story, which inverts the
trajectory of *Romeo and Juliet* by bringing the couple ever closer together
rather than parting them. The play's epilogue evokes an afterlife in which
the couple, '*suddenly younger than we have known them*', appear to each
other as strangers and play through the entire first-sight sequence of I.v;
love and death never part Power's characters (p. 38). More poignantly,
Power's choice to begin at the end implies the characters are regressing
throughout, imagining mental decline as second childhood.

The play invites its audience to recall and rewrite *Romeo and Juliet*,
playing tricks with collective memory by destabilising the familiar and
substituting new memories through the distorted life history of Power's
characters. Speaking of experiencing citation in performance, Margaret
Jane Kidnie writes: 'Citation occupies a strange space in performance. It
belongs to the event, yet seems to arrive from somewhere else, bringing
with it another's voice and authority. This inherent intertextual condition
creates as an effect of language the certainty that quotation, here seemingly
out of place, has an identifiable origin.'[7] The reorganisation and redistri-
bution of lines in *A Tender Thing* insisted on the play's separateness from
Romeo and Juliet, depending on the audience's recognition of famous lines
dislocated from their original context. Characters are not restricted only
to the lines of their corresponding Shakespearean character; perhaps most
notably, Juliet speaks the Queen Mab speech while teasing Romeo immediately before her first collapse. While Power's characters operate as coherent
dramatic entities, they are also fractured through the audience's own active
process of recognition, the pleasure of memory that Anne Ubersfeld identifies as a key pleasure of the theatre: 'The superimposing of the preceding

---

[6] Ben Power, *A Tender Thing* (London: Nick Hern, 2009), p. 8. Subsequent references are given in
parentheses in the text.
[7] Margaret Jane Kidnie, 'Citing Shakespeare', in Peter Holland (ed.), *Shakespeare, Memory and
Performance* (Cambridge: Cambridge University Press, 2006), pp. 117–32 (p. 125).

element on the new one makes a new construction possible, and, there again, the spectator tests how alert his intelligence is in the utilization of an agile memory.'[8] Power's characters both are and are not Romeo and Juliet, at once both textual deconstructions of Shakespearean figures and an elderly couple approaching death.

The agility noted by Ubersfeld is key to a play that repeatedly reminds its audience to remember while staging the traumatic loss of memory in advanced old age. The audience partakes in the attempt to latch on to the 'certainty' of textual origin that Kidnie identifies. In the theatre this can be a distressing experience, mirroring the sense of uncanny dislocation that the ailing and forgetful Juliet experiences. In one of her scenes of confusion, Juliet '*pulls away from*' Romeo and cries out:

> Oh, where's my daughter? I did bid her come,
> And now she is with God.
> On Lammas Eve at night then was she born.
> That was she, marry, I remember it well.
> 'Tis since the earthquake a great many years;
> And she was wean'd – I never shall forget it –
> Of all the days of the year, upon that day. (p. 30)

As Juliet casts about into her fading memory, recalling her lost daughter as a presence, then an absence, Power uses an extended evocation of memory to illustrate precisely what is at danger of being forgotten. Power takes words spoken by the Nurse and Lady Capulet that might be overlooked in performance and foregrounds them in *A Tender Thing* as belonging to Juliet herself. The verbal dislocation emphasises the sense of loss; not only does the audience witness the pain of *A Tender Thing*'s Juliet, but they may experience a moment of cognitive dissonance in imagining Juliet having a child at all. By aligning Lady Capulet, the Nurse and the two Juliets in this moment, Power turns Shakespeare's brief mention of a lost child into an emotional, polyvocal cry.

This dependence on the experience of recognition for dramatic effect cannot operate on all audience members in the same way. Lyn Gardner noted in her review '[f]amiliarity with the original will deepen this experience, even if it never escapes the feeling of being a clever workshop idea', while Dominic Cavendish felt that 'while the verse is

---

[8] Anne Ubersfeld, 'The Pleasure of the Spectator', trans. Pierre Bouillaguet and Charles Jose, in *Performance: Critical Concepts in Literary and Cultural Studies*, 4 vols. (London: Routledge, 2003), vol. II, pp. 236–48 (p. 240).

intoxicating' it was 'shorn of dramatic context'.⁹ Cavendish's experience here contradicts Gardner's assumption. His reaction is based on
the sense of a lack; Power's play of course has dramatic context, but the
experienced reviewer is more attuned to the lack of the specific *original*
dramatic context that, for him, makes sense of the lines. Gardner also
contradicts herself – it is her familiarity with Shakespeare that makes
this play seem like a workshop idea, whereas a less experienced audience
may be freer to experience the emotional impact of Power's story. The
process of recognition may then be a barrier to emotional experience;
the play's strategies work best when, as in the evocation of Juliet's lost
child above, the new narrative does not *depend* on recognition of the
original for its impact.

Power's strategy becomes more manipulative when *A Tender Thing* invites
its audience to remember what was never there, as in the central scene, in
which Juliet insists that Romeo enable her suicide at the appropriate time:

JULIET: Hear me.
　　　I shall not bear it, love, but choose to sleep,
　　　Submitting to that timeless cold embrace,
　　　And ending this unnatural decay.
　　　'Tis better far to sleep, at peace, in love,
　　　Than stretched upon this tortured rack of life.
　　　If, in thy wisdom, thou canst give no help,
　　　Nor no physician cure the sufferings to come,
　　　If thou remember all our happiness past
　　　And if thou loves me, as thou sayst thou dost,
　　　Do thou then call my resolution wise,
　　　And with our hands we'll help it presently. (p. 24)

The final couplet, a paraphrase of *Romeo and Juliet*, iv.i.53–4, may be
recognised as a quotation, and in turn serves to authenticate the preceding lines, which are actually original to this play. One reviewer, while
emphasising the play's use of 'Shakespearean words', even singled out the
phrase 'end this unnatural decay' despite this being entirely original to
Power.¹⁰ Not-Shakespeare becomes Shakespeare through the lack of marked
differentiation, the 'invisible quotation marks around the Shakespearean
language' that Kidnie identifies as necessary for the demarcation of citation

⁹ Lyn Gardner, '*A Tender Thing* – Review', *Guardian*, 4 October 2012; Dominic Cavendish, '*A Tender Thing*, RSC Swan, Stratford-upon-Avon, Review', *Telegraph*, 8 October 2012.
¹⁰ Natasha Tripney, '*A Tender Thing*', *The Stage*, 4 October 2012, www.thestage.co.uk/reviews/2012/a-tender-thing-review-at-swan-stratford-upon-avon/ (last accessed 9 May 2017).

in explicit confrontations with Shakespeare such as those of the Reduced Shakespeare Company.[11] This is not the 'deferential relationship' of citation, nor the 'supportive or questioning' relationship of quotation described by Julie Sanders, but the subtle and potentially (mis)leading utilisation of the pseudo-Shakespearean.[12] The overarching Shakespearean authority implicit in the text's rules of creation is ascribed to the new text; Power's breaking of the rules enables him, effectively, to co-opt Shakespeare's voice to authorise his own writing.

In playing with its audience's assumed memory – for the concept assumes familiarity with *Romeo and Juliet* – *A Tender Thing* demonstrates the inherent metatheatricality of the quotation device, inviting creative interpretive engagement with the ur-text on which it depends. Yet the amalgamation of pseudo-Shakespearean new writing with decontextualised Shakespeare lines also raises the ethical and intellectual question of how far an audience conditioned to recognise Shakespeare will go in constructing the new text as Shakespearean. The constraining superstructure of Shakespeare that governs the rules of the text is also a shorthand for audience accessibility that frees Power from the need to establish character, back-story and poetry. For Power, this freedom enables a creative exploration of issues surrounding ageing, euthanasia and loss that can be judged and contextualised against a Shakespearean standard; the flip-side, as Cavendish's comments reveal, is that knowledge of the Shakespearean context may detract from the purposes of the new text. This tension is exacerbated in the second of my texts, where more rigid restrictions of language align paradoxically with even greater independence from Shakespeare.

let me tell you

Paul Griffiths's short novel *let me tell you* is far stricter than *A Tender Thing* in its execution and its avoidance of recognisable Shakespearean soundbites. The book is a formal experiment, creating both a prequel to *Hamlet* and a back-story for Ophelia in the tradition of Mary Cowden Clarke's 1850 *The Girlhood of Shakespeare's Heroines*, using only those words spoken by Ophelia in *Hamlet*. Creating a corpus of 'Ophelian' from the approximately 480 words across the 1604 and 1623 texts of the play, Griffiths takes literally the idea of allowing a character to tell their story 'in their own

---

[11] Kidnie, 'Citing Shakespeare', p. 129.
[12] Julie Sanders, *Adaptation and Appropriation* (London: Routledge, 2006), p. 4.

words'.[13] This means that the narrator is denied even her own name; while a preface (by Claudius) identifies the speaker as Ophelia, Ophelia – who never speaks her own name in *Hamlet* – refers to herself throughout only as 'O'. O recounts the story of her childhood, her relationships with her brother, father and absent mother, and her early friendship with Hamlet, until finally reaching a moment when she chooses whether or not to become part of the narrative of *Hamlet* or to leave Elsinore. Moving from prose to dramatic dialogue, poetry to song, Griffiths twists Ophelia's words into a variety of shapes.

While the words within this limited corpus recur insistently and music-ally, Griffiths avoids extended collocations derived from the play, resisting individual moments of overt quotation. Instead, he plays with frequen-cies and positioning to make the words in Ophelia's corpus more or less prominent as appropriate. To take some significant examples, the word 'Hamlet' appears twice in Ophelia's dialogue (the 101st most spoken word in a corpus of 1,166 words), both times in reference to the character (1. iii.89, 11.i.76); in Griffiths's text, the word appears only once in a corpus of 39,835 words, and describes a small village (p. 44); Hamlet himself is demoted significantly in Griffiths's novel. The word 'choose' only appears once in each text, but restricting it to a single usage in the much longer *let me tell you* increases its significance; the word is held back to serve as the novel's final word, making the point that the ability to choose is denied to O until this point. Perhaps more significantly, Ophelia's distinctive verbal tags are muted. The collocation 'my lord' appears no fewer than 27 times in Ophelia's dialogue, leading to these words being the 2nd and 5th most spoken words by the character. In *let me tell you*, however, the collocation appears only 8 times, with 'my' slipping to 6th and 'lord' being only the 187th most spoken word. The markers of politeness and deference that mark Shakespeare's Ophelia are absent in O's discourse.

A reader looking for verbal echoes of Ophelia is therefore frustrated by the paucity of distinctive lines or phrases from *Hamlet*. Where these do occur, they are significant – Griffiths himself points to the phrase 'Words, words, words' (11.ii.189), spoken as a prophecy of something Hamlet *will*

---

[13] Griffiths lists 483 'letter strings', of which five pairs duplicate letters with additional punctuation (*a/ 'a', ha/ha', I/i', o/o', 't/t*) (Paul Griffiths, private communication). This number includes plurals; thus, *remembrance* and *remembrances* count as two separate words. Some flexibility is allowed by words such as *th'* and *'s*, which serve as detachable prefixes and suffixes. I am grateful to Griffiths for his extraordinary generosity in discussing his work.

say in the future – but they are few.[14] As with *A Tender Thing*, the process of recognition operates here to equate form with content. While Power's play reorganises whole lines to mimic the unreliable distortions of fragmented memory, Griffiths's strategy evokes the narrative of *Hamlet* through scenes involving prophecy and foreshadowing, but focuses on the plight of a character who neither is allowed to speak, nor has words appropriate to the task. 'My words may be poor, but they will have to do.'

The effect of Griffiths's use of quotation is both to constrain and to liberate O. She is limited by the words she borrows from Shakespeare, and this in turn limits her ability to explain her own experience; she cannot articulate events beyond her own predefined vocabulary. Yet as everything spoken or written by other characters has to be filtered through Ophelia's corpus as well as their own, O has a larger word pool than any other character in the book and thus assumes linguistic privilege. When the young Laertes (designated 'Little' here, as Ophelia never names 'Laertes') complains in a letter to his father about O stealing his mirror, O has to translate for the reader: ' "My grace" – I think he meant "glass" – "is my own. Tell O." ' (p. 62). O/Ophelia has access to the word 'glass' but Little/Laertes does not, ceding to O the responsibility and privilege of elucidating meaning. Far from being controlled by others' words, O controls those of others.

Yet while Griffiths in this example makes clear O's linguistic advantage over Little, he goes on to use *mis*quotation to undermine his narrator. In one key scene, O's father writes letters home from court, including advice that he wishes O to pass on to Little. The letter is composed of words available only in Polonian *and* Ophelian, limiting the word pool further.

> *'It may be that I will not see you all for some time, and if so, there is something I would like you to tell him from me, if and when he must go away from home.*
> *This is what I would say:*
> *' "Give your thoughts no tongue.*
> *' "What men you know, and that show you affection, you should keep by you.*
> *' "Give each lord your shoulder, but no madam your heart.*
> *' "Do not take and do not give. You know what this means.*
> *' "Look good when you go out, but doubt fashion.*
> *' "This most of all: to your own soul be true, and it must come from this, as night from day, you may not then be false to rich, to poor." '* (p. 70)

Griffiths, *let me tell you*, p. 36 (and private communication). Ophelia's use of 'in my mind's eye' (p. 89) is another example.

As O reports this letter (is she reading or retelling?), the restrictions placed on her father's words reconstruct his *sententiae* in words that are familiar to her. At one level this allows O to put into plain speech her father's wordy discourse. Yet the familiarity of Polonius's famous advice from *Hamlet*, 1.iii also excludes O. '*You know what this means*' goes straight over O's head – the father's address depends on Little understanding his subtext, but O has no more words with which to expand on what the ambiguous '*Do not take and do not give*' may mean; she cannot articulate the commonplace 'Neither a borrower nor a lender be' (*Hamlet*, 1.iii.75). The complexity of Polonius's advice to Laertes, in a monologue that ignores Ophelia, is replicated here despite O's linguistic privilege. Even more poignantly, 'to your own soul be true' reveals that O does not have access to the word 'self', and thus implicitly is devoid of self-determination. Throughout Griffiths's novel O wields almost no control over her surroundings, which are determined by characters ranging from a Nurse to her father and brother, to the King and the absent, nameless mother who haunts her memories.

The work of recognition and remembrance instigated by quotation practice here draws attention to what is *not* said. In a later letter from the father to O, one absence becomes very clear:

> '*I was up late at a show. I know you do not like the music I like; still, I think you would like this from what they did:*
>
> Love, love me do,
> You know I love you,
> I'll never be true,
> So PLEASE, love me do.
>
> '*Well, you have to know the music. It's not at all like the king's: I'll play it for you when home – which is where I long to be!*' (p. 71)

Now Lennon and McCartney are transmitted via Polonian and Ophelian, and the fact that *Love Me Do* can still be reconstructed despite the double restriction occasions humour. Yet the evocation of a lyric perhaps as iconic to Griffiths's audience as any Shakespearean passage makes a serious point, the misquotation signalling to the reader that Ophelia/O never uses the word 'always'. 'Never' is a mistake, an intrusion, the incorrect word in an obvious quotation. The text depends on the reader's assumed knowledge of the Beatles song for what should appear in its place, and 'always' becomes the absent ghost haunting the misquotation. Griffiths's other key work in Ophelian is the spoken sound poem *there is still time* (2004), and the lack of 'always' in both belies anxiety over Ophelia's ticking clock. For Ophelia, there is no 'always', and her fate appears prescribed by the nature of the prequel. This culminates in the novel's final lines:

> This time I could make things better for him. I know I could. It does not have to go as they say.
>> I could do that: go home and not go on.
>> I could go on, and find what I still do not know.
>> This way, that way.
>> I have stayed here to think, and then:
>> I choose. (p. 139)

The possibility of her choice is undermined, however, by the restrictions of her vocabulary. Her choices are limited by what she can articulate, and what she can articulate is only what already belongs to Shakespeare's Ophelia. Coupled with the assumption that a prequel necessarily leads into the action of the original, O's 'choice' may be no choice at all. While Griffiths's novel traces a trajectory leading up to a moment of what O experiences as genuine choice, the re-emergence of the ur-text in the final pages (Barnardo and Francisco's opening lines of *Hamlet* are heard through a window) puts the freedom of Griffiths and O in direct tension with the looming inevitability of *Hamlet* itself. The reader's allegiance to O may be in her challenge to the established Shakespearean narrative, or it may be sympathy for her apparent inability to alter events.

Intrusive Shakespeare

Early in *A Tender Thing*, during the characters' only scene of full health together, Power quotes elements of the balcony scene to capture the couple's playfulness; Romeo's 'O, wilt thou leave me so unsatisfied?' (II. ii.125) in this context becomes banter between a husband and wife (p. 12). Here, however, fall the most obvious insertions from outside *Romeo and Juliet*, as lines of remembrance are interpolated from the Sonnets:

> **JULIET:** Let that sun shine and show us as we are.   **(original)**
> That time of year thou mayst in us behold,
> When yellow leaves, or none, or few do hang
> Upon those boughs which shake against the cold,
> Bare ruined choirs, where once the sweet birds sang.
> In me thou seest the twilight of such day,
> As after sunset fadeth in the west,
> Which by and by black night doth take away.   **(Sonnet 73, 1–7)**

ROMEO: To me, fair friend, you never can be old,
For as you were when first your eye I eyed,
Such seems your beauty still.   **(Sonnet 104, 1–3)**

JULIET: And how is that?   **(original)**

ROMEO: Such as would make a man sing like a bird!   **(original)**
Our love was new, and then but in the spring,
When I was wont to greet it with my lays.   **(Sonnet 102, 5–6)**
Dost thou remember how I used to sing?   **(original)** (p. 13)

The importation of Shakespeare from outside the play's source corpus distinguishes this moment, and the creation of iambic pentameter lines by Power to join them serves the function of an additional set of Kidnie's 'invisible quotation marks', demarcating these lines from the surrounding text (drawn from *Romeo*) so that, in de Grazia's words, they 'enclose rather than highlight passages, drawing attention to words that are imported from elsewhere'.[15] This is a more traditional use of citation within the play's broader quoting structure, and implies the insufficiency of *Romeo and Juliet* for Power's purpose at this point. Even though Power's overall project is one of playful pastiche and reconstruction of a 'Shakespearean' tone, his importation of external quotation at this point suggests that a deferential evocation of Shakespeare remains part of the play's premise.

In a similar way, foreign Shakespeare is introduced into *let me tell you*, Chapter 11, although here adhering to the book's rules. In this chapter, Little receives four love letters containing sonnets. The first lines of each may be familiar:

What's mine is yours and what is yours is mine **(Measure for Measure, v.i.529)**
I cannot tell what you and other men **(Julius Caesar, i.ii.93)**
It is not night when I do see your face **(A Midsummer Night's Dream, ii.i.221)**
They do not love that do not show their love. **(The Two Gentlemen of**
    Verona, i.ii.31) (pp. 116–20)

Griffiths's ability to find genuine Shakespearean quotations while still using only Ophelia's words is an unremarked 'Easter Egg' for attentive readers, and his creation of sonnets – themselves a form that highlight creativity under constraint – demonstrate his ingenuity. Nonetheless, these quotations also create an extruding presence, the sonnets (from an unnamed sender) declaring what appears to be a Shakespearean origin.

---

[15] De Grazia, 'Quotation Marks', p. 60.

Griffiths quotes Shakespeare's Ophelia quoting Shakespeare, and in so doing the elsewhere-distorted Shakespearean voice reassumes a momentary prominence.

Both *A Tender Thing* and *let me tell you* are new works, but remain ghosted by Shakespeare. The relationship between Shakespeare and these texts poses interesting difficulties for an analysis of practices of quotation. The restrictions that both texts advertise imply deference, yet both authors resist slavish adherence to their originals, instead creating intertextual palimpsests that playfully insist on the present text's multiplicity while dispersing the Shakespearean voice on which they are premised. By employing quotation *within* quotation, as in the sonnets above, both texts foreground the careful utilisation of words as their key theme, as in the quotation from Griffiths with which I opened this chapter. That passage makes clear that one of O's denied words is 'power'; she has to assert, awkwardly, 'I have the *powers*' (my emphasis). Her restriction is manifest even at the initial moment of celebrated liberation. By working within Shakespeare, both authors cede power in a strategy that I see as political; the restrictions on their own expression map onto the voices of Ophelia and Juliet that struggle for expression in Shakespeare. By turning Ophelia, Juliet and their plays into palimpsests of reorganised quotation, and by creatively exploiting their linguistic dependence on Shakespeare, Power and Griffiths draw attention to the silences in their sources, to the issues of restricted expression and mute suffering that do not themselves provide soundbites for quotation. These constrained words may be poor, but they will (have to) do.

CHAPTER 15

'Beauty too rich for use'? Shakespeare and Advertising

Graham Holderness

The Shakespeare Myth revisited

Sometime in the 1980s, the use of Shakespeare in advertising became something that could be taken seriously. Previously (even though Shakespeare, in *Measure for Measure*, has been credited with having invented the word 'advertise' (1.i.41)), for the dominant schools of literary interpretation, advertising per se was regarded as symptomatic of the decadence of 'mass civilisation', and any quotation of Shakespeare for commercial purposes beneath the dignity of 'minority culture'.[1] Theoretically informed critical interventions such as *Political Shakespeare* (1985) brought popular culture, and with it advertising, within the scope of Shakespearean criticism and analysis.[2] At the same time these theoretical initiatives, grounded as they were in Marxism and Marxist-influenced forms of (what we now call) political correctness, tended to share with the criticism they aimed to supplant a hostile critique of capitalist enterprise and the commercial appropriation of culture. Opening the field of criticism to admit popular culture as an object of enquiry did not necessarily involve any shift away from the anti-capitalist critique previously maintained by F. R. Leavis and L. C. Knights.[3]

The Shakespeare Myth (1988) was the first book formally to incorporate discussions of Shakespeare in advertising and other media of popular culture. In the Preface, I quoted *Romeo and Juliet* to point to the irony of the British £20 note of the time including, in its design, a representation of the balcony scene: 'The choice of play must seem at first glance curiously inappropriate: is not this drama the great poetic protest of romantic passion against mercenary morality and commercialized relationship? Utterances

---

[1] See F. R. Leavis, *Mass Civilisation and Minority Culture* (Cambridge: Minority Press, 1930). See also F. R. Leavis and Denys Thompson, *Culture and Environment* (London: Chatto and Windus, 1933).
[2] Alan Sinfield and Jonathan Dollimore (eds.), *Political Shakespeare* (Manchester: Manchester University Press, 1985).
[3] Knights edited the journal *Scrutiny* (Cambridge, 1932–53) together with Leavis.

of elevated and idealized passion – "Beauty too rich for use, for earth too dear" – juxtapose incongruously and with ironic effect against the sordid and banal symbols of monetary value.'[4] Thus, while *The Shakespeare Myth* made it possible to address Shakespeare-related advertising as cultural production and material text, such phenomena were rigorously contained within the Marxist parameters of the Frankfurt School, and viewed as symptomatic of the ideological impoverishment of culture by commerce in a 'bourgeois' society.[5]

This chapter takes a fresh look at the quotation of Shakespeare in advertising, with particular reference to *Romeo and Juliet*, in the light of subsequent developments in criticism and theory.[6] It argues that advertisements quoting Shakespeare should be taken seriously as independent cultural appropriations and novel textualisations; and demonstrates the stubborn persistence in this context of Marxist-influenced frameworks and methodologies that should really by now have passed into history.

'Romeo, Romeo'

Romeo and Juliet has been extensively used as a source for advertisements, largely as a consequence of its familiarity from school curricula and popular film adaptations, the easy adaptability of its characters and themes to some of advertising's primary demographic targets, and the immediate recognisability of its frequently disseminated iconic images. Advertisements have tended to draw on the play's obvious preoccupations – young love, dangerous passion, social conflict, misunderstood youth, passionate sex – but have also been strongly influenced by film adaptations of the play such as those of Franco Zeffirelli (1968), Baz Luhrmann (1996) and Robert Wise (1957) (see Chapter 11). At its most conventional, this type of appropriation equates 'Shakespeare', via *Romeo and Juliet*, with passion, urban style and love transcending barriers. In 2004, posters for the Swiss radio station

---

[4] Graham Holderness (ed.), *The Shakespeare Myth* (Manchester: Manchester University Press, 1988), p. xii.

[5] There were exceptions of course. Derek Longhurst's chapter 'You Base Football Player! Shakespeare and Popular Culture' in *The Shakespeare Myth* (pp. 59–73), more attuned to the emerging discipline of cultural studies, acknowledged that the use of Shakespeare in advertising could display ingenuity, wit and creative innovation. For my own partial recantation of *The Shakespeare Myth*, see Graham Holderness, 'Stratford Revisited', in Martin Procházka, Michael Dobson, Andreas Höfele and Hanna Scolnicov (eds.), *Renaissance Shakespeare, Shakespearean Renaissances: Proceedings of the Ninth World Shakespeare Congress, Prague 2011* (Newark: University of Delaware Press, 2014), pp. 363–73.

[6] See, for example, Robert Shaughnessy (ed.), *The Cambridge Companion to Popular Culture* (Cambridge: Cambridge University Press, 2008); and Douglas Lanier, *Shakespeare and Modern Popular Culture* (Oxford: Oxford University Press, 2002).

Espace 2 displayed a picture of an inter-racial couple on a train, kissing passionately under the name of 'Shakespeare'.[7] By contrast, one of the wittiest modern appropriations (2008) is a Polish print advert for condoms. An old play-text lies open to display pages containing what purports to be the first scene of *Romeo and Juliet*. A typically Victorian epigraphic illustration shows the lovers kissing at Juliet's window, and the play's title. The image is not a two-dimensional page, however, but a book; and across one of the pages lies a pack of condoms. On closer inspection the text of the play is composed of alternating speeches (the speech-headings capitalised and in square brackets) between Romeo and Juliet, consisting entirely of 'aaahHa! … OooOoooh! … aAaaAhh! … aaA!'. The expectation of quotation is confounded by misquotation. The strapline reads: 'Unimil. Discover pleasure.'[8] As the anticipated Shakespearean poetry is replaced by the irreverent sound-effects of popular pleasure, the incongruous juxtaposition of the play's 'violent delights' (ii.vi.9) with safe sex is part of the humorous misrecognition that constructs this advert as a commentary on, as well as an appropriation of, Shakespeare. The high romance of *Romeo and Juliet* is all very well for page and stage; but a different language is needed for everyday modern living.

The ludic irreverence of such postmodern pastiches is actually nothing new in Shakespearean advertising. Often the sexual passions of the play have been playfully sublimated into other appetites, and cited in the marketing of food. An old advertisement for tinned ox-tongue in the form of a trade card uses an antique picture of Romeo and Juliet with Friar Laurence, with a tin of ox-tongue interpolated into the image. The strapline reads: 'Juliet greets the Friar with Libby, McNeill and Libby's meats.' The Friar's response is 'Romeo shall thank thee, daughter, for us both' (ii.vi.25) (Figure 10). Both visual and literary quotation of the play are folded into a pastiche, with the formal quotation decontextualised and reoriented to refer to the gift of tinned meat. The effect is one of witty and incongruous association between the play and the product the play is used to advertise.

The names of the main characters can be quoted when the desired effect is one of complementary opposites, such as strawberries and cream.[9]

---

[7] Discussed in Douglas M. Lanier, 'Post-Textual Shakespeare', *Shakespeare Survey*, 64 (2011), 145–62.
[8] Available at www.coloribus.com/adsarchive/prints/unimil-condoms-romeo-juliet-12144455/ (last accessed 12 May 2017).
[9] A crêperie in Long Beach serves a heart-shaped 'Romeo and Juliet' crêpe with cream and strawberries. See www.yelp.co.uk/biz_photos/la-creperie-caf%C3%A9-long-beach-5?select=c8sBUDOxiU CFFi1xqMoahQ (last accessed 12 May 2017).

Figure 10   '*Romeo & Juliet* Act II Scene VI: Juliet greets the Friar with Libby, McNeill & Libby's meats. "Romeo shall thank thee, daughter, for us both."'

Staying with the dessert menu, in this example, a misquotation assists the promotion of sugar:

> Sugar, that extraordinarily delightful bedfellow of coffee, is sweet and seductive in equal measure. The smallest addition of sugar transforms espresso into a toasty, caramel affair with a round, smooth finish and heightened notes of cocoa and molasses. As a result, white, brown, raw and artisanal sugars have each taken their turns on cafe tables. Indeed, if Shakespeare's Juliet was with us today, she would be forgiven for tossing the roses aside to ask if sugar by any other name would taste as sweet. In Silvana's Organic Panela, she would have her answer.[10]

This extract from a press release for European Foods Wholesalers promotes an organic sugar by misquoting a familiar tag-line from Shakespeare's *Romeo and Juliet* – 'a rose / By any other name would smell as sweet' (II. ii.47–8) – and converting it to 'sugar by any other name would taste as sweet'. This figure for a quintessential sweetness beyond language is transferred to the quality of the product. Other phrases in the text that are not quotations from Shakespeare nonetheless adopt an allusive quality from that specific contextualisation: 'delightful bedfellows'; 'sweet and

---

[10] Available at www.europeanfoods.com.au/fresh-in-store/view/48/%20 (last accessed 12 May 2017).

seductive'. The quotation seals the advertising copy to a cultural memory of *Romeo and Juliet*, quite possibly obtained from sources other than the text of the play itself, as a rhapsodic celebration of young love, erotic romance and sweet surrender.

More recently the play's investment in the dangers of miscommunication (miscarried messages etc.) has been deployed by mobile phone companies to promote communications media such as phone networks, an analogy elaborated on here by media critics:

> Remember Juliet's cry in the balcony scene, 'Romeo, O Romeo, wherefore art thou Romeo?' (2.2.33). It's the precursor of networked individualism as Juliet wonders why Romeo, a Montague, is moving beyond group boundaries to woo her, a Capulet.
>
> Modern readers might understand Juliet's cry as 'where are you?'. Both meanings suggest how the Triple Revolution – the turn to social networks, the pervasive internet, and the always accessible mobile phone – have changed the ways in which we connect with each other. Nowadays, Juliet would routinely text or call Romeo via their mobile phones: 'What are your feelings about me? Can you get away from your family? When will you be coming?'[11]

An advert for Nextel (2010) features a traditional theatrical performance of *Romeo and Juliet* in a proscenium-arch theatre. The performance is a comical, 'reduced Shakespeare' 30-second rendering of the play from the balcony scene to the deaths of the lovers. The only difference is that all the characters are equipped with mobile phones, and speak to one another through them.[12] T-Mobile (2008) transfers the balcony scene to an American suburban house, with Juliet on a terrace and Romeo appearing below.[13] AT&T (2007) use a simple static statement to mine the play for modern technological wisdom:

> Romeo believes Juliet is dead.
> Juliet dies because Romeo
> Believes that she is dead.
> Communication is very important.

A later version shows Friar Laurence capable of averting the tragedy by texting details to Juliet. Romeo unfortunately doesn't have AT&T, and

[11] Barry Wellman and Lee Rainie, 'If Romeo and Juliet had mobile phones', *Mobile Media and Communication*, 1:1 (2013), 166–171 (p. 166).
[12] Available on YouTube at www.youtube.com/watch?v=M-cZtWefN8s (last accessed 12 May 2017).
[13] Available at www.adland.tv/commercials/t-mobile-romeo-and-juliet-2008-30-usa (last accessed 12 May 2017).

so communication fails.[14] The emphasis here on the vital importance of clarity in securing mutual understanding is performed by the stark simplicity of this bald summary, which replaces Shakespeare's convoluted plot and elaborate language with an unmistakable transparency of expression. For our modern commercial and technological purposes, the advert seems to imply, Shakespeare needs to be not quoted, but translated. An advert for Orange (2009) shows a modern 'Romeo and Juliet' couple exiting out of their upper-storey windows, and walking to meet one another in the air. The only barrier to their love seems to have been the fact that they live in different buildings.[15]

The first three examples cited here handle the source material in a humorous way, displaying an awareness of the mismatch between the play's tragedy of miscommunication, and the communicative utopia promised by mobile phone technology. Quotation is discarded in favour of live immediacy, instant messaging and user-friendly transliteration. The Orange advert is a more elaborate construction. A vivid red rose, the focus of the lovers' yearning, stands out from the pale monochromes of contemporary dress and chic urban interior decor. The narrative is ironically but persuasively accompanied by a musical quotation, Nino Rota's 'love theme' from Franco Zeffirelli's *Romeo and Juliet* (1968). The aerial perambulation of the lovers is compellingly visualised by special effects. Here Shakespeare is quoted as a familiar source for images of beauty, love, the transgression of barriers and a transcendent emotional liberty.[16]

Gradually *Romeo and Juliet* as an advertising source has been shifted away from the ironic incongruity of using the play to promote irrelevant products – tinned ox-tongue or organic sugar – towards the validation of lifestyles, necessarily equipped with the appropriate technology and fashion accessories. In December 2016, a 30-second advertisement for Apple's latest smartphone featured a lush, cinematic performance of *Romeo and Juliet* by two young children. The play is represented in a series of four quotations, delivered with feeling. As Juliet says 'My love is deep, the more I give to thee', and Romeo replies 'A thousand times goodnight' (his voice suddenly echoing, as if heard live rather than on film), the camera pulls away to reveal that Juliet's father is proudly filming

---

[14] Available on YouTube at www.youtube.com/watch?v=mixBMymKqvw (accessed 12 May 2017).

[15] Available on YouTube at www.youtube.com/watch?v=Fgh6tOSm9hk (accessed 12 May 2017).

[16] I am grateful to the creator of the Tumblr blog *Shake and Tumble* for bringing together and reflecting on some of these examples: www.shakespearean.tumblr.com/post/4953845162/shake-speare-in-advertising-romeo-and-juliet (last accessed 9 May 2016).

his daughter's school play: 'your movies look like movies on iPhone 7'.[17] Copy-writers who probably studied Shakespeare themselves have begun to assume a similar knowledge of Shakespeare on the part of their target audience. A familiarity with *Romeo and Juliet* can be assumed as deriving not merely from comedy sketches of the balcony scene, or decontextualised quotations ('Wherefore art thou, Romeo?'), but from a direct acquaintance with the play, read or seen, in a literary or adapted (filmic) form. The reference point shifts away from the quotation, and back towards its source. An example of the latter can be found in an advert for a brand called 'Romeo & Juliet Couture'.

> Whether ironic or romantic, the name is familiar to the old and young alike. Through the line, we present an idea to contrast the tragedy with a universal collection of versatile, comfortable, and fashion-forward apparel. We offer a diverse collection from couture inspired, sophisticated feminine tops, dresses, bottoms and outerwear. Romeo & Juliet Couture sends a positive message of tolerance and love which empowers our youth worldwide to make the right decisions for themselves and to treat everyone with respect and dignity. The line is in-tune with the trends of contemporary fashion, and its ability to evolve with the trends and inspirations within the fast-paced and ever-changing industry is apparent – in both realms of design and quality. Founded in 1999 for the European market and introduced to the US Market in 2002. Spring/Summer 2011 marked our latest addition– Romeo & Juliet Couture Handbags. The full collection is currently available at Neiman Marcus, Saks Fifth Avenue, Fred Segal, Kitson and other fine specialty stores.[18]

The play's title is quoted in the branding of the line, though its familiarity, and implied universality, are such as to render quotation unnecessary ('the name is familiar to the old and young alike'). The play is cited, rather than quoted, as a classic source for a positive parable of 'tolerance and love', which substitutes for Shakespeare's 'tragedy'. Its protagonists are assumed to represent youth, beauty, innocent and transcendent passion, and impeccable style. This seemingly far-fetched analogy in fact formed the basis for one of the most remarkable contributions to date of Shakespeare to advertising, and advertising to Shakespeare.

---

[17] 'iPhone 7 – Romeo and Juliet – Apple', www.youtube.com/watch?v=qStdSMad6TY (last accessed 12 May 2017).
[18] Press release quoted at www.examiner.com/article/tv-s-paul-fisher-promotes-romeo-and-juliet-couture-modeling-contest (last accessed 23 December 2015).

H&M presents *ROMEO & JULIET*

In 2005, fashion retailer H&M launched an advertising campaign for a new line of denim jeans ('&denim'). The campaign was fronted with a 6-minute film by celebrated art photographer and film director David LaChappelle, entitled *H&M presents ROMEO & JULIET*. The advert was posted on H&M's website and broadcast in some US cinemas before its withdrawal following complaints that it glorified gang culture and gun violence. It remains accessible via YouTube postings.[19] The advert's investment in the play extends to an abridged narrative and theatrical adaptation, but its purpose is to market something never mentioned in the play, or ever worn in Renaissance Verona – denim jeans.

The film's structure combines the kind of 'love story' narrative often used in modern adverts (for example, for perfume), with the conventions of the music video (the whole action is keyed to two songs, both from the musical *Dreamgirls*, which recounts the story of the Supremes). The first of these ('When I First Saw You') is sung in person by soul singer Mary J. Blige at a version of the Capulet ball, which visually quotes, in its lurid colours and disco lighting, the MTV 'Renaissance California' of Luhrmann's adaptation of *Romeo and Juliet* (1996). The setting for the rest of the story in the H&M version, however, is darkly urban American, suggesting inevitably the stylised New York of *West Side Story* (1957). Here Romeo and Juliet do of course have mobile phones, but the devices don't seem able to avert tragedy. We see Juliet in her room, responding to a text message from Romeo, going out into the street to meet him. Before she gets there, he is gunned down in a drive-by shooting. Juliet's grieving over his dead body, accompanied by the second song ('I Tell You I'm Not Going'), which she sings herself, makes up the remainder of the film, intercut with flashbacks detailing the progress of their romance.

The advert positions Shakespeare within and beyond its parameters, by a method somewhere between quotation and allusion, perhaps best defined as 'citation'. Citation references the source of a quotation in shorthand, rather than reproducing its exact words. It is not therefore quotation, but neither is it simply allusion to something that exists elsewhere and would need to be independently consulted in order to verify its character. Here Shakespeare is quoted in the title – *H&M presents ROMEO & JULIET* – in the narrative development and denouement of doomed young love,

[19] Available on YouTube at www.youtube.com/watch?v=XY7rMoteGqU (last accessed 12 May 2017).

and pervasively throughout the *mis-en-scène*. Thus the name 'Paris', which would be intelligible only to someone who knows the play, appears sprayed in graffiti on a wall. We see reflected in a window a billboard advertising a film called *The Lady Doth Protest* – a verbal and visual joke that links *Hamlet* with the conventions of the popular cinema thriller – and, on a shop awning, a quotation from *The Merchant of Venice*: 'I will buy with you, sell with you, talk with you' (1.iii.29). 'This *Romeo and Juliet*', as Mark Thornton Burnett and Ramona Wray comment, in a seminal discussion of the advert, 'is acutely responsive to, and self-conscious about, the "sources" of its own existence and the histories of revision that intercede in, and give shape to, its imaginative possibility'.[20]

The film is well aware that it is quoting not just Shakespeare, but the complex legacy of adaptation and appropriation that has brought 'Shakespeare' as a recognisable cultural signifier into the twenty-first-century media environment. Thus the film invokes Shakespeare's play via the key film adaptations – including the film versions of Zeffirelli and Luhrmann – likely to be familiar to its target audience. Iconic images from the play – the masked ball, the balcony scene, the lovers in bed – are multiply quoted by visual reference to the film sources, as well as to the explicit and implicit stage directions of the theatrical text. 'The screen pasts of Shakespeare', in the words of Burnett and Wray, 'are a function of his current comprehensibility'. Here quotation is more likely to be visual than verbal, within 'a context in which it is the icon rather than the word that is prioritised'.[21]

As in Shakespeare's play, the lovers meet at a masked party, and remove their masks to reveal themselves to one another. Juliet appears on a fire escape (the balcony), and blows a kiss down to Romeo in the street (the Capulets' orchard). In one of the flashbacks, Romeo is seen climbing into the window of her room in daylight, where they lie together on the bed and cover themselves with a sheet to shut out the light. Juliet's mourning over Romeo's corpse parallels the same action in the play. The film ends not with golden memorial statues erected in Verona, but with a reprise of Romeo and Juliet lying together on her bed, both stripped to the waist. The camera focuses on the product promoted, their denim jeans. Love is stronger than death, and denim stronger than either.

[20] Mark Thornton Burnett and Ramona Wray (eds.), *Screening Shakespeare in the Twenty-First Century* (Edinburgh: Edinburgh University Press, 2008), p. 3.
[21] *Ibid.*, pp. 2–3.

But the primary source of the film is not Shakespeare (1595), nor Luhrmann's *Romeo +Juliet* (1996), but *West Side Story* (1957). Only in the Robert Wise/Bernstein/Sondheim adaptation is the Romeo character (Tony) killed (by gunfire), while Juliet/Maria survives to mourn and reproach his killer(s). The 'balcony scene' irresistibly recalls neither the Casa di Giulietta, nor Californian-Verona, but *West Side Story*, since it takes place on a fire escape, and Juliet wears a dress reminiscent of Maria's 'I feel pretty' party-dress. Juliet literally floats down to meet Romeo in the street, a motion strikingly reminiscent of the choreography of *West Side Story*. Music and dance form the basic language of the advert, and it has no dialogue. Romeo's clearly Latin appearance (the actor is dancer Gustavo Victor Carr) and signature white jacket invoke both the Puerto Rican Sharks of *West Side Story* and Tony Manero of *Saturday Night Fever*, just as the musical allusions via *Dreamgirls* to Motown and the background of Tamyra Grey (near-miss *American Idol* winner) gesture toward the sociology and culture of American female black music performers.

I have acknowledged the discussion by Burnett and Wray, in their Introduction to *Screening Shakespeare*, as a very effective appreciation of the advert as a complex form of cultural quotation, and as such a representative example of twenty-first-century Shakespeare: 'Shakespeare in the post-2000 period moves among and between a range of screen incarnations, which encompass adaptations, documentaries, cinema advertisements, post-colonial reinventions and mass media citations, and which test the boundaries of conventional idioms and mediums.'[22] Typical of this layered, hybrid discourse is the awareness of a lineage traceable back to 'adaptations' rather than originals, evident in the pastiche and quotation of media, rather than literary or theatrical, versions of Shakespeare. Hence Shakespeare is 'packaged' in a way that locates the drama in relation to some of its other manifestations in popular culture.[23] Even the overriding emphasis on fashion chimes with style statements and visual images familiar from Luhrmann's supremely image-conscious modern-dress film.

At this point, however, Burnett and Wray depart from their positive appreciation of the film as quotation, and of the 'culture of conjuration and pastiche' it represents, and embark on a political interrogation of the advert's treatment of race and ethnicity.[24] *West Side Story*, say Burnett and Wray, shows life as 'an ethnic war zone', whereas the H&M film

[22] *Ibid.*, p. 2.
[23] *Ibid.*
[24] *Ibid.*

'subscribes to a vaguely and ambiguously realised constituency that belies any straightforward identification'. Romeo could be Asian (in fact he is clearly Hispanic) or Latin, while Juliet 'inhabits the aesthetically whitened extreme of the Afro-American experience'. The 'free-floating and cross-cultural ethnicity' symptomatised by a mixed-race model of humanity is then attacked as a concession to the homogenisation of capitalist enterprise.[25] '*Romeo and Juliet* by David LaChappelle models itself along the lines of these "raceless" narratives: devotion to a product ... is seen to be preferable to absorption in a community, and expectations about conflict are resolved in the spectacle of an ethnically diluted, and accessory-driven, homogeneity.'[26] Along these lines it is better to be absorbed in a community, even one at war with another, than devoted to a product. Or rather devotion to a product is a form of fetishism that masks the real fault-lines between communities. Cultural differences that presumably ought to be acknowledged, if not celebrated, such as those between the warring immigrant communities of *West Side Story*, are here flattened out to constitute the archetypal wearer of H&M jeans as racially neutral and ethnically homogenised. Shakespearean universality is also channelled, into music that articulates 'a personal journey that achieves a transcendently communicative efficacity'. The film's 'whitened value system' 'betrays' its own attempt to represent social conflict and transgressive passion, just as H&M now represents itself as a 'worldwide consortium' oblivious to its roots as a modest Swedish clothing outlet.[27] Equally, Tamyra Gray's status as an *American Idol* runner-up serves to endorse nothing more than the 'illusion of traditions of meritocracy'.[28]

In this analysis, the Shakespearean advert, and the Shakespeare quotations within it, can be over-read. For Burnett and Wray, the gunman who kills Romeo is characterised as identifiable in his very anonymity. Because he is hooded, and only his eyes are visible, he is said to recall photographs of Guantanamo Bay detainees, and hence 'Muslim and/or Islamic extremists'. His violence springs, therefore, not from ethnic gang disputes, but from anti-American terrorism. He is the outsider whose otherness must give place to American unity: at the end he reappears, apparently repentant, and thus signifies the post 9/11 US directive of social unity and cultural homogeneity, and 'the aggressive military tactics of the

[25] *Ibid.*, p. 3.
[26] *Ibid.*, p. 4.
[27] *Ibid.*
[28] *Ibid.*, p. 5.

Bush administration'.[29] Likewise, in Burnett and Wray's reading, the visual quotation of a line from *The Merchant of Venice* on a shop awning suggests 'fraternisation rather than rejection, intercourse rather than ostracisation', but also alludes to 'earlier US relations with Iraq, a history of trade in armaments, and a complicity in the engendering and perpetuating of authoritarian regimes'.[30] As Tamyra Gray sings 'We will share the same love, / We both share the same mind', the lyrics are not so much an affirmation of star-crossed love, as a demand that racial alterity surrender to American domination.

The advert asks to be read as indirect quotation of Shakespeare, of *Romeo + Juliet* and of *West Side Story*, since it locates in those cultural antecedents the model for its own irenic message. But the critical analysis of Burnett and Wray sees the film's signifiers as directly expressive of a capitalist ideology that has been imported into Shakespeare by the material socio-economic context of the advert. It should be apparent that these systematic distortions of the visual evidence, and the theoretical movement away from consideration of the advert as a quotation of Shakespeare, are designed to contain it within a politically correct anti-capitalist dogma. The film becomes, in this theoretical paradigm, less a quotation of Shakespeare, and more a quotation of images and ideologies from the US-led 'War on Terror'.

But the killer is clearly black, even in his hooded state (as they later admit, when unmasked he bears 'the film's most conventionally ethnicised appearance').[31] Hence he is a member of the same ethnic group/gang/community as Juliet (who according to Burnett and Wray is really, notwithstanding her skin colour, essentially white). So the killing is clearly motivated, as it is in *West Side Story*, by gang rivalry. The killer is not in police custody at the end (the police show up after him); indeed, he has returned to the scene with the same kind of remorse as that shown by the Sharks over Tony's body. Juliet points Romeo's mobile at the killer in a gesture that recalls Maria's reproachful pointing of the gun at the other gang members at the end of *West Side Story*.

Thus the film is nothing like as ideologically loaded and contaminated as Burnett and Wray argue. In fact, it is a quite faithful quotation of a mediated Shakespeare, accessed via Luhrmann and Wise/Bernstein/Sondheim, which poses, against social division and ethnic violence, a body

[29] *Ibid.*
[30] *Ibid.*, p. 6.
[31] *Ibid.*, p. 5.

of recognisably American liberal and democratic values. Love is better than hatred. Romance is better than conflict. Sexual passion *can* transcend social divisions, as it does across the divide of vendetta in Shakespeare's Verona. The social mobility of American meritocracy is by no means an 'illusion', as testified by the musical allusions to *American Idol* and to the career of the Supremes, who travelled all the way from the Frederick Douglass Housing Projects to global stardom.

All these quite traditional values are then properly deployed to endorse the product. Denim jeans derived from the protective attire of workers. They began to be manufactured in their modern form when German immigrant Levi Strauss, in 1873, patented a means of holding the cloth together with rivets. In time they became a uniquely 'classless and non-gendered' garment.[32] They can of course be very expensive: but it is the mission of stores such as H&M to retail high-fashion jeans to ordinary people at affordable prices. Neither high fashion, nor communication (mobile phones), nor true love, are out of the reach of such ordinary young black and Hispanic people as LaChappelle's Romeo and Juliet.[33]

Although Burnett and Wray set out to embrace quotations of Shakespeare as realised in popular culture and contemporary media, their methods are too ideologically constricted to allow a free and creative reading of this film. Their theoretical and analytical methods remain underpinned by the dogmatic anti-capitalist elitism of the Frankfurt School, as were those deployed decades ago in *The Shakespeare Myth*. High culture rules: mass culture is a systematic degradation and dumbing-down of human potentiality. The USA is said to exist primarily as 'competitive cult of manufactured celebrity' symptomatised by *American Idol*.[34] Despite the demonstration that this Shakespeare quotation is a novel product of its cultural context, in the advert something else called 'Shakespeare' is being ruthlessly manipulated by capitalist greed. 'Shakespeare' is 'packaged' for the 'global garment industry', 'mortgaged to, and deployed in promoting, the narrative's commercial requirements'. The helpless, 'targeted' 'consumer' is a passive victim of the same system of manipulation.[35] He is Herbert Marcuse's one-dimensional man, forced by the relentless pressure of advertising to inhabit an illusory permanence and universality.[36] The

---

[32] Margaret Maynard, *Dress and Globalisation* (Manchester: Manchester University Press, 2004), p. 47.
[33] Or the rest of us. Even low-paid university professors may shop at H&M.
[34] Burnett and Wray, *Screening Shakespeare*, p. 5.
[35] *Ibid.*, pp. 2, 7, 6, 7.
[36] Herbert Marcuse, *One-Dimensional Man: Studies in the Ideology of Advanced Industrial Society* (New York: Beacon Press, 1964).

film shows traces of, but denies the existence of, a destructive and violent American nationalism. This reads like a Marxist analysis, but Marx believed in a classless universalism, not the multicultural promotion of sectarian loyalty.[37]

LaChappelle is not after all, in the view of Burnett and Wray, creating a new Shakespeare, but only paying tribute to an old one, borrowing spurious authenticity in the service of product marketing. 'Films already inscribed with the market stamp of youth culture and urban angst lend their reputation to LaChappelle's advertising utterance, pointing up a modality of articulation and reception in which Shakespeare is "hip" and in which an affiliation with the Bard is as cool and current as the acquisition of the latest designer label.'[38] The accent of contempt here for the hybridisation of Shakespeare and fashion retailing witnesses to a radical disconnect between the critical methods deployed, and the material under consideration. To put it bluntly, however sophisticated, knowing, self-reflexive and postmodern popular culture may be, it is often, at heart, innocent. The film is not primarily about making Shakespeare cool, or even about endorsing jeans by the use of Shakespeare's name. It is rather a romantic quotation and reaffirmation of Shakespeare's premise: that young love, and tragically young death, can operate as litmus tests that challenge and call into question the motives of those involved in social conflicts. The simple pleasures of falling in love, mutually breaking the rules, looking nice for your girlfriend or boyfriend, place on trial the casual slaughter of the drive-by shooting, the hooded black gunman and the ethnic gang culture that supports him.

A conservative reading of Shakespeare, if you like. But the decision to remove the film from circulation on the grounds that it glamourised gun violence in the interests of selling clothes was almost as wrong as Burnett and Wray's castigation of it as a defence of xenophobic American patriotism, the War on Terror and Guantanamo Bay. Both the act of censorship and the critical mauling represent forms of political correctness that stand against freedom. David LaChappelle's film celebrates youthful passion, democratic style, affordable fashion, social mobility and free enterprise. In all of which I happen to believe. Don't you, *hypocrite lecteur*? Don't you?

---

[37] 'Communism [is] the positive transcendence of private property, as human self-estrangement, and therefore [is] the true appropriation of the human essence by and for man.' Karl Marx, *Economic and Philosophic Manuscripts of 1844*, trans. Martin Milligan (New York: Dover, 2007), p. 102.

[38] *Ibid.*, p. 3.

Conclusion

> The 'text of modern life' these days is embedded in a network of text messaging, internet connections, video clips, and file sharing. Shakespeare in our culture is already disseminated, scattered, appropriated, part of the cultural language, high and low ... Shakespeare is already not not only modern but postmodern: a simulacrum, a replicant, a montage, a bricolage. A collection of found objects, repurposed as art.[39]

Marjorie Garber opens her study of Shakespeare and modern culture by showing how far we have moved from the crude 'base and superstructure' model of culture with which the analysis of Shakespeare and advertising began. When we find quotations of Shakespeare in contemporary culture, they are appropriations likely to be drawn from other appropriations rather than from any direct, unmediated, 'original' source. This demonstrates two things: one, that Shakespeare is already part of the culture, albeit in this fragmented, dissipated, disseminated form; and two, that we cannot contain Shakespearean quotation within circumscribed parameters of class, race, gender and power. Shakespearean quotation is freely available both to the advertising industry, and to the people who read its texts and consume the products it promotes. To condemn the texts of advertising, and the retail practices of billions of ordinary people, as mercenary corruptions of culture seems remarkably elitist. As the examples provided above indicate, the quotation of Shakespeare in advertising is capable of producing new, strange, creative initiatives in culture and art. Shakespeareans should be embracing these cultural productions with the appreciation and enthusiasm they deserve.[40]

---

[39] Marjorie Garber, *Shakespeare and Modern Culture* (New York: Random House, 2008).

[40] For an example, see Graham Holderness and Bryan Loughrey, 'Ales, Beers, Shakespeares', in Siobhan Keenan and Dominic Shellard (eds.), *Shakespeare's Cultural Capital: His Economic Influence from the Sixteenth to the Twenty-First Centuries* (London: Palgrave, 2016), pp. 99–125.

CHAPTER 16

Digital Technology and the Future of Reception History

Stephen O'Neill; Balz Engler and Regula Hohl Trillini

QUOTING SHAKESPEARE IN DIGITAL CULTURE

Stephen O'Neill

Shakespeare's words are everywhere online should we choose to notice. Considering our culture of search, synonymous with Google and the myriad social media technologies we use daily, each with their own internal search functions, Shakespearean quotation is part of the quotidian flow of digital networked platforms. Perhaps this is because Shakespeare *is* Shakespeare; or because 'Shakespeare's words stick like velcro on the soul', to quote Jeanette Winterson upon the publication of *The Gap of Time*, the novelist's 'cover version' of *The Winter's Tale*.[1] That a quote about the affective power of Shakespeare's words can be accessed as a tweet, in this instance from publisher Arden Shakespeare, referencing the author's Twitter handle @Wintersonworld, itself evidences how digital platforms are key spaces where Shakespeare not only circulates but is constructed again and again.[2] Digital technologies are bridging the gap between Shakespeares – an amorphous assemblage of mediated and mediatised texts – and a great variety of users. The digital and its denizens converge with the spectral quality of Shakespearean words – 'the return of the expressed' – and variously enable, sustain and alter these Shakespeares' uncanny temporality.[3]

Key to this realisation is the participatory nature of platforms such as Twitter, YouTube and Tumblr, which prompt and promote democratic forms of media engagement, including the use of Shakespearean texts.[4] While Shakespeare studies has attended to new media Shakespeare

---

[1] Jeanette Winterson, *The Gap of Time: The Winter's Tale Retold* (London: Hogarth, 2015), p. xvii.
[2] www.twitter.com/Ardenpublisher/status/677122676348100608 (last accessed 18 May 2017).
[3] Marjorie Garber, *Shakespeare's Ghost Writers* (New York: Routledge, 2010), p. 70.
[4] See Jean Burgess and Joshua Green, *YouTube: Online Video and Participatory Culture* (Cambridge: Polity, 2013); Dhiraj Murthy, *Twitter: Social Communication in the Twitter Age* (Cambridge: Polity, 2013).

productions, the specific practice of quoting Shakespeare has received less attention.[5] In what follows, I suggest that digital cultures represent a significant phase in the long narrative of quoting Shakespeare that the present volume unfolds. Several questions come to mind here. What conditions does the digital world entail that are different and new? Among these we can include screen culture, networked communication and connectivity, agential media users, and shareable or 'spreadable' content. What new practices are discernible when we select examples from the extraordinary surfeit of digital content? What connections might be traced between early modern understandings of quotation, in the form of *sententiae* and commonplaces, and a Shakespeare quotation in a tweet? If a quotation's intertextuality is seen as 'tethering works to the future as well as the past', then in what ways might digitally quoted Shakespeare illuminate or alter what Shakespeare means?[6] Quotation online reveals modes of creative intertextuality and critical misquotation. Moreover, in terms provided by recent media-oriented analyses of Shakespeares, quotation online can be understood as the interrelation of three constitutive agents: Shakespeare (or words marked as 'Shakespearean'), the human user and the technological apparatuses.[7] How and why Shakespeare quotations (re)appear within digital culture is a function of us, the wetware, or 'biosemiotic motor' to media platforms that render 'the textual remains lively once more'.[8]

Framing quotation as an interaction of humans and machines may not be a stark proposition, especially in light of persuasive arguments that humans and technologies are coeval.[9] We need only think of tweet bots that auto-generate quotations from Shakespeare's works line by line, as in the Twitter profile @IAM_SHAKESPEARE, to get a sense of how digitally quoted Shakespeare entails human–posthuman coordination. Here the computational software and hardware, which are human- or wetware-designed in the first instance, become part of the dynamic between sentient humans and the affective resonance of Shakespeare's words, their stickiness in Winterson's sense of 'velcro on the soul'.

---

[5] See Jennifer Ailles, '"Is There an App for That?" Mobile Shakespeare on the Phone and in the Cloud', in Daniel Fischlin (ed.), *Outerspeares: Shakespeare, Intermedia and the Limits of Adaptation* (Toronto: University of Toronto Press, 2014), pp. 75–112.

[6] Douglas Bruster, *Quoting Shakespeare* (Lincoln: University of Nebraska Press, 2000), p. 3.

[7] Kylie Jarrett and Jeneen Naji, 'What Would Media Studies Do? Social Media Shakespeare as a Technosocial Process', *Borrowers and Lenders*, 10:1 (2016), www.borrowers.uga.edu/1794/show (last accessed 18 May 2017).

[8] Richard Burt and Julian Yates, *What's the Worst Thing You Can Do to Shakespeare?* (New York: Palgrave, 2013), pp. 1, 6.

[9] N. Katherine Hayles, *How We Became Posthuman* (Chicago: University of Chicago Press, 2008).

@IAM_SHAKESPEARE creator Joshua Strebel harnesses the computer's inherent capacity for repetition to render Shakespeare as an 'answer to the banality of the everyday tweet'.[10] Quotation, Marjorie Garber reminds us, 'by its very presence offers a critique of the context into which it is summoned'.[11] Shakespeare's words as tweets become networked digital objects that can be easily shared, deployed as conduits for connection, as metacommentaries on the Twittersphere itself, or as expressions of emotion. To think further about how Shakespeare as an assemblage of texts accumulates value through quotation in digital technologies means delving into the superabundance of online content. Within the attention economy of online and digital environments, it is our capacity to notice that becomes the scarce resource: distraction is inevitable, selection necessary.[12] While data mining exercises could enable a quantitative analysis, affording insight into the most frequently quoted lines on particular platforms or in apps, such an approach lies beyond the scope of the present discussion.[13] Instead selection falls into the category of 'what I noticed' as an individual user, although even this category is not exclusively human, since computational algorithms enable the process of search and identify relevance or related digital objects.

Ease and availability constitute the primary, enabling conditions of quoted Shakespeare in digital networked culture. So long as a user has access to a computerised, screen-based device (desktop, laptop, tablet, mobile phone), s/he can access Shakespeare's texts. To Christie Carson and Peter Kirwan's question, 'Are all Shakespeares digital now?', we must surely answer yes, since the entire corpus is available online, with convenient user affordances such as text- and concordance-search functions (*Open Source Shakespeare*) and full hypertext editions (*Folger Digital Texts*).[14] Whatever the different forms digitally quoted Shakespeares take, they involve the interaction of user and computer data. Digital quoted Shakespeare is more than a set of content-examples and more than cultural texts. They are digital objects comprising a cultural and a computational

---

[10] Joshua Strebel, 'William Shakespeare's 450th Birthday: Why I've Tweeted a Line of the Bard Every 10 Minutes for Five years', *Independent*, 23 April 2014, www.goo.gl/1QZMzI (last accessed 18 May 2017).

[11] Garber, *Shakespeare's Ghost Writers*, p. 69.

[12] See Richard A. Lanham, *The Economics of Attention* (Chicago: University of Chicago Press, 2000).

[13] See Matthew P. Simmons, Lada A. Adamic and Eytan Adar, 'Memes Online: Extracted, Subtracted, Injected, and Recollected', *ICWSM*, 11 (2011), 17–21, www.goo.gl/Q555ce (last accessed 18 May 2017).

[14] Christie Carson and Peter Kirwan (eds.), *Shakespeare and the Digital World*, e-book (Cambridge: Cambridge University Press, 2014), loc. 5151; www.opensourceshakespeare.org/ (last accessed 18 May 2017); www.folgerdigitaltexts.org/ (last accessed 18 May 2017).

layer.[15] To a computational network, Shakespeare's words – the cultural layer – are merely binary code and HTML. However, the computational always affects the cultural. One effect is the ease with which computer data in the form of hyperlinks, the organising elements of the internet, allow users to share content.[16] Interfaces such as Twitter and YouTube are further designed to facilitate sharing through embedded share icons. These icons are visual markers of contemporary media's dominant condition: 'spreadability'. In Henry Jenkins, Sam Ford and Joshua Green's formulation, vernacular media interventions are as important and influential as those of large-scale commercial or corporate interests. In a networked culture, there may be no singular reason why individuals or communities of users decide to spread media content but, as the authors elaborate, in so doing 'people make a series of socially embedded decisions'.[17] Whether users produce, share or appraise content for cultural, personal, political or economic reasons, the act itself is generative and may produce new practices and aesthetics.[18] This emphasis on user agency as a catalyst of spreadable media needs to be balanced with an acknowledgement of the non-human facilitator, the computational layer that simultaneously enables the user's manipulation and repurposing of media content. Spreading Shakespeare is an act or decision that is always technologically enabled and situated.

To quote Shakespeare, users do not have to seek out the texts themselves but can find pre-packaged selections as part of general quotation websites, mobile apps or dedicated Shakespeare quote sites. It is possible to select text – a function that combines human and computer as we hold the mouse or touch the tablet screen – and then copy-and-paste it. So habitual as to be unremarkable, the copy-and-paste function is a major affordance of digital media. It may encourage direct over indirect quotation as users opt to reuse existing text rather than create entirely new text.[19] Yet some quote generator sites encourage misquotation. *The Shakespeare Quote Generator* allows users to input a word into a dialogue box, which the app randomly substitutes for a word in the original: entering the word 'digital' returns 'All the world's a digital / And all the men and women

[15] Lev Manovich, *The Language of New Media* (Boston: MIT Press, 2001), p. 46.
[16] Alexander Halavais, 'The Hyperlink as Organizing Principle', in Joseph Turow and Lokman Tsui (eds.), *The Hyperlinked Society* (Ann Arbor: University of Michigan Press, 2008), pp. 39–55.
[17] Henry Jenkins, Sam Ford and Joshua Green, *Spreadable Media* (New York: New York University Press, 2013), p. 13.
[18] *Ibid.*, pp. 35, 177.
[19] Elisabetta Adami, 'The Rhetoric of the Implicit and the Politics of Representation in the Age of Copy-and-Paste', *Learning, Media and Technology*, 37:2 (2012), 131–44 (p. 142).

merely players'; or, if one reloads, 'Our revels now are ended. These our actors, / As I foretold you, were all spirits and / Are melted into digital, into thin digital.'[20] Through the reload icon, as well as the option to click on the question 'Which work was this quote from, and what was the missing word?', the site encourages users to engage in an intertextual game. By contrast, the mobile app *William Shakespeare Quotes* does not provide the source for quotations but rather organises them around thematic headings.[21] The app becomes a digital version of the early modern commonplace book, such as Bodenham's *Bel-vedére; or, The Garden of the Muses* (1600), in which quotes from a range of sources appear unacknowledged and arranged around headings, the implication being that the reader will apply quotes to particular occasions, even engaging in creative misquotation.[22] In both cases, the quote becomes a potentially adaptive thing that is remade through a new medium. In the generator's case, the built-in randomness means that some user-entered words substitute more effectively than others, but what emerges is a new type of Shakespearean line, one that is algorithmically determined and yet takes on a resonance in its accidental metacommentary on our digital moment.

Generated quotes can be pasted into Twitter or any other digital platform, either in their algorithmically generated form, or adapted and repurposed by a user. The sharing and repurposing of available content thus constitute another condition of quoting Shakespeare in the digital age. Questions of originality, user agency and creativity come to the fore: simply to copy the second digital quote, adapted from Prospero's elegiac words, in order to paste into a tweet as a response to #makeaquoteshakespearean, a trending topic on Twitter, may seem entirely derivative.[23] Such modes of participation corroborate assessments of digital culture as a threat to human cognition and memory.[24] Yet the reuse of the computer-generated quote entails user agency because it is both an act of sharing and, since the quote is placed on Twitter in an individual profile and with a hashtag generated by other 'tweeple', also a redetermination of the initial reception context. Posting a quote using the hashtag #makeaquoteshakespearean involves call

---

[20] www.thesurrealist.co.uk/shakespeare.php (last accessed 18 May 2017).
[21] Available at www.play.google.com/store/apps/details?id=william.shakespeare (last accessed 18 May 2017).
[22] Julie Maxwell, 'How the Renaissance (Mis)Used Sources: The Art of Misquotation', in Laurie Maguire (ed.), *How to Do Things with Shakespeare* (Oxford: Blackwell, 2008), pp. 54–76; see also chapters in Part I.
[23] www.twitter.com/hashtag/makeaquoteshakespearean. Trending on Twitter, 31 October 2015 (last accessed 18 May 2017).
[24] See Andrew Keen, *Digital Vertigo* (New York: St Martin's Press, 2015).

and response. It keys individuals into a micro-network structured loosely around Shakespeare and into a collective or community of fellow users. 'Thou hadst me had at Hey Nonny Nonny', as one user puts it, mashing the phrase from *Jerry Maguire* with a song from *Much Ado about Nothing*.[25] As user experience of Twitter temporarily coheres around the hashtag, the Shakespeare quote becomes a mode of and catalyst for *social* media.

Twitter's connections to early modern practices of commonplacing also emerge here. In the description of the commonplace book 'as a memory store of quotations, which could be activated to verbalise present experience in the language of familiar moral paradigms and with reference to a cultural history shared by the writer and reader', we can locate similarities to the tweet-as-quote.[26] *Bel-vedére*'s explanatory address to the reader about its sententious 'flowers', 'each line being severall sentence, and none exceeding two lines at the uttermost', invites us to see it as an early modern precursor to Twitter's promotion of the aphoristic and its mish-mash of cultural references.[27] A further similarity between Twitter and early modern commonplacing is discernible in the former's use of indexical icons such as the retweet button or share arrow and the latter practice's use of typographical markers such as quotation marks and manicules, which alerted the reader to 'sententious passages suitable for transcription into a commonplace book'.[28]

Browsing on Twitter reveals how participation in #makeaquote-shakespearean is shaped by the medium and its culture, not only in terms of Twitter's current 140-character limit but also ironic mash-ups of news and pop culture. On the Twittersphere, #brevityisthesoulofwit. One user tweets 'behold, doth thou know me? Then address me such forth with title!', with a still image of Heisenberg from *Breaking Bad*.[29] Others critique the adaptive logic of the tweets: 'I like this **#MakeAQuoteShakespearean** hashtag, but it reminds me that most people do not actually know how Shakespearean grammar works.'[30] From these examples we can extrapolate some broader insights: tweets are not simply text-based but are intermedial; Twitter makes it easy to upload media, 'coaxing' users into generating

---

[25] www.twitter.com/BrettFishA/status/660341206283612160 (last accessed 18 May 2017).
[26] Ann Moss, *Printed Commonplace-Books and the Structuring of Renaissance Thought* (Oxford: Clarendon Press, 1996), p. v.
[27] *Bel-vedére; or, The Garden of the Muses* (London, 1600), available on *Early English Books Online*, www.eebo.chadwyck.com (last accessed 18 May 2017).
[28] Zachary Lesser and Peter Stallybrass, 'The First Literary *Hamlet* and the Commonplacing of Professional Plays', *Shakespeare Quarterly*, 59:4 (2008), 371–420 (p. 378).
[29] www.twitter.com/MonsignorRenard/status/660547625695973376 (last accessed 18 May 2017).
[30] www.twitter.com/Crowbeak/status/661465603769630720 (last accessed 18 May 2017).

particular types of Shakespeare media texts.[31] The digital thus accelerates a 'post-textual Shakespeare' as the language becomes only one element in what is now a densely intermedial Shakespeare.[32] Users can be understood as performing identity through participation in Twitter and this intermedial Shakespeare. They perform according to the platform's conventions and, through playfulness, irony and ingenuity, demonstrate that they are clued in to its culture. Rewards come in the form of likes, retweets and follows by other tweeple. To criticise users for misunderstanding iambic pentameter is to misinterpret the cultural and medium-specific conditions of quoting Shakespeare in the digital world. The Shakespeare quotation as gift, token and even conduit to connection and community far outweighs (even as it sometimes creatively trades off) concerns for accuracy, textual fidelity and authorial sovereignty.

If, in these examples, quotation seems to dismember Shakespeare, digital cultures also provide examples of traditional forms of quoted Shakespeare as the favourite or iconic quote. @HollowCrownFans, the profile of the fan community around the BBC TV serial drama *The Hollow Crown* (2012, 2016), encourages the sharing of favourite quotes through #ShakespeareSunday. The fans extend the 'intimate public' associated with fandom, issuing a call to the networked public of Twitter.[33] The call is structured around a suggested theme, ranging from 'Hal: From Prince to King' (selected on Sunday 25 October 2015, the 600th anniversary of Agincourt) to the supernatural.[34] Foregrounding temporality, with the added suggestion of the leisure time traditionally associated with Sunday, links the call to foundational moments in the history of Shakespeare commemoration as Israel Gollancz's 'Shakespeare day'.[35] The hashtag acts as a centripetal force, labelling, sharing and showcasing cherished Shakespeare quotations to the networked community: 'Love sought, is good; but given unsought, is better' (*Twelfth Night*, III.ii.147).[36] Or from ShakespeareArgentina, 'The web of our life is of a mingled yarn, good and ill together' (*All's Well that Ends Well*, IV.iii.73–4).[37] These tweet quotes

---

[31] See Aimee Morrison, 'Facebook and Coaxed Affordances', in Anna Poletti and Julie Rak (eds.), *Identity Technologies* (Madison: University of Wisconsin Press, 2014), pp. 112–31.

[32] Douglas Lanier, 'Post-Textual Shakespeare', *Shakespeare Survey*, 64 (2011), 145–62.

[33] danah boyd, 'Social Network Sites as Networked Publics', in Zizi Papacharissi (ed.), *Networked Self* (New York: Routledge, 2011), pp. 39–58.

[34] www.twitter.com/HollowCrownFans/status/657564693981106176 (last accessed 18 May 2017).

[35] Clara Calvo, 'Fighting over Shakespeare: Commemorating the 1916 Tercentenary in Wartime', *Critical Survey*, 24:3 (2012), 48–72.

[36] www.twitter.com/thelifeof_rose/status/696230671614775296 (last accessed 18 May 2017).

[37] www.twitter.com/ShakespeareArg/status/696439708369428480 (last accessed 18 May 2017).

exemplify Maurice Halbwachs's concept of 'collective memory', which alerts us to the nexus of individual/group interests in the history of Shakespeare commemoration.[38] Yet, the hashtag exemplifies the argument that in our digital age, collective memory is increasingly 'connective memory' – a kind of 'mingled yarn' – in the way that technologies not only enable but crucially shape how human users communicate and remember.[39] Shakespeare is being remembered through the interaction of agentive human users and their network of quotes rendered on Twitter as identifiable digital objects spreadable across the 'web (of our life)'.

The language of remembering/dismembering, a feature of adapted Shakespeare, lends itself to a conceptualisation of quotation as a breaking off and severing of the textual corpus, but a suturing too. As with the Shakespeare phenomenon more generally, however, where the 'Thing Shakespeare' uncannily (re)appears through subsequent iterations, so with digital quotation dismembering the lines nonetheless contributes to Shakespeare's currency, sustaining the valency of 'Shakespearean' and creating an appetite for it amidst the copia of online content.[40] 'There's rosemary, that's for remembrance; pray you, love, remember', to quote @ Wwm_Shakespeare.[41] Digital productions provide a mnemonic function but also foreground the everyday currency of Shakespearean words, as in the YouTube video *You're Quoting Shakespeare*.[42] YouTube presents related videos on the right of the interface, among them a TEDx talk *Shakespeare is Everywhere*.[43] YouTube provides a convenient, mutable archive of video assemblages of Shakespearean idioms that remediate a well-known passage by Bernard Levin, widely available online in various formats; it has even been conveniently annotated with hyperlinks.[44] YouTube is an index of the quotidian Shakespeare: in the vlog 'Look at Me, Quoting Shakespeare ... like a Boss ;)' a young woman, reflecting on coming out, remarks 'expectation is the root of all heartbreak'.[45] The vlogger lays claim to a phrase

[38] Quoted in Clara Calvo and Coppélia Kahn (eds.), *Celebrating Shakespeare* (Cambridge: Cambridge University Press, 2015), p. 8.

[39] Andrew Hoskins, 'Digital Network Memory', in Astrid Erll and Ann Rigney (eds.), *Mediation, Remediation, and the Dynamics of Cultural Memory* (Berlin: De Gruyter, 2009), pp. 91–108.

[40] Maurizio Calbi, *Spectral Shakespeares: Media Adaptations in the Twenty-First Century* (New York: Palgrave Macmillan, 2013), p. 6.

[41] www.twitter.com/Wwm_Shakespeare/status/696410920768172033 (last accessed 18 May 2017) (quoting *Hamlet*, v.iv.199–200).

[42] www.youtube.com/watch?v=q33RvElAAc4 (last accessed 18 May 2017).

[43] www.youtube.com/watch?v=LsESSyMnwmU (last accessed 18 May 2017).

[44] Bernard Levin, *Enthusiasms* (London: Jonathan Cape, 1983), pp. 167–8; betterlivingthroughbeowulf. com/we-cant-help-but-quote-the-bard/ (last accessed 18 May 2017).

[45] www.youtube.com/watch?v=U4wzbyhCiL4 (last accessed 18 May 2017).

culturally marked as Shakespearean: 'that's a Shakespeare quote, so I feel really cool when I say it', she remarks, overlapping the conative with the emotive function of language. Shakespeare's traditional imprimatur here sustains Shakespeare's currency in YouTube youth culture, just as the (mis) quote reveals the words, or a version of them, to be embedded in daily life.

Fully to understand quoted/quoting Shakespeare in digital culture is not merely to recognise that, as in offline culture, Shakespearean words have entered into a broad range of language functions, but is also to appreciate new modes and aesthetics in play. The meme is exemplary of a digital culture aesthetic, with its combination of media (text and still or moving image) and irony, or a gag that the recipient easily gets.[46] Shakespeare quotations are being memefied, as they are mashed with the meme-world's tendency toward humour. From the Tumblr profile *Some Random Geek*, for instance: 'Shakespeare walks into a gay bar … Exit pursu'd by a bear'. The setup uses the classic 'X walks into a bar', with the enigmatic stage direction from *The Winter's Tale* supplying the punchline, which is extended through the pun on gay culture types.[47] Tumblr memes assume their own aesthetic and logic: the viewer interprets the codes accordingly, identifying a relation of expectation to reality, as in 'Describe your dating life in a Shakespeare quote', and the answer: 'Full of sound and fury, signifying nothing'.[48] A series of tags ('#apropos of nothing #Shakespeare #Shakespearean quote #dating life #meme') allows these memetic texts to be located and linked to similarly tagged content. A sense of play is evident, but so too is the blogger's gesture to the incidental nature of social media production and participation ('#apropos of nothing').

The Shakespeare quote is becoming a residual cultural form as the meme, the digital environment's cultural dominant, transforms it. As Jenkins has recently suggested, Raymond Williams's paradigm of residual/emergent/dominant, that classic formulation about subtle shifts in cultural tastes and habits, offers us a framework for thinking through the relation of seemingly old texts and new participatory technologies.[49] Tumblr's interactive affordances are revealing here as users call out to other users or followers, inviting them to engage in mimesis and create a similar type of text to their own. The blog *incorrectshakespearequotes* invites followers to submit a parodic adaptation

---

[46] Limor Shifman, *Memes in Digital Culture*, e-book (Boston: MIT Press, 2013).
[47] www.randomgeeknamedbrent.tumblr.com/post/102556022631/shakespeare-walks-into-a-gay-bar (last accessed 18 May 2017).
[48] www.bridgetroll42.tumblr.com/post/131690212634/describe-your-dating-life-in-a-shakespearean-quote (last accessed 18 May 2017).
[49] Jenkins, Ford and Green, *Spreadable Media*, pp. 95–9.

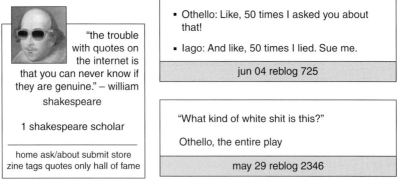

Figure 11   Incorrect Shakespeare blog, 'What kind of white shit is this?'

as *not*-Shakespeare using the format of putative quote and source, as in '"What kind of white shit is this?" Othello, the entire play'[50] (Figure 11). This illustrates Shifman's argument that memes are 'forms of political participation' and express 'critical approaches toward race-based stereotyping'.[51] In its self-referential ironising of ideologies of sexuality and race in Shakespearean texts, this meme simultaneously instances an attenuated relation to Shakespeare and also licenses the validity of such a position. Enacted here is a provocative, potentially productive queering of Shakespeare as tradition, value and cultural capital that complements calls within the field for the scholar to demonstrate an ethical commitment to alternatives to a 'transcendent, homogenised Shakespeare'.[52] However, as with other seemingly Shakespeare-eccentric texts, memetic misquotation may not necessarily signal 'anti-hegemonic, liberatory or otherwise progressive political and social effects'.[53] In the ascendancy of irony that marks the digital, to the point that irony is bereft of its critical edge, perhaps *incorrectShakespearequotes* risks becoming the next cliché, the next target for memetic irony and meta-commentary.

'"[T]he trouble with quotes on the internet is that you can never know if they are genuine." – william shakespeare'.[54] This strapline sums up the conditions of quoting/quoted Shakespeare in digital cultures that this mini-chapter has been tracing. An authenticity discourse surrounding both

---

[50] www.incorrectshakespeare.tumblr.com/post/120224235069/what-kind-of-white-shit-is-this, posted 29 May 2015 (last accessed 18 May 2017).

[51] Shifman, *Memes*, locs. 1239, 223.

[52] Alexa Huang and Elizabeth Rivlin, 'Introduction', in Alexa Huang and Elizabeth Rivlin (eds.), *Shakespeare and the Ethics of Appropriation* (New York: Palgrave, 2014), pp. 1–20 (p. 6).

[53] *Ibid.*, p. 12.

[54] www.incorrectshakespeare.tumblr.com/ (last accessed 18 May 2017).

Shakespeare and the internet is invoked and ironised by the media prosumer, who avails of the low barriers to entry of digital technologies and software. As in this example, so with digital quoted Shakespeare more generally we are always dealing with the interaction of three constitutive agents: user, technological apparatus and Shakespeare as textual assemblage. Noteworthy too is how veracity, accuracy and provenance have less currency in a digital culture structured upon a logic of remix and upon practices of mash-up or creative repurposing. In participatory digital cultures, Shakespeares get quoted insofar as they are texts that can be used and shared in order to generate new meanings. This is not to say that the digital necessarily advances misquotation or misremembering – there are ample resources that give us the thing itself in the form of scholarly digitised texts – but is rather to capture the digital environment's transformative effects, as it leads to creative, metacritical uses of the Shakespearean. The result is a form of quoted Shakespeare that moves away from the anchoring authority of a stable text toward a far more diffuse, democratic understanding of what the Shakespearean encompasses. This diffusion or dispersal should be understood less in terms of loss than as a tethering of Shakespeare's words to the future, as they survive as identifiable digital objects only to (re)appear in platforms yet to be created or in new modes of vernacular media production that are yet to emerge: #notforanagebutforalltime.

BACK TO THE FUTURE: DIGITAL QUOTATION RESEARCH

Balz Engler and Regula Hohl Trillini

Digital technology is transforming quotation research, bringing new material to our attention and questioning the categories we have been using to deal with quotations. Computers enable us to deal with so many texts and to categorise them so efficiently that quantity can become a qualitative dimension. This does not mean that we are leaving a rich tradition of scholarship behind us. The experience of building the *HyperHamlet* database, which entailed researching a substantial corpus of quotations and annotating them for a range of useful parameters, suggests that the contributions of nineteenth- and twentieth-century philology can enrich digital work.[55] In older scholarship as well as in the digital humanities, it is worth thinking about how the way we search determines what we find, and

---

[55] www.hyperhamlet.unibas.ch/ (last accessed 14 May 2017). See also Balz Engler, 'Truly Delivered: The *Hyperhamlet* Project', in Bruce R. Smith (ed.), *The Cambridge Guide to the Worlds of Shakespeare*, 2 vols. (Cambridge: Cambridge University Press, 2016), vol. 1, pp. 1706–7.

which of our finds we consider worth thinking about. The most significant difference made by digital technology may be a richer understanding of intertextuality.

New Methods

Until the late twentieth century, Shakespeare quotation research relied on manual work, often carried out by philologists rather than students of literature. Interest tended to be focused on where a passage had come from, and how its association with its origin affects the text in which it recurs. Many of the results were published in individual *Notes & Queries* articles or in the footnotes and indexes of scholarly editions such as the Princeton Coleridge or the Cornell Wordsworth.[56] Systematic collection of where Shakespeare passages had *gone to* was attempted in a single case, the *Shakspere Allusion Book*. First published in 1874 and updated until 1909, it records Shakespeare echoes dating from between 1591 and 1700 in an essentially Victorian spirit, offering a collection of references to and mentions of Shakespeare or his works as historical evidence. In the Preface to the 1909 edition, John Munro writes: 'These volumes were not made in a day. Thirty years have passed in their compilation … Many willing hands, too, have lent assistance. Antiquaries, scholars, and friendly readers, have all most kindly helped.'[57]

Willing hands continue to take quotation research forward, but since the beginning of the 1990s they are the hands of wiki users rather than letter writers, as more and more texts become available electronically and can be searched more and more easily, even automatically, thanks to webcrawlers. Various initiatives have made available a vast range of texts. Project Gutenberg had already started in 1971. In 1994 the Text Encoding Initiative established standards of transcription, which are still valid, and since then databases have proliferated.[58] To mention just a few: since the year 2000, the Text Creation Partnership has led to the publication of *Early English Books Online*, which contains more than 125,000 titles published

---

[56] Samuel Taylor Coleridge, *The Collected Works of Samuel Taylor Coleridge* (Princeton: Princeton University Press, 1987–2001); William Wordsworth, *The Cornell Wordsworth* (Ithaca: Cornell University Press, 1975–2007).

[57] C. M. Ingleby, L. Toulmin Smith, F. J. Furnivall and John Munro (eds.), *The Shakspere Allusion-Book: A Collection of Allusions to Shakspere from 1591 to 1700*, rev. edn, Shakespeare Library (London: Chatto & Windus, 1909), p. vii.

[58] www.tei-c/index.xml; www.textcreationpartnership.org/; www.eebo.chadwyck.com/home; www.quod.lib.umich.edu/e/ecco/ (all last accessed 14 May 2017).

between the 1470s and 1700, and *Eighteenth Century Collections Online*. *Google Books* aims to make millions of books available as page images, unfortunately with unreliable OCR transcriptions.[59]

Full-text databases and digital search tools offer exciting possibilities to Shakespeare quotation research, but not the easy cornucopia that scholars, in their first enthusiasm, may expect. Even assuming unlimited funds, the tempting wealth of material needs to be managed, as our experience with the pioneering *HyperHamlet* project taught us. First, a suitable edition of Shakespeare's text had to be selected for the basic text. As the focus in such a project is on readers' reactions rather than on textual research, we chose a conventionally acceptable version. The Cambridge edition (1863–6, revised 1891) served as a standard edition for decades and is now in the public domain.[60] Next, the database set-up needed to balance the scholarly wish to be rigorously systematic against the interests of prospective users navigating the site. Search options should be useful rather than exhaust the unlimited possibilities of classification, and tagging criteria had to be established that would usefully catch emerging and developing notions of what should be considered a quotation.

New Results

Once a database is set up, the ability to crunch huge amounts of material makes it possible to push the boundaries of research set by the capacity of 'willing hands'. First, it becomes possible to unearth verbal recyclings that researchers, inevitably limited by their particular cultural and historical perspectives, would not have recognised. Software that registers verbal parallels between texts can overcome the cognitive bias of human readers. A good example is *Tesserae*, which focuses on classical literature but is expanding into other areas such as Shakespeare.[61]

Second, once a sufficiently large, representative if not complete, corpus of verbal parallels has been established, researchers can begin to make evidence-based statements about the use of Shakespeare's plays and poems in other genres and periods, and on his status as a cultural authority. Statistical analysis and evaluative readings can also help to determine whether a passage is to be considered a quotation, meaning to give

---

[59] www.books.google.com/ (last accessed 14 May 2017).
[60] Eric M. Johnson, *Open Source Shakespeare: An Experiment in Literary Technology*, www.opensourceshakespeare.org/info/paper_toc.php (last accessed 14 May 2017).
[61] www.tesserae.caset.buffalo.edu/ (last accessed 14 May 2017).

'the words of another', or whether it is a phrase drawn from the stock of English idioms and proverbs, which is, of course, enriched by many former quotations. It becomes possible to write a reception history based on language use as well as criticism and performance.

Romantic Routine: An Example

In Romantic texts our electronic searches have revealed a combination of high admiration for Shakespeare (bardolatry) and casual deployment of his words ('banal Shakespeare').[62] This complicates the question of what constitutes 'quotation'. The *HyperHamlet* project retrieved thousands of textual overlaps in fictional as well as non-fictional texts. The authors of historical, Gothic, courtship and Silver Fork novels, as well as hundreds of journalists, writers-to-the-day and members of the public, all recycle Shakespearean phrases. Most of these quotations are very lightly marked, signalling an intertextual inset with just inverted commas or an archaism such as 'thee', and not mentioning Shakespeare or the quoted play in any way. The sheer number of such quotations indicates that this use of Shakespeare constitutes a widespread habit, as Lord Byron acknowledged: ' "To be or not to be! that is the question", / Says Shakespeare, who just now is much in fashion.'[63]

An example from Mary Wollstonecraft Shelley's 1826 novel *The Last Man* illustrates this fashion and shows how computer-retrieved data can raise important questions. The narrator has just discussed worrying news about a mentally unstable friend with his sister: 'Have those gentle eyes, those "channels of the soul", lost their meaning, or do they only in their glare disclose the horrible tale of its aberrations? Does that voice no longer "discourse excellent music"? Horrible, most horrible! I veil my eyes in terror of the change, and gushing tears bear witness to my sympathy for this unimaginable ruin.'[64] This short passage includes lines from two different *Hamlet* scenes. The Ghost's 'horrible, most horrible' (I.v.80) comes after a fused echo of two lines from Hamlet's conversation with Rosencrantz and Guildenstern ('discourse most eloquent music' (III.ii.325–6) and 'much music, excellent voice' (III.ii.332–3)). In addition, there is a phrase from

[62] See Kate Rumbold, ' "So common-hackneyed in the eyes of men": Banal Shakespeare and the Eighteenth-Century Novel', *Literature Compass*, 4:3 (2007), 610–21.
[63] Lord Byron, *Don Juan*, IX.xiv, in Jerome McGann (ed.) *The Major Works* (Oxford: Oxford University Press, 2000), p. 681.
[64] Mary Wollstonecraft Shelley, *The Last Man* (London: William Pickering, 1996), p. 37.

Bryan Waller Procter's once-popular play *The Broken Heart* (1819), which makes three quotations by two authors in three consecutive sentences.

What is Mary Shelley doing here? *The Broken Heart* was evidently popular enough for her to count on readers recognising 'channels of the soul' without a title or author's name; but that the phrase should be given quotation marks like 'discourses excellent music', while 'Horrible, most horrible' is not, is remarkable. It is unreasonable to assume that Shelley did not remember the provenance of 'Horrible, most horrible', let alone the fact that it is a borrowed phrase. Whether and how she expected that readers recognise it is less certain; maybe it is meant to be a more integral part of the narrative voice, since its Hamletian meaning is closest to the heightened general emotion of the passage.

Most other evidence points to the distribution of quotation marks being almost random. *HyperHamlet* records forty-eight *Hamlet* quotes from Mary Shelley's works, and twenty-one of them are completely unsignalled, including obvious (if imprecisely rendered) borrowings such as 'the pale hue of resolution' (III.ii.84–5) or 'methodized madness' (II.ii.200).[65] They are so unobtrusive, in fact, that the 1996 Pickering edition of Shelley's *Novels and Selected Works* omits to annotate several of them. In the passage given above, only the two quotations that are in quotation marks are pointed out in a footnote. 'Horrible, most horrible' has escaped an editorial eye (or computer) that may have been scanning for quotation marks only, and thus the phrase remains unacknowledged. But it is without any doubt a borrowing from *Hamlet*. Further examples can be seen in Figure 12, which shows the results of a *HyperHamlet* search for tokens that were identified by full-text searches but are not mentioned in annotated editions or scholarly articles (filtered out by the setting 'Research Field: Fulltext Search'). In fact, all these quotations are neither in quotation marks nor marked by Shakespeare's name, and are thus easy to overlook although they are unquestionably taken from his tragedy.

It is doubtful whether Mary Shelley meant to evoke the context of her quotations. What is certain is that the density and the unreliable marking of quotation are not a personal quirk; they represent a characteristic sample of an intertextual practice that could be called 'Romantic Routine'.[66] The *HyperHamlet* corpus shows a particular way of marking prevalent between the 1780s and the 1830s. First, more than half of all Shakespeare quotations

---

[65] Mary Wollstonecraft Shelley, *The Fortunes of Perkin Warbeck* (London: William Pickering, 1996), p. 31; and Shelley, *The Last Man*, p. 168.

[66] See Regula Hohl Trillini, *Casual Shakespeare: Three Centuries of Verbal Echoes* (Abingdon: Routledge, 2018), pp. 118–41.

Search   Clear Search

Collection   Core   ⬦ Author Mary Wollstonecraft Shelle Title Text Date Motif or Name Language

1   ±more

Contributor Genre Subject Marking Quotation Marking Author Marking Work Intertextuality

Textual Function Voice Line Overlap Modification

2

their glare disclose the horrible tale of its aberrations? Does that voice no longer "discourse
excellent music?" Horrible, most horrible! I veil my eyes in terror of the change, and gushing
tears bear witness to my sympathy for this unimaginable ruin.

   <   Act 1, Scene 5, Line 85, 359 ±Details

[13] Shelley, Mary Wollstonecraft (1826): **The Last Man**

The men shrank back; they seemed afraid of what they had already done, and stood as if
they expected some Might Phantom to stalk in offended majesty from the opening.

   <   Act 1, Scene 1, Line 60, ±Details

[14] Shelley, Mary Wollstonecraft (1826): **A Visit to Brighton**

No conjecture was too extravagant which could afford solution to the enigma of a park at
Brighton; but as experiment in this case was of more worth than any theory, I walked up
Egremont-place towards the mysterious Park. An arched entrance! It was not Trajan's
"Hyperion to a Satyr:" wooden gates - two-pence to pay on going in. I have passed the
Rubicon, and stand within the Park, An hollow in the hills, overlooked by their bald tops, is
railed in, and some drab-coloured grass clothes the slopes.

   <   Act 1, Scene 2, Line 142 ±Details

[15] Shelley, Mary Wollstonecraft (1826): **The Last Man**

Even in the Elysian fields, Virgil describes the souls of the happy as eager to drink of the
wave which was to restore them to this mortal coil. The young are seldom in Elysium, for
their desires, outstripping possibility, leave them as poor as a moneyless debtor.

   <   Act 3, Scene 1, Line 75 ±Details

[16] Shelley, Mary Wollstonecraft (1830): **The Fortunes of Perkin Warbeck**

For good or ill, we are in the hands of a superior power:

" There's a divinity that shapes our ends,
Rough-hew them how we will."

We can only resolve, or rather endeavour, to act our parts well, such as they are allotted to
us.

   <   Act 5, Scene 2, Line 10, 11, ±Details

[17] Shelley, Mary Wollstonecraft (1830): **The Fortunes of Perkin Warbeck**

All then was over! his prophetic soul had proved false in its presumed foreknowledge;
defeat, dishonour, disgrace tracked his steps.

© Department of English, University of Basel, Switzerland

Figure 12   A screenshot of search results from *HyperHamlet* showing *Hamlet* quotations
by Mary Wollstonecraft Shelley.

are marked in some way (quotation marks, italics, archaisms etc.). Second,
the majority of marked quotations do not mention either Shakespeare
or *Hamlet*; they are marked for quotation only. This indicates in the
Romantic era a still unimpaired awareness of quotations as quotations
(which declines after 1840) but without the self-conscious wish to signal
Shakespeare (which is evident in marking by name earlier in the eighteenth

century). Such symptoms of routine intertextuality pervade most contemporary writing.

Romantic Routine is a mass phenomenon with distinctly individual shapes. William Hazlitt, for example, put 4 out of 5 of his 2,000 Shakespeare quotations in quotation marks, while Lord Byron is closer to 50 per cent, and Maria Edgeworth marks only a third of her references. The three *Hamlet* phrases in the following passage from her novel *The Absentee* are not marked at all:

> Mrs Dareville … gave full scope to all the malice of mockery, and all the insolence of fashion. Her slings and arrows, numerous as they were and outrageous, were directed against such petty objects … that, felt but not seen, it is scarcely possible to register the hits, or to describe the nature of the wounds. Some hits, sufficiently palpable, however, are recorded for the advantage of posterity.[67]

These phrases are comparable to the brief quotations – sometimes consisting of only a couple of words, but recognisable on account of the play's familiarity – discussed elsewhere in this volume (see especially Chapter 6). The thousands of similarly casual references from the period that have been thrown up by electronic research make it impossible to dismiss such examples as individual quirks or the anonymous idioms they may have become later. Shakespeare permeated the literary and journalistic discourse of the period to an extent that makes it probable that even weak echoes were consciously made, but at the same time diminishes the literary, allusive weight of every single item.

Outlook

Revealing that the extent of 'banal Shakespeare' quotation justifies speaking of a 'Romantic Routine' is just one example of what digital quotation research can do. Full-text searches can widen our knowledge of other periods and fields of reception history but also reveal the earlier life of phrases traditionally ascribed to Shakespeare's creative genius and quoted as such. Many collocations existed in the discourse before Shakespeare reused (quoted?) them. (For a full discussion of Shakespeare as a quoter, see chapters 1 to 4.) These collocations at first continued to be used independently and came to be considered quotations from

---

[67] Maria Edgeworth, 'The Absentee', in *The Novels and Selected Works*, 12 vols. (London: Pickering and Chatto, 1999), vol. v, pp. 1–203 (p. 31). Cf. *Hamlet*, iii.ii.58: 'slings and arrows of outrageous fortune'; iii.ii.73: 'the insolence of office'; v.ii.257: 'a palpable hit'.

Shakespeare only later. As with quotations from Shakespeare, the number of intertextual borrowings *in* his works, spotted and pointed out by philologically knowledgeable readers, has been considerably enlarged by electronically retrieved material. A case in point is the phrase 'To be or not to be' (*Hamlet*, III.i.56), which was (including variants such as 'to love or not to love') in use before as well as after Shakespeare. The markings that accompany its seventeenth-century occurrences show that it acquired the character of a quotation over the course of several decades, from Abraham Cowley in 1656:

> Oh Life, thou Nothings younger Brother!
> So like, that one might take One for the other!
> What's Some Body, or No Body?
> In all the Cobwebs of the Schoolmens trade,
> We no such nice Distinction woven see,
> As 'tis To be, or Not to Be.

to Daniel Defoe in 1726:

> Attempts to square th' Extent of Souls,
> As Men mark Lands, by Butts and Bounds,
> Wou'd the Great *Be*, and *not to Be* Divide,
> And all the Doubts of *Entity* decide.[68]

Here the phrase 'has become so much of a noun-like "item" that it has an adjective of its own'.[69]

As Marshall McLuhan has reminded us, new technologies introduced to perform a traditional task more efficiently change the ways in which we interpret the world.[70] We live in a period of such change and may speculate on how the availability of texts in electronic form and databases of the kind described will produce new ways of reading. Instead of moving sequentially, in a linear fashion, we study networks of cross-references, quotations and allusions, taking seriously Julia Kristeva's claim that '[a]ny

---

[68] Abraham Cowley, 'Life and Fame', in *The Works of Mr Abraham Cowley*, 2 vols. (Cambridge: Cambridge University Press, 1905), vol. II, pp. 201–3; Daniel Defoe, *A hymn to peace. Occasion'd, by the two Houses joining in one address to the Queen. By the author of The true-born English-man* (London: John Nutt, 1706), p. 10.

[69] Regula Hohl Trillini, 'Hamlet and Textual Re-Production 1550–1650', in Indira Ghose and Denis Renevey (eds.), *The Construction of Textual Identity in Medieval and Early Modern Literature*, Swiss Papers in English Language and Literature (SPELL) (Tübingen: Narr, 2009), pp. 163–76 (p. 171).

[70] For example, in Marshall McLuhan, *The Gutenberg Galaxy: The Making of Typographic Man* (London: Routledge and Kegan Paul, 1962); *Understanding Media* (London: Routledge and Kegan Paul, 1964).

text is constructed as a mosaic of quotations; any text is the absorption and transformation of another'.[71] In a reading that moves from one quotation to the quotation that is its source, and so on, the authority of the source, 'the words of another', according to the definition of the *OED*, will be diminished, and a passage may gradually become quasi-anonymous – a process that may affect both Shakespeare the quoter and Shakespeare the quoted.

As Douglas Lanier put it, Shakespeare the text will be replaced by 'the vast web of adaptations, allusions and (re)productions that comprises the ever-changing cultural phenomenon we call "Shakespeare"'.[72] The rhizome is a useful theoretical model for this: 'To think rhizomatically about the Shakespearean text is to foreground its fundamentally adaptational nature – as a version of prior narratives, as a script necessarily imbricated in performance processes, as a text ever in transit between manuscript, theatrical and print cultures, as a work dependent upon its latter-day producers for its continued life.'[73] In consequence, it may be useful to replace the *OED*'s definition of quotation by a range of intertextual possibilities.[74] Electronic search lends itself to dealing with this issue: it registers linguistic features, which in different bundles are useful in mapping the rich continuum of verbal and motivic overlaps that exist between texts – from undoubted references, such as 'Brevity is the soul of wit, according to Shakespeare' in Stephen King's *Hearts in Atlantis*, to highly dubious stuff like this entry in John Clarke's *Pareomiologia Anglo-Latina* of 1639: '*A trout hamlet with foure legs*. Soterichi lecti'.[75]

Intertextual references come in many shapes: the conventions of academic quotation are verbatim repetition, with quotation marks and full information on author and work, while 'allusion' should have none of these features, and 'literary quotation', whether casual or full of referential intent, is excused from both precision and full information. An electronic research medium can manage unprecedented numbers of parallels

---

[71] Julia Kristeva, 'Word, Dialog and Novel', in Toril Moi (ed.) *The Kristeva Reader* (New York: Columbia University Press, 1986), pp. 34–61 (p. 37).

[72] Douglas Lanier, 'Shakespearean Rhizomatics: Adaptation, Ethics, Value', in Huang and Rivlin, *Shakespeare and the Ethics of Appropriation*, pp. 21–40 (p. 29).

[73] *Ibid.*

[74] See Sixta Quassdorf, '*A little more than kin': Quotations as a Linguistic Phenomenon. A Study Based on Quotations from Shakespeare's 'Hamlet'* (Freiburg im Breisgau: University of Freiburg, 2016).

[75] Stephen King, *Hearts in Atlantis* (London: Hodder and Stoughton, 2000), p. 407; John Clarke, *Paroemiologia Anglo-Latina: In usum scholarum concinnata* (London: F. Kyngston for R. Mylbourne, 1639), p. 71. Munro *et al.*, *The Shakspere Allusion-Book* discusses this passage at length (p. 433).

or overlaps between texts so that specialists can decide whether a passage should be considered a quotation as defined by the *OED* or in the wider sense suggested here. Such judgement will be made on a much larger range of evidence than has hitherto been available; if we are too selective, we may miss interesting things.

Afterword

Margreta de Grazia

Let us return to the anecdote Craig Raine calls 'a parable of transmission' (p. 179), for it nicely epitomises the subject of this uniquely capacious collection: the passage of quotations from Shakespeare into language, ordinary as well as literary, through different genres, media and technologies, to different effects and purposes, over the course of the last four centuries. In the anecdote, a woman in her eighties, after experiencing *Hamlet* for the first time, is surprised to find that such a famous work is chock-full of quotations. Expecting something fresh and original, she encountered instead expressions she had been hearing all her life: 'Woe is me', 'Sweets to the sweet', 'The rest is silence.' Obviously the truth is just the reverse: it is not that *Hamlet* is made up of commonplaces but rather that over time Hamlet has become commonplace.

But the obvious truth looks quite different when we reset the details of the anecdote to correspond to the time and place of the earliest quarto of *Hamlet* (Q1). According to the title page, it was published in 1603 and performed not only in the city of London, but at the universities of Oxford and Cambridge. Let's also replace the old woman with an aspiring young man, from one of those universities. He might have left the theatre with the very same impression: so many quotations! But instead of being disappointed, he would have been delighted. If he had his table book with him, as we know theatregoers often did, he would have jotted down as many as he could in the rapid fire of delivery. Eager for more, he might have found a copy at the bookstalls and been thrilled to see printed in the margins several inverted commas, indicators used to mark *sententiae*, but typically only in classical works. Their presence in a vernacular play indicated that like the tragedies of Sophocles or Euripides, it contained precepts of philosophical, theological or stylistic value, to be spotted and marked in his own hand and transcribed for future use, in writing or conversation. This was definitely a text worth owning, not for its new ideas and turns of phrase but for its ready-made units of meaning and expression, in

the time before the next century, when *sententiae* would become sententious, and commonplaces commonplace.

With that bookish youth in mind, let's take a look at Hamlet himself, in the act of delivering his most frequently quoted soliloquy, 'To be
or not to be'. That same earliest edition (Q1) requires that Hamlet enter
holding a prop. As he approaches, the king comments to his counsellor,
'See where he comes, poring upon a book.' Now suppose Hamlet once left
alone continues poring over that book, not thinking aloud but reading
aloud. Scholars have long noted how this soliloquy echoes a number of
works, classical and Christian. The dilemma of whether to remain alive
in misery or to face the uncertainty of unknown death turns out to be
quite traditional. The following works have been proposed as possible
sources: Plutarch's *Moralia*; Cicero's *Tusculan Disputations*; Augustine's *De
libero arbitrio*; Cardano's *De Consolatione*; Montaigne's *Essays*; Charron's
Of Wisdom; and the homily given regularly in services, *Against the Fear of
Death*. Might one of these books be the one he has in hand?

Or, perhaps, better still: might the book be his own table book,
containing extracts from all those books? We know he has a table book
because he whips one out after the appearance of his father's ghost to
reveal who murdered him: the king, whom we have just seen smile his way
through several court crises. 'One may smile and smile and be a villain',
Hamlet sets down in his tables. If they are organised thematically, as tables
often were, he might file it under the heading 'Hypocrisy', along with
other commonplaces on the topic. Perhaps in his melancholy he has been
collecting under the heading 'Suicide' or 'Self-slaughter' various stock
epithets – 'dreams of death', for example, or 'the undiscovered country'.
Indeed Hamlet's soliloquy reads like a patchwork of commonplaces cul-
minating in a fully fashioned one that rejects the option: 'conscience makes
cowards of us all' (Q1). Is this then a staging of Hamlet not thinking aloud
but reading generic thoughts aloud?

This recasting of the most quoted textual stretch in the language comes
of reading Part I of *Shakespeare and Quotation*. In the context of its discussion of the early modern period as a culture of quotation, quite a few
practices look quite different: theatregoing, reading, writing, literature,
even bookselling. Shakespeare looks different, too, when cast as an author
who not only quoted but, as these essays suggest, may have correlated
quotation with both literary fame and dramatic popularity. The sonnets
resonating with Ovid are those that lay claim to the immortality of art.
Perhaps he chose to write a revenge play, *Titus Andronicus*, as his first
tragedy in the hope that its Senecan sententiousness might win quick

popularity. (According to one of Shakespeare's contemporaries, 'English Seneca read by candlelight yields many good sentences.'[1]) But memorable lines have an attraction even if their only authority is their familiar ring. Why else name comedies *All's Well that Ends Well* and *Much Ado about Nothing*?

As this collection's long historical view also demonstrates, the tables turn: the Shakespeare who quoted becomes the Shakespeare who is quoted. (And not only in English, of course. 'Shakespeare and Quotation in Translation' also deserves a volume.) The technologies for storing and retrieving quotations too have changed, from Shakespeare's table book to present-day digital databases. Part II traces the numerous printed collections that appear between script and digital technologies, beginning with anthologies of English verse such as *Bel-vedére; or, The Garden of the Muses* (1600), where Shakespeare's verses are included but not attributed to him. By the mid eighteenth century, Shakespeare's pre-eminence has been secured, and the first volume of quotations devoted to his work alone is published: William Dodd's *The Beauties of Shakespear* (1752), indexed for easy access by topics from 'Action' to 'Worldliness'. Similar compendia flood the Victorian book market, either as companions to editions of the complete works or, as a substitute, for those many readers short of cash, space or time: why settle for anything less than a distillation of Shakespeare? Even on stage, what Pope dubbed 'shining passages' are highlighted. Celebrity actors such as Kemble, Siddons and Kean would – after their virtuosic delivery – pause for applause, interrupting the action, as clowns on Shakespeare's stage were accused of doing with their antics.

More than the works themselves, these compendia encouraged the practice of quotation; in them, quotes are offered up for use. No doubt there were some readers who were happy to curl up with their copy of *Bartlett's Familiar Quotations*, experiencing perhaps a sense of intimacy with what might be taken for Shakespeare's thoughts and feelings, especially when the names of their dramatic speakers were removed. More commonly, though, these quote books would have served as reference works in which readers would seek out the quote they needed. The chapters in this volume describe the great variety of such uses over the centuries: to demonstrate literacy, to enrich the vernacular, to cultivate taste and judgement, for moral instruction and spiritual enlightenment, to pass exams, to impart a

[1] Thomas Nashe, 'To the Gentlemen Students of Both Universities', in Robert Greene (ed.), *Menaphon: Camillas Alarum to Slumbering Euphues* (T. O. for Sampson Clarke, 1589), sigs. **1r–A3r (sig. **3v).

sense of community or nationhood (and not always English nationhood), to enhance letters and speeches, to sell products. Even novelists, such as Richardson and Austen, as we discover, made use of quote books, putting the words of Shakespeare's dramatic characters into the mouths of their own fictional ones, often not without irony. But even when quote books are cast aside, the habit of using Shakespeare in snatches remains. Keats might speak for the Romantics more generally when he sees himself as one who 'gathers Samphire, dreadful trade', with Shakespeare overhead peering down from the cliff of Dover. Editors also gather up Shakespeare quotes in order to annotate them, an especially dreadful task when they are as intricately embedded as in the modernist verse of T. S. Eliot or W. H. Auden.

Yet however much is appropriated from the works, the store remains undiminished, as if in compliance with John Locke's dictum that 'enough and as good [be] left in common for others'. Indeed, as Part III observes, the supply has increased over time – exponentially with digitisation and the world wide web. Quotes fly faster and further from their quarto and Folio embeddings. And while our editions of those texts are committed to their assiduous reproduction, no such fidelity is required of quotes lifted from those works. Once detached from their context, they have no responsibility to their source. In whatever form they occur – high or low, cultural or commercial – no regulations govern their usage. One is free to quote Shakespeare out of context, inaccurately, without attribution, with omissions and substitutions, and to any purpose. But in the wake of these chapters, which discover such fecundity in this licence, one might also ask, is there such a thing as abuse? The editors in their introduction twice risk reproducing one dark example, already gone viral: a marine quotes a line from Hamlet's soliloquy while killing a wounded captive. The atrocity backed by Shakespeare cannot be ignored, of course, as an earlier age might have done in the name of decorum or decency. But if we as literary critics are to address ourselves to such an atrocity, we might need to ask what we are doing when we reproduce one merely as an example of Shakespeare's ubiquity or of quotation out of context.

Such a consideration brings us to a final thought on *Shakespeare and Quotation*: how do we in our criticism use quotation? Literary criticism is hardly imaginable without it. We use it at every turn, often as if it had the evidentiary status of facts, data and statistics. And unlike creative writing, criticism allows no liberties with quoted material. The integrity of texts must be respected as well as the work of authors. Quotations must be given verbatim, in context, with full citation, verse and prose properly formatted, who-said-what clearly demarcated. These mechanical conventions are easily mastered. But criticism also involves the greater stylistic and intellectual challenge of quotation as a matter of voice: when a critical voice introduces a literary one, the two modes of writing meet head-on. If a piece of literary criticism works, it is in no small part the result of how quotes from literary texts have been selected, marshalled and incorporated into their critical surrounds. All the more reason to wonder, as the editors do in their introduction, why literary studies has largely neglected the practice of literary quotation. With the publication of *Shakespeare and Quotation*, there can be no excuse.

Index